REQUIEM
OR REVIVAL?

The Promise of
North American Integration

ISABEL STUDER
CAROL WISE

Editors

BROOKINGS INSTITUTION PRESS
Washington, D.C.

For Olivier,
and to the memory of George Graham

Copyright © 2007
THE BROOKINGS INSTITUTION
1775 Massachusetts Avenue, N.W., Washington, D.C. 20036
www.brookings.edu

Library of Congress Cataloging-in-Publication data

Requiem or revival? : the promise of North American integration / Isabel Studer and
Carol Wise, Editors.
    p.   cm.
    Summary: "Within NAFTA, explores interactions between regionalism and
multilateralism, the impact of the 'new trade' agenda, and unresolved problems—
migration, security, and energy. Discusses NAFTA's relationship to the Free Trade
Agreement of the Americas negotiations and the Doha Development Round and various
ways in which NAFTA could be revamped or improved"—Provided by publisher.
    Includes bibliographical references and index.
    ISBN-13: 978-0-8157-8201-8 (pbk. : alk. paper)
    ISBN-10: 0-8157-8201-2 (pbk. : alk. paper)
    1. North America—Economic integration. 2. North America—Economic policy. 3.
Free trade—North America. I. Studer, Isabel. II. Wise, Carol. III. Title.

    HC95.R46 2007
    337.1'7—dc22   2007024063

9 8 7 6 5 4 3 2 1

The paper used in this publication meets minimum requirements of the
American National Standard for Information Sciences—Permanence of Paper
for Printed Library Materials: ANSI Z39.48-1992.

Typeset in Adobe Garamond

Composition by Cynthia Stock
Silver Spring, Maryland

Printed by R. R. Donnelley
Harrisonburg, Virginia

CONTENTS

Preface

By 2008 the North American Free Trade Agreement (NAFTA) will have met its prime objectives. At this time, some 99 percent of goods and services in those sectors covered by NAFTA will flow duty-free between Canada, Mexico, and the United States, and the explicit goals of increasing trade and foreign investment in North America will have been met. Yet, at least from the standpoint of Canada and Mexico, NAFTA has fallen short of its original expectations on the regional integration front. First, despite the stipulation of article 24 of the General Agreement on Tariffs and Trade that a preferential trade agreement such as NAFTA should remain open to new members, there have been no additional accessions since the formal launching of NAFTA in 1994. Second, while all three members initially colluded in the decision to forgo the creation of strong regional institutions, ironically, this has prevented NAFTA from evolving into a more compelling regional project. The lack of a sound institutional framework has, in other words, hampered progress in key issues areas (migration, energy, regional infrastructure, border security) that are intrinsic to the integration process but have instead been treated as externalities. Third, Canada's efforts to counterbalance U.S. dominance over NAFTA through the negotiation of a broader hemispheric accord, or Free Trade Area of the Americas (FTAA), have been patently thwarted.

Up until mid-2006 trade policymakers and analysts in North America had held out hope that the completion of the Doha Development Round at the World Trade Organization would provide the necessary impetus for addressing NAFTA's unfinished business and that domestic politics in the three member countries would converge more closely in the tackling of migration and energy challenges, in particular. However, as this book goes to press, both Doha and the FTAA negotiations have been relegated to the back burner, at least until after the 2008 presidential election in the United States.

From the standpoint of the Western hemisphere, this suggests that the U.S. strategy of seeking bilateral free trade agreements in the future with "willing and interested partners" (for example, Central American countries, Colombia, Ecuador, and Peru) will prevail indefinitely. Thus the timing on this collection of essays is such that the authors are able to look back on both the accomplishments and the shortcomings of NAFTA and to speculate on the possible paths forward for trade reform and regional integration.

Acknowledgments

The challenges of uniting a truly trinational set of specialists to write these essays are such that we have gathered a long list of benefactors and sponsors who warrant recognition. This project began as a two-day seminar organized by Isabel Studer at the Facultad Latinoamericana de Ciencias Sociales (FLACSO) in Mexico City, which was supported generously by the Subsecretaría para América del Norte (SRE), the Canadian Embassy in Mexico City (with special thanks to Ambassador Gaëtan Lavertu), and by the U.S. Embassy in Mexico City (with special thanks to Ambassador Antonio O. Garza). The editing and finalization of the chapters were supported by the Carleton University Fulbright in North American Studies in Ottawa, Canada; the Fulbright-García Robles Fellowship at the Universidad de la Américas in Puebla, Mexico; and by the Canada Institute at the Woodrow Wilson Center for International Scholars in Washington, D.C.

Additional support for this project was provided by CEMEX, the Center for International Studies at the University of Southern California (USC), the Center for International Business Education and Research at USC's Marshall School of Business, the Faculty Development Research Fund at USC's College of Letters, Arts, and Sciences, the Earhart Foundation, and the Haynes Foundation of Los Angeles. Thanks also to Katherine Baldwin, Marcela Lopez, and Victor Meza for their able research assistance.

Finally, we wish to thank the Brookings Institution Press and its incredibly capable editorial and production staff, including Larry Converse, Chris Kelaher, Mary Kwak, Anthony Nathe, and Janet Walker. As always, Susan Woollen has honored us with a cover design that perfectly captures the theme of this book.

Isabel Studer   Carol Wise
Mexico City   Los Angeles

ABBREVIATIONS

AD/CVD:	antidumping/countervailing duties
APEC Forum:	Asia-Pacific Economic Cooperation Forum
Aramco:	Saudi Arabian Oil Company
CAFTA:	Central American Free Trade Agreement
Caricom:	Caribbean Community
CGE model:	computable general equilibrium model
CFR:	Council on Foreign Relations
CG18:	Consultative Group of Eighteen
CREST:	Center for Renewable Energy Systems Technology
Cocex:	Interministerial Commission on Trade Policy in Mexico
Coece:	Foreign Trade Business Coordination Council of Mexico
Conapo:	National Population Council, Mexico
CTD:	Committee on Trade and Development, World Trade Organization
CUSFTA:	Canada-U.S. Free Trade Agreement
DGMCA:	General Directorate for Mexican Communities Abroad
EC:	European Commission
EEC:	European Economic Community
EFTA:	European Free Trade Association

EPA:	Environmental Protection Agency, United States
EU:	European Union
FDI:	foreign direct investment
FSC:	foreign sales corporation
FTA:	Free Trade Agreement
FTAA:	Free Trade Area of the Americas
G7/G8:	Group of 7 / Group of 8 most developed nations
G20/G21:	Group of 20 / Group of 21 developing country bloc, World Trade Organization
GAO:	Government Accountability Office, United States
GATT:	General Agreement on Tariffs and Trade
GDP:	gross domestic product
GHE:	greenhouse emissions
GPT:	General Preferential Tariff, Canada
GSP:	Generalized System of Preferences
H-O:	Heckscher-Ohlin trade theorem
IADB:	Inter-American Development Bank
ICT:	information and communication technology
IEA:	International Energy Agency
IFI:	international financial institutions
ILO:	International Labor Organization
IMF:	International Monetary Fund
IPRs:	intellectual property rights
IRCA:	Immigration Reform and Control Act, 1986
ISI:	import-substitution industrialization
LAC:	Latin America and the Caribbean
LDCs:	less developed countries
LNG:	liquefied natural gas
MDGs	millennium development goals, United Nations
META:	Middle East Trade Area
Mercosur:	Southern Cone Common Market
MFA:	Multi Fiber Arrangement
MFN:	most-favored nation
MRE:	Ministry of Foreign Affairs, Brazil
MSC:	multiple service contract
MTN:	multilateral trade negotiations
NACEC:	North American Commission for Environmental Cooperation
NACLC:	North American Commission for Labor Cooperation
NADBank:	North American Development Bank

NAEWG: North American Energy Working Group
NAFTA: North American Free Trade Agreement
NAMA: nonagricultural market access
NGO: nongovernmental organization
NSF: National Science Foundation
OAS: Organization of American States
ODA: official development assistance
OECD: Organization for Economic Cooperation and Development
OPEC: Organization of Petroleum Exporting Countries
PAN: National Action Party, Mexico
Pemex: Petroleos Mexicanos (Mexico's state-owned oil company)
PRD: Revolutionary Democratic Party, Mexico
PRI: Institutional Revolutionary Party, Mexico
Prosec: Sectoral Development Program, Mexico
PSA: public service agreement
R & D: research and development
RTA: regional trade agreement
SARE: Rapid System for Company Establishment Program, Mexico
SDT: special and differential treatment
SMEs: small- and medium-sized enterprises
SPP: Security and Prosperity Partnership of North America
TAA: trade adjustment assistance
TFP: total factor productivity
TIEA: Trade and Investment Enhancement Agreement
TPA: Trade Promotion Authority, U.S. president
TRCB: trade-related capacity building
TRIPS: trade-related aspects of intellectual property rights
TRIMs: trade-related investment measures
UN: United Nations
UNHCR: United Nations High Commission for Refugees
UR: Uruguay Round
URAA: Uruguay Round Agreement on Agriculture
USAID: United States Agency for International Development
ODA: official development assistance, United States
USTR: United States trade representative
WCSB: Western Canadian Sedimentary Basin
WMD: weapons of mass destruction
WTO: World Trade Organization
WTO-DSU: World Trade Organization's Dispute Settlement
            Understanding

1

No Turning Back

Trade Integration and the New Development Mandate

CAROL WISE

S ince the Uruguay Round of negotiations of the General Agreement on Tariffs and Trade (GATT) in 1986, hemispheric and subregional trade negotiations have proliferated and have interacted with this more established multilateral venue in unpredictable ways. First was the uncharacteristic willingness of the United States to venture outside of GATT in search of bilateral free trade agreements (FTAs). Frustrated with the slow pace of the Uruguay Round, the United States launched bilateral accords with Canada and Israel in the latter part of the 1980s. The Canada-U.S. deal, in turn, invoked Mexico's request to negotiate a similar bilateral agreement with the United States, which resulted in a second anomaly—and the main focus of this book: the 1994 launching of the North American Free Trade Agreement (NAFTA). NAFTA was unprecedented in that it linked a middle-income developing country seeking to lock in ambitious market reforms and thus willing to forgo developing country status at the negotiating table (Mexico) with a small but highly developed market of the Organization for Economic Cooperation and Development (Canada) and the the wealthiest and most competitive market in the world (the United States).

Concomitant with the launching of NAFTA, new subregional schemes were being created, such as the four-member South American Mercosur bloc

(Argentina, Brazil, Paraguay, Uruguay), and preexisting schemes in Central America, the Caribbean, and the Andean region were revived. A third surprise was the apparent compatibility of these arrangements, both within the Western Hemisphere and also in terms of ongoing multilateral trade goals; like Mexico, countries further to the south were ready to jettison long-standing protectionist biases in favor of trade and investment liberalization. Finally, as NAFTA's negotiators secured commitments that reached beyond GATT's accomplishments in such areas as services, investment, intellectual property rights, and dispute settlement, NAFTA spurred GATT's members to return to the multilateral negotiating table and wrap up the Uruguay Round accord in late 1993, albeit with equivocal results.

From there followed the 1995 creation of the World Trade Organization (WTO), meant to replace, expand on, and better enforce the provisions of GATT. Later that same year, the Clinton administration announced its intention to negotiate a free trade agreement among all thirty-four democratically elected countries in this region. It was envisioned at the outset that the Free Trade Area of the Americas (FTAA) would subsume NAFTA and the other emerging subregional accords into one large hemispheric bloc, while also exerting pressure for further progress at the multilateral level.[1] In less than a decade more regional and subregional deals had been negotiated than ever before.[2] These apparent synergies and virtuous cycles among global, hemispheric, and regional integration instilled considerable optimism that items on the "old" (market access for agricultural and industrial goods) and "new" (services, investment, and intellectual property rights) trade agendas could be constructively addressed by the WTO.

A new round of multilateral trade talks was thus launched in Doha, Qatar, in November 2001, the ninth in a series that dates back to the founding of GATT in 1947 and the first since the formalization of trade negotiations under the WTO. In recognition of the need to more firmly address issues of vital importance to developing countries, most of which had been sold short or ignored in the Uruguay Round,[3] this ninth set of negotiations came to be known as the Doha Development Round. This designation reflected the explosion in the number of developing countries that were now active in international trade, many of which are recent members of GATT/WTO.[4] This explains the heightened pressures from nongovernmental organizations (NGOs) for a true development orientation of the kind witnessed at the WTO's ill-fated Ministerial Conference in Seattle in 1999.

Yet despite the WTO's expressed commitment to negotiate a Doha package that would directly address North-South asymmetries and work to incorporate developing countries into the global trading system on more equitable terms, the Doha Development Round collapsed in mid-2006.[5] The outcome was the continued reticence of the developed countries to offer authentic concessions on the old trade agenda—market access for agricultural and labor-intensive manufactured goods—while insisting on commitments to deep liberalization on new trade issues. But neither were the wealthier developing countries willing to budge sufficiently on the latter. Added to this was the failure of the OECD bloc to firmly specify and commit to the kinds of assistance and exemptions—or "special and differential treatment"—necessary to bridge the North-South divide at the WTO.[6] A similar collective action standoff had stalled the FTAA negotiations a year earlier as the two most important protagonists, the United States and Brazil, failed to agree on the terms for incorporating both old and new trade agenda issues into that accord.

This dissipation in momentum and commitment toward economic integration within the multilateral and hemispheric arenas has prompted some to suggest that these logjams might once again be broken at the subregional level.[7] It is this juncture that forms the departure point for this collection of essays. From the perspective of North America, this volume unites a group of renowned specialists from the three NAFTA countries, the goal being to evaluate the different, although not mutually exclusive, options and integration dynamics from the standpoint of each NAFTA partner. While the disappointments of Doha and the FTAA may render the prospects for deeper North American integration more likely, some of these authors also elaborate on the various ways in which NAFTA itself is in need of revamping. For example, although the agreement has readily delivered on higher levels of trade and investment among the three member countries, and key sectors like autos, electronics, and computers are tightly integrated across this region, NAFTA has patently failed to move forward as a trinational integration project.

Of particular concern is the inability of Mexico to sustain any momentum in the growth of wages, formal employment, and per capita income—a trend that contradicts those neoclassical economic assumptions upon which the design and pace of trade liberalization under NAFTA were based.[8] Obviously, not all of Mexico's growth lag can be attributed to NAFTA, as the country's initially ambitious domestic economic reform trajectory ground to a near halt under the Fox administration (2000–06).[9] But neither has there been much commitment on the part of the United States and Canada to foster regional institutions or comparable mechanisms that could directly tackle the asymmetries and promote competitiveness as part of a larger NAFTA endeavor. Thirteen years into NAFTA there is still no cohesive organizational framework to manage spillover effects in such areas as energy security and the massive northward flow of undocumented Mexican migrants into the U.S. labor market. Despite the stipulation of GATT's article 24 that membership in a subregional scheme such as this should remain open, not one new member has been admitted to NAFTA.[10]

By virtue of its NAFTA membership Mexico has gone farther than any other developing country in striking a balance between the liberalization of issues on the old and new trade agendas.[11] However, to date the prospective costs of a deep liberalization of items on the new trade agenda are more evident than the supposed benefits gleaned from greater market access in those sectors that define the old trade agenda. From the standpoint of the developing country bloc within the WTO, this demonstration effect goes to the heart of the current impasse: with the developing countries now representing a majority of the 150 countries that belong to the WTO, and with powerful emerging market economies like Brazil, China, India, and South Africa participating as never before, demands that the Doha development mandate be addressed must soon be met.

Although the chapters in this volume emphasize that NAFTA-style regionalism has been no panacea, this experiment nevertheless offers insights into possible paths forward for trade integration. This is so both in terms of Mexico's learning curve as a developing country that has aggressively integrated with the fiercely competitive North American market and in terms of assessing viable options for advancing global trade liberalization given the obstacles that have arisen. To put this differently, it seems that "big-think" proposals for deep and rapid economic integration, which marked the 1990s, are giving way to a gradual reconciliation of developing country demands for fair trade with the adjustment costs of further liberalization. In acknowledgment of this trend, and from the vantage point of North America, the authors in this volume address the following themes that have dominated the academic literature and recent trade policy debates:

—The interaction between regionalism and multilateralism, including the crucial role of institutions for enabling the developing countries to comply with their obligations, as herein lies the critical link between economic integration and development

—The question of how the "new trade agenda" (liberalization of trade in services and investment, government procurement, enforcement of intellectual property rights, and support for labor and environmental standards) has altered the classic theory of economic integration, which focuses mainly on questions of trade creation versus trade diversion and the welfare effects of regional trade

—Within North America, the importance of addressing pressing issues that directly relate to NAFTA (migration, energy security) but that were omitted from original negotiations because of their political sensitivity

Regionalism, Multilateralism, and the Development Challenge

In 1991, when the U.S. Congress gave the green light to the senior Bush administration to move forward with the negotiations for a North American Free Trade Agreement, the notion of tightly integrating Mexico with these two OECD markets was both daring and controversial. Daring, because this marked the first U.S. free trade agreement that included a developing country, and one that wanted to join the agreement badly enough to waive considerations for special and different treatment; controversial, because the very disparities between Mexico and its two prospective partners immediately raised concerns about the possible deleterious effects of NAFTA on Mexico. However, as all three member governments agreed that NAFTA would remain a free trade agreement in principle and would avoid the "Brussels bureaucracy" of supranational institutions and adjustment assistance that characterizes the European Union (EU), Mexico basically signed on to a rigorous, market-based restructuring program with the thinnest of safety nets.

At the time, labor markets and the environment were the concerns most raised by a diverse coalition that formed the core opposition to NAFTA, the result being the attachment of side accords and the creation of separate trilateral entities to oversee both of these issues. On the eve of the 1993 NAFTA vote in the U.S. Congress some last-minute doubters on Capitol Hill raised concerns about the larger development challenges engendered by Mexico's entry into NAFTA, and these were assuaged by the Clinton team's offering of the North American Development Bank (NADBank) to be funded jointly by the United States and Mexico. This was essentially it, in terms of the incorporation of a development mandate into NAFTA. Inching slowly along, the impact of the separate commissions for labor and the environment has been hampered in that the enacting legislation applies only to the upholding of national laws within each NAFTA country and not to the generation and application of NAFTA-wide standards. The NADBank, after approving just five loans in its first five years, is gaining more steam, but its scope is limited to environmental infrastructure projects along the U.S.-Mexico border.[12]

While one can rightfully debate whether an EU-style adjustment effort would have made a dent in the enormous gap between Mexico and its partners, it can be more convincingly argued that the absence of a sound institutional framework is now prohibiting the three countries from moving forward in deepening NAFTA as a regional project. As Gary Hufbauer and Jeffrey Schott observe, "NAFTA's skeletal institutional structure has impeded the achievement of core objectives. . . . The NAFTA Commission—composed of trade ministers of each country—is neither seen nor heard. . . . The NAFTA Secretariat is responsible for administering the dispute settlement processes [and] it also provides day-to-day assistance to the working groups and the commission. It has insufficient funds to do either job well."[13]

Within North America the tendency has been to work around NAFTA in suboptimal ways, rather than to strengthen NAFTA's institutions and expand on its economic accomplishments. Such was the case with the Security and Prosperity Partnership of North America (SPP) launched in 2005, a trilateral effort to strengthen cooperation and information sharing within the region, and also with the numerous counterproductive migration and guest worker proposals. In the case of the SPP, which was basically dead on arrival, at least half of the designated issue areas (for example, manufactured goods, financial services, information and communication technologies, and agriculture) overlap with the NAFTA text and side agreements; moreover, the working groups tasked with linking prosperity and security within the selected issue areas are themselves poorly coordinated. Tellingly, the three NAFTA member governments avoided terms like *integration* and *community* in the context of the SPP and instead relied on "agenda, process, framework, and mechanisms for tri-national dialogue."[14]

In short, even though Mexico's entry into NAFTA was considered an insurance policy for locking in market reforms and NAFTA membership has been an indisputable boost for the creation of higher levels of trade and investment, NAFTA has done little to foster higher levels of productivity and competitiveness on the Mexican side.[15] In chapter 2, I explore the bases for these unfulfilled promises and argue that the record is more mixed than the negative portrait painted by NAFTA's critics.[16] In fact, I argue that macroeconomic variables (inflation, interest rates, exchange rates, aggregate growth) in North America have converged favorably toward OECD standards. Mexico, however—after doubling its per capita growth performance between 1995 and 2000—has hit a virtual plateau in the rise of real income. And although Mexico's average aggregate growth rate of 2–3 percent during the NAFTA era is respectable and in step with Canada and the United States, this rate is well below the average growth rate for other Latin American emerging markets like Argentina, Chile, and Peru during the same time period.

What accounts for the bottleneck in Mexico's growth rate of both aggregate and per capita GDP since 2000? Part of the answer is bad luck, given China's forceful entry into the U.S. market in the 2000s, but Mexico's falling behind is also policy induced. Be it cheaper costs for labor and utility inputs, a broader supplier base, or much lower corporate tax rates, China has gradually outpaced Mexico in U.S. markets once considered the cornerstone of North American integration (telecommunications, computer peripherals, and sound and television equipment). First, Mexico's microeconomic underperformance can be attributed to the gulf between neoclassical trade theory, which assumes a state of perfect competition and constant returns to scale under NAFTA, and the concrete empirical obstacles that underpinned its launching back in the early 1990s.[17] The obstacles include, for example, organizational weaknesses, deeply engrained barriers to competition, and sizable skill and technology deficits that typically characterize a developing economy like Mexico's.

Second, I part ways with those NAFTA critics who place sole blame on the agreement itself for these shortcomings and suggest that the roots of economic underperformance in Mexico lie as much in the frailties of domestic politics, political institutions, and policymaking. The pending reform tasks inherited by the Fox administration, although straightforward, were waylaid by the unexpected difficulties of managing economic liberalization in the context of a minority government and a divided Congress. Thus the delay of crucial measures toward energy sector modernization, fiscal restructuring, labor market mobility, and technical support and credit for small and medium-size firms is just as much to blame for Mexico's current growth trap. In hindsight, I suggest that Mexico's weaknesses going into NAFTA were exacerbated not only by policymakers' embrace of the agreement as a tool to lock in incipient market reforms back in the early 1990s but also by their miscalculation concerning the benefits to be gained from Mexico's geographic proximity to the U.S. market.[18]

I underline the costliness of the six-year reform hiatus that beset the Fox team and the urgency of relaunching comprehensive competitiveness-enhancing reforms by the current administration of Felipe Calderón (2006–12).[19] On this count, my analysis confirms that the classic Vinerian justification for joining an FTA—aggregate welfare gains and trade and investment creation as opposed to diversion—has been trumped by new growth theories that emphasize the importance of an FTA in promoting scale economies, intra-industry specialization, and technological adaptation.[20] This insight goes to the heart of Mexico's willingness to sign on to the new trade agenda in 1994, which in turn helped render NAFTA an innovative model and deal maker for completing the Uruguay Round. Yet the experience since 1994 also shows that political elites and policymakers in all three countries have yet to fully seize these opportunities, which has relegated NAFTA's whole to much less than the sum of its parts.

Even if NAFTA's operational tendencies are still more akin to two bilateral deals that have basically been cobbled together, Isabel Studer reminds us that the possibilities for a more dynamic and compelling regional project remain. In chapter 3 Studer argues that the very creation of NAFTA shows that trilateral coordination is possible when it is based on the national interests of the three trade partners. She disputes the traditional explanations offered by international relations theorists, which hold that the enormous asymmetries among the North American partners explain the preference of each for a more pragmatic association with minimal institutions and supranational oversight.

As standing theories hold, under conditions of extreme asymmetry the weakest states have no interest in formalizing cooperation because formal agreements only further disempower them.[21] This standard explanation, she argues, begs the question of why Canada and Mexico were willing to negotiate and sign on to NAFTA in the first place. It also fails to account for Mexico's about-face at the outset of the Fox administration, whereby Fox proposed a NAFTA-plus strategy, which among other things would seek to constructively address the secular northward flow of undocumented Mexican migrants to the United States and establish a U.S.$20 billion development fund to invest in infrastructure corridors to better connect the North American region.

Although the NAFTA-plus proposal was widely endorsed by nongovernmental actors across the region as the most effective way to mitigate the huge asymmetries between Mexico and its two northern neighbors, it met with little success in the governmental corridors of Ottawa and Washington. The opposition of the United States, in particular, to the creation of more vibrant institutions to promote Mexico's integration with the North American market (that is, financial and technical support for the expansion of regional infrastructure, human capital investments, and industrial restructuring) is visceral, and this has clearly slowed progress in bridging NAFTA's development gap. As a way of addressing these shortcomings, Studer argues that the three countries need to enhance the existing regional institutional structure and, based on those adjustments, to seek new forms of cooperation rooted in their respective national interests.

Along similar lines, in chapter 4 Jeffrey Schott encourages all three NAFTA countries to use the impasse at Doha and the FTAA to work together to advance their common interests. By collaborating more closely in the resolution of mutual concerns, he argues, the NAFTA countries could reap substantial gains both within the North American context and in building the requisite consensus to conclude the WTO and FTAA negotiations. In this interim, Schott emphasizes, the success of future negotiations will also depend on the willingness of each country to undertake substantive domestic reforms in areas that relate directly to the bottlenecks surrounding both the old and new trade agendas.

The remaining chapters that touch on this theme of regionalism and development are those by Jaime Zabludovsky and Sergio Gómez, Gordon Mace, and Glauco Oliveira (chapters 5, 6, and 7). Respectively, these authors explore the past efforts and perceived options for the expansion of the North American integration model into a larger hemispheric project and the possibilities for mutual reinforcement between the two. Despite the embrace of the FTAA concept in Latin America as a means for collectively countering U.S. hegemony and advancing on the old and new trade agendas with a smaller set of more homogeneous actors, Zabludovsky and Gómez characterize Mexico's initial attitude toward the FTAA as one of aloofness. With little incentive to share its privileged access to the U.S. market, Mexico instead used the advantage of its NAFTA membership to advance at the bilateral level.

The result by 2005 was Mexico's completion of an ambitious network of FTAs in the hemisphere as well as its proactive stance at the WTO. This more or less mirrored the U.S. strategy of "competitive negotiations," which sought to address some of the rules on the new trade agenda through the negotiation of bilateral FTAs in the region while simultaneously participating in multilateral negotiations. Zabludovsky and Gómez cite two main drawbacks to this bilateral approach for Mexico. First, Mexico's trade protectionism and the related transaction costs of customs valuation rose steadily in relation to countries with which it did not have a preferential FTA in place. Second, these bilateral maneuvers greatly diluted the incentives for countries to participate in FTAA negotiations. Whereas the Latin American and

Caribbean (LAC) countries originally perceived the FTAA as the fastest way into the North American market, many instead succeeded in securing a bilateral deal with the United States.

Yet after the inauguration of the George W. Bush administration in 2001, which showed a greater willingness to move ahead bilaterally with any number of interested takers, Mexico began to feel a tighter pinch from this U.S. competitive negotiating strategy. The combination of China's 2001 entry into the WTO and the rapidity with which Chinese producers began outpacing Mexican exporters in key U.S. markets confirmed that preferential access to the prized U.S. market was no longer a strictly North American perquisite. For Mexico, apart from more seriously tackling its own reform backlog, the challenge is to streamline its non-FTA trade regime and to expand its trade and investment horizons beyond the U.S. market. In this vein, Zabludovsky and Gómez present a compelling argument for the negotiation of a continental free trade zone that would join the NAFTA bloc with the nine other countries that have secured (or are in the process of securing) FTAs with the United States.

By virtue of having already negotiated these FTAs, they argue, the countries involved (from the Andean, Central American, and Caribbean subregions) have made a sound commitment to trade liberalization and regional integration. Moreover, the smaller number of actors could mean a higher probability for constructive collective action. From the standpoint of strengthening Mexico's export-led development strategy, this twelve-member continental zone could also help stanch future losses incurred by Mexico within regional markets due to the implementation of these new FTAs. Though compelling, there are at least three possible glitches to the realization of this proposal, besides the 2006 mid-term election of a congressional majority not in favor of free trade. As one of its first points of trade business the new Democratic-led House Ways and Means Committee sent a letter to the Office of the U.S. Trade Representative demanding the incorporation of binding guarantees on labor rights in the still-pending U.S. FTAs with Colombia and Peru.[22] The House of Representatives also promptly voted down a measure to establish normal trade relations with Vietnam.

In the grander scheme of things, the proposal by Zabludovsky and Gómez raises three concerns. First, it is not clear that deeper liberalization involving the proposed twelve-member zone would resolve the development shortcomings of Mexico and most of its Latin American neighbors.[23] Second are the concerns and conflicting interests of Canada, the only other developed country to sit at the FTAA negotiating table. Third, while the current political climate in the Southern Cone may not favor the inclusion of these countries in the proposed continental zone, it is difficult to imagine the exclusion of the region's largest and most powerful economy, Brazil, from such an arrangement. Brazil, having played a pivotal role in stalling the FTAA negotiations, could help render the creation of a continental zone that is more than just a matter of maintaining perks in the U.S. market, as is the case with the current twelve-member lineup.

As for Canada, the twelve-member proposal reinforces its worst fears: the greater consolidation of the U.S. economy as the regional hub, and a regulatory framework that would accommodate U.S. preferences and interests but not necessarily those of Canada. In his chapter, Gordon Mace explains that the Canadian government originally agreed to the FTAA concept as part of its own efforts to counterbalance an increasingly asymmetrical Canada-U.S. relationship. From the start, Ottawa saw that the pursuit of a series of bilateral accords with its LAC neighbors would be insufficient given Canada's wish to craft regional rules that could help rein in U.S. trade practices and contingent protectionism.

But Canada's overriding concern at the FTAA negotiations was to establish a sound regulatory framework to govern the new trade agenda in the hemisphere (services, competition policies, investment). This is because Canadian exports to LAC have remained constant since 1994, with about 1 percent going to Mexico and 1 percent to the rest of the region, even though the value of Canadian foreign direct investment in LAC (excluding Mexico) has increased considerably. With services now accounting for 70 percent of Canadian GDP, an agreement on WTO-plus rules to govern hemispheric foreign direct investment and services was of the essence.

In light of the importance of foreign direct investment for Canada, Mace emphasizes that Mercosur—which is not factored into the Zabludovsky-Gómez proposal—is the one LAC subregion that offers any promise for expansion. For example, from 1990 to 2005 Canadian foreign direct investment increased from U.S.$125 million to U.S.$4.6 billion in Argentina, from U.S.$1.7 billion to U.S.$8.0 billion in Brazil, and from U.S.$265.0 million to U.S.$5.6 billion in Chile (an associate member of Mercosur). Between the start of the official FTAA negotiations in 1998 until the 2003 Miami FTAA Trade Ministerial, Canada participated on the grounds that the projected trade agreement would comprehensively cover the old and new trade agenda—including WTO-plus rules around foreign direct investment.

For Canada the failure of the FTAA was the shift away from striking a comprehensive accord and toward a two-tiered approach in 2003, whereby, in tier one, participating governments would agree on a common approach to tariff reductions and, in tier two, governments could choose to address the new trade agenda within a more flexible venue, including bilateral and "plurilateral" deals. With this proposal an unacceptable option from the Canadian standpoint, and with the twelve-member FTA proposed by Zabludovsky and Gómez lacking appeal given its exclusion of Mercosur, Canadian officials are readjusting their sights on how to accomplish national goals through further integration.

As for Brazil's exclusion from the proposed continental zone, in his chapter Glauco Oliveira makes clear that Brazil has hardly given up on trade negotiations despite various impediments and setbacks. Even if a majority coalition of domestic elites has yet to see the potential for dynamic gains from conceding on the new trade agenda via closer Mercosur-NAFTA ties, Oliveira argues that the U.S.-Brazil economic bond is strong enough to bring both sides back to the negotiating table at some point. For example, manufactured products and intra-industry trade now account for 70 percent of U.S. exports to Brazil and almost 75 percent of Brazilian exports to the United States. Be it within Doha, the FTAA, or the continental zone proposed by Zabludovsky and Gómez, these higher value-added goods would be trading according to similar rules, which is a compelling case for a sizable increase in foreign direct investment in Brazil.[24]

Ultimately, Oliveira concludes, there is little structural logic to Brazil's current focus on integrating with the G20 countries, where, outside of Argentina, its economic ties are all but nil.[25] As the costs of protectionism increase for those Brazilian producers with a comparative advantage for exports to the United States, some—including powerful agricultural interests—have pushed for a more ambitious regional accord that would involve important concessions on the new trade themes. This, however, would require that the United States open up those very agricultural sectors that triggered the breakdown of the FTAA negotiations. With the George W. Bush administration moving in the opposite direction—raising trade barriers for sugar, orange juice concentrate, and cotton in the 2002 farm bill—Brazil and its Mercosur partners remain understandably wary of U.S. intentions at any of the various trade negotiating tables discussed here.

With the recent entry of the anti-U.S. Venezuela into the Mercosur bloc, the viability of the FTAA as a regional option seems remote, at least until after the 2008 U.S. presidential election.[26] The venue may not be clear, Oliveira argues, but the best strategy would be to deal with the new trade issues while continuing to push for much more favorable terms on agriculture and market access.

Developing Countries and the New Trade Agenda

Although the new trade agenda is generally seen as a main obstacle to the conclusion of the latest round of hemispheric and multilateral negotiations, the chapters in this volume broaden this explanation and address the role of cumulative tensions between North and South. Over the long run there is a pattern of OECD dominance in the previous eight multilateral trade rounds and the perpetual postponement of issues, like agriculture, that are of primary concern to the large contingent of developing countries now belonging to the WTO. As Schott notes in his chapter, agriculture holds the key to a successful Doha Round—not because of its importance in international trade (which is less than 10 percent) but because it is the sector with the highest trade barriers and largest potential welfare gains for developing countries. For example, farm products still account for 30–60 percent of GDP in the developing world, while farm subsidies within the OECD continue to approach 50 percent of all farm production.[27]

At the same time, 90 percent of world trade is in industrial goods and services, for which developing countries face average manufacturing tariffs in developed country markets that are three times higher than those faced by other developed country exporters to these same developed country markets. Schott therefore cautions that a farm deal, however difficult, will not be sufficient to secure the Doha Round. The final accords must also include substantial results in the other key areas under negotiation: nonagricultural market access (NAMA), services, trading rules (for example, subsidies, countervailing and antidumping measures, trade facilitation), and special and differential treatment (SDT) for developing countries. These demands for SDT lie in the fact that up to ninety developing countries in the WTO have still not met the costs of their Uruguay Round obligations in areas such as customs valuation and the protection of intellectual property rights.

In fact, at both the WTO and the FTAA negotiating tables SDT has become a developing country demand for authentically tackling North-South asymmetries.[28] In the Western Hemisphere, such demands are further driven by the mixed results of the market reform programs launched since the early 1990s. The heightened participation in commercial negotiations by LAC countries at all levels reflects the crucial role that trade liberalization has played in this overall reform scenario. Yet despite the diversity in timing, content, and implementation of these market reforms, aggregate outcomes in productivity and competitiveness conform most readily to Mexico's mediocre performance.[29] In the case of Doha, the hard economic realities of fully complying with demands for further liberalization seemed to have catalyzed a developing country consensus that no agreement would be better than one that extracts further commitments with no solid promises for the financial and technical assistance that would be necessary to fully comply.[30]

In chapter 8 Theodore Cohn highlights the complex ways in which the Doha Development Round represents new terrain for countries in both North and South. Until the early 1960s, he argues, GATT functioned as a Northern club that sought to preserve its influence over the global trading system. To this day, key issues on trade governance are discussed in the WTO's elite "green room" sessions, with participation limited to the director general and about twenty-five prominent trading states. Part of the disaster surrounding the 1999 Seattle WTO Ministerial Conference stemmed from developing country protests over their exclusion from green room sessions held beforehand, and some developing countries continue to decry their inadequate representation in draft declarations issued by the chair of the WTO General Council to facilitate negotiations in the 2001 Doha and 2003 Cancún ministerial meetings. Cohn's analysis clarifies that the new trade agenda refers not just to the substantive issues at hand but also to the need for a process that is more inclusive, accountable, and transparent.

Cohn also argues that substance and process are linked and that the North must accept that it cannot dominate Doha Round negotiations to the degree that it has controlled earlier rounds. Already the formation of the G20 developing country bloc within the Doha Round has effectively pressured the developed countries, and particularly the EU, to agree to the removal of agricultural export subsidies. To reach an agreement on these and other sensitive issues, the North will have to offer more concessions than in previous rounds. Apart from North-South cleavages over these issues, Cohn details the ways in which G20 demands have also caused rifts among OECD countries in the Doha Round. Persistent tensions between the United States and the EU over a limited-versus-comprehensive Doha agenda, respectively, have caused an attendant lack of leadership in global trade governance as well as an inability to effectively respond to the South's demands.

This is especially relevant in the realm of SDT, where Cohn cites the changes being sought by the developing countries: more flexibility in the offering of exemptions from certain trade rules, stricter guarantees on access to industrialized markets, technical assistance to enable the South to implement WTO agreements, and procedures to monitor and enforce SDT commitments. However, a main obstacle to reaching agreement along these lines is the collective failure to define what constitutes a development agenda for the WTO. A growing body of academic evidence and trade policy analysis confirms the importance of trade for development, but there is still little consensus about the specific linkages that would constitute a prodevelopment stance at the WTO. Beyond the legal issue of discerning which government measures are WTO compliant, some of the items on the developing countries' SDT wish list resonate too closely with long-standing battles over the role of industrial policy in promoting development.

In principle, the OECD bloc at the WTO stands together in advocating open, nondiscriminating economic policies and positive technological spillovers from liberal trade and foreign direct investment as the most expedient ways to spur productivity and an efficient allocation of resources. In practice, obviously, there is wide disparity among OECD countries in their willingness to maneuver around the WTO's neoclassical economic paradigm—hefty U.S. agricultural subsidies and high EU farm tariffs being prime examples. In the case of the United States, these contradictions seem to define the inability of the George W. Bush administration to be proactive at the Doha Round. As Mac Destler argues in chapter 9, the United States has shown little enthusiasm for SDT, and despite the flurry of FTAs that it has negotiated with small developing countries, most SDTs offer minimal concessions on market access.

For Destler the collapse of the FTAA talks can be traced to U.S. intransigence on subsidy cuts for sugar and oranges; the persistence of U.S. cotton subsidies is also partly to blame for the stalemate at the Doha Round. To break this pattern, Destler says, U.S. trade negotiators will need to win new access to both goods and services markets in emerging economic powerhouses like Brazil and India. In other words, both sides will have to give much more than they have offered thus far. Destler details an erratic pattern of trade policymaking under the George W. Bush administration, which has intermittently tackled the challenges at hand, exacerbated them with protectionist concessions to domestic interests to secure legislation like the president's Trade Promotion Authority (TPA), and then dropped all efforts to promote U.S. trade strategy. In mid-2004, for example, U.S. leadership helped produce a supposedly groundbreaking WTO document that produced substantive and procedural accords on agriculture (cotton in particular), nonagricultural market access, services, trade facilitation, and a range of development-related issues. In the months after Bush's November 2004 election victory, however, U.S. commitment to this trade agenda simply ceased.

Destler notes the considerable political groundwork that remains to be done in order to make U.S. market-opening concessions possible. At home, the Office of the U.S. Trade Representative will have to build a domestic constituency of stakeholders, much like the winning coalition that secured congressional approval of NAFTA and TPA; further, the executive office will have to bridge the rancorous ideological rifts over trade policy that have come to divide members in both houses of Congress along rigid party lines. Abroad, the completion of the Doha Round will require a revival of U.S. leadership and U.S. collaboration with nations committed to this same task. With the July 1, 2007, expiration of TPA looming, and the renewal of U.S. agriculture legislation coming due at the same time, Destler emphasizes that time is of the essence for reviving U.S. trade policy. Unfortunately, and as noted earlier, the trade wariness of the newly elected Democratic Congress runs counter to this imperative.

On the side of the wealthier emerging market countries, the chapters by Oliveira and by Antonio Ortiz Mena L. N. (chapters 7 and 10, respectively) speak not only to similar collective action bottlenecks on the domestic front in Brazil and Mexico but also to the inclination of both countries to place greater faith in the multilateral arena. As Oliveira explains, capital- and knowledge-based factors are scarce in Brazil, prompting the owners of these scarce factors to call for a gradual liberalization of those sectors that compose the new trade agenda. But Oliveira also cites studies that convincingly show considerable long-run competitive gains for Brazil, assuming the liberalization of services in selected sectors (health insurance, credit export insurance, land transportation, engineering, accounting, and legal services). The initial adjustment costs would obviously be steep, given the complex domestic regulatory framework that now governs Brazil's services sector, and this is where the calls for SDT and a two-tiered FTAA are loudest. This is also the very juncture at which the old and new trade agendas collide.

If Brazil has played a leadership role in challenging U.S. hegemony and in calling for G20 solidarity at the WTO, Mexico, as a result of its concessions on the new trade issues within NAFTA, has frequently been at odds with other developing countries at the WTO. However, Ortiz Mena also points to the pivotal role that Mexico has played in advancing developing country interests in the new trade agenda. Mexican leadership includes its chairing of the working group on trade-related intellectual property (TRIPs) at the

WTO's Fourth Ministerial Conference; its brokering a deal to allow the export of generic copies of patented drugs to the poorest countries; its endorsing efforts to reach multilateral agreement on investment rules; its resisting the linkage of environmental and labor considerations; and its opposing developed country proposals that the wealthier developing countries be excluded from technical assistance and trade capacity building.

Ortiz Mena notes that domestic pressures have increasingly pushed Mexico into the G20 camp. He cites a 2004 opinion poll that shows that just 34 percent of Mexicans view globalization as a positive force, 66 percent disagree that rich countries trade fairly with poor countries, and less than half believe that Mexico should comply with unfavorable WTO rulings on trade disputes. This public sentiment accounts for the September 2004 implementation of a law on international economic agreements that grants unprecedented oversight powers to the Mexican Senate. Because Mexico's some forty FTAs are basically faits accomplis, this law applies mainly to its future multilateral trade commitments. This said, an equally difficult dilemma for Mexico lies in the regional realm, where tough NAFTA-related issues like energy and migration have been relegated to partial and ineffectual bilateral solutions, almost in spite of the preexisting regional framework.

Energy and Migration: The Need to Endogenize NAFTA's Externalities

The final chapters analyze pressing regional concerns that center on energy security and undocumented migration, issues that have nagged all three NAFTA members to varying degrees and that will continue to do so regardless of the revival of the Doha Development Round. While understandably omitted from the original NAFTA talks and side agreement negotiations due to their domestic political sensitivities, these issues are far from extraneous; rather, they are part and parcel of the North American integration process. Yet the reluctance of political leaders and elite decisionmakers to draw on the NAFTA framework in addressing challenges that arose with regard to these key areas suggests the further marginalization of NAFTA as a regional project.

In the case of energy security, although ostensibly a pillar of the 2005 SPP, there are few signs that this particular venue will prevail in shifting the usual pattern of parallel bilateral problem solving onto a more continental track. In chapter 11, on the prospects for forging a continental energy policy, Isidro Morales analyzes the fundamentally different domestic approaches to energy development that now characterize North America. For example, U.S. proposals for enhanced energy security are rooted in a market-oriented model that seeks to establish incentives for conventional and nonconventional resource development but with strong regulatory oversight at the federal level. This complements the Canadian energy framework, especially with the latter's emphasis on the development of nonconventional oil resources (tar sands, bitumen, and synthetic oil) in western Canada. If anything, with the emergence of Canada as an oil power and the development of its huge nonconventional petroleum resources, Canadian policymakers and private sector actors seek to deepen market integration in oil and gas with the United States.

Mexico is again the outlier in North America, as the bulk of its energy sector remains under state control. As sensible as it might be from an efficiency standpoint for Mexico to now expand the coverage of NAFTA's disciplines to its energy sector, a large swath of domestic public opinion continues to oppose market solutions in the production of oil and natural gas.[31] Felipe Calderón, the winner of the 2006 presidential race and former director of the state oil company, Pemex, has taken former President Fox's stance in arguing that NAFTA treatment must be expanded to upstream gas and oil activities but without privatizing Pemex. This proposal, although not optimal, would allow for the further integration of energy markets under an arrangement that links Pemex more closely with private firms.

According to Morales, this proposal best suits American and Canadian interests, since energy firms in these countries are eager to participate through any means in new opportunities for private energy investment in Mexico. Further, although any opening of Mexico's energy sector would require a constitutional amendment, this process could be regulated by the principles and obligations now written into NAFTA—a credibility commitment that is lacking in the SPP. Under this scenario, Mexico's energy sector would move closer to a market-based governance approach, and sales to the United States could be increased without requiring major political or strategic concessions. The question is, in what ways could U.S. and Canadian leadership reverse a long-standing and nationalist collective action stalemate that has literally run Mexico's energy sector into the ground?

The answers are surely not easy; in the continued absence of dynamic North American leadership in constructing a truly continental approach to energy security, Morales cautions that the United States can no longer take Mexico for granted as a steady energy supplier. Moreover, with a divided Mexican congress and contrasting energy proposals put forth by the three main political parties on whether and how to open Mexico's energy sector to private participation, Mexico's own energy security is increasingly at stake. With little domestic consensus on how to fully tap the development of Mexico's energy potential, and with the central government's gutting of Pemex coffers to compensate for chronically low domestic tax collections, Mexico's energy stability merits more regional attention than it has thus far been afforded.

In chapter 12 Charles Doran reinforces these insights from the international angle, and in so doing he emphasizes that the threat to North American energy security is not just a regional one. Doran challenges the conventional notion that the U.S. energy supply is secure because U.S. energy imports come mainly from two reliable local suppliers, Canada and Mexico; in reality, only a third of U.S. energy imports come from these neighbors. According to data from the International Energy Agency, Canada provides about 24 percent of U.S. imported oil and natural gas, and Mexico provides about 8 percent of U.S. imported energy needs. That leaves some two-thirds of U.S. energy imports coming from other parts of the world, some of which are clearly less reliable than those in North America.

Given the North American supply and demand situation and the diversity in commercial and political perspectives, Doran reviews how each North American energy partner is likely to perceive the issue of global energy vulnerability. Despite a highly interdependent North American energy market, the United States is the most vulnerable of the three countries, because it alone is a net importer of energy. In Mexico, as the population and economy continue to grow, national energy supplies will increasingly be depleted, especially if domestic legislation banning foreign investment in the energy industry remains in effect. Mexico could thus become a net importer of petroleum and natural gas unless it accelerates the development of its reserves. Canada, because of its large oil sands reserves, is likely to remain a net energy exporter for some time to come. Yet Doran warns that technical and environmental constraints surrounding the exploitation of Canada's western oil sands have limited production to about a half million barrels a day.

Underlined by the reality that North America alone accounts for 29 percent of world energy demand, the problem of energy vulnerability is large and troublesome. In the face of a severe supply disruption, not all governments in North America would be affected equally. But based on the assumption that each member of the NAFTA community seeks a stable international political environment wherein the continuous supply of energy to the global economy is a foundational principle, Doran endorses the need for both greater market efficiency and integration within the NAFTA bloc and a more aggressive energy policy, one that promotes the development and adaptation of alternative fuel sources at competitive prices as substitutes for petroleum and natural gas.

The authors of the final two chapters on migration and citizenship in North America emphasize that a myopic approach to labor mobility and citizenship rights under NAFTA has worked against productivity and political cohesion. While the main headliner on this front is the massive flow of undocumented Mexican workers into U.S. labor markets, and the accompanying acrimonious exchange between the U.S. and Mexican governments over immigration policy, in chapter 13 Tamara Woroby points to the lost opportunities inherent in the status quo. She argues that, given that Canada and the United States are net receiving countries, the differences between Canadian and U.S. immigration policies are instructive.

In Canada the most important criterion is whether a prospective immigrant has the economic skills that Canada requires. Based on a point system, some 60 percent of documented immigrants entering Canada do so based on their skill levels, whereas only one-fifth of documented workers enter the United States on these same grounds. Approximately two-thirds of documented immigrants enter the United States on the basis of family reunification criteria, although economic motives obviously drive the decision to migrate in the first place. Especially since the 2000 recession, economic pressure to migrate has exploded against a backdrop of strong U.S. labor market demand and lackluster growth in jobs and wages in Mexico. The annual inflow of undocumented migrants to the United States may be as high as 500,000 over the past five years, and it is estimated that at least half of these come from Mexico.

Along with Woroby, Christina Gabriel and Laura Macdonald (chapter 14) argue that the failures of U.S. immigration policy have exacerbated these illicit labor flows. First, the narrow fixation on border security and strengthening barriers to entry along the U.S.-Mexico border ignores the fundamental laws of supply and demand under which undocumented northward migration has flourished. This is confirmed by the heavy reliance of U.S. industrial, agricultural, and service sectors on cheap Mexican labor to fill less-skilled employment niches. For Mexico, remittances (earnings sent home by the country's foreign laborers) are greater than the total share of foreign direct investment, tourism, and agricultural exports in the country's balance of payments. These complementary trends confirm the difficulty of separating economic development issues from migration patterns, although this reality has not fully resonated with U.S. policymakers.

Second, although there has been no shortage of proposals for how to cope with migration pressures within NAFTA, there has been little progress in the area of reforms to clarify and strengthen mobility rights. Mexico's calls for a more rational and humane legal framework to capture the benefits of labor market mobility, while also controlling its excesses, have gone unheeded by Washington. One plausible solution is to create an intermediate immigrant category, something between unauthorized and legal resident status. This could be followed by the granting of temporary status (as in a guest worker program), which would also help to bring unauthorized workers out into the open. Conditions for proof of economic contribution, such as a required number of years in active employment before applying for change of status to legal resident, could then be set forth.

The alternatives, suggest Gabriel and Macdonald, as reflected in the barrage of border security proposals emanating from Capitol Hill, run directly against the grain of NAFTA's original justification. That logic, put forward by Mexican and U.S. political leaders in the early 1990s, holds that Mexico's entry into NAFTA provides a magnet for domestic jobs and investment and thus limits the northward flow of illicit migrants. Instead, these northward flows have continued at an unprecedented pace; employer demand for migrants who lack strong skills has broadened the economic underclass in the United States. Further, unauthorized Mexican workers have been vulnerable to discrimination and workplace violations and lack many basic social rights. In the post-9/11 era undocumented Mexican migrants who are able to penetrate the U.S. border are more likely to stay rather than to engage in the circular pattern of migration that characterizes past economic survival strategies.

In the end, although vital issues like energy security and intrabloc labor migration were considered too politically volatile for inclusion in the NAFTA negotiations of the early 1990s, each of these issues has become impossible to ignore. The ability of each of the three NAFTA members to see its way toward continental solutions is imperative to the resilience and credibility of NAFTA. With decisive U.S. leadership and commitment to a regional project, the range of available solutions could easily take on an aura of viability. Without this leadership, NAFTA could easily fade into the shadows of assertive experiments with regionalism in the Asia-Pacific. Although the prospect of more competitive regional integration across Asia will most likely bring the Doha Round back to life, North America will still be left to face various regional challenges.[32]

Notes

1. Fernando Masi and Carol Wise, "Negotiating the FTAA between the Main Players: The U.S. and MERCOSUR," in *MERCOSUR and the Creation of the Free Trade Area of the Americas,* edited by Marcel Vaillant and Fernando Lorenzo (Washington: Woodrow Wilson Center for International Scholars, 2005).

2. World Bank, *Global Economic Prospects: Trade, Regionalism, and Development* (Washington: 2005).

3. Richard Steinberg, "In the Shadow of Law or Power? Consensus-Based Bargaining and Outcomes at the GATT/WTO," *International Organization* 56, no. 2 (2002): 339–74.

4. John S. Odell, "Introduction," in *Negotiating Trade: Developing Countries in the WTO and NAFTA,* edited by John S. Odell (Cambridge University Press, 2006).

5. Pascal Lamy, "What Now, Trade Ministers?" *International Herald Tribune,* July 28, 2006, p. 6.

6. Joseph E. Stiglitz and Andrew Charlton, *Fair Trade for All: How Trade Can Promote Development* (Oxford University Press, 2005), p. 88.

7. Tom Wright, "Collapse of Global Trade Talks: Regional Deals Move to the Forefront," *International Herald Tribune,* July 26, 2006, p. 1; "In the Twilight of Doha," *Economist,* July 29, 2006.

8. Timothy J. Kehoe, "Assessing the Economic Impact of North American Free Trade," in *The NAFTA Debate: Grappling with Unconventional Trade Issues,* edited by M. Delal Baer and Sidney Weintraub (Boulder, Colo.: Lynne Rienner, 1994).

9. Manuel Pastor and Carol Wise, "The Lost *Sexenio*: Vicente Fox and the 'New' Politics of Economic Reform in Mexico," *Latin American Politics and Society* 47, no. 4 (2005): 135–60.

10. Bruce Ackerman and David Golove, "Is NAFTA Constitutional?" *Harvard Law Review* 108, no. 4 (1995): 799–929.

11. Sylvia Maxfield and Adam Shapiro, "Assessing the NAFTA Negotiations: US-Mexican Compromise on Tariff and Nontariff Issues," in *The Post-NAFTA Political Economy: Mexico and the Western Hemisphere,* edited by Carol Wise (Pennsylvania State University Press, 1998).

12. As of December 2004 the NADBank had approved U.S.$697 million, from its U.S.$3 billion callable capital base, for loans and grants for eighty-five infrastructure projects, although just 57 percent of these were planned for the Mexican side of the border. See Gary Hufbauer and Jeffrey Schott, *NAFTA Revisited* (Washington: Institute for International Economics, 2005), pp. 174–76.

13. Ibid., p. 61.

14. Marcela Celorio, "The North American 'Security and Prosperity Partnership': An Evaluation," Working Paper (Center for North American Studies, American University, March 2006), p. 10.

15. Organization for Economic Cooperation and Development, *Getting It Right: OECD Perspectives on Policy Challenges in Mexico* (Mexico City: Centro de la OCDE en México para América Latina, 2007), pp. 59–63.

16. See, for example, John Audley and others, *NAFTA's Promise and Reality* (Washington: Carnegie Endowment for International Peace, 2003).

17. On neoclassical trade theories, see Kerry A. Chase, *Trading Blocs* (University of Michigan Press, 2005).

18. See, for example, Manuel Pastor and Carol Wise, "The Origins and Sustainability of Mexico's Free Trade Policy," *International Organization* 48, no. 3 (1994): 459–89.

19. Chappell H. Lawson, *Mexico under Calderón: The Challenges Ahead* (Los Angeles: Pacific Council on International Policy, 2006).

20. For more on this debate, see Jacob Viner, *The Customs Union Issue* (New York: Carnegie Endowment for International Peace, 1950); Kerry A. Chase, "Economic Interests and Regional Trading Arrangements," *International Organization* 57, no. 1 (2003): 137–74.

21. Blanca Torres, "Rowing Upstream," in *Greening the Americas: NAFTA Lessons for Hemispheric Trade,* edited by Carolyn L. Deere and Daniel C. Esty (MIT Press, 2002), p. 203; Stephen Krasner, "México y Estados Unidos," in *Interdependencia ¿Un enfoque útil para el análisis de las relaciones México-Estados Unidos?* edited by Blanca Torres (Mexico City: El Colegio de México, 1990).

22. Sibylla Brodzinsky and Peter S. Goodman, "Latin Americans Wonder if Democrats Are Traders," *Washington Post,* November 23, 2006, p. A1.

23. Kenneth C. Shadlen, "Exchanging Development for Market Access? Deep Integration and Industrial Policy under Multilateral and Regional-Bilateral Trade Agreements," *Review of International Political Economy* 12, no. 5 (2005): 750–75.

24. Albert Fishlow, "Brazil: FTA or FTAA or WTO?" in *Free Trade Agreements: US Strategies and Priorities,* edited by Jeffrey Schott (Washington: Institute for International Economics, 2004).

25. Members of the G20 (actually G21 with Uruguay's recent joining) are Argentina, Bolivia, Brazil, Chile, China, Cuba, Egypt, Guatemala, India, Indonesia, Mexico, Nigeria, Pakistan, Paraguay, Philippines, South Africa, Tanzania, Thailand, Uruguay, Venezuela, Zimbabwe.

26. "Mercosur's Summit: Downhill from Here," *Economist,* July 29, 2006, p. 52.

27. Stiglitz and Charlton, *Fair Trade for All,* p. 50.

28. Norberto Iannelli, "Achievements, Prospects, and Challenges of Hemispheric Cooperation," INTAL-ITD Occasional Paper 38 (Washington: Inter-American Development Bank, June 2006), pp. 7–8.

29. Barbara Stallings and Wilson Peres, *Growth, Employment, and Equity: The Impact of the Economic Reforms in Latin America and the Caribbean* (Brookings, 2000), pp. 1–71.

30. Stiglitz and Charlton, *Fair Trade for All,* p. 60.

31. Antonio Ortiz Mena L. N., "Getting to No: Defending against Demands in NAFTA Energy Negotiations," in *Negotiating Trade: Developing Countries in the WTO and NAFTA,* edited by John S. Odell (Cambridge University Press, 2006).

32. See, for example, Fred Bergsten, "Plan B for World Trade: Go Regional," *Financial Times,* August 16, 2006.

PART I

THE NORTH AMERICAN FREE TRADE AREA

Achievements and Limitations

2

UNFULFILLED PROMISE
Economic Convergence under NAFTA

CAROL WISE

It is estimated that around 230 subregional integration schemes have cropped up across Asia, Africa, the Middle East, and the Western Hemisphere since 1990, but this chapter is concerned with one of the more unusual features to have emerged within the current generation of regional trade agreements (RTAs): the sweeping elimination of economic barriers between the less developed countries and the developed countries.[1] Ireland, Greece, Spain, and Portugal made this leap when joining the European Economic Community (EEC) between 1973 and 1986, and Mexico, the focus of this analysis, later followed with its entry into the North American Free Trade Agreement (NAFTA) with Canada and the United States in January 1994.

By definition, these more recent North-South deals—all of which involve shorter liberalization timelines and much higher levels of asymmetry and heterogeneity—invoke a more development-oriented set of questions and concerns.[2] First, today's underdeveloped RTA members are poorer than their European predecessors were at the time of accession. In the latter cases, all but Portugal registered at least double the levels of per capita income before joining the EEC/European Union (EU) than did Mexico on the eve of NAFTA.[3] The EU, moreover, coupled mutual market access for these poorer entrants with development assistance, free movement of labor within the EU

27

bloc, and other measures meant to compensate for the steep asymmetries at hand.[4] Not so NAFTA, which means that any bridging of the huge gap between Mexico and its NAFTA partners—or for that matter between the United States and any number of its newest RTA partners (for example, the Central Andean or Central American blocs)—has fallen to market forces.

Second, along with the laissez-faire ethos that has underpinned this latest wave of North-South integration, the accompanying discourse both within Mexico and among the three NAFTA partners raised expectations for rapid development gains. From the start, neoclassical theories of trade and growth held sway, arguing that a country like Mexico—the least developed and most protected member of the RTA—would be expected to undergo a more painful adjustment but would also reap disproportionate gains in the way of higher growth, productivity, and overall welfare.[5] In the short run, it was expected that the elimination of barriers to the free flow of goods, capital, and services within the RTA would enable all three countries—but especially Mexico—to better capture the benefits of regionalism (scale economies related to greater specialization, increased technological capabilities, and a more rapid and efficient deployment of those endowment factors for which Mexico has a comparative advantage) and trigger a dynamic process of income convergence among the three members.[6]

It was also envisioned that NAFTA's competitive potential in the long run would rest on the dynamic blending of Mexico's abundant factors (natural resources, comparatively cheap labor, and proximity to the U.S. market) with the abundance of capital, technology, and know-how that Canada and the United States brought to the table. Yet from the start there were doubters concerned about both NAFTA's impacts on labor and the environment and the plausibility of this neoclassical economic scenario. For example, because Mexico had already unilaterally liberalized the bulk of its tariff lines before joining the General Agreement on Tariffs and Trade (GATT) in 1986, technical estimates cautioned that the overall impact of North American integration on Mexico would amount at most to 5–8 percent of Mexico's GDP.[7]

Experience has borne out some of the predictions. However, none of the forecasters fully captured the essence of what has come to pass: Mexico's short-lived surge under NAFTA and the uneven pattern of convergence between Mexico and its NAFTA partners and within Mexico itself.[8] Whether measured in absolute (growth) or relative (distribution) terms, or by comparing macro- versus microeconomic indicators, the expectations for higher sustainable growth and dynamic gains have yet to fully materialize. In particular, Mexico has struggled to compete with China since its entrance into U.S.

markets upon accession to the World Trade Organization (WTO) in 2001.[9] Granted, theories of growth and development have yet to fully come to grips with the rapid and remarkable ascendance of China in the world economy. Yet many of these same theories held that Mexico, by virtue of its privileged access to the U.S. market since 1994, should be able to hold its own against such incursions.

Despite a growing and dynamic literature that debates both the impetus and the obstacles to convergence, these insights take us just so far in explaining Mexico's inability to fully exploit its unique status as a member of NAFTA.[10] What's missing is a broader political explanation, one that probes the interests, ideologies, and policies that have underpinned North American integration from both a regional and a domestic standpoint. I begin here with a brief examination of the institutional design of NAFTA and note how the agreement itself intentionally overlooks Mexico's economic status and the steep asymmetries that distinguished it from the outset. The following section reviews the convergence/divergence debate with regard to NAFTA and Mexico and analyzes the empirical data that have been used to tout both the benefits and the costs of asymmetrical integration. The final sections of the chapter critique the potential role of NAFTA as a development tool and argue that the asymmetries call for a more proactive regional strategy.

NAFTA in Perspective: Anglo-Saxon Regionalism

Although there are distinctions between NAFTA and the EU in terms of regional integration strategies, EU strategies have affected U.S. integration debates since the onset of NAFTA negotiations in 1991 in the sense that a majority of U.S. policymakers, legislators, and public opinion shapers have sought to define EU integration strategies in terms of how *not* to proceed. At least from the standpoint of Washington, the main areas of contention with the EU model concern the web of supranational institutions (or "Brussels bureaucracy") that governs political and economic integration in Europe, the equating of the EU's extensive harmonization and standardization measures with a misguided industrial policy, and the strong role that public policy has played in the provision of social and infrastructure funds to smooth the adjustment costs of EU entry for weaker members and regions.[11]

Thus while in principle NAFTA and the EU may embrace similar goals in the promotion of growth, productivity, and overall welfare gains, the shadow of the past has meant markedly different policy choices. The EU approach to integration reflects the ideological and pragmatic concerns that gave rise to the European social welfare state in the wake of World War II.[12] In the United States historic preferences have similarly prevailed, but in favor of a laissez-faire integration strategy that casts responsibility for overall welfare in individualistic terms.[13] At least in Washington's lexicon, the EU's supranational institutions impinge on state sovereignty, and the EU's public policy is too interventionist and solicitous of the less developed members.

These differences can be framed in terms of the four-stage taxonomy used in the literature on regionalism.[14] Since 1957 the EEC/EU has evolved from a six-member free trade area (wherein barriers to trade in goods are eliminated but each member maintains independent tariffs with nonmembers) to a customs union (which sets a common external tariff on all trade between members and nonmembers); then to a twenty-five-member common market (which deepens the customs union by allowing for the free flow of labor and capital); and then to a full economic union in which a majority of members share a common currency and seek to coordinate macroeconomic policies. Within this scheme, NAFTA is a free trade area in which the flow of goods, capital, and services has been liberalized over a fifteen-year time schedule. It is the dominant preference of U.S. and Canadian policymakers, as well as of vested interests in North America, that this arrangement remain at the level of a free trade area, an arrangement that has been rightly labeled Anglo-Saxon regionalism.[15]

Other features of NAFTA further justify this classification, including the primarily private sector impetus for its negotiation and the anti-institutional biases inherent in the agreement. On the role of the private sector in lobbying for NAFTA, Kerry Chase argues convincingly that it was the high preexisting levels of intra-industry trade and production sharing across borders in intermediate goods, as well as the possibilities for exploiting economies of scale, that prompted producers in NAFTA's key sectors (autos, computers, office equipment, electronics, machinery and parts) to push for regional liberalization. "Because barriers to regional trade and investment restrict opportunities to take advantage of differences between countries in wages, skills, or capital costs, firms seek regional arrangements if they can redeploy intermediate production between labor-rich and labor-scarce areas."[16] With Mexico and Canada accounting for 60.5 percent of U.S. intrafirm trade in 1989, regional liberalization clearly offered producers the opportunity to reduce manufacturing costs and realize higher profit margins.

Because each of the three members maintains its own independent trade relationship with nonmembers, NAFTA includes detailed rules of origin in key sectors to prevent imports from third countries from entering the free trade area through the member country with the lowest tariffs. To deter outsiders from free riding, the three biggest North American auto producers, blue chip computer companies such as Hewlett-Packard and IBM, and large textile firms, among others, sought and won guarantees that competitors from Asia and the EU, in particular, would contribute to their own restructuring costs by paying North American content duties as high as 62.5 percent. Under GATT/WTO, these stiff entry requirements in the form of rules of origin are permitted conditionally within RTAs but not at the multilateral level.

None of these explanatory factors detracts from the oft-told narrative regarding the choice and design of NAFTA. As this story goes, all three countries were reeling from the global economic shocks of the 1970s and the international recession of the early 1980s. As noted above, bilateral trade and cross-border production with U.S. companies was of increasing importance for both Canada and Mexico, although one main U.S. response to the rising debts and deficits of the mid-1980s was an increase in protectionism. Of necessity, Canada and Mexico had each begun a gradual process of economic liberalization and macroeconomic restructuring to address the cumulative shortcomings of decades of high protectionism, but these respective reform strategies could only be locked in domestically via secure access to U.S. markets.[17] As the Uruguay Round negotiations were clearly lagging, U.S. policymakers conceded, first, to negotiate a bilateral Canada-U.S. Free Trade Agreement (CUSFTA), which was implemented in 1989, and then the trilateral NAFTA, which was launched in 1994.

Apart from offering its own brand of protectionism-cum-industrial policy—that is, breathing room for cross-border producers in North America to restructure behind stiff content rules—NAFTA also facilitated certain liberalization inroads that had been heretofore blocked in the multilateral arena. Such was the case with the liberalization of services and investment, provisions for strengthening intellectual property rights, and the design of dispute settlement mechanisms for trade and investment conflicts. From the U.S. viewpoint, the creation of dispute settlement mechanisms and a rotating NAFTA secretariat sufficed in terms of an institutional foundation for NAFTA. Given the huge disparities within North America, both Canada and Mexico correctly perceived that the design of supranational institutions would require each to concede sovereignty to the United States in ways that reached beyond their respective political comfort zones. Thus all three countries colluded in favor of a minimalist institutional framework.[18]

In the interim between the completion of the NAFTA negotiations by the outgoing Bush administration in 1992 and the inauguration of the Clinton administration in January 1993, grassroots opposition to this minimalist institutional approach swelled in the United States. Domestic civic constituencies demanded additional institutional guarantees in terms of environmental protection and labor rights as a quid pro quo for their support of the proposed agreement. Civil society was highly successful in politicizing the debate over NAFTA, winning institutional concessions for labor and the environment and for the creation of the North American Development Bank (NADBank). Unfortunately, the resulting institutions—the North American Commission for Labor Cooperation, the North American Commission for Environmental Cooperation, and the NADBank—"were left with such minimal mandates and meager funding that they barely meet original expectations."[19]

Through a kind of ad hoc intergovernmental consensus, ruling elites in all three countries have certainly avoided the programmatic redundancy and bureaucratic creep that also characterizes the EU. However, the adamancy against institutionalizing NAFTA has been such that there is no central headquarters or trinational staff to coordinate the work of the NAFTA secretariat. Dispute settlement procedures are thus decentralized, and panel members are chosen on a revolving basis. At most the labor and environmental side agreements obligate each member to uphold and implement its own national laws and to play mainly a consultative role. As the following section argues, this insistence that NAFTA remain a free trade area in the absence of sound institutional moorings has limited NAFTA's success to the narrow parameters by which it has been defined.

Convergence/Divergence: The Debate and the Data

The tenth anniversary of NAFTA in 2004 was met with a spate of assessments, most of which judged its success or failure according to the growth of intrabloc trade and investment flows, the net employment effects on each member country, and the accompanying distributional impacts.[20] In brief, these analyses found that total intrabloc merchandise trade had grown by more than 200 percent and that the stock of foreign direct investment in Mexico had increased fivefold from its pre-NAFTA levels.[21] On the downside, labor markets and wage trends had turned increasingly volatile, and distribution had somewhat worsened. Perhaps most troubling was the World Bank's finding that Mexico's foreign direct investment performance "was not significantly above the Latin America norm."[22] Neither were its aggregate or per capita growth rates. When analyzed from these vantage points, NAFTA's reviews ranged from unfavorable to mildly beneficial.[23]

The continued lack of enthusiasm or consensus over NAFTA's purpose and impacts reflects the gulf between the wishful theoretical thinking and the concrete empirical asymmetries that underpinned its launching in the early 1990s. As the guiding principle for North American integration, neoclassical theory assumed a state of perfect competition and constant returns to scale under an RTA such as NAFTA. As mentioned earlier, it was expected that over time the elimination of barriers to the free flow of goods, capital, and services within the RTA would enable all three countries—but especially Mexico—to better capture the benefits of regionalism (scale economies related to greater specialization, increased technological capabilities, and a more rapid and efficient deployment of those endowment factors in which Mexico has a comparative advantage) and would trigger a dynamic process of income convergence among the three members.[24]

The fact that NAFTA has yet to measure up to this scenario of buoyant dynamism and steady convergence among the three countries in many respects vindicates the earlier doubters of neoclassical trade theory.[25] The obstacles they pointed out include, for example, institutional weaknesses, deeply engrained barriers to competition, and sizable skill and technology deficits that characterize a developing economy like Mexico's. Yet even Canada, with its advantage as a G8 country, has lagged in this regard. For example, although Canadian income distribution is the most equitable in North America, Canada's purchasing power per capita remains about 74 percent of that of the United States, and productivity and investment ratios are similarly trailing.

The data do lend equivocal support to the champions of neoclassical analysis in that both Canada and Mexico have converged toward the more highly developed U.S. standard in terms of broad macroeconomic performance—inflation, interest rates, aggregate growth, and exchange rate stability—even if the microeconomic track record has been uneven. This microeconomic point is driven home in tables 2-1 and 2-2, which show a respectable upward convergence of GDP growth rates for the three NAFTA countries but a troubling lag in the rise of per capita incomes. Real income in Mexico, after doubling its per capita growth between 1995 and 2000, hit a virtual plateau. And while Mexico's average aggregate growth rate of 2–3 percent during the NAFTA era is respectable and in step with Canada and the United States, it is well below the average growth rate for other Latin American emerging markets like Argentina, Chile, and Peru.

The indisputable successes in the macroeconomic realm include Mexico's ability to radically reduce inflation and interest rates to levels already achieved by Canada and the United States. As tables 2-3 and 2-4 show, both

Table 2-1. *Annual GDP Growth, United States, Canada, and Mexico, Select Years, 1980–2005*

Percent

Year	United States	Canada	Mexico
1980	(0.2)	1.3	9.2
1990	1.7	0.2	5.1
1995	2.7	2.8	(6.2)
1997	4.5	4.2	6.8
1998	4.3	4.1	5.0
1999	4.1	5.5	3.6
2000	4.2	4.6	6.6
2001	0.3	1.5	(0.3)
2002	3.5	4.3	0.7
2003	4.9	5.2	1.3
2004	0.7	6.5	4.4
2005	3.6	3.0	3.0

Source: *International Financial Statistics* (Washington: IFS, various years).

Table 2-2. *GDP per Capita, United States, Canada, and Mexico, Select Years, 1980–2004*

US$

Year	United States	Canada	Mexico
1980	21,000	16,539	3,282
1990	26,141	19,229	3,187
1995	27,404	20,117	2,637
1997	30,096	21,287	4,165
1998	31,357	20,402	4,068
1999	32,870	21,677	4,958
2000	34,445	23,537	5,799
2001	35,163	23,048	6,326
2002	36,033	23,535	5,956
2003	37,423	27,403	5,878
2004	39,722	31,030	6,478

Source: *International Financial Statistics* (Washington: IFS, various years).

Table 2-3. *Consumer Prices, Annual Change, United States, Canada, and Mexico, 1995–2004*
Percent

Year	United States	Canada	Mexico
1995	2.81	2.17	35.00
1996	2.93	1.58	34.38
1997	2.34	1.62	20.63
1998	1.55	0.99	15.93
1999	2.19	1.72	16.59
2000	3.38	2.75	9.50
2001	2.83	2.53	6.36
2002	1.59	2.25	5.03
2003	2.27	2.77	4.55
2004	2.68	1.83	4.69

Source: *International Financial Statistics* (Washington: IFS, various years).

Table 2-4. *Interest Rates, United States, Canada, and Mexico, 1993–2005*
Percent

Year	United States	Canada	Mexico
1993	6.00	4.11	22.04
1994	7.14	7.43	20.38
1995	8.83	5.79	59.43
1996	8.27	3.25	36.39
1997	8.44	4.50	22.14
1998	8.35	5.25	26.36
1999	7.99	5.00	23.74
2000	9.23	6.00	16.93
2001	6.92	2.50	12.80
2002	4.68	3.00	8.20
2003	4.12	3.00	6.91
2004	4.33	2.75	7.22
2005	6.18	3.50	9.90

Source: *International Financial Statistics* (Washington: IFS, various years).

of these indicators dropped to the single-digit range, after a prolonged period of double-digit inflation and high interest rates following the country's 1994 financial meltdown. Given Canada's tighter integration with the United States and its G8 status at the outset of NAFTA, its macroeconomic performance has been even more impressive. Although some of Canada's uninterrupted growth has been due to the luck of high commodity prices since 2001, it is also policy induced.

As the country's long-standing mercantilist policies had virtually imploded by the late 1980s, Canadian policymakers met the challenge of heightened competition from the U.S. market by executing major fiscal cuts and deep structural reforms through the 1990s. Although these bold moves were anathema to most Canadians at the time, they have paid off. Since 1997 Canada has been the fastest growing G8 economy, registering a fiscal surplus for seven consecutive years; net public debt has been reduced by nearly 30 percent of GDP, and the public pension and health care systems are on sound fiscal footing.

The gap between Canada's sound macroeconomic performance and its less dynamic microeconomic returns is reflected in table 2-5, which shows Canada falling behind the United States on five competitiveness indicators. A 2005 report from Canada's Institute for Competitiveness and Prosperity notes some complacency in this respect, stating that Canadians have simply not been "as successful as their U.S. counterparts in creating value from our labor, intellectual, physical, and natural resources."[26] The tackling of this tenacious gap (such as tax incentives that spur rather than deter investment; increased ties between R&D, universities, and private initiative; and the application of more advanced technology to the production of goods) emerged as one of the policy commitments made by the winning conservative candidate, Stephen Harper, in Canada's January 2006 parliamentary elections.

A main puzzle here concerns Mexico's microeconomic progress in table 2-5, which is notable, although the inroads recorded defy the rapid trend toward its displacement by China in the U.S. market (as reflected in tables 2-6 and 2-7). As table 2-5 shows, the proportion of high-tech exports as a percentage of GDP nearly tripled for Mexico, outpacing Canada's improvement—and with no change at all on this count for the United States. The number of patents granted to Mexico increased at a faster rate than did those of the United States, while Canadian patents actually decreased. Moreover, Mexican productivity easily outgained that of both the United States and Canada in the post-NAFTA years. While Mexico trailed in the growth rate of

Table 2-5. *Competitive Indicators, United States, Canada, and Mexico, Various Years*

Indicator and year	United States	Canada	Mexico
High-tech exports as percent of GDP			
1990	33.0	13.0	8.2
2000	33.0	18.6	22.0
R & D as percent of GDP			
1996	2.5	1.7	0.3
2001	2.8	2.1	0.3
Patents granted			
1999	153,487	13,778	3,899
2000	157,496	12,125	5,519
2001	166,038	12,019	5,479
Internet users per 1,000 population			
1994	49	25	0.4
2001	551	512	36
Productivity (output per hour, 1990 = 100)			
1994	100	100	100
2001	146.1	124.2	177.8

Sources: World Trade Organization and International Labor Organization.

Table 2-6. *Exports to the United States from China and Mexico, 1995–2004*

	China		Mexico	
Year	Exports in U.S.$ billion	Percent change	Exports in U.S.$ billion	Percent change
1995	45.6	17.5	61.7	24.7
1996	51.5	13.0	73.0	18.2
1997	62.6	21.5	85.9	17.7
1998	71.2	13.8	94.7	10.3
1999	81.8	14.9	109.7	15.8
2000	100.1	22.3	135.9	23.9
2001	102.3	2.2	131.4	−3.3
2002	125.2	22.4	134.7	2.5
2003	152.4	21.7	138.1	2.5
2004	196.7	29.1	155.8	12.9

Source: *TradeStats* (Washington: International Trade Administration, various years).

Table 2-7. *Top Ten U.S. Imports from Mexico, 2004*

Rank and commodity[a]	Value in U.S.$ billion	Percent of total
1. Electrical machinery and equipment and parts thereof; sound recorders and reproducers, television image and sound recorders and reproducers, and parts and accessories of such articles (85)	37.4	24.00
2. Vehicles other than railway or tramway rolling stock and parts and accessories thereof (87)	26.1	16.78
3. Machinery and mechanical appliances; electrical equipment; parts thereof; sound recorders and reproducers, television image and sound recorders and reproducers, and parts and accessories of such articles (84)	20.0	12.86
4. Mineral fuels, mineral oils, and products of their distillation; bituminous substances; mineral waxes (27)	19.7	12.65
5. Optical, photographic, cinematographic, measuring, checking, precision, medical, or surgical instruments and apparatus; clocks and watches; musical instruments; parts and accessories thereof (90)	6.0	3.88
6. Furniture; bedding, mattresses, mattress supports, cushions, and similar stuffed furnishings; lamps and lighting fittings not elsewhere specified or included; illuminated signs, illuminated nameplates, and the like; prefabricated buildings (94)	5.1	3.30
7. Special classification provisions (98)	4.7	3.00
8. Articles of apparel and clothing accessories not knitted or crocheted (62)	4.1	2.65
9. Articles of apparel and clothing accessories knitted or crocheted (61)	2.7	1.74
10. Edible vegetables and certain roots and tubers (07)	2.4	1.54
All other	27.4	17.60
Total	155.8	100.00

Source: *TradeStats* (Washington: International Trade Administration, various years).

a. As of 2003 exports from China to the United States in ranks 1, 3, 6, 8, and 9 now exceed those of Mexico.

Internet users and in the ratio of R&D to GDP, these facts too support the assumptions of neoclassical trade theory: Mexico did better at increasing productivity than at increasing R&D because its comparative advantage is in labor, not science, and not in the capital required for fast Internet expansion.

As estimated by Daniel Lederman and his colleagues at the World Bank's Latin America and Caribbean Division, "Mexico's global exports would have been about 50 percent lower and foreign direct investment would have been about 40 percent less without NAFTA. Also, the amount of time required for Mexican manufacturers to adopt U.S. technological innovations was cut in half. . . . NAFTA made Mexico richer by about 4 percent of its gross domestic product per capita."[27] Mexico, moreover, has leveraged its NAFTA membership to shift from a heavy dependence on oil exports toward a diversified mix of higher value-added goods. In light of these gains, what accounts for the bottleneck in Mexico's growth rate of both aggregate and per capita GDP? How is it that China has so readily cut into Mexico's supposed long-touted advantage in the U.S. market? And why would nearly half of the electorate support a presidential candidate in 2006 who vowed to backtrack on many of the country's commitments to a NAFTA-style development model?

Mexico: The Politics of Divergence

In the early 1990s the eagerness of Mexican policymakers to close the NAFTA deal was such that former president Carlos Salinas de Gortari vowed to forgo Mexico's developing country status at the NAFTA negotiating table. While a similar elite-level decision would have been unthinkable in more democratic polities like those of Argentina or Brazil, in Mexico the peculiarities of hegemonic, single-party politics basically rendered the country's entry into NAFTA a fait accompli. At the same time, the United States made it clear from the start that this North American project would remain distinct from the EU: it would remain a free trade agreement with no aspirations to become a fully integrated political and economic union. True to its Anglo-Saxon roots, the goal set for NAFTA was mainly an economic one. This in itself is a political decision, though cast in apolitical terms by the executives of all three countries.

Thus according to these minimalist criteria of trade and investment expansion, NAFTA clearly measures up to the narrow standards imposed by its creators. In short, although Mexico may arguably have been worse off had it not joined NAFTA, counterfactual analysis (such as comparisons of Mexico with other Latin American emerging markets that did not join NAFTA) and the post-2000 growth trap that appears in table 2-1 suggest a pattern of underperformance. Or to put it differently, Mexico's competitive inroads displayed in table 2-5, although impressive in and of themselves, have not been dynamic enough to trigger the development leap envisioned by NAFTA's architects. Mexico's reform record suggests that the roots of divergence lie not only with the agreement itself but also with the frailties of domestic politics, institutions, and policymaking.[28]

In the remainder of this section I focus on the three main factors that have contributed to Mexico's underperformance within NAFTA: the use of an RTA as a tool to lock in incipient market reforms without adequate preparation; the unexpected difficulties of managing economic liberalization in the context of a hegemonic, single-party system; and a miscalculation concerning the benefits to be gained from Mexico's geographic proximity to the U.S. market.

The Limits to Mexico's Liberalization-cum-Integration Approach

In contrast to the reform preparation and adjustment assistance afforded to less developed entrants into the EU before their accession, Mexico's own market restructuring program was still gathering steam when NAFTA was launched in 1994. As the country's political and economic elite seized NAFTA entry as a way to permanently lock in a liberal development strategy, the risks inherent in this liberalization-cum-integration approach were made evident by the December 1994 peso crash. It would be difficult to exaggerate the adverse effects of this financial crisis over the longer term.[29] To this day the distributional fallout and lingering risk adversity have partially deterred Mexico from achieving the higher growth and per capita gains that have pushed EU developing countries like Ireland and Spain closer to the front of the global pack.

As tables 2-3 and 2-4 show, it took Mexico nearly a decade after the peso debacle to stabilize inflation and join step with its NAFTA partners in terms of macroeconomic performance. This victory did not come cheaply, as it ties policymakers to a tight monetary and fiscal regime that works directly against job creation and improvements in per capita growth.[30] The battle for macroeconomic stability also diverts resources and policymaking talent away from the pressing competitive tasks shown in figure 2-1, including the kinds of institutional modernization required to support a meaningful competition policy. However, despite the real or imagined confines of Anglo-Saxon regionalism and its simplistic penchant for laissez-faire, nothing in this doctrine has stood in the way of those institutional reforms needed to bolster

Figure 2-1. *Factors of Institutional Strength: Canada, the United States, and Mexico*

Variable ranges from −2 to +2 for all countries

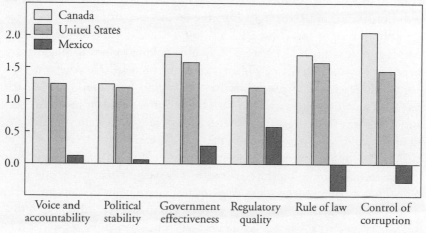

Source: D. A. Kraay and M. Mastruzzi, *Worldwide Governance Indicators: 1996–2005* (Washington: World Bank, 2006)

Mexico's gains from NAFTA. Rather, the country's growth bottleneck appears to be homegrown and deeply engrained in domestic politics.

Divided Government and the Reform Backlog

For Mexico, NAFTA entry catalyzed the long overdue political liberalization, which culminated in 2000 in the first opposition presidential victory that the country had seen since the installation of the heavy-handed Institutional Revolutionary Party (PRI) in 1929. When elected to the presidency in 2000, National Action Party (PAN) candidate Vicente Fox inherited a formidable list of reform tasks, but he also inherited a democratic dividend that seemed to promise high levels of political support for tackling the reform agenda. At the top of this list was the need for energy sector modernization and improvement of the country's transportation and communications infrastructure; fiscal restructuring to raise tax revenues as a percent of GDP; technical support and credit for those small and medium-size firms that provide the bulk of Mexican employment; greater labor market mobility; and a deepening and expansion of human capital investments in education and health.

Candidate Fox had aptly identified this cluster of reform tasks as the prime requirements for reviving economic growth, wage gains, and international competitiveness. Unfortunately, the country's acclaimed 2000 democratic transition fell short of a cohesive majority coalition to usher Fox's reform agenda through the legislature, the result being that the executive was immobilized early on. Those PRI technocrats responsible for negotiating Mexico's entry into NAFTA were no doubt looking to lock in single-party hegemony along with the new liberal economic model.[31] However, the subsequent interaction between political and economic liberalization in Mexico has been anything but static, and the failure of the president's party to capture a majority in the legislature was just one of several indicators of Mexico's dramatic political transformation in the NAFTA era.

Along with the advent of minority government was a concomitant shift from a seemingly omnipotent executive to a weakening presidency and from a hegemonic party system to a multiparty and increasingly fractionalized one. The Mexican Congress, moreover, evolved from a mere rubber stamp to a more independent and active legislative body. Heightened party competition and congressional coming of age have greatly diminished the Mexican executive's constitutional authority over the legislative process. In other words, gone are the days of strictly elite-level consultation and autocratic implementation of major economic initiatives, including something as fundamental as the country's entry into NAFTA.

This situation, while effectively thwarting Fox's reform agenda, need not prove fatal in itself. But it does mean "that future presidents will have to be very effective coalition builders given the country's institutional tendencies toward separation of purpose and the dearth of legislative powers."[32] This point has become increasingly important for Mexico, as minority governments could prevail indefinitely given a similar outcome in the 2006 presidential elections.

Research suggests that legislative success rates for executives operating within presidential systems under the constraints of minority government over the post–World War II period were not all that different from the success rates of those who led majority governments: a 61 percent success rate for the former versus a 72 percent success rate for the latter.[33] But indefinite minority government in Mexico places a premium on the ability of the executive to negotiate, compromise, build alliances, and forge majority coalitions that can advance the reform agenda.

On this count, the Fox administration folded like a bad hand; the resulting reform delays are reflected in figure 2-1. The challenge for Mexico will be to break out of the costly collective action gridlock that held policymakers hostage for Fox's entire six-year term, to further modernize the country's political and economic institutions, and to orchestrate a more integrated proactive strategy that links the various macro- and microeconomic variables discussed here in ways that directly tap the country's competitive potential. Earlier on, PRI technocrats saw NAFTA membership as a shortcut for achieving these goals. Now the electorate and those politicians and policymakers who represent it still face many of the same reform tasks that awaited them at the outset of NAFTA.[34] The lesson: privileged access to the U.S. market cannot substitute for the deep structural reform that Mexico requires to fully compete and to prosper from an RTA.

The Chimera of Geographical Advantage

Certainly there were doubters within the Mexican business community who questioned their own ability to survive heightened competition from U.S. and Canadian imports under an RTA. Yet NAFTA's architects were able to quell these fears by touting Mexico's geographical advantages—its proximity to the U.S. market and rich natural endowments—as the country's ticket for success. Even today, when faced with evidence that the combined effects of trade integration and geographical proximity have failed to achieve high sustainable growth, prominent business representatives in Mexico continue to express hope that geography will pay off once the country's pending structural reforms are completed.[35]

Such wishful thinking flies in the face of the historic gains that China has made in terms of per capita income growth and penetration of the U.S. market—and in the absence of geographical advantages or the privileged access that Mexico has enjoyed for more than a decade under NAFTA. Table 2-6 shows some of the gains that China has made at Mexico's expense in terms of the dollar amount of exports to the United States. China has outpaced Mexico in sectors once considered core to NAFTA: a broad range of machinery and parts and electronics, including telecommunication, computer peripherals, and sound and television equipment. These two categories grew from 13 percent of Chinese exports to the U.S. market in 1990 to some 20 percent in 2004.

China's rapid advances over Mexico may have a simple explanation, such as China's lower costs for utility inputs to industrial production, its greater labor market mobility, its more conducive tax incentives, and its education system, which is turning out some 600,000 engineers and thousands of other qualified professionals each year.[36] But there is also a deeper institutional story to be told here, one that begins with the counterproductive role played by Mexico's political institutions, as discussed above. The literature on the economics of growth probes the broader institutional sources of economic divergence within the international system, and the more compelling arguments point toward the range of institutional measures shown in figure 2-1 as a more complete explanation for the drag on Mexican growth and international competitiveness.[37]

Has China made more convincing progress on these politico-institutional variables? Perhaps not. But as Yingyi Qian argues, Chinese policymakers have pursued institutional reforms that not only directly address their designated economic goals but also are designed to improve economic efficiency within the range of what is politically feasible.[38] One example of this is dual-track reform, under which some prices are liberalized at the margins but without entirely departing from the central planning model. Similar strategies involve private asset ownership with built-in incentives to dissuade the state from expropriating these assets. Although a far cry from the state-of-the-art practices that have been recommended to emerging market reformers by international financial institutions, China's heterodox approach to institutional reform serves it well.

Ironically, in the name of orthodoxy (and given the high political costs associated with the reforms mandated by the international financial institutions laid out in figure 2-1), Mexico has not achieved much in the way of institutional reform. Insights from the literature on economic growth confirm that institutional innovation can help even the most geographically disadvantaged countries (for example, Botswana, Chile, Mauritius) raise per capita GDP.[39] But in the absence of such institutional creativity, the benefits of Mexico's proximity to the U.S. market have proved ephemeral. Even under the most successful domestic reform scenario, Mexico will still require considerable technological guidance and development assistance from its NAFTA partners. Given that the very design of NAFTA works against any such help, Mexican policymakers are faced with the reality that they are on their own with regard to engineering a full-blown economic transformation.

NAFTA as a Development Tool?

The dilemma for the North American political economy is that those markets at risk (see table 2-7) are not just Mexico's to lose. The North American automobile sector is a pressing case in point, where tightly linked cross-border production and intrafirm trade have helped to retain regional market share in the face of rising Chinese competition, even though this sector still lacks an explicit continental strategy. Mexico, in particular, has yet to fully integrate its productive clusters in autos and transport equipment. Here, and even within the narrow confines of Anglo-Saxon regionalism, the kinds of dual-track endeavors identified by Yingyi Qian (that is, measures that improve economic competitiveness without raising the usual political hackles) could help preserve the North American market advantage. For starters, and this is just one of any number of examples, the three NAFTA governments could coordinate the setting of much stricter fuel efficiency standards, which would deter the production of gas-guzzling autos and sports utility vehicles, a move the Chinese government is now taking.

Would a dual-track approach help to whittle down the asymmetries that appear in tables 2-1, 2-2, and 2-5 or jump-start Mexico's domestic reform effort? Probably not, although some Chinese-style tinkering at the margins of the NAFTA model could perhaps slow the outflow of jobs and investments in those sectors that face displacement. "Big-think" proposals have dominated in this realm, NAFTA-plus being one example.[40] NAFTA-plus would update the RTA so as to more directly address the profound changes that have occurred since 1994 (security concerns related to the 9/11 attacks, China's rise as a global trader, migration along the U.S.-Mexico border). Yet no one member government or cross-border coalition seems able or willing to spend the political capital to lead such an endeavor.

In fact, despite the concrete demand for regional public goods—regulatory reform, regional infrastructure, a more orderly and humane immigration framework, and cohesive policies to enhance competition—those vested interests in all three countries that originally lobbied for NAFTA have been remarkably disengaged. Thus any impetus for change over the past decade has taken the shape of a series of bilateral development accords, including a security-oriented Smart Borders Declaration between the United States and Canada, the more development-based Mexico-U.S. Partnership for Prosperity, and the Mexico-Canada Alliance.[41] In its own way, each of these initiatives is meant to compensate for NAFTA's shortcomings. Recall that the initial justification for the negotiation of NAFTA was to lower transaction costs via the harmonization of regulatory standards and the regionalization of infrastructure networks; jobs, growth, and income gains were expected to increase across North America as a result of these synergies.

Yet in the post-9/11 era NAFTA's laissez-faire approach to lowering these barriers and capitalizing on these economies of scale has been exhausted. The explosion of intrabloc trade has swamped regional transport systems, and this—along with heightened security concerns and divergent regulatory standards—has lengthened, not shortened, delays at the border. Contrary to the vision of NAFTA as a magnet for job growth within Mexico, put forth originally by NAFTA's proponents, illicit labor flows from Mexico to the U.S. job market have increased exponentially. The question thus remains as to how the original rationale for NAFTA—the realization of higher productivity gains and greater international market share based on the merging of Mexico's plentiful supply of cheap labor with the abundance of capital, technology, and know-how in Canada and the United States—can be reinvigorated.

The most recent attempt to address these unpleasant realities was the creation of the Security and Prosperity Partnership of North America (SPP), announced in Waco, Texas, by the leaders of all three countries in March 2005. SPP represents the first trilateral endeavor undertaken since the creation of the North American Environmental Cooperation Commission in 1993 and the first trilateral executive-level meeting since 2001. Of interest here is the "prosperity" side of this venture, whereby trilateral working groups have been appointed to promote regional competitiveness across nine designated areas, ranging from transportation to financial services to information and communication technologies.[42] But SPP already appears to be just more of the same: it mirrors rather than deepens NAFTA and offers no new institutional innovations or major commitment of funds with which to promote North American competitiveness.

A March 2006 follow-up SPP meeting held in Cancún, Mexico, did create the North American Competitiveness Council and assigned it a private-public consultative role meant to bolster sectors most at risk (autos and transportation, steel, manufacturing, and services). However, this gesture similarly piles on tasks with no new organizational mechanisms or significant financial allotments for implementing them. The possibilities for enhancing North American competitiveness by reaching creatively across borders, and in ways that respect WTO guidelines, are immense. But in the NAFTA case, the specific menu of policy development tools is not the issue.[43] Be they production-related grants to promote cross-border clustering of small entrepreneurial companies or horizontal incentives to link regional firms in the realm of tax rebates, interest rate concessions, or technology transfer, the solutions to North American barriers to competition are political and ideological.

In the end, then, SPP and all of the other above-mentioned initiatives are mainly window dressing for NAFTA: Canada and Mexico will continue to work bilaterally with the United States on competitive measures and the facilitation of cross-border trade and investment, and each of the three members will continue to rely on its own domestic legal and institutional backdrop.[44] In this vein, some ad hoc advances have been made, most notably the lowering of rules of origin since 2003 for some twenty product lines that account for around U.S.$20 billion in annual trilateral trade.[45] This matters for at least two reasons; first, these content rules have slowed the flow of business to the extent that eligible producers are willing to forgo their tariff exemptions in order to avoid further delays at the border; and second, they have deterred privileged sectors like autos and textiles from adapting to changing market conditions and done little to halt the loss of market share in North America, as demonstrated in tables 2-6 and 2-7. A more plausible alternative to these content rules would be to establish a common import tariff at most-favored-nation rates.[46] This debate, however, is nowhere in sight.

Hence policy change within NAFTA is moving at a glacial pace, especially in light of the swiftness with which China is conquering key North American markets. Given China's cost advantages in North America, the most immediate task will be for Mexico to move further along the industrial learning curve into higher value-added activities that are at once complementary to and competitive with the lower-end market niches increasingly occupied by China. At a minimum this would mean tackling the abysmal numbers for Mexican competitiveness that appear in table 2-5. The problem is how to get from here to there, as Canada and the United States, in particular, continue to eschew designing institutions to properly focus the integration process or to build an assistance fund to finance a truly trilateral competition policy. Important work on Mexico's competitive potential has been undertaken in that country by select federal government agencies, the Senate, academia, and the private sector, although few of these insights made it onto the campaign platforms of the three leading presidential candidates in 2006.

Certainly NAFTA could provide a forum for pursuing dual-track measures whose economic benefits would be expected to greatly outweigh the political costs—for example, the modernization of border infrastructure and the harmonization of regulatory norms across the three countries. Even when the political costs are relatively high, as in the case of coming to terms with undocumented immigration at the U.S.-Mexico border, NAFTA should ostensibly be part of the solution. For some Washington policymakers, dual-track reforms will no doubt resonate too closely with the EU approach to integration; and the use of NAFTA as a venue for immigration reform would clearly stoke long-standing fears about national sovereignty. But these worries skirt the main point, which is the urgent need to increase the provision of public goods under NAFTA by infusing its orthodoxy with just a tinge of heterodoxy.

Conclusion

This chapter offers three conclusions. The first concerns insights into the way that NAFTA has differentially benefited Canada and Mexico, the so-called spokes to the U.S. hub. Canada, obviously, enjoyed better economic circumstances at the outset, and inductive analysis of its economic performance since entering into an RTA with the United States confirms that G8 membership has been conducive to convergence in GDP growth and per capita income gains. This analysis also emphasizes the ways in which Canada has used its privileged access to the U.S. market as an opportunity to restructure its economy and change its historically mercantilist trade strategy. Mexico, in contrast, seized NAFTA membership as a way of locking in a new market-oriented reform model, one for which there has been insufficient preparation or follow-up. The data presented here hint at the one-shot nature of Mexico's gains under NAFTA and confirm that since 2000 Mexico seems to have squandered its preferential access to the U.S. market.

As tempting as it has been for policymakers in Canada and Mexico to point the finger at the United States and at NAFTA itself as the main perpetrators of Mexico's slow economic growth, the literature on economic growth seems to toss this particular ball back into Mexico's court. To questionable avail, Mexico placed almost blind faith in neoclassical trade dictums and the power of geographical advantage to trigger higher sustainable growth and lift its population out of poverty. Although China's eventual displacement of Mexico in certain North American sectors was just a remote possibility at the time of NAFTA's negotiation, the quick culmination of China's structural shift is testimony to the importance of domestic institutional reform and experimentation. While the EU has built-in incentives and requirements for institutional reform for its less developed members, the three NAFTA countries eschewed this strategy as too interventionist. Thus despite clear evidence of its shortcomings, Anglo-Saxon regionalism seems to have prevailed by default, with all three members stuck in a classic collective-action stalemate.

My final point concerns the future of North American integration. As innovative as NAFTA was at the time of its 1994 implementation, it may well have peaked in terms of its original goal of maximizing trade and investment ties among the three member countries. And while NAFTA helped trigger innovative breakthroughs in the liberalization of services and investment and the strengthening of intellectual property rights, these trade issues are now firmly embedded in the multilateral trade agenda. With China now advancing in the U.S. market, NAFTA seems to have lost its way as a regional project. A revival of NAFTA would require that regional leaders agree to a continental strategy that taps labor markets across the three borders, tackles the huge asymmetries that continue to divide Mexico from its partners, and invests more vigorously in infrastructure and technology transfer. Otherwise, NAFTA's very divergence will continue to eat away at this particular brand of regionalism.

Notes

1. On subregional integration schemes, see World Bank, *Global Economic Prospects: Trade, Regionalism, and Development* (Washington, 2005), p. 30.

2. Paolo Giordano and others, eds., *Asymmetries in Regional Integration and Local Development* (Washington: Inter-American Development Bank, 2005).

3. Werner Baer and Larry Neal, "Introduction," *Quarterly Review of Economics and Finance* 43 (2003): 714.

4. For a full discussion of the differences between NAFTA and the EU, see Robert Pastor, *Toward a North American Community: Lessons from the Old World to the New* (Washington: Institute for International Economics, 2001).

5. For a good overview of these neoclassical assumptions, see Timothy J. Kehoe, "Assessing the Economic Impact of North American Free Trade," in *The NAFTA Debate: Grappling with Unconventional Trade Issues,* edited by M. Delal Baer and Sidney Weintraub (Boulder, Colo.: Lynne Rienner, 1994).

6. Jeffrey Sachs and Andrew Warner, "Economic Convergence and Economic Policies," Working Paper 5039 (Cambridge, Mass.: National Bureau of Economic Research, 1995); Sebastian Edwards, "Openness, Productivity and Growth: What Do We Really Know?" *Economic Journal* 108 (1998): 383–89.

7. These pre-NAFTA estimates are summarized in Aaron Tornell and Gerardo Esquivel, "The Political Economy of Mexico's Entry into NAFTA," in *Regionalism versus Multilateral Trade Arrangements,* edited by Takatoshi Ito and Anne O. Krueger (University of Chicago Press, 1997).

8. Enrique Dussel Peters, *Polarizing Mexico: The Impact of Liberalization Strategy* (Boulder, Colo.: Lynne Rienner, 2000).

9. Enrique Dussel Peters, *Economic Opportunities and Challenges Posed by China for Mexico and Central America* (Bonn: German Development Institute, 2005).

10. M. Ayhan Kose, Guy M. Meredith, and Christopher M. Towe, "How Has NAFTA Affected the Mexican Economy? Review and Evidence," Working Paper (Washington: Research Department and Western Hemisphere Department, International Monetary Fund, 2004).

11. Pastor, *Toward a North American Community,* pp. 28–39; Philippe C. Schmitter, "Neo-functionalism," in *European Integration Theory,* edited by Antje Wiener and Thomas Dietz (Oxford University Press, 2004), p. 47.

12. A comprehensive analysis of these distinctions can be found in Peter Hall and David Soskice, eds., *Varieties of Capitalism* (Oxford University Press, 2001).

13. Bernard Silberman, *Cages of Reason: The Rise of Rational States in France, Japan, the United States, and Great Britain* (University of Chicago Press, 1993).

14. Jeffrey A. Frankel, Ernesto Stein, and Shang-Jin Wei, *Regional Trading Blocs in the World Economic System* (Washington: Institute for International Economics, 1997); World Bank, *Global Economic Prospects,* p. 28.

15. Stephanie Golob, "Beyond the Policy Frontier: Canada, Mexico, and the Ideological Origins of NAFTA," *World Politics* 55 (2003): 361–98.

16. Kerry Chase, "Economic Interests and Regional Trading Arrangements," *International Organization* 57 (2003): 141. This argument was developed earlier by Paul Krugman, "Intra-Industry Specialization and the Gains from Trade," *Journal of Political Economy* 89 (1981): 959–73; Gene Grossman and Elhanan Helpman, "The Politics of Free-Trade Agreements," *American Economic Review* 85 (1995): 667–90; Helen Milner, "Industries, Governments, and Regional Trade Blocs," in *The Political Economy of Regionalism,* edited by Edward Mansfield and Helen Milner (Columbia University Press, 1997).

17. See, for example, Carol Wise, "Introduction: NAFTA, Mexico, and the Western Hemisphere," in *The Post-NAFTA Political Economy,* edited by Carol Wise (Pennsylvania State University Press, 1998); Pastor, *Toward a North American Community,* pp. 23–25; Gary Hufbauer and Jeffrey Schott, *NAFTA Revisited* (Washington: Institute for International Economics, 2005), pp. 1–8.

18. Louis Bélanger, "An Unsustainable Institutional Design: Incompleteness and Delegation Deficit in NAFTA," in *Regionalism and the State: NAFTA and Foreign Policy Convergence,* edited by Gordon Mace (Aldershot, U.K.: Ashgate, 2007).

19. Hufbauer and Schott, *NAFTA Revisited,* p. 62.

20. See, for example, John Audley and others, *NAFTA's Promise and Reality* (Washington: Carnegie Endowment for International Peace, 2003); Hufbauer and Schott, *NAFTA Revisited;* Daniel Lederman, William F. Mahoney, and Luis Servén, *Lessons from NAFTA for Latin America and the Caribbean* (Stanford University Press, 2005); Miguel D. Ramirez, "Mexico under NAFTA: A Critical Assessment," *Quarterly Review of Economics and Finance* 43 (2003): 863–92; Sidney Weintraub, "Trade, Investment, and Economic Growth," in *NAFTA's Impact on North America,* edited by Sidney Weintraub (Washington: Center for Strategic and International Studies, 2004).

21. Hufbauer and Schott, *NAFTA Revisited,* pp. 22–36.

22. Lederman, Mahoney, and Servén, *Lessons from NAFTA,* p. 18.

23. On the unfavorable side, see Audley and others, *NAFTA's Promise and Reality,* and Jeff Faux, *The Global Class War* (New York: Wiley, 2006); for a more favorable assessment, see the essays in Sidney Weintraub, ed., *NAFTA's Impact on North America* (Washington: Center for Strategic and International Studies, 2004).

24. Sachs and Warner, "Economic Convergence and Economic Policies"; Sebastian Edwards, "Openness, Productivity and Growth: What Do We Really Know?" *Economic Journal* 108 (1998): 383–89.

25. Paul Mosley, "Globalisation, Economic Policy, and Convergence," *World Economy* 23 (2000): 613–34; Marcus Noland, "Chasing Phantoms: The Political Economy of USTR," *International Organization* 51 (1997): 365–87; Robert Wade, "Is Globalization Reducing Poverty and Inequality?" *World Development* 32 (April 2004): 567–89.

26. Roger L. Martin, foreword to *Realizing Canada's Prosperity Potential* (Toronto: Institute for Competitiveness and Prosperity, 2005).

27. Lederman, Mahoney and Servén, *Lessons from NAFTA,* p. 2.

28. Among those blaming NAFTA are Audley and others, *NAFTA's Promise and Reality.*

29. The economic team at that time closely pegged the peso to the U.S. dollar as a main way to combat inflation; however, the simultaneous opening of the trade and capital accounts in the late 1980s and a massive inward flow of U.S. portfolio investment attracted by Mexico's higher interest rates (see table 2-4) placed upward pressure on the exchange rate. Investors fled, as Mexico's economic fundamentals in late 1994 indicated an inevitable need for a sizable downward adjustment in the peso.

30. Celso Garrido, "Mexico's Financial System and Economic Development," in *Confronting Development,* edited by Kevin Middlebrook and Eduardo Zepeda (Stanford University Press, 2003).

31. Maxwell Cameron and Carol Wise, "The Political Impact of NAFTA on Mexico: Reflections on the Political Economy of Democratization," *Canadian Journal of Political Science* 37 (September 2004): 301–23.

32. Matthew Shugart and Stephan Haggard, "Institutions and Public Policy in Presidential Systems," in *Presidents, Parliaments, and Policy,* edited by Stephan Haggard and Mathew D. McCubbins (Cambridge University Press, 2001), p. 99.

33. This unpublished study was conducted by Sebastian Saiegh at New York University's Department of Political Science and is cited in Gerardo Munck, "Democratic Politics in Latin America: New Debates and Research Frontiers," *Annual Review of Political Science* 7 (2004): 443.

34. Manuel Pastor and Carol Wise, "The Lost *Sexenio*: Vicente Fox and the 'New' Politics of Economic Reform in Mexico," *Latin American Politics and Society* 47 (2005): 135–60.

35. This is the case, for example, with Luis Gutiérrez, president of Grupo Acción, which is the largest infrastructure provider to companies operating in Mexico's export processing zones. Luis Gutiérrez, interview with author, Mexico City, November 2005.

36. José Ignacio Martínez Cortes and Omar Neme Castillo, "La ventaja comparativa de China y México en el mercado Estadounidense," *Comercio Exterior* 54, no. 6 (2004): 516–28.

37. Lederman, Mahoney, and Servén, *Lessons from NAFTA,* pp. 41–49. See also Daron Acemoglu, Simon Johnson, and James Robinson, "Reversal of Fortune: Geography and Institutions in the Making of the Modern World," *Quarterly Journal of Economics* 117

(2002): 1231–94; Dani Rodrik, A. Subramanian, and F. Trebbi, "Institutions Rule: The Primacy of Institutions over Geography and Integration in Economic Development," *Journal of Economic Growth* 9 (2004): 131–65; Dani Rodrik, ed., *In Search of Prosperity: Analytical Narratives on Economic Growth* (Princeton University Press, 2003).

38. Yingyi Qian, "How Reform Worked in China," in *In Search of Prosperity: Analytical Narratives on Economic Growth,* edited by Dani Rodrik (Princeton University Press, 2003). Also see Chaohua Wang, ed., *One China, Many Paths* (London: Verso, 2003); Minxin Pei, *China's Trapped Transition: The Limits of Developmental Autocracy* (Harvard University Press, 2006).

39. See, for example, Dani Rodrik, "Introduction," in *In Search of Prosperity: Analytical Narratives on Economic Growth,* edited by Dani Rodrik (Princeton University Press, 2003).

40. Council on Foreign Relations, *Building a North American Community,* Independent Task Force Report 53 (New York: 2005), pp. 6–8.

41. For example, the Smart Borders Declaration between Canada and the United States is based on a thirty-point plan to secure border infrastructure, share information, and facilitate the secure movement of people and goods in the wake of the terrorist attacks of 9/11. The United States also drew up a twenty-two-point Border Partner Agreement with Mexico and modeled it along similar lines as that with Canada. See Marcela Celorio, "The North American 'Security and Prosperity Partnership': An Evaluation," Working Paper (Center for North American Studies, American University, 2006).

42. SPP report submitted by the economic, security, and foreign policy ministries of Canada, Mexico, and the United States, June 2005 (www.usembassycanada.gov/content/can_usa/spp_ottawa_report.pdf).

43. Marcelo de Paiva Abreu, "Which 'Industrial Policies' Are Meaningful for Latin America?" INTAL-ITD Working Paper SITI 11 (Washington: Inter-American Development Bank, 2006).

44. Celorio, "The North American 'Security and Prosperity Partnership,'" p. 8.

45. Hufbauer and Schott, *NAFTA Revisited,* pp. 60–61.

46. Council on Foreign Relations, *Building a North American Community,* p. 35.

3

Obstacles to Integration
NAFTA's Institutional Weakness

ISABEL STUDER

When he took office in 2000 President Vicente Fox promoted the idea of a deeper integration of North America, one that would include the free transit of not only goods, services, and capital, but also labor. He also proposed establishing a U.S.$20 billion development fund equivalent to Europe's cohesion funds to invest in, among other things, infrastructure corridors to better connect the North American region. More generally, Fox proposed the European Union process of integration as a model for North America. This approach, also known as NAFTA-plus, was seen by many as the most effective way to mitigate the huge asymmetries between Mexico and its two northern neighbors—a gap that has lingered tenaciously since the 1994 implementation of the North American Free Trade Agreement (NAFTA) among Canada, Mexico, and the United States.

Fox's proposal met with little success in Canada and the United States, leaving the much less ambitious programs that had been established since 1994 to cope with the asymmetries. Among these programs are the agreement to broaden the mandate of the North American Development Bank (NADBank); the Alliance for Prosperity Program, meant to channel private investment into marginalized areas of Mexico that export migrant labor; and the trinational Security and Prosperity Partnership of North America (SPP), launched in 2005 with the aim of providing a comprehensive framework for enhancing both the competitiveness and the security of the region.

The commonly held view that the events of September 11, 2001, reduced the political possibilities for advancing Fox's proposed North American agenda is an accurate but partial explanation for where things now stand. In the absence of such tragic events, perhaps, the United States would not have turned its attention toward matters of global security and Canada would not have focused mainly on its bilateral relationship with the United States. But even then, other structural, economic, geopolitical, and especially sociocultural factors would still stand in the way of deepening North American integration. This is the basic argument of my chapter.

The analysis is divided into four parts. The first section differentiates NAFTA from the world's other large integration scheme, the European Union (EU), and in doing so sets a baseline for my argument. The second and third sections of the chapter focus on how domestic political dynamics in the United States are determining factors for the anti-institutional bias and organizational deficits that underpin NAFTA. The fourth section deals with the resistance to formal integration with the United States on the part of Canada and Mexico and suggests that the shadow of the past also accounts for NAFTA's weaknesses.

Two Models of Integration

The aim of this analysis is not to fully compare the two forms of integration in North America and Europe but rather to note some basic differences between the two. While NAFTA seeks trade and investment liberalization and adopts a minimalist institutional framework, the European process has more ambitious social and political objectives and supranational institutions that support these objectives. The European institutional framework (including the European Parliament, the European Court of Justice, the European Council, and the European Commission) is a multilevel system in which decisionmaking competence in several key policy areas resides in Brussels, not in the national capitals, and aims at solving common transnational problems and advancing the integration process. This framework also addresses inequalities inside the countries and among states at the regional level.

In North America the predominant stance is that the market will deepen the process of economic integration and will thus rectify long-standing inequalities in the long run. The only two standing North American institutions, the North American Commission for Environmental Cooperation and the North American Commission for Labor Cooperation, were created with the implicit objective of monitoring Mexico's enforcement of environmental and labor law (mainly through citizens' complaints), rather than the more proactive goal of solving common transnational problems from a position of institutional strength. At best, these institutional mandates regarding trilateral cooperation are diffuse. In the absence of clear political objectives to address the challenges of deeper integration, these institutional settings reflect an overly cautious state-centric approach, in which most relevant decisions are left to open-ended diplomatic solutions.

Thus beyond the bounds of trade and cross-border investment, most transnational problems in North America (environment, migration, security) tend to be resolved unilaterally. When bilateral solutions are pursued they tend to be ad hoc, and very few issues are handled from a trilateral, or North American, perspective, despite the advanced levels of economic integration that now exist. Take for example the missed opportunities in the realm of demographics and labor markets. Canada and the United States will see the first of the baby boomers reach the age of sixty-five during the decade that begins in 2010. Together with declining fertility rates and rising longevity, widespread retirements in Canada and the United States will slow the growth of the labor force and raise elderly dependency ratios in both countries.[1] Canada is aging ever faster than the United States. (Mexico, which is still a demographically young country, will not exhibit elderly dependency ratios similar to those of its northern neighbors until 2050.)

This slowdown in the growth of the Canadian and U.S. workforces will necessitate the continuation of hiring labor from abroad if these countries are to avoid slower economic growth. But as Tamara Woroby argues (chapter 13), immigration has proven to be a highly controversial and complex issue in both recipient and sending countries. Since Mexico will not begin to face the aging of its population until the 2030s, it has a window of opportunity to turn this demographic advantage into higher economic growth. Rather than the single-minded pursuit of bilateral or trilateral agreements to ensure a steady and secure flow of migrants to the north, Mexico simultaneously needs to exert a stronger and sustained effort to boost the skills and productivity of its labor force during this interim. Labor force quality is indeed a key contributor to productivity, particularly in an era in which information technology has become a defining feature of the workplace. Mexico lags behind other developing countries like China and India in its human capital development.

NAFTA has created the know-how for conducting business in North America and a secure legal framework for investment across borders, thereby facilitating the emergence of regional systems of production. The countries in North America could turn these existing economic interdependencies and demographic complementarities into positive synergies by developing cooperative training and education programs that could enhance core labor competencies in North America's fastest growing sectors. For instance, the aging of the population in Canada and the United States will soon generate a high demand for workers in health care and related services. Mexico's investment in a well-trained workforce that could meet this U.S. and Canadian demand would translate into not only a positive solution to the migration issue but also a way to attract badly needed foreign direct investment into Mexico. Such cooperation would, however, require a sustained effort to coordinate bureaucratic entities in the three countries, including the ministries of labor, the economy, and education as well as the private sector.

Although the three countries would benefit largely from adopting a trilateral, institutionalized approach to their common challenges, the United States and Canada have been especially resistant to rely on existing regional institutions or to build new ones. This has partly to do with the ineffectiveness and conflictive nature of the North American commissions on labor and the environment in the last decade and is also partly explained by the high degree of economic asymmetry in North America.

As Robert Pastor points out, the differences in size and power among the member states of the EU were never as great as those among the member states of NAFTA when it was signed.[2] And as international relations theory has long argued, the enormous asymmetries among the North American partners would explain the preference of each of the three countries for a pragmatic association, with few institutions.[3] In other words, under conditions of extreme asymmetry, the weakest states have no interest in formalizing cooperation because formal agreements will further disempower them.[4] However, this standard explanation begs the question of why Canada and Mexico were willing to negotiate and sign on to NAFTA in the first place. What's more, it cannot account for the change in policy preferences over time within Mexico. Why, for instance, did the Salinas administration (1988–94) prefer a minimalist approach to institutionalizing Mexico's relations with its North American partners while Fox's objective was to adopt a European model of integration in North America?

A more complex take on the relationship between power and institutions in North America would suggest that both more and less powerful states have strong incentives to participate in formal agreements and are willing to institutionalize their behavior with that of other states as long as these arrangements favor their self-interests. A powerful state has an interest in establishing international, particularly multilateral, institutions for two reasons. The first is that such institutions can resolve collective action problems by reducing the kinds of compliance and transaction costs that impede effective and mutually beneficial exchange.[5] The second, following the work of G. John Ikenberry, is that states are willing to pay the price in terms of their autonomy and sovereignty precisely due to the asymmetries involved. The more powerful state has incentives to lock in the behavior of less powerful states through international institutions and thus avoid having to continually use its power to force these states to act according to the larger state's preferences.[6] The weaker state has incentives to restrict the larger state from using its power arbitrarily and indiscriminately. For this negotiation to work, the behavior of the weaker state or states involved in the creation of international institutions must have repercussions for the more powerful state, which in turn must have the ability to influence the weaker states but also the self-restraint not to abuse that ability.[7]

From this perspective, it is not difficult to understand how the United States emerged as the driving force behind the multilateral institutional framework after World War II. As Ikenberry argues, "No other great power has advanced such far-reaching and elaborate ideas about how institutions might be employed to organize and manage the relations between states. But despite the enthusiasm for creating institutions and a rule- based international order, the United States has been reluctant to tie itself too tightly to these multilateral institutions and rules."[8] In other words, this ambiguity is due to the fact that the United States operates within these institutions when it can dominate them and evades or resists them when it cannot.

However, as Ikenberry acknowledges, it is difficult to specify beforehand the concessions that states will make in choosing between political autonomy and heightened accountability of its own policies via membership in regional institutions. That is, one can identify the dilemma that states face when they agree to create institutions but not the concessions they will make or the kind of rules and norms they may be willing to adopt.[9] The literature on institutions skirts this question, since state preferences for certain rules and the kind of international institutions that will be negotiated are exogenous to institutional models, which themselves are embedded largely in rationalist frameworks.[10]

In sum, the reference to structural asymmetry in North America is insufficient for understanding why the three NAFTA member countries had strong preferences for developing a "primitive" institutional framework like the one that emerged.[11] Moreover, the conditions of structural asymmetry do not explain why the United States and Canada are so reluctant to invest in supranational or simply regional institutions geared toward redressing inequalities in North America, or why Mexico has come around to the opposite stance. What explains the change in Mexico's position, from accepting the minimal institutional framework established by NAFTA to proposing ten years later an institutional framework similar to that of Europe?

In the following sections I offer a simple answer, one that reaches past structural explanations and rationalist models in identifying the incentives that states have for creating international institutions. My point is that we must look to history, values, and domestic politics; that is, we must look to those factors that shape state preferences about the kind of international institutions—strong or weak, supranational or not—that should govern North America.

U.S. Exceptionalism

The U.S. bias against the creation of international institutions has spawned a rich literature that highlights the historic and sociocultural underpinnings of U.S. exceptionalism. From the standpoint of institutions, Edward Luck summarizes four characteristics of U.S. exceptionalism: the desire to act independently and an apparent immunity to pressure and criticisms from others; the supposition that its national values are universally valid and that its political positions are moral and appropriate, not simply opportunistic; the heavy weight of domestic politics in determining positions in international forums and a desire to adopt national legislation over the rules and responsibilities imposed by international agreements; and the belief on the part of decision-makers and legislators that they have other options for achieving national interests and that multilateral institutions are only one option and not an obligation.[12]

A strong adherence to seventeenth- and eighteenth-century liberal ideology makes the U.S. experience very different from that of other countries of the West. For Louis Hartz, Seymour Martin Lipset, and Samuel Huntington the absence of feudalism in the development of the state is the basis for U.S. exceptionalism. The lack of a strong, centralized state, such as the ones that evolved across Europe, meant that the U.S. state was perceived in even parts as both a threat to and a protector of individual rights. Thus individual liberty turned into the fundamental political value, which explains why neither socialism nor extreme conservatism developed.[13] Liberal ideology spawned a

uniquely American ethos, and antistatism was thus translated into anti-insti-
tutionalism, giving rise to a legalist, litigious political culture.

From this liberal ideology there emerged in the United States a belief that
sovereignty was vested solely in the people. This explains why Congress, as an
expression of that sovereignty, plays a fundamental role in designing U.S.
international policy and implementing it on the basis of local concerns and
interests.[14] These combined elements have fueled a negative bias within the
U.S. political establishment against the creation of international institutions,
particularly supranational ones. Entrenched political and economic interests
have thus been germane to the dilemmas faced by the United States in both
the creation of and its participation in international institutions.

One response to the U.S. dilemma vis-à-vis international institutions has
been the quest for an international order with low costs in terms of limitations on U.S. political sovereignty. Since 1945 U.S. policymakers have promoted the idea of an "automatic" international order, which would require a
direct but minimal intervention by the United States because it would be
based on the liberal economic principles favored by the United States.[15] For
example, the General Agreement on Tariffs and Trade (GATT) was created
with a minimal bureaucracy and promoted U.S. interests in the world without the United States having to compromise its autonomy. This less binding
commercial regime had broad support from both the U.S. public and Congress as a driving force for economic growth and postwar prosperity.[16]

With globalization and the heightened investment by U.S. firms in world
markets, the U.S. predicament with regard to international institutions has
only intensified. Evidence of this is the strong opposition both from the conservative right and the center-left in the U.S. Congress to the 1995 creation
of the World Trade Organization (WTO), based on the perception that it
would make decisions harmful to U.S. sovereignty.[17] Chief among these fears
was the effect that a rigorous application of free trade principles would have
on U.S. autonomy in the realm of environmental, labor, health, and other
contentious domestic issues. The authority of a new international bureaucracy over the U.S. Congress was of particular concern to the Republican
Party, which opposed the replacement of GATT by the WTO—a stronger
international organization in which the United States would have less
power.[18] Some within Congress went so far as to compare the WTO's decisionmaking structure to that of the United Nations, arguing that at least the
United States had the right to a veto in the UN Security Council. But opposition to the WTO was mainly expressed by a minority fringe of both political parties, making it difficult to strike up an alliance between them. As

Judith Goldstein argues, U.S. groups that advocate fair trade over free trade and that have opposed multilateral initiatives like the WTO in the name of distributive concerns have not managed to influence the decisions of the political elite or to build predominant collective coalitions.[19]

However, although congressional passage of the enacting legislation to join the WTO reflected the economic interests of the United States, the opposition did secure a stipulation that every five years a commission would review all dispute resolution decisions that went against the United States at the WTO. The aim here was to prevent the WTO from exceeding its authority or acting in an unjustifiable manner, with Congress threatening to withdraw the United States from the WTO in the event of an unfavorable commission review.[20]

The international trade regime that the United States fostered in the post–World War II era also reflects the basic values of antistatism and liberal individualism. Political elites and the U.S. public have always seemed more comfortable than their European counterparts in supporting capitalism and the preeminence of the market. And U.S. policymakers have resisted the need to "manage" capitalism along European lines. Kevin Featherstone and Roy H. Ginsberg posit the following:

> Individualism in a growing economy fostered the belief that the U.S. was a land of opportunity, based on meritocracy rather than privilege. . . . The belief in individual opportunity and limited government has meant there has been much less support for welfare and redistributive policies than is typically found in Europe. There is a strong commitment to equal opportunity, but this is to be in the competition of a laissez-faire economy, and not via strong government.[21]

Although the differences between the United States and Europe should not be exaggerated, some opinion polls show that, in general, Americans tend to give less support to redistributive measures and the promotion of equal opportunities than do the Europeans.[22] As Lipset notes, "The United States continues to be exceptional among developed nations in the low level of support it provides for the poor in welfare, housing, and medical care. As a result, though the wealthiest country in the world, the proportion of its people living in poverty is the highest among the developed nations."[23]

In the 1990s the United States participated in the construction of international institutions with a regional character. The participation of the United States as the only superpower in regional bodies that fostered trade liberalization like NAFTA and the Asia-Pacific Economic Cooperation Forum (APEC

Forum) was partly due to strategic considerations. U.S. objectives were many, including jump-starting the stalled Uruguay Round of trade negotiations and promoting policy reforms among developing countries that would in the long run guarantee the opening up of their markets.[24] In the case of Mexico and the negotiation of NAFTA, the central aim of the United States was to foster the economic and political stabilization of its neighbor. From Washington's vantage point, NAFTA as an international treaty would force future Mexican administrations to uphold liberal rules on free trade and foreign direct investment.[25]

Following its historic preference for institutions that promote U.S. values without compromising U.S. sovereignty, the United States promoted a laissez-faire and legalistic institutional framework for NAFTA. The agreement, as such, leaves little margin for future interpretation and shuns the delegation of sovereign authority to intergovernmental, let alone supranational, bodies.[26] With the exception of a supranational mechanism to protect investors, NAFTA's dispute resolution mechanisms do not commit beyond the review of rules operating in the national context of each member country. The United States was thus able to fulfill the objectives it planned for NAFTA: greater market access, guarantees to investors, the political and economic stabilization of Mexico, and a revival of the Uruguay Round's stalled multilateral trade negotiations in Geneva.

All of this was accomplished without having to invest in strong North American institutions. In a context of sizable asymmetries, Canada and Mexico, as the smaller partners, had no incentives for creating strong or supranational institutions, which could end up being dominated by the United States. Instead, they preferred to reduce uncertainty and the indiscriminate, unilateral wielding of power by their omnipotent neighbor through a regimen that would leave little room for interpretation.

NADBank, created upon NAFTA's approval, is an example of the predominance of this market ideology, even in matters linked to economic development. In the last phase of negotiations between President Bill Clinton and the U.S. Congress to approve NAFTA, Representative Esteban Torres (D-Calif.) demanded the creation of a development bank to invest in environmental infrastructure along the Mexico-U.S. border as a condition for his pro-NAFTA vote. The original proposal was a bank with a U.S.$1 billion capital base that could generate U.S.$15 billion for projects favoring social integration. The European model was the inspiration for a development bank that would offer guarantees and low interest rates for environmental projects, an infrastructure beneficial to trade, and social support to promote growing businesses.[27]

But NADBank ended up with a much smaller capital base and a weaker mandate than the original design called for. To date it only has U.S.$450 million in capital, which can generate U.S.$2 billion in loans, compared with World Bank estimates that it will require a U.S.$25 billion infusion annually over ten years in order for Mexico to modernize its sagging infrastructure. In addition, NADBank's mandate is restricted to financing environmental infrastructure and offering loans at market rates. In Mexico these rates are not accessible, and in the United States they are not competitive.[28]

A market focus has prevailed even in the reform of NADBank's mandate, which was proposed and designed as a response to Vicente Fox's North American initiative. In March 2002 the presidents of Mexico and the United States agreed to broaden NADBank's mandate, including the expansion of the eligible geographical jurisdiction in Mexico to 300 kilometers (186 miles) from 100 kilometers (62 miles) from the border. The offering of credit programs at a preferential rate and subsidies concentrated within the 100-kilometer area was also increased to U.S.$50 million. This contrasts with the European structural cohesion funds allocated between 2000 and 2006, which came to U.S.$190 billion. For the 2007–13 period, the European Parliament approved a total of EUR 308 billion for structural funds, or 35.7 percent of the total EU budget.[29]

The Society for Prosperity, a Mexico-U.S. program launched in March 2002 to foster development in low-growth, migrant-worker-sending regions in Mexico, is another example of NAFTA's market bias. The ultimate aim is to improve productivity, particularly in regions of Mexico that have not grown and that serves as home to many of those who migrate to the United States.[30] Another commitment was to create a U.S.$50 million fund to set up thirty-five exchanges between institutions of higher learning in both countries and to offer scholarships for student exchanges and graduate studies in the United States.

What tends to be forgotten is that the institutions created by NAFTA also include the parallel accords on labor and the environment. The latter implies the creation of the only trilateral institution, the North American Commission for Environmental Cooperation; although this commission lacks broad supranational powers, it does introduce "independent" functions for its secretariat and the permanent representation of nongovernmental organizations in bodies like the Joint Public Advisory Committee and the National and Governmental Advisory Councils, which seek to ensure the enforcement of environmental legislation in North America and in Mexico in particular. The very existence of these institutions teaches us, then, that despite its ideological ambivalence toward international institutions, the United States is willing to support these institutions and even some supranational gestures when these work to appease domestic political demands and concerns.

U.S. Domestic Politics

The negotiation of parallel environmental and labor accords was the result of a political situation that forced the proponents of NAFTA to accept the demands of groups close to the Democratic Party, particularly the unions, that opposed a treaty based strictly on trade and investment.[31] At the same time, the side agreements on labor and the environment offered political cover to members of the Democratic Party and thus secured their vote for NAFTA in the U.S. Congress, even though these accords fell far short of the kinds of institutionalized framework that would be required for their success. Groups opposed to NAFTA went so far as to propose a social charter that would model the process of North American economic integration along European lines. However, the Mexican government, business interests on both sides of the border, and conservatives in the Republic Party all opposed an EU-style social charter as a pretext for introducing protectionist measures.[32]

It was the U.S. political situation, and particularly the election of Democratic Party candidate Bill Clinton in 1992, that rendered the side accords a make-or-break deal for NAFTA. During the campaign Clinton vowed to review NAFTA to ensure that it adequately addressed environmental protection and workers' rights. With support for NAFTA by the U.S. Congress hinging on these conditions, Mexico and Canada were forced to accept the parallel accords. Congress did approve NAFTA by a relatively broad margin (234 to 200) in November 1993.

But the heated debate over the treaty continues today, as groups opposed to free trade across North America are further galvanized by the weakness of the NAFTA side accords in truly defending environmental protection and workers' rights. It is largely this antipathy toward NAFTA that delayed the U.S. Congress for a decade from granting the president fast-track authority (now called Trade Promotion Authority, or TPA) to negotiate future trade agreements. The strength of these "blue-green" coalitions in opposing other free trade agreements has been clear since the November 1999 Seattle demonstrations, which virtually shut down the WTO ministerial meeting held there.

In short, the lingering bitterness over NAFTA has sorely tested the historic bipartisan and inter-institutional consensus between Congress and the White

House concerning the promotion of free trade the world over. NAFTA emerged at a unique political juncture, in which domestic concern for the competitiveness of the U.S. economy predominated, particularly with regard to Japan and the Asian Tigers (South Korea, Taiwan, and Hong Kong), and multilateral trade negotiations were enshrouded in pessimism. U.S. union leaders seized upon NAFTA as a chance to recover the political influence they had lost through outsourcing, import competition, and dwindling membership. In their view, the ultimate result was a deterioration of labor standards in the United States and the rest of the world.

Environmental groups, frequently at odds with their union brethren, now saw their interests as complementary. Like organized labor, the environmental coalition expressed its conviction that trade liberalization would further undermine environmental standards and demanded the side agreement as a quid pro quo for supporting NAFTA. From their perspective, free trade can undermine international environmental regulations since competition among developing countries to attract investment triggers a race to the bottom in terms of these regulations.

Unfortunately, although the side agreements on labor and the environment won the vote for NAFTA, these have not mitigated the polarization of the U.S. electorate over free trade. In fact, policymakers themselves remain deeply divided. In 1994, when the Office of the U.S. Trade Representative proposed that legislation to implement the Uruguay Round include the extension of fast-track authority and labor and environmental standards, the business community, which had supported NAFTA, strongly opposed the measure and managed to get the White House to withdraw the request. As was shown by several Clinton administration attempts to secure fast-track authority to negotiate further trade agreements, a proposal that did not include labor and environmental issues was destined to fail to get the support of the Democrats; a proposal that did include them would be rejected by the Republican majority in Congress.

The 1994 devaluation of the Mexican peso and the negative effect that this had in Latin American markets and in the U.S. Congress also contributed to President Clinton's failure to secure fast-track authority. The crisis spurred NAFTA's opponents in the United States to launch a campaign against free trade agreements and to block a plan to admit Chile into NAFTA.[33] The conservative Republican congressional majority elected in 1994 was more interested in its agenda for domestic politics than in foreign policy issues. These Republicans opposed offering a bailout plan for Mexico and showed no interest in promoting a new trade initiative after the tortuous legislative history of NAFTA. Other events that complicated the political panorama were the mid-1997 Asian crisis, the 1998 moratorium on the payment of Russia's foreign debt, and the 1999 devaluation of the Brazilian real.

President Clinton finally sent his request for fast-track authority to Congress in September 1997, but he had to withdraw it for lack of support from his own Democratic Party. When he reintroduced it a year later, it was defeated 243 to 180. His proposal did not include labor issues, showing that there was still no bipartisan consensus with regard to the aims of U.S. foreign trade policy. While many Republicans insisted that environmental and labor issues should not be dealt with in fast-track legislation, for most Democrats this was a priority.

In the summer of 2002 President George W. Bush won congressional approval for TPA, which allowed him to negotiate a new WTO round, the Free Trade Area of the Americas (FTAA), and other bilateral accords. Even with TPA in hand, however, the consensus that existed over the goals of U.S. foreign trade policy for decades—and that made it possible to promote free trade throughout the world—has not been rebuilt. In a context in which the public continues to have a negative perception of NAFTA and of free trade in general, the powerful private sector coalition that supported and made approval of NAFTA possible has not been revived. A high price was paid for the approval of TPA: hefty concessions to protectionist groups (agriculture, textiles, and steel, for example) as well as the sacrifice of the relative independence of the executive for negotiating accords through the creation of a new congressional supervisory mechanism.

The controversy about environmental and labor issues in the House of Representatives did not repeat itself in the Senate, where the debate was dominated by labor matters, particularly the discussion about trade adjustment assistance and the guarantee that U.S. rules for trade remedies (antidumping and compensatory tariffs) would prevail. The Democrats wanted assistance for workers displaced by trade competition to be substantial. Senators from steel-producing states wanted guarantees that the TPA would not weaken U.S. antidumping legislation. They were concerned about the Bush administration's decision to accept the issue as part of the negotiations in the new, multilateral Doha Round. To get the authority to negotiate trade agreements, Bush levied tariffs of up to 30 percent on most steel imports. With that, he won Senate approval for TPA.

In this polarized context, it is difficult to imagine U.S. acceptance of big initiatives that would signal the negotiation of more formal institutional mechanisms to bolster NAFTA's weaknesses. Institutional proposals based strictly on the furthering of economic integration under NAFTA continue to run up against the opposition of unions and environmental groups and, therefore, the majority of Democrats in the U.S. Congress. On the other side of the aisle, the Republicans would oppose any strengthening of institutional measures more favorable to the interests of these same groups.

I. M. Destler concludes his seminal study of U.S. trade policy on an optimistic note, expressing trust that U.S. leaders can cope with these conflicting domestic pressures and continue to promote free trade.[34] Implicit in his book is the idea that a number of options are viable from the standpoint of U.S. trade policy: multilateral pursuits at the WTO, the NAFTA venue, or even the participation of the United States in international trade agreements or bodies in which it does not have veto power, as long as U.S. interests are reflected in these accords. The key factor is leadership from the U.S. executive to undertake an international project that resonates and unites the dispersed and localized interests expressed in Congress.

My argument, nevertheless, is that the resolution of obstacles arising out of the NAFTA accord would still conform to U.S. preferences for a minimalist institutional framework in North America. This U.S. focus will also prevail with prescriptions on how to deal with problems of inequality. The difficulties in fundamentally reforming the NADBank is an example of the tenacity of U.S. preferences for maintaining a market approach for dealing with matters linked to economic development.

Other Barriers to Institutionalizing North American Integration

The integration of the three North American nations through regional institutions has met with at least two other obstacles. One is the preference of Mexico and Canada for bilateral interaction with the United States. The other is the historic ambivalence of both Canada and Mexico to openly share a common future with the United States.

The Defense of Sovereignty in Canada and Mexico

As Robert Pastor argues, another obstacle to the institutional deepening of North American integration is the preference of Mexico and Canada for bilateral interaction with the United States. "This is also a perfectly natural reaction by two countries that can barely see each other over the giant elephant that sleeps or stampedes between them."[35] Pastor attributes this bilateral focus to the economic disparity between Mexico and its two trade partners given that cultural differences have diminished. It is this disparity that has shaped very different bilateral agendas: while migration and drug trafficking are central issues in Mexico-U.S. relations, Canada's bilateral agenda with the United States is dominated by trade conflicts in sectors linked to fishing, forests, and cultural industries.

However, and precisely because of these asymmetries, Mexico did propose an institutional design for North American integration that followed the European model. The Canadian prime minister at the time, Jean Chrétien, was patently unenthusiastic about the proposal. The Canadian government has subsequently held fast to this stance on the trilateral cooperation agenda. To be fair, the Canadian federal government's attitude is slightly more favorable toward NAFTA than that of some sectors of Canadian society, particularly intellectuals. At the same time, these circles believe that the focus of North American integration should be two-dimensional to reflect the radical differences between Canada's and Mexico's agendas with the United States. This vision has been reinforced since September 11, 2001.

Overall, since the signing of NAFTA, both Canada and Mexico have become less insistent about promoting links among the three societies and about making sure that the United States sees deeper integration and coordination with its neighbors as a way to solve common problems. Their neglect of North American integration is understandable given the historic tendency of both Mexico and Canada to see the diversification of their respective international ties as a natural counterweight to U.S. influence, as I will explain. No sooner had the ink dried on NAFTA than the various sectors in Mexico demanded a diversification of Mexico's economic relations. This ambiguity was also clear in the Fox administration's proposal to advance simultaneously with the integration of North America and with multilateralism.

In any case, the terrible events of September 11 prompted a more marked return to bilateral approaches. Despite the fact that this political shock presented an opportunity to develop a joint security plan, Canada maintained its preference for dealing with the United States through silent diplomacy. From that perspective, the more shallow NAFTA option continued to be the preferred one for Canada. Deep-rooted historic and cultural reasons continue to shape Canada's attitude of not automatically embracing President Fox's proposed North American initiative. These same factors also help to explain Mexico's ambivalence about North American integration, particularly on the part of some of its elites.

Thus in both Canada and Mexico nationalist sentiments are a barrier to following the European model and even to gradually advancing institution building and deepening integration in North America. Ironically, the fundamental condition of being neighbors with the United States has fueled conceptions of nationalism and fears of being eclipsed by U.S. might. Both countries, for example, are part of the U.S. strategic sphere of influence; both depend on its huge market and the inflow of U.S. investments; and both are subject to a growing—if highly asymmetrical—economic interdependence with their powerful neighbor.

In the post–World War II context, Mexico became relevant to the United States because of its strategic location and also because of U.S. concern over Mexican domestic political instability. This concern became the basis for a special relationship between Mexico and the United States within the already existing special relationship the latter had conferred on Latin America for security reasons. For Mexico this relationship meant preferential treatment for Mexican exports and "the willingness of [the United States] to cooperate in resolving Mexico's economic problems."[36] It also meant U.S. acceptance of the Mexican government's use of foreign policy and nationalist pronouncements as a means to legitimize itself domestically.

Canada also received special treatment from the United States but based on different considerations. Internal political stability or the ideological bent of various Canadian administrations were not sources of concern for U.S. security. What was at issue was the defense of continental air space. In exchange for Canadian military and diplomatic support for the defense of U.S. continental and international strategic interests, the United States offered Canada both economic concessions and exceptions to certain of its policies that could affect Canadian interests.[37]

Canada and Mexico showed unconditional adherence to the Western bloc during the cold war. However, that association and the growing economic interdependence with the United States created a dilemma for the two countries: striking a balance between the main objectives of averting costly conflicts with the United States and of maintaining national autonomy. From this emerged a tacit understanding with the United States: it would recognize and accept Mexico's and Canada's right to steer an independent course in their foreign policy as long as they did so regarding matters that were not of fundamental importance to the United States. In exchange, Canada and Mexico cooperated on issues that, though not a priority for them, were fundamental from the U.S. standpoint.[38] For decades, however, these two countries sought to maintain a certain distance, particularly a political distance, from a powerful neighbor with which they gradually but inexorably strengthened economic ties.

Limited Convergence in North America

In the 1980s advances in the consolidation of European integration, the prolonged stagnation of the Uruguay Round talks, and growing U.S. protectionism in part explain the gradual convergence between Mexico and Canada with regard to the negotiation of the North American Free Trade Agreement. This is why the Conservative Party Canadian prime minister, Brian Mulroney (1984–94), pushed to finalize the Canada-U.S. Free Trade Agreement (CUSFTA) in 1987 and why Mexican president Carlos Salinas de Gortari (1988–94) proposed a similar accord with the United States in 1990. The new direction was a fundamental departure from a past in which both Canada and Mexico refused to accept the idea of a common future with the United States.

In an about-face, Prime Minister Mulroney made the reestablishment of the special Canada-U.S. relationship a priority objective of his foreign policy; the bond had existed after World War II but had been broken off in the volatile 1970s.[39] Support for the Reagan administration's Strategic Defense Initiative and the proposal to negotiate a free trade agreement between the two countries were some of the signs of the new turn in Canadian foreign policy. Although this rapprochement has been attributed by some to the ideological affinities between Mulroney and Reagan, the adverse international context for Canadian security—above all economic security—was a determining factor. This included resurgence in East-West tensions, a protectionist spirit that had settled over the U.S. Congress and the European Community, and a badly managed set of multilateral negotiations at GATT.

Like Canada, Mexico proposed negotiating a free trade agreement with its powerful neighbor as a defensive strategy. Although several factors explain Mexico's economic opening and its government's unprecedented diplomatic move toward the United States, two were fundamental: the volatile international economic context and the success of the trade liberalization measures that had been previously introduced, including Mexico's entry into GATT in 1987.[40] In the early 1990s the Mexican government seemed to have arrived at the conclusion that the international situation offered few options for diversifying the country's trade. Given the planned expansion of the EU and the recent CUSFTA, Mexico considered it necessary to exploit the advantages of proximity and considerable integration with the United States by negotiating guaranteed access to that market for Mexican products.[41] Above all, NAFTA was seen as a strategy to attract desperately needed investment for Mexico's economic recovery.

NAFTA, then, institutionalized Mexico's commitment to economic opening as a development model proper, and it cinched the government's determination to maintain closer relations with the United States. In exchange, Mexico ensured its place in the U.S. market, which was key to the success of the new export model and inflow of investment, without which economic modernization would be impossible. From the Mexican perspective NAFTA preserved national sovereignty because Mexico negotiated as an equal partner with its two more developed partners. For example, nowhere in NAFTA is Mexico given special or differential treatment for being a developing country or for the enormous difference in its level of development compared to its two trade partners. The broad, detailed text served the interests of the Mexican government at the time because no supranational institutions were created that would show the predominance of its northern neighbor.

However, with the advent of the Fox administration in 2000, it became clear that NAFTA had done little to create a consensus in the Mexican population concerning the country's closer relations with the United States. If anything, NAFTA has exacerbated Mexico's historic ambivalence toward its northern neighbor. Witness the mixed signals sent by the Fox administration in offering its solidarity to the U.S. government at the time of the September 11 attacks and, above all, its refusal to support the U.S. military intervention in Iraq even though Mexico was a member of the UN Security Council at the time of the March 2003 invasion. While the Mexican business elite was in favor of expressing its solidarity and supporting the United States unconditionally, political elites and the general public were divided.

Fox's proposal to shift North America onto a more constructive plane was based, first, on the philosophy of change that he espoused since the beginning of his administration: the alignment of Mexican foreign policy with the reality of the country's situation and that of the world, which had changed profoundly since the end of the cold war. Second, Fox's proposal was based on the recognition that, a decade after NAFTA came into effect, although Mexico's growing economic integration with the North American region had increased trade and investment, the well-being of all Mexicans still had not improved.[42] In fact, inequality inside Mexico had further deepened.[43]

This is why Fox's suggestion to pursue a European-style integration strategy in North America became relevant, in particular with regard to structural regional development and social cohesion funds that could be oriented, as in Europe, to less favored regions (those with no comparative advantage) in order to compensate for the flows of foreign direct investment that naturally go to more developed areas in Mexico. More than direct compensation to these regions, there was a special interest in better understanding the experience of countries like Ireland, Spain, and Portugal and the role that EU support has played in bolstering public investment in infrastructure and the promotion of human capital through educational programs and labor regulations. For example, some studies suggest that these cohesion funds can help contain migratory flows in disadvantaged regions as long as some part of this public funding goes to education and the development of human capital.[44]

Final Considerations

Formidable political obstacles stand in the way of the three countries of North America deepening their integration along European lines. However, the most important political impediments exist in the United States, where deeply engrained biases against the creation of supranational institutions prevail, particularly in Congress. Neither is there any commitment to establish mechanisms to reduce inequality across the North American region, beyond measures that are based on the logic of the market. These obstacles, while formidable, are still not set in stone.

A favorable scenario for deepening integration depends both on the lineup of political forces in the U.S. Congress and on the determination of the U.S. executive to assume leadership in North America. The European model certainly rubs against U.S. preferences for market-based solutions; but at the same time, the experience since 1994 shows the limits of this model. As a first step toward addressing its shortcomings, the three countries should begin by recognizing how their failure to act collectively is undermining the potential benefits accrued from their complementarities and the already high levels of integration in North America. New forms of cooperation and policy coordination are certainly in the realm of the possible, but the essential ingredients are political leadership and the kinds of collaboration and commitment between the public sector and the private sector that brought NAFTA to life in the early 1990s. In the absence of these factors, and of a more institutionalized framework, it is difficult to imagine how the NAFTA countries can resolve common transnational problems in such strategic areas as migration and labor markets, climate change, and energy.

Notes

1. An increase in fertility rates is not a short- or medium-term option to spur the growth of the workforce because the past decline of the total fertility rate has already

reduced the number of women of childbearing age. The increase in absolute birth rates would thus be limited. During the 1990s and early 2000s, immigrants already accounted for about one-half to two-thirds of the growth in the U.S. and Canadian workforces, respectively. Present projections indicate that this trend will persist into the near future.

2. Robert Pastor, *Toward a North American Community: Lessons from the Old World for the New* (Washington: Institute for International Economics, 2001), pp. 36–39.

3. Joseph M. Grieco, "Systemic Sources of Variation in Regional Institutionalization in Western Europe, East Asia, and the Americas," in *The Political Economy of Regionalism,* edited by Edward D. Mansfield and Helen V. Milner (Columbia University Press, 1997); Andrew Hurrell, "Regionalism in Theoretical Perspective," in *Regionalism in World Politics,* edited by in Louise Fawcett and Andrew Hurrell (Oxford University Press, 1995); Robert E. Baldwin, "Changes in the Global Trading System: A Response to Shifts in National Economic Power," in *Protectionism and World Welfare,* edited by Dominick Salvatore (Cambridge University Press, 1993); Peter J. Katzenstein, ed., *Tamed Power: Germany in Europe* (Cornell University Press, 1997).

4. Those who have made this argument for the Mexican case include Frederick W. Mayer, *Interpreting NAFTA: The Science and Art of Political Analysis* (Columbia University Press, 1998); Blanca Torres, "Rowing Upstream," in *Greening the Americas: NAFTA Lessons for Hemispheric Trade,* edited by Carolyn L. Deere and Daniel C. Esty (MIT Press, 2002); Stephen Krasner, "México y Estados Unidos," in *Interdependencia ¿Un enfoque útil para el análisis de las relaciones México-Estados Unidos?* edited by Blanca Torres (Mexico City: El Colegio de México, 1990).

5. The literature on this point is extensive. See, for example, Robert O. Keohane, *International Institutions and State Power: Essays in International Relations Theory* (Boulder, Colo.: Westview, 1989); Robert O. Keohane, *Power and Governance in a Partially Globalized World* (London: Routledge, 2002).

6. G. John Ikenberry, "State Power and the Institutional Bargain: America's Ambivalent Economic and Security Multilateralism," in *US Hegemony and International Organizations,* edited by Rosemary Foot, S. Neil MacFarlane, and Michael Mastanduno (Oxford University Press, 2003).

7. Ibid., p. 53.

8. Ibid., p. 49.

9. Ibid., p. 70.

10. Steven Weber, "Institutions and Change," in *New Thinking in International Relations Theory,* edited by Michael W. Doyle and G. John Ikenberry (Boulder, Colo.: Westview, 1997), p. 243.

11. Sydney Weintraub, *NAFTA: What Comes Next?* (Washington: Center for Strategic and International Studies, 1997), pp. 62–67.

12. Edward C. Luck, "American Exceptionalism and International Organization: Lessons from the 1990s," in *US Hegemony and International Organizations,* edited by Rosemary Foot, S. Neil MacFarlane, and Michael Mastanduno (Oxford University Press, 2003), p. 27.

13. Louis Hartz, *The Liberal Tradition in America* (San Diego: Harvest Books, 1955), p. 43; Samuel Huntington, "American Ideals versus American Institutions," in *American Foreign Policy*, edited by G. John Ikenberry (New York: Longman, 1999); Seymour Martin Lipset, *El excepcionalismo norteamericano: Una espada de dos filos* (Mexico City: Fondo de Cultura Económica, 1996).

14. Pastor, *Toward a North American Community*, p. 149.

15. Judith Goldstein, "Ideas, Institutions, and American Trade Policy," in *The State and American Foreign Economic Policy*, edited by G. John Ikenberry, David Lake, and Michael Mastanduno (Cornell University Press, 1988).

16. Luck, "American Exceptionalism and International Organization," p. 38.

17. I. M. Destler, *American Trade Politics*, 3d ed. (Washington: Institute for International Economics/Twentieth Century Fund, 1997), p. 223.

18. See Luck, "American Exceptionalism and International Organization," p. 38.

19. Goldstein, "Ideas, Institutions, and American Trade Policy," p. 41. In the end, Goldstein notes that the congressional vote on the WTO was 288 in favor to 146 against (121 votes for and 56 votes against in the Republican camp and 167 votes for and 89 votes against in the Democratic camp; in the Senate, the final vote was 76 to 23).

20. Destler, *American Trade Politics*, p. 223.

21. Kevin Featherstone and Roy H. Ginsberg, *The United States and the European Union in the 1990s: Partners in Transition* (New York: St. Martin's Press, 1996), p. 208.

22. Ibid., p. 210. Derek Bok, *State of the Nation* (Harvard University Press, 1998), p. 157, quoted in Pastor, *Toward a North American* Community, nn. 25, 35.

23. Seymour Martin Lipset, *Continental Divide: The Values and Institutions of the United States and Canada* (New York: Routledge, 1990), p. 39.

24. As an answer to the difficulties encountered in the Doha Round negotiations at the WTO and on a hemispheric level, the United States has adopted a strategy similar to the one it used in the early 1990s. The current strategy, competitive bilateralism, is ostensibly oriented toward promoting advances on a multilateral level.

25. For the United States it was just as important to achieve the opening of the Mexican market to investment and U.S. products as it was to ensure economic "discipline" and to cement the process of liberal reform that had begun in the 1980s. The ultimate aim was to maintain economic and political stability in Mexico in order to put an end to recurring economic crises. The hope was that this treaty and the reforms accompanying it could also liberalize the political system and contribute to Mexico's development.

26. Pastor, *Toward a North American Community*, p. 30. Also see Louis Belanger and Gordon Mace, "What Institutional Design for North America?" in *Free Trade in the Americas: Economic and Political Issues for Governments and Firms*, edited by Sidney Weintraub, Alan M. Rugman, and Gavin Boyd (Cheltenham, U.K.: Edward Elgar, 2004), p. 115.

27. Albert Fishlow, Sherman Robinson, and Raúl Hinojosa-Ojeda, "Proposal for a North American Regional Development Bank," paper prepared for the Federal Reserve Bank of Dallas conference, Dallas, June 14, 1991.

28. The bank also manages the nonrefundable resources of the Environmental Protection Agency for the Border (the Border Environmental Infrastructure Fund, or BEIF), earmarked for technical assistance, institutional strengthening, and training. Thus of a total of U.S.$1.143 billion invested in forty-three projects up until 2002, the bank lent U.S.$24 million and managed U.S.$355 million of the BEIF.

29. See European Parliament news (www.europarl.europa.eu/news/expert/infopress_ page/059-9473-185-07-27-910-20060628IPR09333-04-07-2006-2006-false/default_en.htm).

30. White House, *Fact Sheet,* March 22, 2002.

31. Destler, *American Trade Politics,* pp. 199–200.

32. Ibid., p. 222. See also Frederick Mayer, *Interpreting NAFTA: The Science and Art of Political Analysis* (Columbia University Press, 1998).

33. Richard Feinberg, "Comparing Regional Integration in Non-Identical Twins: APEC and the FTAA," *Integration and Trade* 4, no. 10 (2000) (www.2-irps.ucsd.edu/ faculty/rfeinberg/feinberg.pdf); Jeffrey Schott, *Prospects for Free Trade in the Americas* (Washington: Institute for International Economics, 2001).

34. Destler, *American Trade Politics,* p. 279.

35. Pastor, *Toward a North American Community,* p. 150.

36. Commission on the Future of Mexico-U.S. Relations, *El desafío de la interdependencia: México y Estados Unidos* (Mexico City: Fondo de Cultura Económica, 1988), p. 25.

37. See John W. Holmes, *Life with Uncle: The Canadian-American Relationship* (Toronto University Press, 1981); Charles Doran, *Forgotten Partnership* (Johns Hopkins University Press, 1984).

38. See Mario Ojeda, *Alcances y límites de la política exterior de México* (México: El Colegio de México, 1076), p. 93; David Leyton-Brown, "Managing Canada–United States Relations in the Context of Multilateral Alliances," in *America's Alliances and Canadian-American Relations,* edited by Lauren McKinsey and Kim Richard Nossal (Toronto: S. L. Summerhill, 1988).

39. David Leyton-Brown, "A Refurbished Relationship with the United States," and Michael K. Hawes, "Canada-US Relations in the Mulroney Era: How Special the Relationship?" in *Canada among Nations: The Tory Record 1988,* edited by Brian W. Tomlin and Maureen Appel Molot (Toronto: James Lorimer, 1989).

40. See Blanca Torres and Pamela S. Falk, eds., *La adhesion de México al GATT: Repercusiones internas e impacto sobre las relaciones México-Estados Unidos* (Mexico City: El Colegio de México, 1989).

41. For a more detailed explanation of the reasons to negotiate a free trade agreement with the United States, see Emilio Zebadúa, "Del Plan Brady al TLC: la lógica de la política exterior mexicana, 1988–1994," *Foro Internacional* 34, no. 4 (1994): 626–51.

42. The increase in intraregional trade has been spectacular, soaring 200 percent between 1993 and 2004, while extraregional trade grew 42 percent. Mexican exports to the United States grew at an average of 14 percent annually in that same period; U.S.

exports to Mexico grew about 10 percent a year. Mexico received an average of U.S.$4 billion in foreign direct investment annually between 1980 and 1993, a figure that jumped to U.S.$13 billion in the first decade of NAFTA. Thanks to the agreement, Mexico rapidly recovered from its 1995 financial crisis. Without the agreement, Mexico would not have been able to take full advantage of the rapid growth of the U.S. economy.

43. Isabel Guerrero, Luis Felipe López-Calva, and Michael Walton, "The Inequality Trap and Its Links to Low Growth in Mexico" (Washington: World Bank, 2007).

44. Pastor, *Toward a North American Community,* pp. 141–42.

4

TRADE NEGOTIATIONS AMONG NAFTA PARTNERS

The Future of North American Economic Integration

JEFFREY J. SCHOTT

N orth American economic integration long predates the creation of the Canada-U.S. Free Trade Agreement (CUSFTA) and the North American Free Trade Agreement (NAFTA). Several of the authors whose work appears in this volume have contributed importantly to the integration process—some for longer than they would like to admit. But there's still more work to do to ensure that regional integration achieves its ultimate purpose: to improve the standard of living of all the people in our societies.

This chapter traverses what has been achieved by building bridges—literally and figuratively—to link the three countries. North American economic integration has a rich history, which Gary Hufbauer and I document in our 2005 book, *NAFTA Revisited.*[1] I here address only a small but central aspect of that experience—how the three NAFTA partners can use trade negotiations to advance their own economic agendas and to deepen regional integration. But first an important caveat.

Trade and other intergovernmental initiatives do not operate in a vacuum. Macroeconomic events—the Mexican peso crisis of 1994–95, the U.S. high-tech boom of the 1990s, Canadian budget and monetary discipline over the past decade—clearly have shaped the depth and pace of economic integration. Domestic economic reforms will continue to determine how well firms and workers in each country can take advantage of trade and investment opportunities in the broader regional marketplace. Indeed, an open secret of trade policy is that many of the gains from trade derive from what countries do to change their own policies and practices. Now let me turn to trade negotiations and the NAFTA countries.

A Three-Dimensional Trade Strategy

Each NAFTA country is implementing what I call a three-dimensional trade strategy—that is, a mix of bilateral, hemispheric, and multilateral negotiations—to propel growth in its economy and to address the unfinished and new agenda of regional economic integration (including services, investment, government procurement). This strategy is often labeled multitrack, but that term doesn't convey the idea that these trade talks are interrelated—and, if done properly, are mutually reinforcing.

Why pursue such a complex trade strategy? It clearly runs counter to economic theory, which strongly favors multilateral negotiations based on the principles of nondiscrimination and most favored nation (MFN) treatment. The short answer is that this differentiated approach to trade negotiations is better suited to the current international economic environment, the challenges of competing in an era of globalization, and the new complexities of doing business at the World Trade Organization (WTO), where decisions generally require consensus among the 150 member countries. Moreover, WTO negotiations no longer accommodate the broad range of economic and foreign policy objectives that the NAFTA countries now pursue in trade negotiations. For example, the United States has broad-ranging negotiating objectives, set out in the Trade Act of 2002, encompassing "traditional" issues like tariffs and quotas as well as trade-related policies on intellectual property, labor, and the environment—many of which are not on the WTO negotiating agenda.

A three-dimensional negotiating strategy offers numerous advantages, though it poses some risks as well.[2] On the plus side, pursuing negotiations on several fronts can build momentum for new trade reforms. In some areas, progress is more feasible within smaller free trade agreements (FTAs) than at the WTO, especially on issues like intellectual property rights and services that involve complex regulatory policies; in other areas, results are only possible through agreement on multilateral disciplines (for example, domestic farm subsidies). Some issues have been excluded from the WTO agenda altogether (labor practices, investment, and competition policy) and currently can be vetted only at the level of bilateral or regional talks. In those cases, FTA provisions could establish precedents for possible future WTO accords. However, adding those issues to WTO talks would likely require a "rebalancing" of the negotiating agenda to include issues of priority to developing countries such as fundamental antidumping reform and new exceptions to obligations on intellectual property rights.

On the negative side, bilateral and regional initiatives can divert trade and distort investment flows, raise transactions costs inter alia by imposing different customs rules for different trading partners, and hinder WTO talks by diverting negotiating resources and political attention away from the multilateral forum. Moreover, while some precedents that were developed in the course of negotiating FTAs could be usefully advanced in WTO talks (such as new rules on e-commerce included in the U.S.-Chile FTA), others do not merit emulation (U.S.-Chile provisions on short-term capital controls).

The key challenge for policymakers is to ensure that the various trade initiatives promote consistent objectives and are mutually reinforcing. These bilateral initiatives can help catalyze broader regional reforms and build alliances in support of multilateral initiatives at the WTO. Success in furthering multilateral trade liberalization at the WTO in turn could minimize the adverse effects of trade diversion generated by FTA trade preferences and help ensure that bilateral and regional initiatives complement the objectives of the multilateral trading system. The challenge, of course—and well documented in the academic literature—is to minimize the distortions that arise in trade and investment flows from FTA trade preferences and discriminatory rules of origin. Through good design and complementary WTO reforms, FTAs can provide net benefits for the entire trading system.

The United States, Canada, and Mexico have all been active in the WTO's Doha Round, in negotiations for a Free Trade Area of the Americas (FTAA), and in negotiations for other FTAs, of which the most important by far is NAFTA. At the WTO and hemispheric talks, they are working cooperatively, though not in concert. One of the virtues of being in an FTA instead of a customs union is that an FTA allows each country to pursue an independent trade policy. In the North American arena, negotiations among the NAFTA partners continue to be pursued to revise rules and augment trade reforms. Some issues are dealt with trilaterally (such as revised rules of origin for specific industries). But the most important problems generally are dealt with through "dual bilateral" channels between the principal protagonists–either because of Mexico's more limited economic and administrative capabilities or because NAFTA's institutional mechanisms are quite weak.

Independently, but in parallel fashion, each of the North American partners has been pursuing a three-dimensional trade negotiating strategy since NAFTA entered into force in 1994. The following subsections summarize what each country is doing.

U.S. Trade Strategy

The United States continues to give priority attention to the conduct of multilateral trade negotiations. The United States was the demandeur of all of the rounds of both the WTO and the General Agreement on Tariffs and Trade (GATT) and has played a leadership role throughout the current Doha Round. The importance of the WTO to U.S. trading interests explains why former U.S. trade representative Robert Zoellick spent so much time trying to revive the talks in 2004 after the fiasco at the Cancún Ministerial; why his successor, Rob Portman, appointed Peter Allgeier—his most experienced and knowledgeable deputy—to take charge of the Doha Round talks in Geneva in June 2005; and why Susan C. Schwab, who replaced Portman in May 2006, spent the first six months of her term trying to revive the talks after negotiations collapsed in July 2006.

The Doha Round continues to be the most important trade initiative pursued by the United States. Early in the talks U.S. negotiators proposed radical reforms for agriculture, the elimination of industrial tariffs by 2015, and the liberalization of services in sectors such as finance, telecommunications, air transport, energy, and environmental services. U.S. officials need to bring home a big package of concessions from both industrial and middle-income developing countries in order to garner sufficient political support in Congress to reform the few but notable U.S. trade barriers, especially subsidies and border barriers in agriculture, that will be required as part of the U.S. contribution to the overall Doha Round accords. The difficulty in crafting such a big package, and in convincing major developing countries to improve their offers in tandem with the United States and the European Union, is an important reason that the Doha Round was still in jeopardy as of year-end 2006.

For the past two decades U.S. officials have supplemented efforts at the negotiating table in Geneva with bilateral and regional trade pacts designed to bolster U.S. trading interests and reinforce the multilateral trading system. Much of this activity has focused on the Western Hemisphere. After concluding the CUSFTA and NAFTA, U.S. officials proposed the FTAA and then initiated a series of FTA negotiations with FTAA participating countries to accelerate the process of economic integration between North and South

America. As of December 2006 the United States had ratified pacts with Israel, Canada, Mexico, Jordan, Chile, Singapore, Australia, Morocco, five Central American nations (CAFTA-5) and the Dominican Republic, Bahrain, and Oman; had concluded negotiations with Peru and Colombia; and was continuing FTA talks with Panama, the United Arab Emirates, South Korea, and Malaysia. Negotiations with Thailand, Ecuador, and the five-member Southern African Customs Union, as well as the FTAA, have been at least temporarily suspended. Current and prospective FTA partners (not including other FTAA participants) account for almost 44 percent of total U.S. merchandise trade and more than half of U.S. merchandise exports.[3]

Last but not least, the United States and its NAFTA partners recommitted themselves at the Crawford, Texas, summit on March 23, 2005, to enhancing their cooperation through the upgraded Security and Prosperity Partnership of North America. Originally, the United States saw NAFTA as an economic opportunity to capitalize on a growing export market to the south and as a way to support political pluralism and democratic processes in Mexico. It was also hoped that the pact would contribute to a long-term response to chronic migration from Mexico to the United States. Today, extended NAFTA talks are perhaps most needed to address new economic and security challenges confronting the region in the aftermath of the terrorist attacks of September 11, 2001.

Mexico's Trade Strategy

Mexico has pursued a three-dimensional trade strategy perhaps more diligently than even the United States. It has been an active participant in multilateral talks since its GATT accession in 1986 and was the host country for the Special Summit of the Americas in Monterrey and for hemispheric trade talks in Puebla. And of course Mexico is perhaps most famous as the instigator of NAFTA as well as many other FTAs with countries around the world—including key industrial markets such as the European Union (EU), the European Free Trade Association (EFTA), and Japan. In addition, Mexico entered into FTAs with Bolivia, Chile, Costa Rica, El Salvador, Guatemala, the G3 (Colombia, Mexico, and Venezuela), Honduras, Israel, and Nicaragua during the period January 1995 to June 2001.[4] Mexico has many more FTAs than the United States, and these pacts—along with the FTAA—are an integral part of Mexico's broader development strategy.

Like the United States, many of Mexico's FTA partners are Western Hemisphere neighbors. In a sense, Mexico is crafting its own FTAA through an agglomeration of bilateral FTAs with trading partners in the region.

These agreements are key to its strategy to attract European and Asian investment to build up Mexico as the locale for servicing the broader hemispheric market. Such investments benefit from more open and secure access to Latin American markets as well as the NAFTA region. Yet there still is a confused debate on whether the FTAA is good for Mexico. Some observers claim that the FTAA would erode Mexico's preferences in the U.S. market, and thus Mexico should hinder the evolution of the hemispheric trade pact in order to preserve its relative preferential status in the U.S. market. But such arguments ignore the fact that NAFTA preferences are being devalued every year as the United States negotiates other FTAs and reduces its MFN trade barriers.

Canada's Trade Strategy

Canada has been a stalwart supporter of the postwar multilateral trading system. Over the past two decades, however, it has also diversified its approach to trade negotiations: it was the instigator of the CUSFTA, a reluctant NAFTA partner, and more recently, a signatory to several inconsequential FTAs. In addition, Canada has been an active player in the FTAA, though mainly for foreign policy rather than for economic reasons.

For Canada, two trade channels have paramount importance: bilateral talks with the United States and multilateral negotiations to deal with issues that it has not been able to resolve with the United States on a bilateral basis (subsidies, contingent protection). The latter explains why, though more than 75 percent of Canadian trade is with the United States, Canadian policy has always had a multilateral bent—in large measure to develop global rules to help manage relations with its unwieldy neighbor. Canadian ventures into other FTAs have been less productive. It has emulated U.S. deals with Chile, Costa Rica, and Israel and has pursued talks with EFTA as well as other Latin American and Caribbean countries that have negotiated or are negotiating with the United States.[5] In some cases, these pacts include provisions that Canada has sought to apply to broader regional and WTO accords, with little success to date, particularly in the area of antidumping.

In sum, each NAFTA partner in its own way is engaged in a rich mixture of trade negotiations. At present, however, these negotiations seem to be underperforming at all levels. The Doha Round negotiations are plagued by modest expectations; the Cancún fiasco in September 2003 illustrates the problems of developing a consensus among the large and diverse membership; and subsequent talks—despite the procedural progress made in Geneva in July 2004—only reinforce concerns that politically sensitive reforms will, once again, be deferred. The Doha Round still risks being the first ever "failed" round that substantially damages the multilateral trading system.

Like the WTO talks, the FTAA negotiations are burdened by an ambitious mandate and impeded by sharp divisions over agricultural trade reforms. As emphasized by several authors in this volume, the Western Hemisphere talks have not advanced since the Miami Ministerial Meeting in November 2003. Like the Doha Round, the FTAA talks effectively have been suspended; unlike the WTO initiative, however, little effort has been made to put the talks back on track.

Finally, the prospects for expanding NAFTA discussions to address new initiatives (energy, security, labor migration) continue to be burdened by disputes in sensitive areas (trucking, sugar, softwood lumber) that negotiators have not been able to resolve for years. At the same time, infrastructure deficiencies and new security imperatives complicate the processing of goods and people across the U.S.-Canada and U.S.-Mexico borders, impeding the process of North American economic integration.

Working Together, Negotiating Apart

Some observers suggest that the three NAFTA countries should follow the European model and integrate—or at least coordinate—their trade policies to maximize their leverage in international trade negotiations. Others argue for a U.S.-Canada customs union, omitting Mexico until its economic development appreciably advances.[6] Practical politics, however, dictates a more pragmatic approach. The U.S. Congress is wary of sharing control over U.S. trade policy with the U.S. executive branch and would flatly reject a Canadian or Mexican voice in U.S. policy. The best approach for the NAFTA partners is to work together in trade negotiations to advance national priorities that, over time, will redound to the benefit of the entire region.

Let me summarize the key challenges now facing the negotiation of the Doha Round accords, the FTAA, and initiatives to update NAFTA and how the three NAFTA partners can work together to advance their common interests.

The Doha Round

The Doha Round offers the prospect of the biggest economic payoff; it is also the only venue to confront the subsidies and the contingent protection problems that have long plagued North American intraregional trade. Moreover, WTO talks present the best chance to achieve substantial cutbacks in agricultural subsidies and import barriers, which would have the additional benefit of removing some complications to restarting and advancing negotiations on an FTAA.

The successful conclusion of the Doha Round will turn on the ability of WTO members to deal with problems that have survived the eight previous attempts at GATT liberalization. Some intractable problems remain, particularly in agriculture (European farm tariffs and nontariff barriers, Japanese rice tariffs, U.S. cotton subsidies, and Canadian dairy restrictions) and services (transportation and labor services), but also involving compliance with WTO norms (Chinese protection of intellectual property, restrictions on genetically modified crops, and operations of state-trading enterprises). In these areas, bilateral initiatives have not been sufficient to overcome strong domestic political resistance to reform these foreign practices. Progress on these matters will require a bigger deal, which can be crafted only in multilateral negotiations.

Agriculture holds the key to a successful Doha Round negotiation—not because of its importance in international trade (less than 10 percent of global merchandise trade) but because it is the sector with the highest trade barriers and largest potential welfare gains for developing countries. A farm deal, however difficult, still will not be sufficient to secure the Doha Round. To counter opposition from protectionist lobbies, the final accords must also include substantial results in the other key areas under negotiation: nonagricultural market access, services, trading rules (subsidies, countervailing and antidumping measures, trade facilitation, disciplines on regionalism), and special and differential treatment for developing countries. Otherwise, it will be hard to sell the Doha Round accords to national legislatures.

Whether the Doha Round will succeed is still an open question. Progress on agriculture has been insufficient to spur worthwhile offers on manufactures and services, especially from the handful of big emerging-market countries that will enjoy the most growth over the next decade: China, Brazil, India, Indonesia, South Africa, and Thailand. Without substantive offers outside of agriculture by both developed and developing countries, the United States, the EU, and Japan will not be able to maintain—much less augment—their offers on farm reforms. While Brazil, India, and other developing countries may step forward with new offers on manufactures and services, their proposals are likely to contain only minor reforms that would fall well short of what could energize farm talks. Those countries remain wary that key farm reforms will be excluded or subject to lengthy deferment in the Doha Round negotiations.

The Doha Round can still produce a comprehensive package of agreements by the end of 2007. However, this result will require the U.S. Congress to renew Trade Promotion Authority (TPA), which expires on July 1, 2007. Without this legislative mandate, U.S. officials will have difficulty offering substantive reforms in U.S. policies, and consequently the Doha negotiations probably would go into deep hibernation. Reviving the Doha Round is, in my view, a prerequisite for congressional consideration of TPA, since the Bush administration will have to be able to delineate why such authority is needed.

To revive multilateral negotiations member countries will need to agree on specific numbers or ranges for cuts in agriculture and in nonagricultural market access and to agree, also, on the specific areas in which they will augment their obligations under the General Agreement for Trade in Services (GATS).[7] Only then can negotiators develop a final package of agreements—limiting exceptions and special treatment for sensitive products—a task that will take at least another year and that may require the intervention of heads of state to initiate those reforms needed to put the deal together.

What could a WTO deal do for North American economic integration? The clearest benefits would emerge from an agreement to cut farm subsidies and to discipline state trading enterprises. Such reforms would "level the playing field" for intraregional trade in farm products, especially field crops, dairy products, and sugar. In addition, new rules on antidumping and countervailing duties could provide guidelines for resolving long-standing North American disputes on steel.

The Free Trade Area of the Americas

The FTAA talks are important for both economic and foreign policy reasons. The FTAA is the economic engine that drives hemispheric cooperation on more than twenty initiatives undertaken by leaders at the ongoing Summit of the Americas, launched in 1994 by the Clinton administration. The FTAA would provide the first major trade accord between the United States and Brazil and its partners in the Southern Cone Common Market (Mercosur). At the same time, the hemispheric FTA would help harmonize the separate free trade regimes that have been negotiated among regional trading partners.

That said, the negotiations effectively have broken down. The United States and Brazil, the cochairs of the FTAA talks and the leading economies of North and South America, have been unable to bridge their differences and offer concrete new opportunities for exporters and investors in each other's markets (see chapter 7 by Glauco Oliveira). The targeted deadline for concluding the FTAA passed largely unnoticed in January 2005; since then, the talks have been in suspended animation awaiting progress at the WTO on agricultural subsidies and other issues.

What impact would the FTAA have on North American economic integration? Mexican and Canadian farmers would face more competition in the U.S. market, but industries in those countries would find new opportunities to export to South America (thus enhancing their own investment prospects). But the pact clearly would have less impact than a WTO accord or upgrading of NAFTA.

Upgrading NAFTA

By most standards, NAFTA has been a great success for all three countries, contributing to unprecedented growth in regional trade and investment.[8] Intraregional merchandise trade in North America now exceeds U.S.\$700 billion annually, and cross-border direct investment is extensive.

However, the NAFTA partners now face new challenges to economic integration in an increasingly competitive and security conscious global environment. Residual restrictions continue to impede regional trade and investment; the region remains vulnerable to volatile energy prices and supply shortfalls; illegal immigration still confronts political leaders on both sides of the Rio Grande; and long-standing labor and environmental problems continue to fester, particularly in the U.S.-Mexico border region. In addition, heightened security measures since September 11, 2001, have made it more costly and cumbersome to move goods and people across borders and pose a particular challenge to businesses that have integrated their operations on a regional basis—one of NAFTA's great virtues. The Smart Borders Declaration between the United States and Canada and the Border Partner Agreement between the United States and Mexico have been a good start in addressing the new security needs of the post-9/11 world.

However, much more needs to be done to ensure continued prosperity for the three countries, which depend on each other for their economic prosperity and security. For the United States, improving prospects for economic growth in Mexico is critical to strengthening security on its southern border, while deeper cooperation with Canada on border security initiatives is essential to ensure the efficient flow of goods and people across the long northern border. Mexico's economic prospects depend both on the continued health of the U.S. economy and on its own domestic reforms, particularly tax and energy policies to generate funds for investment in oil and gas field development and in power generation and distribution. For Canada, maintaining an open U.S. border is crucial for its economic well-being; trade and security pacts can help forestall the reinstatement of stringent U.S. border restrictions imposed in the wake of the 9/11 terrorist attacks, which were so disruptive to Canadian production and commerce.

Updating and deepening North American economic integration thus merits priority attention for both economic and security reasons. New initiatives in the areas of trade, energy, and migration could help deal with pressing problems in each country while promoting closer security ties to better handle the aftershocks of future terrorist attacks.

How can the NAFTA partners work together to advance their common interests? First, the NAFTA countries should deepen the trade bargain. While creating a customs union may not be feasible, the partners could move toward a common external tariff by lowering and gradually harmonizing their MFN tariffs. A common external tariff would have several advantages:

—It would reduce the cost of imported goods.

—It would mitigate concerns about the protectionist impact of NAFTA's rules of origin (since cutting MFN tariffs dilutes the value of the regional tariff preferences that are conditioned on meeting the origin rules).

—It would promote liberalization that could also contribute to the success of the Doha Round.

However, a common external tariff would not resolve vexing problems long immune to negotiated fixes (most notably regarding wheat and sugar) as well as other countervailing and antidumping problems.

Second, the NAFTA countries should jointly develop a North American energy security policy that promotes regional production and trade as well as the buildup of strategic reserves and production capacity in the event of overseas supply disruptions. The United States, Canada, and Mexico share a common interest in expanding regional energy production, especially oil and natural gas:

—The United States accounts for about a quarter of global consumption of oil and gas; its energy import bill totaled U.S.$175 billion in 2004. Additional supplies worldwide redound to its advantage by dampening price increases.

—Canada has bountiful reserves and a willingness to supply more oil and gas to regional and world markets if labor and regulatory constraints can be addressed. Exploitation of new energy reserves will spur economic growth at home and contribute to a narrowing of energy demand and supply imbalances in North America.

—Mexico is energy rich but suffers from power shortages due to inadequate investment in exploration, development, and distribution networks. Mexico's problems derive from tax policies that drain the state oil company (Pemex) of investment funds and the Mexican constitution's prohibition against foreign participation in the exploitation of oil and gas. Recognizing the political roadblocks, Mexico will nonetheless have to rethink its tax and energy policies in the near future—with or without constitutional amendments—to avoid major brownouts and to ensure the success of its development strategies.

Third, the three countries should coordinate more closely regarding their immigration regulations, starting with common visa standards for most non-NAFTA visitors and immigrants. This goal is highly significant from a security standpoint. For people arriving from outside the NAFTA region, the North American countries need a shared system for excluding non-NAFTA nationals who pose a security threat. NAFTA partners also should develop common document and biometric identification standards for all non-NAFTA visitors. More broadly, reforms in U.S. immigration policies could create a better environment for U.S.-Mexico cooperation across the bilateral agenda. However, immigration reform that focuses on increased U.S. border patrols to deter illegal immigration from Mexico, as proposed by President Bush in May 2006, could well generate the opposite result.

In sum, bilateral, regional, and WTO negotiations all are important for the NAFTA partners and for the process of regional economic integration, though each country has different priorities among them. Cooperation among the NAFTA partners can help build the requisite consensus to revive and conclude the WTO and FTAA negotiations. At the same time, the three countries could reap substantial gains by working together within the NAFTA context to resolve both lingering problems and new challenges to North American economic integration. In all these initiatives, successful negotiations will ultimately depend on the willingness of each country to undertake substantive reforms of domestic tax, expenditure, and regulatory policies.

Notes

1. Gary Clyde Hufbauer and Jeffrey J. Schott, *NAFTA Revisited: Achievements and Challenges* (Washington: Institute for International Economics, 2005).

2. For an analysis of the pros and cons, see Jeffrey J. Schott, ed., *Free Trade Agreements: US Strategies and Priorities* (Washington: Institute for International Economics, 2004), chap. 1.

3. For a detailed analysis of these agreements and U.S. policy, see ibid.

4. Herminio Blanco and Jaime Zabludovsky, "FTAA: The Scope of the Negotiations," Working Paper SITI-01 (Washington: INTAL, Inter-American Development Bank, 2003).

5. Danielle Goldfarb, "U.S. Bilateral Free Trade Accords: Why Canada Should Be Cautious about Going the Same Route," Commentary 214 (Toronto: C.D. Howe Institute, 2005).

6. Bill Dymond and Michael Hart, "Policy Implications of a Canada-U.S. Customs Union," Discussion Paper (Ottawa: Canada Policy Research Institute, 2005).

7. Labor services, where commitments will need to be tailored to safeguard security interests and to avoid conflict with immigration policies, should be included.

8. This section draws heavily on Hufbauer and Schott, *NAFTA Revisited,* chap 9.

PART

II

THE HEMISPHERIC CONTEXT

*From NAFTA to the Free Trade
Area of the Americas*

5

Beyond the FTAA

Perspectives for Hemispheric Integration

JAIME ZABLUDOVSKY AND SERGIO GÓMEZ LORA

I t has been more than ten years since the heads of state of the thirty-four democratically elected governments in the Western Hemisphere launched negotiations for a Free Trade Area of the Americas (FTAA), the most ambitious foreign policy initiative the region has seen in decades. The 1994 Miami Summit of the Americas gave birth to the FTAA concept, raising expectations that the long-standing desire for hemispheric integration seemed possible at last. Since the Miami Summit, significant progress has been achieved, even though macroeconomic problems and political crises have plagued several of the participating countries. Despite the effort of FTAA leaders to keep the initiative alive, the originally agreed 2005 deadline for completion of the FTAA has passed and negotiations remain stalled.

To understand the evolution of the FTAA over the last decade and the current impasse, it is best to analyze it in two stages: the period 1994–2000 and the period 2001–04.[1] During the first six years of the FTAA, from 1994 to 2000, no real negotiations took place. The reason is simple: with the 2005 target date for the agreement's completion so distant in the future, no country was willing to make a serious offer, knowing in advance that all substantive discussions would have to wait for the closing stage of the negotiations. Moreover, the most important players, with the exception of Canada and Chile, had other priorities during this period.

In the United States, after the approval of the North American Free Trade Agreement (NAFTA) in 1993 and the conclusion of the eight-year Uruguay Round negotiations in 1994, the Clinton administration rested on these laurels for the remainder of the 1990s. The United States, in other words, basically abdicated the leadership role that it had long played in international trade negotiations. Opposition to further trade liberalization from labor unions, environmentalists, and key actors in the Democratic Party made it difficult for the Clinton trade policy team to maintain the momentum it had gathered to pass the NAFTA bill. The collapse of the World Trade Organization's (WTO's) Trade Ministerial in Seattle in November 1999 and President Clinton's continued failure to obtain the fast-track negotiating authority from the U.S. Congress are just two of the problems faced by his administration in this area.

For the Mercosur (Southern Cone Common Market) countries (Argentina, Brazil, Paraguay, and Uruguay), the FTAA was not a high priority during the 1990s, because most of them were concerned with their own macroeconomic and political crises and their own regional integration efforts. Early on in the FTAA process, Mexico, having secured privileged access to the U.S. market via NAFTA, had little incentive to share this privilege with other countries in the region.[2] Mexico has instead used the advantage of its NAFTA membership to advance at the bilateral level, developing an ambitious network of trade agreements in the hemisphere. Meanwhile, Canada and Chile, although they maintained an active commitment to the FTAA process, also took advantage of the vacuum left by the U.S. lack of leadership to sign free trade agreements (FTAs) with regional partners.

The second stage of the FTAA process started in 2001. Upon assuming office that year, the new administration of George W. Bush sought to revive U.S. leadership in trade negotiations. It invested the political capital needed to obtain the fast-track negotiating authority (now called Trade Promotion Authority, or TPA), which enables Congress to vote up or down on a trade bill without amending it, and the Bush trade policy team provided the leadership to launch a new multilateral round of trade negotiations in Doha in 2001. Last but not least, the United States implemented the competitive negotiations strategy, which sought to address some of the FTAA rules that appeared to hamper progress but which also included the launching of a series of bilateral negotiations with a broad geographical range of countries.

On the need to revive the FTAA process, in 1998 in San José, Costa Rica, the FTAA countries had agreed on the following language: "The initiation, conduct and outcome of the negotiations of the FTAA shall be treated as parts of a single undertaking which will embody the rights and obligations as mutually agreed upon. . . . The rights and obligations of the FTAA will be shared by all countries."[3] In practice, this 1998 single-undertaking principle proved to be a major constraint on FTAA negotiations, as it extended a de facto veto power to each participant regardless of its size or its commitment to the initiative. The single-undertaking principle and its original consensus rule meant that the pace of negotiations was dictated by the slowest trade reformer in the pack and that the scope of the intended agreement was defined by the least ambitious country among the participants.

Once the U.S. executive obtained TPA in August 2002, the Office of the U.S. Trade Representative (USTR) launched its competitive negotiations strategy, one goal being to change these unfavorable incentives within the FTAA process. Since this time, the United States has concluded bilateral FTAs with Singapore, Chile, Australia, Bahrain, Morocco, Central America, and Dominican Republic and has announced the beginning of negotiations with the Southern Africa Customs Union, Thailand, and Malaysia. (As of 2007, U.S. negotiations with Thailand and the Southern Africa Customs Union have been suspended.) Later on, at the 2003 FTAA Ministerial meeting in Miami, separate negotiations for FTAs between the United States and Panama, Colombia, Ecuador, and Peru were announced and have been completed (although they have not been approved by all of the respective legislatures).

The U.S. competitive negotiation approach indeed modified the incentives for countries to participate in FTAA negotiations. Before the adoption of this new U.S. strategy, the Latin American and Caribbean (LAC) countries perceived that the FTAA was not only the fastest way but also the only way to secure an FTA with the United States. However, with the new U.S. strategy, it became evident that the United States was not willing to wait for the LAC countries to move collectively on the hemispheric initiative, and many of these countries began scrambling to negotiate bilaterally with the United States, which had signaled its willingness to move ahead on multiple fronts on the continent. Mexico, in essence, followed suit by adopting a similar strategy of negotiating FTAs with willing partners. Our questions are, Can this strategy of negotiating bilateral FTAs shake the hemisphere out of its doldrums? And what role might Mexico play in this process?

Mexico: Achieving an FTAA by Other Means?

Since Mexico's bold unilateral trade opening in the mid-1980s and its accession to the General Agreement on Tariffs and Trade (GATT) in 1986, its policymakers had been primarily occupied with the Mexico-U.S. bilateral relationship and the country's leadership role at the Doha Round. As mentioned above, after securing bilateral assurances regarding U.S. market access with the launching of NAFTA in 1994, Mexico turned its attention toward the negotiation of a larger network of bilateral agreements, beginning with Costa Rica and Bolivia in 1995 and culminating with the Mexico-Japan FTA in 2005. Until the reawakening of trade leadership in the Office of the USTR in 2002, as signaled by President Bush's gaining TPA from Congress, Mexico's privileged access to the U.S. market was such that it could rise above the plurilateral tensions that have plagued U.S.-Mercosur relations and the broader FTAA negotiating context.

Since 2002, however, Mexico's position in the U.S. market has become much less certain. First is the success with which any number of other countries (Australia, Chile, and Jordan) have followed the Mexican path of securing a bilateral FTA with the United States. Second is the ability of U.S. trade negotiators to finesse a minilateral deal in the form of the U.S.–Central American Free Trade Agreement (CAFTA), which further confirms that preferential access to the prized U.S. market is no longer a strictly North American perk. Third, as confirmed by the data presented in chapter 2 by Carol Wise, is the rapidity with which Chinese producers are outpacing Mexican exporters in sectors that once defined the U.S.-Mexico trade relationship (sectors such as telecommunications, computer peripherals, and sound and television equipment). Together, these trends raise questions concerning the range of viable policy options—including the FTAA—for facing this challenge.

On the upside, Mexico's FTAs with the United States, Japan, and the more than fifteen members of the European Union (EU), completed between 2000 and 2005, mean that Mexico has now secured market access with forty-three countries, accounting for some 65 percent of global trade. On the downside, as table 5-1 shows, rising levels of protection toward the rest of the world have accompanied Mexico's pursuit of ambitious liberalizing agreements. Some of these higher tariffs are vestiges of the country's severe 1994-95 financial crisis, which is the case with textiles, clothing, and shoes. In other cases, like the electronic product lines mentioned earlier, protectionism has been a main response to the intense competitive pressure that China is now exerting on Mexico. Finally, some tariff hikes are due to the demand for higher fiscal revenues, as subsequent Mexican administrations have failed to pass a badly needed tax reform package.

The main result of the trends shown in table 5-1 is that Mexico's most favored nation (MFN) tariff levels (tariffs applied on imports from countries

Table 5-1. *Mexico's Trade Protection, 1993–2004*
Percent

Year and number of FTA trade partners	Average tariff MFN	Average weighted tariff MFN	Tariff dispersion	Tariff level	Import controls	Trade with FTA
1993: 1	13.5	14.5	9.7	28	n.d.	0.3
1994: 3	12.9	13.0	10.5	25	4.3	78.5
1995: 7	13.0	10.3	7.2	7	2.2	82.5
1996: 7	12.5	9.5	7.6	7	2.7	83.2
1997: 7	12.5	9.6	7.7	9	4.1	83.4
1998: 9	12.4	9.7	7.8	10	4.4	83.7
1999: 9	15.4	12.9	8.0	17	3.6	84.1
2000: 20	15.4	14.2	8.0	18	6.2	90.1
2001: 27	15.5	15.1	8.0	17	6.1	88.7
2002: 27	15.5	15.8	8.1	18	5.9	86.7
2003: 27	15.4	15.6	8.0	18	5.9	86.5
2004: 42	14.8	14.2	8.4	16	4.7	83.7

Source: Mexican Ministry of the Economy.

for which Mexico has no FTA in place) are now among the highest in the Western Hemisphere. For example, Mexico's average applied MFN tariff on nonagricultural products was 14.2 percent in 2004. This, along with a 14.7 percent tariff for this same category of goods within Mercosur, sets the hemispheric record. Apart from provoking a negative reaction from its trade partners that currently enjoy no special privileges in the Mexican market, but which account for approximately 23 percent of Mexico's foreign trade, this upward spike in tariffs has raised transaction costs and reduced transparency, thus greatly complicating Mexico's customs administration.

As we see it, Mexico's trade regime is in need of two major reforms. One is to launch another ambitious round of unilateral liberalization; another is to expedite and improve the technical operation of NAFTA, Mexico's primary FTA, but also to pursue FTAs with countries that have a bilateral FTA with the United States. With or without the FTAA, this seems the most promising means for gradually establishing a free trade zone that encompasses increasingly larger chunks of the hemisphere. We return to the question of the FTAA and the potential for such a strategy to jumpstart this process in the final section of the chapter.

Back to the Basics: Mexico's Need to Deepen Unilateral Liberalization

With the 2005 conclusion of the Mexico-Japan FTA, Mexico accomplished its main goals on the bilateral agenda. One remaining venue would be the Mercosur bloc, with which Mexico might pursue a minilateral accord. Although there may seem to be little structural logic to this option, as Mexico's trade with Mercosur accounts for just 2.5 percent of its total foreign trade, at a deeper level, Mexico shares some of the same problems with Mercosur that have impeded U.S.-Mercosur trade negotiations on the U.S. side (as discussed by Glauco Oliveira in chapter 7).

For example, in terms of Mexican imports, those agricultural products for which the Mercosur bloc has a strong comparative advantage (grains, beef, dairy) are precisely the most sensitive for Mexican producers in this sector. As for Mexico's exporting prospects to Mercosur, its strengths lie in electronics, computers, and the auto industry—sectors that are the most protected and politically sensitive in the Southern Cone. In light of these adverse product complementarities, and given Mexico's high tariff levels for non-FTA partners, a sound argument can be made for deeper unilateral liberalization as the most sensible path forward for Mexico at this time. This seems the most direct route for streamlining burdensome administrative procedures at the border, for reducing contraband and tax evasion, and for promoting the efficiency and competitiveness of the Mexican economy. Mexico's tariffs from some 9,824 product lines, shown in table 5-2, illustrate the problem.

High levels of protection against the products of countries outside of Mexico's FTA network place domestic producers at a disadvantage with regard to their competitors from countries where these inputs enter more cheaply. The Mexican government has responded by creating a sectoral development program (Prosec) for some twenty-two domestic industries and by partially liberalizing imports for electronics production, a sector that has been under siege from Chinese competition for the past few years. But the burgeoning administrative burden at the border threatens to erode these efforts. Among other things, Mexico's customs administration oversees tariff collection on twelve FTAs, on MFN tariff rates, on the export-processing zones (*maquilas*), and on antidumping quotas and compensatory taxes. Our argument is that further unilateral liberalization could greatly ease this burden.

Although there are strong similarities in the rules of origin that have been negotiated under Mexico's various FTAs, there is still the question of individual certification and administration of each set of rules. Additionally, the value added computations can become quite complicated. For example, a

Table 5-2. *Mexico's Tariffs, Most Favored Nations*

Tariffs (percent)	Product lines (number)	Tariffs (percent)	Product lines (number)
0	1,750	14	14
5	77	15	2,723
7	4	20	1,343
7.5	1	23	13
9	187	35	483
10	3,192	50	37

Source: Mexican Ministry of the Economy.

product that is manufactured in its entirety by a joint venture between the United States and the EU, but without meeting the rule-of-origin requirements under NAFTA or the Mexico-EU agreement, would still have to pay the MFN tariff as it enters Mexico.

Clearly, Mexico's elimination of the MFN tariff would go a long way toward simplifying ongoing customs procedures. This would render obsolete the use of certificates of origin and the reliance on ad hoc mechanisms to buffer certain subsectors from the negative impacts of this particular brand of protectionism. The opportunities for corruption would be mitigated, and the overall costs of doing business in Mexico could be significantly lowered. Our estimates show that 83 percent of Mexico's imports now come from FTA partners; hence the maintenance of the costly and complex regime just described pertains to around one-fifth of the country's foreign purchases. It would be difficult to argue that the benefits outweigh the costs.

The inevitable pain that unilateral liberalization of these tariffs would inflict on some Mexican producers could be properly addressed through staggered timelines and temporary adjustment assistance. The goal, obviously, would be to improve efficiency for those producers who are so disposed or to facilitate the reassignment of resources to other sectors in the case of those who cannot survive the heightened competition.

Mexico's Need to Negotiate Further Trade Liberalization

As noted above, Mexico's privileged access to the U.S. market has been gradually whittled away both by the remarkable advance of China into U.S. sectors once deemed exclusively North American and by the determination of the U.S. trade policy team to negotiate bilateral accords with willing and interested partners. Mexico would be well advised to couple a strategy of unilateral liberalization with one of deepening its trade ties with the following eighteen FTAs:

—Central America, Dominican Republic, and the United States, whose FTA entered into force in 2004.

—Canada and Central America, whose FTA is in advanced negotiation.

—Chile and the United States, whose FTA entered into force in 2003.

—Canada and Costa Rica, whose FTA entered into force in 2002.

—Central America and Chile, whose FTA entered into force in 2002 (Chile is in the process of extending its agreement to Guatemala, Honduras, and Nicaragua).

—Mexico, El Salvador, Guatemala, and Honduras, whose FTA entered into force in 2001.

—Chile and Mexico, whose FTA entered into force in 1999.

—Mexico and Nicaragua, whose FTA entered into force in 1998.

—Canada and Chile, whose FTA entered into force in 1997.

—Costa Rica and Mexico, whose FTA entered into force in 1995.

—Canada, Mexico, and the United States, whose FTA entered into force in 1994.

—Central American Common Market (Costa Rica, El Salvador, Honduras, Guatemala, and Nicaragua), which entered into force in 1960.

—Mexico and Bolivia, whose FTA entered into force in 1995.

—Mexico, Colombia, and Venezuela, whose FTA entered into force in 1995; Venezuela dropped out in 2006.

—Chile and the Andean countries of Bolivia (1993), Colombia (1994), and Ecuador (1995).

—Andean Community (Colombia, Peru, and Ecuador), which entered into force in 1997.

—United States and Panama, whose FTA is still pending.

—United States and the Andean countries of Colombia, Peru, and Ecuador, whose FTA is waiting for legislative approval.

For Mexico to assume a leadership role in integrating more tightly with these accords—referred to in the literature as the "spaghetti bowl" due to the suboptimal FTA patchwork that is now evolving—would raise the possibility of unifying its own trade regime with these other U.S. partners and provide a badly needed impetus for the streamlining of rules of origin and other barriers across this broad geographical swath.

As the list shows, Mexico, the United States, Chile, Guatemala, Honduras, El Salvador, Nicaragua, and Canada have in one way or another established FTAs among themselves, amounting to twelve free trade zones in all.[4]

The finalization of the U.S.-Andean FTAs (Colombia, Peru, and Ecuador) will bump this number higher. For Mexico, which has seven separate continental FTAs with Bolivia, Colombia, Chile, Uruguay, Costa Rica, Central America (Honduras, El Salvador, and Guatemala), and Canada–United States, a first step forward would be to negotiate with the same Andean countries that are now in the process of completing bilateral FTAs with the United States. The only other outlier would then be the Dominican Republic, which has negotiated an FTA with the United States as part of the CAFTA accord. In order to be included in a consolidated, twelve-member, continental zone, the Dominican Republic would have to negotiate FTAs with Chile, Canada, and Mexico.

To create a subregional free trade zone of twelve countries, the following FTAs would have to be taken into account:
—Mexico and Dominican Republic
—Mexico and Ecuador
—Mexico and Peru
—Chile and Dominican Republic
—Central America and Andean countries
—Canada and Andean countries
—Canada and Dominican Republic
—Panama, Andean countries, Mexico, and Canada

The appeal of this proposed continental free trade zone lies in the much smaller number of actors at the negotiating table (twelve countries instead of thirty-four at the FTAA) and thus its higher probability for constructive collective action. The countries involved, moreover, have already made a sound commitment to trade liberalization and regional integration. There is obviously no guarantee as to Mexico's ability to successfully lead this process, as that will depend on governments, producers, and domestic legislatures in the countries involved. However, Mexico does emerge as the natural leader for such a project, both in terms of its size and in terms of the sound leadership record it has shown in the context of free trade agreement negotiations in the region.

Given the stalemate to which the FTAA has succumbed, all signs point to a continued bilateral negotiating strategy on the part of the United States. Our point is that Mexico cannot afford a passive stance in the face of this reality. First are the cold facts concerning Mexico's displacement by China in U.S. sectors in which it once had a firm foothold, and this is being exacerbated by the flurry of FTAs that the United States is now signing, for example, with Central America and the Andean countries. Second is the increased loss of Mexico's market share in those same continental markets where the United States is busy securing privileged access. The advantages for Mexico in promoting the subregional free trade zone detailed above would be the opportunity to harmonize and reduce rules of origin across this bloc, the realization of greater specialization and economies of scale within this zone, and the administrative simplification of Mexico's own trade regime as part of this reform process.

Although there is increasing consensus concerning the entry barriers and inefficiencies surrounding NAFTA's rules of origin, there is less agreement on how to rectify this problem. A trinational task force report published in 2005, for example, advocates the establishment of a North American Customs Union with a common external tariff similar to the scheme that prevails in the European Union.[5] Yet we would argue that such an arrangement is foreclosed by the absence of a common commercial policy toward outside members under NAFTA, a situation that is readily reflected in the differing tariff levels set by each of the three countries and by the numerous FTAs that each NAFTA member has gone on to negotiate since 1994.

A more viable option would be for the three NAFTA members to expand preferential tariffs to those countries included above in the proposal for a twelve-country free trade zone. Furthermore, the United States and Canada could make important strides in phasing out NAFTA's rules of origin by eliminating their MFN tariffs in certain products. This would obviously have to be negotiated among the NAFTA countries, and given the resistance to further unilateral liberalization by the G-8 bloc within the context of the Doha Round, it could be a tall order.

Yet we envision the setting of two main conditions that could render this proposal viable. The first would be a reduction in MFN tariffs of about 5 percent; the second would be the limitation of unilateral trade concessions by Canada and the United States to those continental members already incorporated into the bilateral FTA network of each country. Since these countries already have fairly free access to North American markets, the reductions would be fairly modest. This is not to downplay the future gains from this strategy, as it bolsters our proposal for greater harmonization and liberalization within the twelve-member regional zone. None of this is meant to entirely jettison the FTAA project; rather, our analysis is geared toward exploring the possibilities for achieving similar ends but by slightly different means. In the following section we elaborate on the main bottlenecks and summarize the debates for overcoming them.

The Main Challenges to Completing the FTAA

Without underestimating the relevance and challenges for all of the countries participating in the hemispheric initiative, the differences between the United States and Mercosur, and the United States and Brazil in particular, emerged as the major stumbling block for the negotiations. The core offensive and defensive interests of FTAA members are summarized below in table 5-3 (defensive interests try to preserve the status quo and are generally associated with protecting the domestic market; offensive interests aim at liberalizing, or imposing new disciplines on, markets with their main trade partners).[6]

As the table shows, the United States has regular or strong offensive interests in eight of the nine negotiating groups and strong defensive interests in just two: antidumping and agriculture, with the latter pertaining to domestic subsidies and market access for a group of products that benefit from significant protection such as sugar, tobacco, citrus fruits, and peanuts. These two highly sensitive issues for the United States are precisely the main offensive interests for Mercosur. In the rest of the FTAA negotiating agenda, the South American bloc has adopted a defensive position, specifically on market access for industrial goods, investment, services, intellectual property, and government procurement.

Obviously, Mercosur's defensive agenda also clashes with the offensive interests of the United States. The United States aims to dismantle Mercosur's high levels of industrial protection (with average tariffs of around 15 percent) and seeks South American adoption of strict intellectual property rights, investment, services, and government procurement disciplines. Given that the United States is already a relatively open economy, the substantive concessions that it can offer Mercosur are few and are concentrated in extremely sensitive sectors: apparel, textiles and footwear, and some agricultural products (such as sugar, tobacco, citrus). Mercosur countries have indicated that, in any case, these concessions will be possible only if the United States agrees to adopt new disciplines for agricultural subsidies and trade remedy measures within the FTAA framework.

However, the inclusion of these two issues presents serious technical and political difficulties. Domestic support programs for agriculture are, by definition, applied across the board, regardless of the final destination of the subsidized commodity. It is impossible to eliminate the subsidy exclusively for exported products, and therefore it is not realistic to assume that the United States would agree to modify its agricultural support policy in the framework

Table 5-3. *FTAA and Offensive and Defensive Interests*[a]

Country/group	Market access	Agriculture	Investment	Services	Government procurement	Intellectual property	Anti dumping and countervailing duties	Competition	Dispute settlement
United States	D	DDD		D			DDD		
	OOO	OOO	OOO	OOO	OOO	OOO		OO	OO
Canada	D	D	DD						
	OOO	O	OO	OOO	OO	OO	OOO	OO	OO
Mexico	DD	DDD	D	D					
	OO	O	OO	O	OO	OO	OOO	O	OO
Chile	D	DD	D	D	D				
	O	OOO	O	OOO		O	OOO	OO	OO
Central America	D	DD	D	D	D	D		D	
	OOO	OOO					OO		OO
Mercosur	DDD	D	DDD	DD	DD	DD		D	
	O	OOO					O	OOO	O	OO
Andean Community	DD	D	DD	D	DD	DD		D	
	OO	OOO					OOO		OO
Caribbean	DDD	D	DD	D	DD	DD		D	
	OO	OOO					OO		OO

Source: Blanco and Zabludovsky, "Free Trade Area of the Americas."

a. Defensive interests (D) are those that try to preserve the status quo and are generally associated with protecting the domestic market; offensive interests (O) aim at liberalizing (or imposing new disciplines on) markets with their main trade partners. One letter indicates a weak interest; two letters indicate a regular interest; and three letters indicate a strong interest.

of a regional negotiation. Accordingly, the United States has indicated that this issue should be addressed in the WTO and not in the FTAA.

The reluctance of the United States to modify its trade remedies regime is more a political constraint than a technical one. In every recent trade negotiation the U.S. Congress has expressed its opposition to any modification that could undermine the "effectiveness" of current protection measures like antidumping and countervailing duties. Thus in the best scenario, any reform to U.S. antidumping legislation would have to be part of a broader package, one ample enough to offset those protectionist interests in the United States that have perpetuated the trade remedy legislation. It does not seem that the FTAA could generate such support. Therefore, antidumping is also an issue that would best be addressed in the Doha Round. In this context, the negotiating approach taken by the participating countries of the FTAA will be a crucial determinant of its success.

Two distinct approaches come to mind in terms of how LAC countries can come to terms with the United States. The first would be to take the FTAA negotiating impasse as an opportunity to promote economic reforms that have their own rationale regardless of the concessions received in exchange. This is the approach that Mexico and countries such as Chile and the Central American nations have adopted in order to succeed in their respective negotiations with the United States. These countries gained preferential access to the U.S. market in exchange for their liberalization efforts and the adoption of strong market-oriented disciplines. In all cases, these countries were convinced of the benefits of the reforms implicit in the FTA and the credibility obtained by locking these in to an international agreement with the United States.

A second approach would be to treat FTAA negotiations as an accounting exercise, whose results would be evaluated in terms of concessions gained and concessions extended. Under this approach, however, it would be extremely difficult to find a balance between offensive and defensive interests in any trade negotiation with the United States, given the inevitable asymmetries. The U.S. economy has relatively few concessions to make apart from access to its agricultural market and the elimination of a few industrial tariff peaks. Given the long list of U.S. offensive interests—elimination of high agricultural and industrial tariffs; liberalization of services, investment, and government procurement regimes; and strict intellectual property rights—the figures just don't add up.

The Current Impasse

The original agreement to conclude the WTO's Doha Development Round by 2005 opened up the possibility for synergies between the FTAA and WTO negotiations. Such synergies could have helped overcome some of the major obstacles that had become evident on the hemispheric level. For example, the possibility that domestic agricultural support programs and antidumping remedies could have been dealt with in Geneva, while the rest of the FTAA agenda was addressed at the hemispheric level, provided an opportunity to strike a balance among the participants in regional negotiations. Unfortunately, this opportunity disappeared in the wake of the failed WTO Ministerial meeting in Cancún in 2003, which only accentuated the imbalance of interests among FTAA nations.

Two months after the Cancún meeting, in November 2003, the hemisphere's trade ministers met again in Miami. It was a key session not only for its proximity to the FTAA target deadline but also because the participants recognized that the Cancún failure could contaminate hemispheric negotiations and create major difficulties for the completion of the FTAA. The trade ministers in attendance showed pragmatism in Miami and sought to rekindle the FTAA initiative by relaxing some of the principles previously agreed to, which were placing a damper on negotiations. In particular, in Miami 2003 the single-undertaking principle was modified. Hemispheric trade ministers agreed that, as a result of the negotiations, countries could adopt different levels of commitment. The main implication of this new rule is the elimination of the veto power that each country had under the original scheme, in which the failure of any participant to undertake a particular commitment precluded any others from doing so.

The Miami 2003 mandate, however, did not specify the route by which the "common set of rights and obligations . . . shared by all countries" was to be developed. Thus during 2004 the negotiating teams tried to implement the instructions with no success. As a result the FTAA process stalled, and the 2005 deadline for concluding negotiations expired without any progress being made. To date, no new deadline has been agreed upon, and no working program has been established. It is this current state of limbo that renders the smaller, twelve-bloc free trade zone appealing, at least as an interim measure, to advance reforms that require immediate attention.

In the medium to longer term, the possibilities for achieving the original vision of a thirty-four-member FTAA include the à la carte scenario, the spaghetti bowl scenario, and the docking station scenario.

In the FTAA à la carte scenario, countries would implement the Miami 2003 Ministerial mandate, undertaking different levels of commitments. There would be a common set of rights and obligations shared by all countries and plurilateral arrangements for participants willing to assume additional commitments. Although this approach could be implemented with the aid of some general principles, such as stand still and transparency, an FTAA à la carte does not solve the imbalance and enormous asymmetries between the United States and Mercosur.[7]

If the so-called new trade issues were to be excluded—intellectual property rights, government procurement, services, and investment—it is unlikely that the United States would be in a position to eliminate agricultural protection for products such as sugar, orange juice concentrate, and tobacco. And without these concessions, it is difficult to imagine that Mercosur would be willing to give up, among other things, the opening up of its industrial sector.

Under the spaghetti bowl scenario, the United States would keep negotiating bilateral or subregional free trade agreements in the hemisphere in tandem with the FTAA. Free trade negotiations with three Andean countries are at an advanced stage, which would leave only Mercosur, Venezuela, Bolivia, and the Caribbean nations outside of the U.S. free trade network in the region. This is the most probable scenario but also the most costly for the region. In the spaghetti bowl scenario, the United States would become the continental hub. Countries in the region having FTAs with the United States would be the spokes—but with considerable difficulty in building a strong export momentum to the biggest market in the world. This scheme would imply cumbersome bureaucratic costs and high efficiency losses associated with the administration of so many FTAs.

The docking station concept would build on the flexibilities achieved at the Miami 2003 Ministerial meeting, where different speeds and scopes were agreed to. Under this scenario, there would be hemispheric disciplines for trade in goods, but the rest of the negotiating agenda (including the new trade issues) would be bilateral. Countries would agree on common rules of origin, a dispute settlement mechanism, and other institutional issues necessary to put in place a free trade agreement.

Through bilateral negotiations, nations would progressively incorporate into a docking station, which would be a free trade zone for goods based on accumulation of origin. Again, disciplines not related to trade in goods—such as investment, services, government procurement, and intellectual property—would not be included in the free trade zone but would be part of the bilateral relationships established between its members. Rules of origin, dispute settlement procedures, and resolution of institutional issues would be common to all participants, and might be visualized as a common dock (see figure 5-1). Tariff dismantling schedules, although negotiated bilaterally, would be part of the common rules through accumulation of origin. Meanwhile, nontariff disciplines would be included in bilateral agreements between the members of the docking station, with no legal relation between or among these agreements. Figure 5-1 shows the twelve countries as boats tied up at a dock.

Under current circumstances, the United States would be the logical center of gravity, or the dock. Having negotiated or being in the process of concluding FTAs with all but Mercosur, Venezuela, Bolivia, and the Caribbean countries, the emergence of the United States as a docking station constructed by it and all of its regional FTA partners could be feasible, especially

Figure 5-1. *The Docking Station Approach to a Twelve-Member Free Trade Zone*

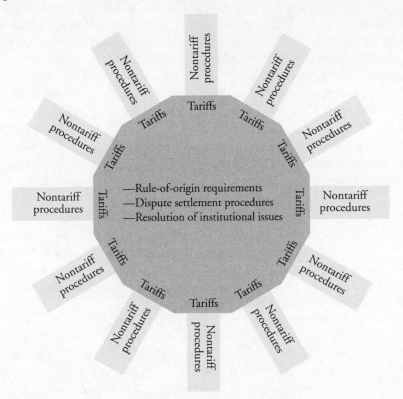

if the current FTAA impasse is not overcome. Under this scenario, NAFTA rules of origin would have to be renegotiated, although NAFTA would remain as is. The new rules of origin might follow CAFTA's rules of origin, given that CAFTA is the most up-to-date U.S. free trade negotiation.

Conclusion

A relaunching of the FTAA process would require that all participants embrace a more pragmatic and flexible stance than exhibited the first time around. All should also keep in mind that the main reason to participate in a free trade area is that economic liberalization makes sense on its own merit. The negotiation of an FTA is one of those rare exchanges where a "concession" made at the negotiating table basically amounts to trade reforms that countries should be unilaterally adopting anyway. At the same time, the major economic partners should lead the process, recognizing that substantive concessions in their sensitive sectors will be necessary to render the agreement politically feasible for the rest of the parties. The United States in particular must resume the leadership role that prompted the Clinton administration to launch the FTAA in the first place.

For the interim, and given the low probability of renewed U.S. commitment until after the 2008 presidential changeover, why not work toward the consolidation of a twelve-member free trade zone that encompasses those countries that have already committed to an FTA with the United States? Here is where a country like Mexico can play the leadership role that it has displayed thus far in the context of free trade agreement negotiations in the region. Equally important, many of the tough issues that have held up the FTAA from the standpoint of Mercosur have already been hammered out as a part of completing those FTAs that would form the base for such a twelve-member zone.

Notes

1. This chapter draws on the following publications: Herminio Blanco and Jaime Zabludovsky, "Free Trade Area of the Americas: Scope of the Negotiation," Working Paper SITI-01 (Buenos Aires: Integration and Regional Programs Department, Inter-American Development Bank, 2003); Herminio Blanco, Jaime Zabludovsky, and Sergio Gómez Lora, "A Key to Hemispheric Integration," Occasional Paper SITI-03 (Buenos Aires: Integration and Regional Programs Department, Inter-American Development Bank, 2004); Jaime Zabludovsky, "The Long and Winding Road to Hemispheric Integration: Ten Key Elements in Understanding the FTAA," in *Free Trade in the Americas: Getting There from Here* (Washington: Inter-American Dialogue, 2004).

2. Canada and Israel were the only other countries to benefit from such access through free trade agreements with the United States.

3. Summit of the Americas, Fourth Trade Ministerial Meeting, Joint Declaration, San José, Costa Rica, March 19, 1998.

4. Canada and Central America are in the advanced stages of negotiating an FTA, and CAFTA is now wending its way through the legislatures of the countries involved.

5. Council on Foreign Relations, *Building a North American Community,* Independent Task Force Report 53 (Washington: Council on Foreign Relations, 2005), pp. 6–8.

6. For more on the interests of FTAA participants, see Blanco and Zabludovsky, "Free Trade Area of the Americas."

7. *Stand still* is the partial maintenance of the status quo, while *transparency* in this context refers to the codification of current levels of liberalization.

6

THE FTAA STALEMATE

Implications for Canadian Foreign Policy

GORDON MACE

If the FTAA stumbles, Canada could be left by the wayside . . . we will lose some of our place in the world.

Pierre S. Pettigrew

The above declaration by the former Canadian minister for international trade attests to the profound disarray concerning the results of the November 2003 Free Trade Area of the Americas (FTAA) Ministerial Meeting held in Miami. Instead of laying the groundwork for the last stretch of a negotiation leading to a comprehensive agreement, this meeting of trade ministers resulted in a significant reorientation of the institutional trajectory of the FTAA. What remained was a seriously watered-down version of the original project. How can we explain Canada's somewhat dire reaction to this turn of events, especially given Canada's still low rates of investment and trade in the Latin American region? Why was the move from a comprehensive to a "lite" FTAA considered a setback not only for Canadian trade goals in the region but, more important, for the essence of Canadian foreign policy in the Americas?

This chapter offers answers to these questions along the following lines. First, I analyze the importance for Canada of building a regional system of the Americas. Second, I discuss the significance of the original FTAA project for Canada. I then assess the implications of a more watered-down FTAA initiative from a Canadian point of view. I conclude with some possible scenarios concerning Canada's future participation in hemispheric trade.

The Importance of Building a Regional System in the Americas

It would be difficult to understand why a country like Canada has given such strong support to a comprehensive FTAA project without first considering the reasons behind Canadian involvement in the Americas. Before the 1990s Canada was not an important player in hemispheric affairs. In 1972 the Canadian government sought and obtained observer status at the Organization of American States (OAS) and started to develop bilateral relations with some of the larger countries of the region. But up to the mid-1980s Canada's relations with its neighbors south of the United States were not at all significant.[1]

Canadian perceptions of the Americas started to shift in the second part of the 1980s as a result of changes in the regional and international environment. The most important factor that explains Canadian involvement in the Americas in the late 1980s was the concern of political elites regarding Canada's weak influence on the world stage. After fifteen years of actively pursuing a strategy to diversify its external relations and mitigate its economic dependence on the United States, the government in Ottawa had to face the fact that the country's ties with the United States had not diminished but had in fact increased to the point where one had to question the capacity of the federal government to pursue a truly independent foreign policy. In the bigger scheme of things, the evolution of the international system since the 1950s resulted in a significant decline in Canada's diplomatic profile.[2] By the 1980s Canada's self-proclaimed "golden age" of foreign policy had waned.

With around 35 percent of Canadian GDP generated by foreign trade, and 85 percent of that trade oriented toward the United States, Canada had become increasingly vulnerable to events occurring in the international arena. At the same time, the outside world had become more forbidding for Canada during the mid-1980s. The government feared that the national economy could be adversely affected by rising protectionism in the United States, itself a reaction to perceived unfair trade practices by Japan and the European bloc.[3] These tensions between regional trade blocs meant that the changing international economic environment could adversely affect Canada.[4]

This consideration, more than anything else, explains Prime Minister Brian Mulroney's decision to propose the negotiation of a free trade agreement to U.S. president Ronald Reagan in the early 1980s. The Canada-U.S. Free Trade Agreement (CUSFTA) came into force in January 1989, formalizing a process of integration between the Canadian and U.S. economies that had long been under way. It was at this juncture that the rest of the Americas became more of a consideration for Canada. CUSFTA provided secure access to the U.S. market for Canadian products, which was the basic reason for negotiating this deal from Ottawa's point of view. However, it also signaled to the rest of Canada's trade partners that it had finally cast its economic fate within North America, something the country had tried so hard to avoid for most of the twentieth century.[5] The signing of the North American Free Trade Agreement (NAFTA) in 1992 would further reinforce that message. To this day the fear lingers that without some degree of trade diversification Canada's near-complete North American vocation could just as easily become a North American entrapment.[6]

The Canadian government therefore reached out to other states in the Americas as a way to counterbalance an increasingly asymmetrical Canada-U.S. relationship. Canadian policymakers viewed the Americas as likely allies because the political and economic landscape there was finally changing after a decade of efforts to rebound from the 1982 debt crisis. By the early 1990s civilian regimes were established everywhere but Cuba, and the region had engaged in a substantial process of democratization. Furthermore, the old import substitution model, which had dominated Latin American economic policymaking since the 1930s, was gradually being replaced by new and more open economic policies in line with those in Canada and the United States. This prospect of a lasting regional transformation enabled the government in Ottawa to convincingly sell the "new look" of its Latin American policy to the Canadian public.[7] In particular, these changes in economic policies and attitudes led to expectations of economic gains for Canadian business.

For Canadian diplomats, this new emphasis on the Americas differed from the government's "third option" foreign policy approach of the 1970s.[8] Whereas the old approach sought to increase trade and economic relations with a few significant world actors in Europe and Asia, the new approach implied a commitment to building a regional system of the Americas. This was the signal that Canada meant to send to the other governments of the Americas when it decided to become a full member of the OAS in 1990. Both then and now, government officials and interested observers believed that this more active participation in the Americas would give Canada more influence in the region.[9]

At a more fundamental level, the importance for Canada of a well-established, efficient, and inclusive regional system of the Americas related directly to policymakers' concerns about promoting Canadian sovereignty. In the first instance, it was clear to Canadian decisionmakers that political and economic relations with the region would develop more smoothly and efficiently if conducted inside a normative institutional framework that had been mutually agreed upon. Even though the OAS was established as the basis for such a system, it has no economic policy mandate and is in dire need of financial and organizational reforms.

A second consideration for Canada was to avoid being boxed into a highly asymmetrical Canada-U.S. relationship. From the start, Ottawa saw that bilateral accords with its neighbors in Latin America and the Caribbean (LAC) would be insufficient, given Canada's goals to fully institutionalize political and economic affairs in the hemisphere.[10] As the Canadian government had done traditionally in multilateral forums, its goal was to craft as best it could a larger hemispheric framework to limit and constrain the behavior of the U.S. government through a set of regional rules.[11] Thus although proposals for an FTAA originated as part of the earlier Bush administration's 1990 Enterprise for the Americas Initiative, and were formalized by the Clinton economic team in 1994, Canada had its own motives for endorsing the negotiation of a full hemispheric accord.

Canada's Support for a Comprehensive and Inclusive FTAA

What role has a comprehensive FTAA project played in the strategic calculus of Canadian foreign policymaking? In the first place, the decade-long pursuit of a regionalist project in the Americas has brought Canada's goals clearly into focus: free trade and economic gains resulting from greater access to the U.S. market.[12] This is also the prime point of coincidence between Canada and its LAC neighbors. Since the completion of the Uruguay Round of multilateral trade negotiations in 1993, most LAC governments have found it difficult to maneuver in an international environment where their products still face barriers in industrialized country markets. Given the shared goal across the Americas of greater access to the U.S. market, Canada has played an important leadership role in keeping the FTAA project alive and focused.

A second reason for Canada's foreign policy orientation toward the Americas had to do with the growing conviction that there is greater strength in numbers. Ottawa's overriding goal was to balance the asymmetrical Canada-U.S. relationship in the context of the Americas, and thus the negotiation of a comprehensive FTAA framework was as much a political as an economic goal for the Canadian government. However, economic imperatives were also clearly at play. These had to do with not only traditional trade concerns like market access and agriculture but also new issue areas like services and investment. Services, for example, account for almost 70 percent of Canada's GDP. As for trade in goods, Canada exports mostly machinery and industrial equipment, motor vehicles and parts, industrial supplies, and energy products.[13] The Canadian economic profile is therefore very different from that of most LAC countries, but the possibilities for capitalizing on the complementarities between Canada and the Americas had become more enticing.

Canadian negotiators had pushed for the start of the official FTAA negotiations at the Second Summit of the Americas in Santiago, Chile, in 1998, and they were eager for the discussions to be completed by the designated 2005 deadline. At the negotiating table, Canada—though willing to compromise on technical procedures—was more rigid when it came to making concessions on the content of the agreement.[14] The Canadian government did not want anything less than a World Trade Organization–plus (WTO-plus) kind of arrangement. Naturally, this meant focusing on the old agenda of tariff reductions in which the majority of LAC governments were more interested. But that was only a part of the equation.

More important, Canada's commitment to a WTO-plus FTAA implied the incorporation of the "new trade agenda" (rules on investment, services, subsidies, and intellectual property rights) that was introduced during the Uruguay Round and now formed part of the regular business of multilateral trade negotiations.[15] Given the structure of Canada's external trade relations, it was important to secure a comprehensive *and* inclusive FTAA agreement with as wide a regulatory framework as possible for the expansion of trade and economic relations in the hemisphere. The other significant consideration for Ottawa was to harmonize its positions within NAFTA, at the WTO, and within a future FTAA.

The Significance of an FTAA "Lite" for Canada

What was the significance of a more watered-down version of the FTAA for Canada? Between the start of the official FTAA negotiations in 1998 and the Miami Trade Ministerial in 2003, it gradually became clear that the final design of the FTAA would not be the NAFTA-plus or the WTO-plus format that the United States originally proposed. As initially envisioned, the projected trade agreement would be comprehensive and the negotiations guided by two basic principles: consensus and a single undertaking. The projected FTAA would involve all countries of the region with the exception of Cuba and would include items dealing with the traditional trade agenda (tariff reductions, market access) as well as items related to the new, more comprehensive trade agenda.

The 2003 Miami Ministerial, however, resulted in a significant change of course. For example, article 7 of the Ministerial Declaration states that member countries could now "assume different levels of commitments." A "common and balanced set of rights and obligations" would be determined for all participating countries. But governments that wanted to do so could, within the FTAA framework, decide to "agree to additional obligations and benefits."[16] What this meant was that the projected FTAA would now be a two-tier agreement.[17] There would be a first tier in which participating governments would agree on a common denominator dealing essentially with tariff reductions. The new agenda would be addressed as a second tier, where governments that chose to do so could engage in comprehensive trade deals on a bilateral basis or, as the Ministerial Declaration states, within "plurilateral negotiations."

Why is this outcome negative for Canada? To answer this question we must look at economic as well as political and diplomatic considerations. On the economic front, recall that trade in goods was not the main objective when the Canadian government first decided to participate in FTAA negotiations. Canadian exports to the Americas during the period 1990–2006 tripled to reach U.S.$12 billion, one-third of which were to Mexico. Canada's imports from LAC over this same time span increased sixfold to U.S.$38 billion, with Mexico representing close to half of this figure.[18] The proportion of Canadian exports to the hemisphere is still dominated by NAFTA, with 98 percent going to the United States, 1 percent to Mexico, and 1 percent to the rest of the LAC countries. In the case of the LAC countries, the proportion has even decreased from 1990 to 2006, from 2 percent to 1 percent.

Clearly, trade in goods, although still important for the Canadian economy, was not the central concern when Ottawa committed to negotiating the FTAA agreement. LAC countries were not important export markets for Canadian goods; and in any case, these markets were expected to open up eventually as a result of multilateral trade negotiations. What really mattered for the Canadian government was the laying down of a sound regulatory framework to govern the new trade agenda in the hemisphere (services, competition policies, investment). Rules concerning foreign direct investment (FDI) were particularly important, as Canadian FDI had increased considerably in the region since 1989.

The value of Canadian FDI in the Americas reached C$83 billion in 2005—a tenfold increase over 1990 levels. Granted, although some C$60 billion was parked in four Caribbean tax shelters by 2005 (in the Bahamas, Barbados, Bermuda, and the Cayman Islands), LAC has still become more important for Canadian FDI over the past fifteen years.[19] For example, from 1990 to 2005 Canadian FDI increased from C$125.0 million to C$4.7 billion in Argentina, from C$1.7 to C$8.0 billion in Brazil, and from C$265.0 million to C$5.6 billion in Chile.[20] These numbers illustrate how important the hemisphere has become for Canadian FDI over the past fifteen years.

Consequently, and in light of Canada's FDI inroads with LAC, policymakers perceived an FTAA "lite" as undermining the significant economic benefits that would result from having a regulatory framework that secured the new investment and trade agenda for Canadian business in the LAC region. Not having a comprehensive agreement signaled an uncertain environment in which Canadian FDI would be less secure. Another serious drawback, from an economic point of view, concerned the bilateral or plurilateral agreements that the U.S. government was in the process of concluding with other governments in the region, at least partially a result of the November 2003 FTAA ministerial stalemate. The Office of the U.S. Trade Representative (USTR) had already completed negotiations for a free trade agreement (FTA) with Chile and another with the Central American countries. Negotiations were also well advanced with Andean and Caribbean countries.

These trends raised at least three problems from the Canadian perspective. First, by signing all of these bilateral or plurilateral FTAs, the U.S. government was in the process of designing a regulatory framework for a large part of the hemisphere that would nicely accommodate U.S. preferences and interests but not necessarily those of Canada. Given the weight of the United States in the region, it is highly probable that the nature and scope of these FTAs will become the model for economic relations across the hemisphere. The Canadian government will then have to adjust and adapt its preferences to conform to this evolving pattern.

The second problem for Canada is that Canadian business may have more difficulty increasing its market shares in the region or could even lose market shares because the U.S. government is moving fast to conclude bilateral or plurilateral FTAs. Canada's only FTAs are with Chile and Costa Rica. Discussions have been going on with the Caribbean Community (Caricom) and

Andean and Central American countries, but no formal agreements have been struck.[21] It is clear that the Canadian government will have to increase the pace substantially if it wants to keep up with U.S. initiatives in this regard. Otherwise, there will be a potential cost for Canadian business in terms of lost opportunities.

The third and more fundamental economic problem is the emergent hub-and-spoke pattern resulting from the multiplication of bilateral and plurilateral FTAs. This is the pattern that Canadian authorities always feared in terms of Canada's location in the hemisphere and one it sought to avoid by joining NAFTA. Because of the immense attraction of the U.S. market for most Latin American and Caribbean countries, a hub-and-spoke pattern of trade deals, with the United States as the hub and LAC countries as the spokes, may very well isolate Canadian business from these emergent trade and economic corridors. In other words, the huge draw of the U.S. market will make it difficult for LAC economic actors to keep Canadian trade and investment opportunities on their radar screen.

From an economic point of view, therefore, the change from a comprehensive and inclusive FTAA to a much more limited trade agreement represents a considerable setback. Canada is clearly a loser in this emerging scenario, because Canadian business will have difficulty fitting into the new pattern of regional trade and economic relations. Furthermore, as FTAA negotiations remain stalled at the start of 2007, the region itself may lose the attractiveness that it once had for Canadian entrepreneurs, who are already setting their sights eastward toward Europe and Asia.

Alongside these economic problems, FTAA "lite" gives rise to a number of strategic and diplomatic considerations for Canada. As mentioned earlier, Canada's increased involvement in the Americas was motivated by the overriding necessity to avoid being a marginal spoke to the U.S. hub. However, the current trade trajectory within the Americas that resulted from the 2003 Miami Trade Ministerial is completely different from what the Canadian government anticipated and has worked toward since joining the OAS in 1990. The new institutional design, composed of an eventual two-tier FTAA coexisting with a patchwork of bilateral and plurilateral trade agreements, lacks the inclusive character that was deemed necessary by Canadian diplomats to support a strong regional system. Without such a system, Canada faces the same hub-and-spoke prospect and possible strategic and diplomatic isolation that it has worked against since the 1980s when deciding to negotiate CUSFTA.

Even though some governments in the hemisphere continue to go through the motions, it is clear that the hemispheric integration process has been in a lull since the end of 2003 despite the Special Monterrey Summit held in Mexico in January 2004 and the Summit of Mar del Plata held in Argentina in November 2005. The failure at Miami in November 2003 is not the sole reason for the difficulties of hemispheric integration, but it is an important element in the explanation. Canadian foreign policy by itself cannot do much to jump-start the FTAA process. Nevertheless, one contribution that Canadian foreign policy is still hoping to make is the technical expertise and know-how necessary to break through the policy gridlock that now plagues trade negotiations within both multilateral and regional organizations. This is where Canadian diplomacy is at its best.[22]

Given the new order of things in the Americas since November 2003, what are the possible scenarios concerning Canada's future involvement? Will Canada pursue separate bilateral agreements with Latin American countries? Or will it instead concentrate on NAFTA and seek to deepen that agreement's effectiveness in promoting the new trade agenda? A debate has already started in Canada concerning possible scenarios for an Americas policy and the pros and cons of choosing one scenario over another. In the next section, these scenarios are examined in terms of their viability for Canada's diplomacy in the Americas.

Scenarios for the Future

According to the recent literature and integration debates, Canada's options in terms of trade and foreign economic policy can be grouped into four scenarios. Each of these scenarios and its respective implications in terms of foreign policy options are reviewed below.

The WTO Scenario

Those promoting a WTO scenario for Canada base their analysis on the observation that, although economic relations among countries in the Western Hemisphere have strengthened over the past twenty years, outside of North America the region remains only a small market for Canadian goods and services.[23] What happens in the hemisphere in terms of the FTAA is far from negligible for Canada, but it will never carry the importance of developments on the world scene. Consequently, Canada's foreign economic policy should concentrate on the WTO, as negotiations there have more important consequences for Canada's trade relations than what happens in other regional forums. Furthermore, the salience of multilateral participation becomes evident in light of the role the WTO has played in the management of Canada-U.S. trade relations. As Andrew Cooper notes, the Canadian government has traditionally relied on multilateral channels such as GATT and the WTO, not only to avoid direct head-on conflicts with the United States but also to constrain U.S. behavior.[24]

In this scenario, Canada would of course still participate in any future FTAA negotiations, but as an interested party, and in a monitoring mode, rather than one of leadership. Canadian diplomats would not push too hard concerning disciplines for the new trade agenda that face opposition from many LAC governments, especially Brazil and Argentina, since antagonizing these governments would serve no useful purpose. After all, Mercosur is the main LAC region that offers sound economic potential for Canada. The Canadian government would also seek to conclude bilateral or plurilateral trade agreements in addition to those already concluded with Chile and Costa Rica—for example, with Caricom and the Andean and Central American subregions.

The NAFTA-plus Scenario

There is no single origin for the NAFTA-plus idea. As a political objective, it is mostly associated with the former Mexican president Vicente Fox, who initially proposed to transform NAFTA into a common market. In February 2001, shortly after his inauguration, Fox managed to convince President George W. Bush to endorse a joint communiqué in which the two leaders agreed to consult the Canadian prime minister on eventual changes to NAFTA.[25] Unfortunately, the terrorist attacks of September 11, 2001, pushed this proposal off the North American agenda, despite efforts by the former Mexican foreign affairs minister, Jorge Castañeda, to give life to the initial proposal with a new Security and Prosperity Partnership (SPP) initiative.[26]

Robert Pastor put the academic version of the NAFTA-plus idea forward in a widely acclaimed book on the North American community.[27] Pastor's fundamental argument is that NAFTA, as initially designed, is not equipped to deal with the increasingly complex issues of interdependence in North America. "What's wrong with NAFTA is not what it did, but what it omitted. The agreement did not envisage any unified approach to extract NAFTA's promise, nor did it contemplate any common response to new threats."[28] What NAFTA needs is sound trilateral institutions that have the capacity to adopt plans and policies for the development and tighter integration of key North American sectors such as transport, energy, and labor markets.

In Canada the idea of a NAFTA-plus strategy is mostly associated with an April 2002 proposal developed by the economist Wendy Dobson and supported by the CD Howe Institute, a think tank at the University of Toronto. The proposal calls for bold initiatives by the Canadian government to convince Washington to move a step further with regard to North American integration. Among other things, Dobson argues in favor of a customs union, and even a common market, in addition to new Canada-U.S. security arrangements, including Canadian participation in North American defense operations.[29]

The majority of Canadian nationalist writers criticized the proposal, and even the editorial team of the country's major newspaper, *Globe and Mail,* expressed doubts.[30] But others were more supportive, including the former Canadian ambassador to the United States and high-ranking diplomat, Allan Gottlieb, who had in the past been closely associated with a more nationalist strategy.[31] Dobson's proposal also received a certain degree of official support when a committee of the House of Commons recommended that the Canadian government propose to its North American neighbors a framework for trilateral cooperation in which heads of state and foreign affairs ministers would meet every year to discuss questions of common interest.[32]

So there is obviously a strong interest in Canada for some form of deeper cooperation in the North American context and especially in the framework of the Canada-U.S. relationship. But what form this cooperation will take remains uncertain since the January 2006 change of government in Canada. What is more likely is that any change will not entail profound modifications to NAFTA, which are opposed by U.S. policymakers and legislators. Furthermore, even if modifications—like the transformation of NAFTA into a customs union—were possible, they would necessitate new regional institutions to deal with the new complexities.[33] And even if the Canadian government would consider a serious revamping of NAFTA, which is not at all certain, it is very doubtful that the U.S. administration would accept more powerful regional institutions. More likely, the three NAFTA leaders would discuss administrative measures to streamline trade and improve economic cooperation, measures that would not necessarily require new legislation. But neither would such measures constitute anything close to a NAFTA-plus strategy.

The Diversification Scenario

Canadian foreign policy outside of North America has become "essentially symbolic" for some observers.[34] However, the idea of returning to a diversification strategy akin to that of the 1970s seems to appeal to Canadian public opinion. Canada is thus again trying to increase its trade and economic relations with Europe and Asia. Canadian representatives are negotiating a free trade agreement with the European Free Trade Association (EFTA), and a framework has been concluded between Canada and the European Union on coming negotiations for a Trade and Investment Enhancement Agreement (TIEA).[35] Negotiations on the TIEA will deal with an ambitious agenda concerning the new trade issues, including among others competition policy, trade and investment facilitation, and financial services.

This new push for diversification does not, however, resemble the diversification strategy of the 1970s. Rather, the current effort seeks the opening of trade and economic channels with Europe and Asia after having secured access to the North American region. But it is far from certain that these new trade initiatives will generate better results than the original diversification efforts on the part of the Canadian government. Consequently, this scenario should be seen as no more than a complement to the preceding one.

The Hemispheric Broker Scenario

In this scenario, the Canadian government would renew its efforts to help relaunch the negotiations for an inclusive FTAA according to the criteria discussed earlier in this chapter. Canada would act as a broker of sorts, with the objective of building a coalition that could help bridge the differences between the United States and Brazil (addressed in detail by Glauco Oliveira, chapter 7, this volume). With the Doha Round having hit its own impasse with the breakdown of negotiations in mid-2006, a renewed FTAA could hold some appeal for regional leaders. From the standpoint of Canadian diplomacy, three considerations come to mind.

First, given that Canada has already invested more than a decade in FTAA diplomacy with seemingly meager results, the economic gains of a revived effort would have to be convincing both to public opinion and to stakeholders. Second, Canada would need support from the Mercosur countries, especially Brazil. However, Canada-Brazil relations have been plagued for some time by the thorny Bombardier-Embraer conflict. The two aircraft industries are so strategic for their respective economies that the back-and-forth fight over domestic subsidies could taint the bilateral relationship for some time. But more important, the two countries have seen their approach to the world system move in different directions: Brazil has been globalizing its economic relations, while Canada, despite efforts to pursue a similar strategy, has become increasingly embedded in North America.[36] These divergent paths are not mutually exclusive, although they do beg the question of just how Brazil and Canada would overcome a limited but tense relationship, with few interests in common.

Third, while it seems unlikely that the Canadian government will adopt a high-profile role in trying to resurrect the stalled FTAA negotiations, Canadian diplomats will be active players if the trade negotiations should resume. This is because these negotiations could determine rules for access to the U.S. market, and as was the case with the NAFTA negotiations, Canadian negotiators will seek to protect Canadian interests. At the end of the day, Canada is still a North American country with the fate of having to manage a dynamic but asymmetrical relationship with the United States.

Concluding Remarks

The thrust of this chapter has been to demonstrate the consequences for Canada of the move toward an FTAA "lite," that is, a reduction of commitments regarding issues that define the new international trade agenda. One possible impact may be reduced Canadian involvement in institution-building efforts in the Americas. Another may be Canada's more isolated position in the Western Hemisphere as a result of the hub-and-spoke structure that could emerge from the patchwork of bilateral and plurilateral trade arrangements that the United States is now launching within the region.

But Canada is not the only country that may be affected by the acceptance of reduced commitments to trade disciplines. As pointed out by Donald Mackay, the fact that governments in the Americas—including the United States—agreed to discard the single-undertaking and comprehensive approach to the FTAA could well have a deleterious effect on multilateral trade negotiations. That is, the strain on the WTO's Doha Round could become heavier and impede the revival of those negotiations.[37]

In the Americas, most other countries could also be negatively affected by the change in trajectory of hemispheric economic integration. A one-on-one negotiation, or even a plurilateral one involving U.S. officials, will not be to the advantage of the other negotiating party or parties given the intraregional disparities in expertise and resources to negotiate trade agreements and monitor them afterward. At a future date, the cost of negotiating a deal between such asymmetrical actors may become very steep for the societies involved in terms of economic growth and political stability. In this context, the management of an already fragile inter-American system may become much more complex. And in the absence of an integrated system of the Americas, the whole LAC region itself, with the exception of Brazil and maybe Argentina, could become less relevant for U.S. foreign policy and in world affairs more generally.

However, things have yet to be settled conclusively. FTAA negotiations have stalled for the moment but have not been officially abandoned altogether. From Canada's standpoint the FTAA is necessary for establishing a strong and efficient regional system in the Americas. Politics, obviously, are another matter, and it remains uncertain whether interested parties may still succeed in pressuring their governments to return to the negotiating table. Given the enormous disparities in power between the United States and the other countries of the region, a hemisphere-wide system would clearly be more advantageous than would a go-it-alone strategy for dealing with Washington.

Notes

The author thanks Nicolas Foucras for his very useful research assistance.

1. See, for example, James Rochlin, *Discovering the Americas* (University of British Columbia Press, 1994), pts. 1 and 2.

2. See, for example, Kim R. Nossal, *The Politics of Canadian Foreign Policy,* 3d ed. (Scarborough, Ont.: Prentice Hall Canada, 1997), 22–36. See also Andrew Cohen, *While Canada Slept: How We Lost Our Place in the World* (Toronto: McClelland and Stewart, 2003).

3. On U.S. economic policy at the time, see, among the vast literature, Stanley D. Nollen and Dennis P. Quinn, "Free Trade, Fair Trade: Strategic Trade and Protectionism in the U.S. Congress, 1987–88," *International Organization* 48 (1994): 491–525. See also Pierre Martin, "The Politics of International Structural Change: Aggressive Reciprocity in American Trade Policy," in *Political Economy and the Changing Global Order,* edited by R. Stubbs and G. R. D. Underhill (Toronto: McClelland and Stewart, 1994).

4. Diana Brand, "Regional Bloc Formation and World Trade," *Intereconomics* 27, no. 6 (1992): 274–81. See also Frans Buelens, "The Creation of Regional Blocs in the World Economy," *Intereconomics* 27, no. 3 (1992): 124–32.

5. Andrew F. Cooper, *Canadian Foreign Policy: Old Habits and New Directions* (Scarborough, Ont.: Prentice Hall Alwyn and Bacon Canada, 1997), pp. 261–63.

6. Allan Gottlieb, "The United States in Canadian Foreign Policy" (Ottowa: Department of Foreign Affairs and International Trade, 1991). "This is why I also believe it is in Canada's interest to promote the widening of the Western Hemisphere free trade area and to build common consultative and quasi-judicial institutions in the economic area. A wider grouping will contribute to greater balance and counterweight in the North American economic space," p. 12. Gottlieb was the Canadian ambassador to Washington in the 1980s.

7. Edgar J. Dosman, "Canada and Latin America: The New Look," *International Journal* 47, no. 3 (1992): 529–54.

8. Gordon Mace and Gérard Hervouet, "Canada's Third Option: A Complete Failure?" *Canadian Public Policy/Analyse de politiques* 15 (1989): 387–404.

9. Peter McKenna, *Canada and the OAS* (Carleton University Press, 1995), p. 159; Jean Daudelin and Edgar J. Dosman, "Canada and Hemispheric Governance: The New Challenges," in *Canada among Nations 1999: Leadership and Dialogue,* edited by F. O. Hampson and M. A. Molot (Oxford University Press, 1998), p. 213; John Graham, "The Quiet Americans," *Ottawa Citizen,* June 12, 2003; Canadian Foundation for the Americas (Focal), "Canadian Foreign Policy for the Americas. Submission to the Hon. Bill Graham, Minister of Foreign Affairs, Foreign Policy Review, 2003" (Ottawa: 2003), p. 2.

10. On this point, Mexican officials are of a like mind, as reflected by comments made by former Mexican ambassador to Argentina, Rosario Green. See Rosario Green, "La union sudamericana es solo una quimera," *La Nacion* (Argentina), December 15, 2004, as reproduced in Latin American Trade Network, *News Review International Trade and Negotiations,* December 17, 2004, pp. 1–2.

11. Cooper, *Canadian Foreign Policy,* p. 248.

12. Gordon Mace, "The Origin, Nature and Scope of the Hemispheric Project," in *The Americas in Transition: The Contours of Regionalism,* edited by G. Mace and others (Boulder: Lynne Rienner, 1999), pp. 32–34.

13. Economist, *World in Figures* (London: Profile Books, 2004), pp. 33, 122–23.

14. Gordon Mace, Jacques Paquet, Louis Bélanger and Hugo Loiseau, "Asymmétrie de puissance et négociations économiques internationales: la zone de libre-échange des Amériques et le rôle des puissances moyennes," *Revue canadienne de science politique/Canadian Journal of Political Science* 36, no. 1 (2003): 129–58.

15. Stephen Woolcock, "The Multilateral Trading System into the New Millennium," in *Trade Politics: International, Domestic and Regional Perspectives,* edited by B. Hocking and S. McGuire (London: Routledge, 1999).

16. Free Trade Area of the Americas, Eighth Ministerial Meeting, "Ministerial Declaration," November 20, 2003 (www.ftaa-alca.org/ministerials/miami_e.asp).

17. Pablo Bustos, "Réquiem para el ALCA?" *Estudios sobre el ALCA,* April 19, 2004, pp. 1–8.

18. Jean Daudelin, "Canada and the Americas: A Time for Modesty," *Behind the Headlines,* 64, no. 3 (2007): 19.

19. Ibid, p. 18.

20. Statistics Canada, Direct Investments Abroad, CANSIM table 376-0051, May 2006 (www.dfait-maeci.gc.ca/eet/pdf/fdi-outward-stocks-counry). Investments are in both traditional sectors (financial services, mining, natural resources, and energy) and new sectors (oil, telecommunications, information technologies, and agribusiness).

21. International Trade Canada, "Regional and Bilateral Initiatives," 2006 (www.dfait-maeci.gc.ca/tna-nac/and-en.asp).

22. "As a middle power, our role is more constructive if it is played not in isolation but in association with many other countries. . . . For us, international associations . . . are of supreme importance. Without them we are impotent." John Holmes, cited in Tom Keating, *Canada and World Order: The Multilateralist Tradition in Canadian Foreign Policy* (Toronto: McClelland and Stewart, 1993), p. 18.

23. Jean Daudelin and Maureen Appel Molot, "Canada and the FTAA: Leadership or Folly?" *Carta Internacional* 76, no. 7 (1999): 12–15. See also from the same authors, "Canada and the FTAA: The Hemispheric Bloc Temptation," *Policy Options Politiques* (March 2000): 48–51.

24. Cooper, *Canadian Foreign Policy,* pp. 77, 248. The renowned Canadian trade expert Michael Hart is also a firm proponent of the WTO scenario. See for example Canadian Foundation for the Americas, "Una Gran Familia? Hemispheric Integration after the Santiago Summit" (Ottawa: Focal, 1999), p. 8.

25. "Toward a Partnership for Prosperity: The Guanajuato Proposal," joint communiqué, February 16, 2001 (www.presidencia.gob.mx).

26. Jorge Castañeda, "It Takes Three to Tango," *Globe and Mail,* March 4, 2002, p. A13.

27. Robert A. Pastor, *Toward a North American Community: Lessons from the Old World for the New* (Washington: Institute for International Economics, 2001).

28. Ibid., p. 2.

29. Wendy Dobson, "Shaping the Future of the North American Economic Space," commentary (Toronto: CD Howe Institute, 2002); Wendy Dobson, "The Next Big Idea: Trade Can Brush in a New Border," *Globe and Mail,* January 21, 2003, p. A15; Anne Golden, "Building a New Partnership," *Globe and Mail,* March 5, 2003, p. A11.

30. For a critique of the Dobson proposal and the borders papers project, see James Laxer, "Wake Up Time," 2006 (www.canadiandimension.mb.ca/v36/v36_6jl.htm); "Big Bargain: Trading Economy for Security," *Globe and Mail,* April 22, 2002, p. A12; Stephen Clarkson, "What's in It for Us?" *Globe and Mail,* May 6, 2002, p. A15.

31. Allan Gottlieb and Jeremy Kinsman, "Sharing the Continent: Reviving the Third Option," *International Perspectives* (Nov.–Dec. 1981), p. 2-5. Also see Allan Gottlieb, "Why Not a Grand Bargain with the U.S.?" *National Post,* September 11, 2002, p. A16; Michael Hart and William Dymond, *Common Borders, Shared Destinies: Canada, the United States and Deepening Integration* (Ottawa: Centre for Law and Commercial Policy, 2001).

32. Comité permanent des affaires étrangères et du commerce international, *Partenaires en Amérique du Nord. Cultiver les relations du Canada avec les Etats-Unis et le Mexique* (Ottawa: Travaux Publics et Services gouvernementaux Canada-Edition, 2002), p. 317.

33. Gordon Mace and Louis Bélanger, "What Institutional Design for North America?" in *Free Trade in the Americas: Economic and Political Issues for Governments and Firms,* edited by S. Weintraub, A. M. Rugman, and G. Boyd (Cheltenham, U.K.: Edward Elgar, 2004).

34. Jean Daudelin, "Trapped: Brazil, Canada and the Aircraft Dispute," in *Canada among Nations 2002: A Fading Power,* edited by N. Hillmer and M. Appel Molot (Oxford University Press, 2002), p. 268.

35. "Trade Negotiations and Agreements" (www.dfait-maeci.gc.ca/tnc-nac/eu_en.asp).

36. Daudelin, "Trapped," pp. 268–69.

37. Donald R. Mackay, "FTAA: The Common Tragedy of Losing the Single Undertaking," *Focal Point* 3, no. 9 (2004): 11.

7

WHAT WENT WRONG?

Brazil, the United States, and the FTAA

GLAUCO OLIVEIRA

The failure to meet the deadline to establish a Free Trade Area of the Americas (FTAA) by January 2005 threw this project into limbo and confirmed the lack of common objectives and unresolved rivalries between Brazil and the United States, the two main players at the regional negotiating table. At the heart of this standoff lie the U.S. determination to negotiate new trade themes such as services, investment rules, government procurement, and intellectual property rights and Brazil's concern with facilitating market access for traded goods, including agriculture, and trade remedy measures (antidumping).

Underpinning these important substantive differences is considerable discord over the possible format for the FTAA. At the November 2003 Miami Summit, Brazil and Argentina proposed a model in which topics would be discussed on separate tracks instead of the single-undertaking approach proposed by the United States and Canada. The alternative framework would tackle the liberalization of trade in goods on track one; the second track would allow countries the option of joining, at their own pace, deeper integration arrangements involving the above-mentioned new trade themes. Because these new trade themes were also being discussed at the multilateral level within the Doha Round of the World Trade Organization (WTO), the

South American countries argued that this second track would gain momentum within the multilateral venue.

Such an FTAA à la carte was met with skepticism by U.S. and Canadian negotiators, and even some analysts in Brazil complained that the plan would be counterproductive and would fail to gather traction.[1] Sensing a possible stalemate, and in line with its increasingly bilateral approach to foreign economic policy, the United States then proceeded to complete free trade agreements (FTAs) with other Latin America countries (U.S.-Chile, U.S.-Colombia, U.S.-Peru) and subregions (U.S.-Central America) while still going through the motions of negotiating the FTAA. Brazil countered by attempting to negotiate an FTA between the United States and Mercosur, the so-called four-plus-one approach, which appears to have fallen into the same void as the FTAA.[2]

This chapter analyzes the political and economic issues at stake for Brazil and the United States, issues that are relevant for understanding both the impasse that has arisen and the hurdles that still await any possible completion of either the four-plus-one approach or the FTAA. My main point is that the stalemate in FTAA negotiations is related to the asymmetries among the countries involved and that, unlike Mexico, which was willing to forgo its developing country status when negotiating NAFTA, South America is not willing to set aside such asymmetries. The result is that in Brazil the FTAA discussion has become contentious and highly politicized, especially concerning the country's ability to commit quickly to the new trade themes, and in the United States the FTAA has been relegated to a low policy priority.

In the bigger scheme of things, Brazilian negotiators would need to take a more objective stance with regard to the costs and benefits of signing on to a project such as the FTAA. In other words, although a market opening for trade in goods is important, the achievement of this goal would inevitably require inclusion of the deep integration issues favored by the United States. After all, the original justification for pursuing the FTAA was the prospect it held for achieving WTO-plus outcomes within the new trade issues areas; in the absence of these outcomes, the FTAA has become a moot point.

Brazilian and U.S. Domestic Political Interests in the FTAA

In analyzing the position adopted by Brazilian and U.S. actors at the FTAA negotiations, I rely on three political economy explanations found in the recent literature: endogenous trade policy, new growth theories, and political science models concerning bureaucratic politics. This section reviews these theories as they apply to the varying trade stances of Brazil and the United States.

Endogenous Trade Policy Models

Endogenous trade theories seek to explain domestic trade policy and politics by applying economic models to political scenarios. The domestic political economy is treated as a market in which there is supply and demand for protectionist or liberal trade policies. Ronald Rogowski, for example, was one of the first to use a neoclassical model like Heckscher-Ohlin (H-O) to explore how trade affects the political behavior of domestic actors; in doing so, he shows how endogenous trade theory can serve as a useful explanatory tool.[3] According to the H-O model, those political actors who own the less abundant factors of production (for example, some combination of capital, labor, or land) will lobby against openness and regional integration. Those political actors who own the abundant factors, however, will support trade liberalization and will lobby in favor of negotiating an FTA. The H-O theorem asserts that openness will decrease the welfare of the owners of scarce factors and increase that of the owners of abundant factors.

Endogenous trade policy models thus allow for variations in domestic political responses. The model by Stolper-Samuelson recognizes, for example, that lobbying activity may occur along factor lines (such as capital versus labor), while the Ricardo-Viner-Carnes model holds that lobbying can also fall along industry lines (importing-competing versus export-oriented sectors).[4] Stephen Magee interprets trade policy outcomes within the context of a democratic regime, whereby competing parties declare their respective positions, industries then lobby and make party donations that will advance their own welfare gains, and the parties then use this campaign financing to influence misinformed voters.[5] In another variation, Gene Grossman and Elhanan Helpman explain protectionism as a function of the structure of industrial organization, trade dependency, and the elasticity of import demand or export supply.[6] The Magee approach suggests that trade policy may vary markedly with a change in government, while the Grossman-Helpman model implies that political capture by vested interests perpetuates a stable or more slowly changing equilibrium for trade policy.[7]

Endogenous trade policy offers potentially important insights for analyzing the U.S. and Brazilian cases. Although most often applied to political behavior within sectors involving traded industrial goods, endogenous trade policy models can also shed light on political positions assumed within the new trade issues, such as services and intellectual property rights. In the case of Brazil, where capital and knowledge-based factors are scarce, the owners of these scarce factors have resisted all but a gradual liberalization in these sectors. Otaviano Canuto, Gilberto Lima, and Michel Alexandre have analyzed the possible impact of the liberalization of services within an FTAA on selected Brazilian sectors (health insurance, credit export insurance, land transportation, engineering, accounting, and legal services), all of which are characterized by low levels of foreign investment.[8]

Their study suggests that the liberalization of these service lines would bolster the ability of Brazilian companies to compete in hemispheric markets but that the adjustment costs would be steep. This is because U.S. and Canadian companies would be fully positioned to dominate the national market and the majority of Brazilian firms are not prepared to meet their challenge. The study concludes that the kinds of regulatory harmonization intrinsic to an agreement in services under an FTAA would benefit those companies already adhering to international regulatory standards and offers them competitive advantage vis-à-vis Brazilian companies. Political behavior was not considered in this study, although one could infer that the highly complex domestic regulatory framework that now governs Brazil's services sector, including constitutional clauses against foreign participation (such as in health services), presents high barriers to entry and strong protection of Brazilian interests.

Magee's electoral hypotheses are less compelling in terms of the Brazilian case, as foreign trade policy still does not hold much appeal for the political parties and a large share of the electorate. Most often, trade discussions are confined to specialized groups. The Grossman-Helpman assumptions about political capture seem more apropos for Brazil, as trade policy debates are basically limited to those with ready access to small pockets of the Brazilian bureaucracy that deal with trade and industrial policy. Broadly speaking, the agencies and ministries responsible for foreign trade policy have been stacked with political rather than technical appointees. The bias toward protection is reflected in higher tariffs for value-added sectors such as electronics in Brazil and exceptions for the automotive sector under Mercosur.[9] As the costs of protectionism increase for those producers with a comparative advantage for exports, such as agriculture and select industries, some are pushing for a more ambitious and realistic approach to trade policy, including the willingness to concede in negotiating over the new trade themes.[10]

In terms of the U.S. case, Marcus Noland applies endogenous trade theory to the behavior of the Office of the U.S. Trade Representative (USTR) during the administrations of Reagan, Bush (1988–92), and Clinton.[11] He finds that there is no policy variation among these administrations: all of them used retaliatory actions against other countries according to the size of the trade deficit a given country was running with the United States. Despite the fact that the stakes are lower than those involving big markets such as the European Union (EU) and Japan, the same pattern of behavior held in U.S. commercial relationships with developing countries: it engaged in similarly protectionist legislation, for example, against Brazil in the late 1980s with regard to disputes over intellectual property rights.

Within the FTAA process this easy resort to protectionism has also been apparent, especially with U.S. apparel, textiles, steel, and agriculture.[12] Endogenous trade policy logic thus seems to hold for the United States, the agricultural sector being a case in point. Technological advances have rendered some products (soy and corn) competitive with Brazil's, but not others (orange juice concentrate, sugar, cotton). U.S. producers of these latter crops would be worse off under an FTAA; they therefore pushed and won further protection under the rubric of the 2002 U.S. Farm Bill. In the Western Hemisphere, Argentina and Brazil have been especially harmed by U.S. agricultural measures, causing Latin American negotiators to be wary of the United States at the FTAA negotiating table. Despite the fact that the Bush administration bears high fiscal costs for its agricultural policy, the executive branch committed only to a slow phaseout of agricultural subsidies through the Doha Round negotiations at the WTO. Not surprisingly, these too collapsed in mid-2006, and U.S. reticence over further agricultural cuts was a large part of this story.

Ultimately, the impulse for further trade opening in the United States will come from representatives of the services and knowledge-intensive sectors. As the owners of abundant factors—knowledge and capital—these groups will largely benefit from the liberalization of trade in services, including telecommunications, banking, insurance, and investment. A coalition of these groups helped secure the Trade Promotion Authority (TPA) bill for President George W. Bush at the outset of his administration, and their protrade lobbying for the FTAA kept this initiative alive in the United States until recently.[13]

Summing up, endogenous trade policy models provide convincing explanations for the respective Brazilian and U.S. stances in the FTAA. This is especially true for the differing attitudes of Brazilian industrial and technological companies, which fear integration because they are less competitive compared to their U.S. counterparts, whereas those same groups in the United States welcome a stronger hemispheric trade and regulatory environment. The same logic applies to U.S. sectors that are labor intensive, which stand to lose by liberalizing trade with labor abundant sectors in Latin America. A main oversight of endogenous trade policy analysis is that it does not consider the importance of intra-industry trade and spillover effects in knowledge-intensive sectors, which can provide much of the rationale for trade integration.

New Growth Theories: Economic Dynamics and Political Cleavages

Despite the asymmetries between the United States and Brazil, and with proper preparation and reform of the sectors at hand, new growth theory holds that with a combined increase in research and development (R & D), technology adaptation, and competition policies, Brazil could achieve higher levels of sustainable growth by completing the FTAA. This is partially because of the high levels of intra-industry trade between Brazil and the United States. The international political economy literature convincingly portrays the role of intra-industry trade as an impetus for liberalization. (However, few political economy analyses focus on the role of intra-industry dynamics in shaping trade policy in Brazil. The point of view is mostly from the standpoint of the United States; a considerable literature, for example, assesses the influence of intra-industry trade in the U.S. decision to pursue NAFTA, as transnational companies sought to access markets and lower their input costs.)[14]

In FTAA discussions those sectors and industries that have pushed for a more comprehensive liberalization of services, investment, and intellectual property rights tend to belong to the most dynamic and knowledge-intensive sectors of the U.S. economy. Ostensibly, these same sectors should be lobbying for an FTAA in Brazil, since they are dominated by multinational companies that similarly favor trade integration as a way to maximize on technology, productivity, and specialization. While political constraints have overshadowed the enthusiasm of an FTAA in both the United States and Brazil, the latter has begun to take some concrete steps in these areas.

For example, the Brazilian government launched a new industrial policy to stimulate the linkage between R & D and the private sector. Also, a new innovation bill was approved before the Brazilian Congress, and a debate on how to better foster R & D investment by the private sector is under way.[15] By the same token, the government encourages new investments in infrastructure through partnerships between private and public agents.[16] Partly due to these efforts, Guilhon de Albuquerque notes that those sectors that are more exposed to international competition since the first years of liberalization (agriculture, shoes, and textiles) are gradually realizing the advantages of

Brazil's membership in the FTAA, such as cheaper access to capital goods, production inputs, and technology.[17]

Yet there is still not enough understanding of the way issues of economic competitiveness and the new trade themes are connected with Brazil's broader trade strategy. On the contrary, some in the Brazilian diplomatic corps continue to argue that the inclusion of new trade themes in the hemispheric integration agenda would only "put the future of the country in jeopardy."[18] Despite the fact that intra-industry trade is an important part of Brazil's bilateral exchange with the United States, and that the Mexican market is an increasing destination for automotive exports from Mercosur, closer ties with the NAFTA countries in the FTAA are not regarded by many in the Brazilian diplomatic or business community as important for the country's competitive upgrading.

In the United States the issues intrinsic to new growth theories are part and parcel of the integration debate. Business sectors in the United States perceive that outsourcing low-wage production and value added services, such as software and call centers, are welfare maximizing and resource saving. As trade liberalization and intra-industry production have placed a premium on increased economies of scale and the clustering of factor inputs, U.S. policy preferences have changed.[19] The case of NAFTA shows that U.S. companies in leading North American sectors like autos and electronics moved their operations to Mexico in search of more cost-effective production curves.

In the FTAA the same incentives are present, as reflected by the lead role that knowledge-based and service-oriented industries in the United States have taken in lobbying for it. For the U.S. business sector, the liberalization of regulatory frameworks in Latin America would make it possible to invest in several sectors currently characterized by high barriers to entry, such as energy, mining, and communications. The main incentive for U.S. sectors is that the FTAA would allow for the design of more comprehensive rules and would involve considerably fewer actors than the Doha WTO negotiations.

Because the potential gains from an FTAA would outweigh the losses, there are grounds for cautious optimism. This prediction is bolstered by the results of recent quantitative research (using computable general equilibrium, or CGE, models), which estimates the welfare gains of trade liberalization under unilateral, multilateral, and regional scenarios. The Michigan model of world production and trade, which covers eighteen economic sectors in twenty-two countries or regions and incorporates aspects of trade with imperfect competition in manufacturing and services, is one of these computational analyses; this model shows that an FTAA would increase the economic welfare of member countries by U.S.$118.8 billion, with the largest increases accruing to the United States (U.S.$67.6 billion) and South America (U.S.$27.6 billion).[20]

Nontrade benefits and costs, such as foreign direct investment or institutional aspects, are, however, more difficult to gauge. Furthermore, trade liberalization entails sweeping domestic adjustments, such as labor displacement, and FTAs inevitably involve some degree of trade diversion. Ultimately, economic theory predicts that trade liberalization under FTAs may spur dynamic growth and enhance productivity, but a more precise assessment is not possible without several years of experience. At the same time, quantitative models do capture static effects, and these clearly register welfare gains. For the Brazilian economy, which is still characterized by trade restrictiveness, liberalization under an FTAA would provide net gains for the national economy.[21] These gains would be greater still for the poorest households and the owners of the country's most abundant factor, unskilled labor.

Based on recent global trends and due to the untapped dynamic possibilities, capital-intensive industries may also stand to reap significant gains. For example, figures from the U.S. State Department show that technology-intensive goods are now the largest export sector of middle-income developing countries.[22] According to this same source, information and communication technologies represent U.S.$450 billion in exports from the developing nations, compared with U.S.$235 billion for raw materials and U.S.$405 billion for low-technology goods. Latin America fits this very mold, as data from the National Science Foundation in the United States show an increase in high-technology exports from this region, with the United States as the main importer.[23]

The National Science Foundation report also notes that there has been an increase in private R & D expenditures in the region, as the subsidiaries of U.S. companies increased their share of investment fourfold between 1990 and 1996. In Brazil, for instance, such investments grew from U.S.$113 million to U.S.$489 million during this time span. With regard to the particular relationship between the United States and Brazil, manufactured products and intra-industry trade now account for 70 percent of U.S. exports to Brazil and almost 75 percent of Brazilian exports to the United States.[24] Although numerous factors help shape a given investment decision, the fact that countries in the region would be trading higher value added goods and operating according to the same rules within an arrangement like the FTAA indicates a better probability that foreign direct investment will increase.

Overall, these data show that the forces of economic dynamism, driven by intra-industry trade and technological spillover effects, are already at work in the relationship between the United States and Brazil. In principle, this structural logic provides at least some incentive for U.S. actors to engage in closer trade and investment ties with Brazil. To the extent that these sectors have failed to mobilize sufficient support to keep the FTAA negotiations alive has less to do with economic modeling and projected welfare gains and more to do with the inability of these sectors to influence entrenched bureaucracies in Brasilia and Washington.

Bureaucratic Politics and Ideological Inclinations toward Free Trade

The bureaucratic politics model, in which competition among bureaucracies determines foreign policy outcomes, can be useful for understanding U.S. and Brazilian trade policies and the position of each country on the FTAA.[25] Daniel Drezner takes this approach in analyzing the interaction between institutions and ideas in the making of foreign policy, which is clearly relevant for understanding the domestic political dynamics that have played out thus far with the FTAA. In terms of the interaction between bureaucracies and ideas in explaining trade policy, Drezner notes that the weight of ideas in determining foreign economic policy outcomes will be limited unless those beliefs are carried out by individuals or groups with political clout.[26] Only when a system of beliefs supporting free trade is rooted in domestic institutions with a political stake in implementing such a policy, can it be brought to life.[27] If an administration is committed to the idea of free trade, as the Clinton and George W. Bush administrations appeared to be, then a concerted effort will be made to use the necessary political instruments to reach the desired objective.

Within Brazil's foreign economic policy apparatus any equivalent commitment to free trade is incipient at best. If not exactly a competition between bureaucracies, there is a noticeable informal system of specialization in the government's international organizations; in particular, financial and monetary affairs are distinct from the trade policymaking apparatus. This format was institutionalized over the last two decades due to the necessity of gaining monetary and fiscal stability to support the country's efforts at inflation stabilization and structural adjustment. Those bureaucratic segments that deal with macroeconomic and monetary policy were granted a good deal of autonomy and have been insulated from the bureaucracy at large. The responsibility for macroeconomic and international issues was concentrated in the upper advisory ranks of the Finance Ministry and the Central Bank.

These particular bureaucracies involve a considerable degree of professionalism and institutionalization. Important technical appointments within them are filled by professionally trained economists or by politicians with sound economic backgrounds.

On the trade side, however, such professionalism is less evident. Currently, the responsibilities for international trade policy are scattered across at least five ministries (Finance, Industry and International Trade, Planning and Budget, Agriculture, and Foreign Affairs). The degree of expertise and institutional robustness of some of these bureaucracies has traditionally been low, particularly in the Ministries of Agriculture and Industry and International Trade. These trade-related ministries have improved over the last ten years, but there remain unfinished reforms that pertain to them in the way of administrative and public service career tracks. Legally speaking, the economic ministries (Finance; Planning; Development, Industry, and Trade) should play a leading role in the country's trade talks. However, the Ministry of Development, Industry, and Trade has historically been a weak and unstable bureaucratic entity, dominated by political appointees, who manage subsidies for the private sector. As such, this ministry has been subject to lobbying from the business community and plagued by a high turnover of staff. The Ministry of Finance, albeit more professional and institutionalized, has been only marginally involved with Brazil's trade policy and negotiations.

Thus it has fallen to the Ministry of Foreign Affairs, probably the most traditional governmental bureaucracy in Brazil, to take the lead on trade policy. Its rigid hierarchical career track based on merit and seniority and its organizational coherence have allowed this ministry to dominate Brazil's trade negotiations. The fact that Mercosur has been designated as one of Brazil's top foreign policy priorities has much to do with political preferences within Foreign Affairs. In short, this ministry has set the pace and defined the substance of trade policy in Brazil.

The Ministry of Foreign Affairs is also the institutional locus for the generation of ideas about foreign economic policy. Its position on commercial policy is directly related to its worldview of Brazil's international status. In this respect, Brazilian foreign policy intersects with its current trade strategy in the sense that the country seeks to carve out its own autonomous space both globally and within the Western Hemisphere. There is, understandably, a constant effort to reinforce Brazil's autonomy vis-à-vis the United States, a tension that has been consistently present in trade negotiations at both the international and regional levels. Although some Brazilian administrations may have preferred a closer alignment with the United States in various issue areas, in trade forums the discourse and pursuit of autonomous positions has been unwavering.

Thus clashes between the United States and Brazil in multilateral trade talks are not new, nor did they start with the advent of the Doha Round in 2001 or the election of the left-leaning Lula administration in 2002. As Albuquerque points out, even during the more market-oriented administration of President Fernando Henrique Cardoso (1994–2002), the initial years of FTAA negotiations were characterized by a defensive position on the part of the Foreign Affairs Ministry.[28] This trend has increased under Lula, because the leading senior diplomats appointed from his Labor Party are now formulating Brazilian foreign policy and remain biased in favor of an import substitution industrialization strategy.[29] This said, Brazilian international relations in recent years, and the position of the Foreign Affairs Ministry as well as parts of civil society, have been characterized by a high degree of dogmatism and even anti-Americanism on certain issues, trade being one of them. Given that the Ministry of Foreign Affairs has had the higher profile in FTAA negotiations, it is no wonder that the trade talks have faltered.

Regarding U.S. trade policymaking, there are some similarities with Brazil but also some important differences. The U.S. trade bureaucracy is similarly spread across several departments, such as Commerce, Treasury, Agriculture, Labor, State, and the USTR. Executive-level advisers in the cabinet also play an important role in foreign economic policymaking. But at the end of the day, and as Mac Destler discusses in chapter 9 in this volume, the executive office is instrumental in bringing trade policy to center stage. Along with the institutional landscape, the economic ideology of a given administration can therefore be crucial for the importance that trade will assume on the national agenda. The Clinton years proved, for example, that an administration's commitment to the idea of free trade can transcend opposition within the president's own party.

The U.S. Congress is certainly more powerful in influencing trade policy outcomes than is the Brazilian legislature. This is evident in U.S. protectionist legislation that has had considerable impact on the regional trade negotiation process and that confirms that parochial interests are never far from the surface of U.S. congressional politics. As noted in a 2005 issue of the *Economist,* U.S. trade policy has suffered at the hands of the George W. Bush administration, despite its rhetorical commitment to liberal economic principles.[30] This appears to be due, first, to the USTR's lack of leverage within the administration and to the turnover of two trade representatives between 2005 and 2006; and second, to the low levels of international economic expertise within the Bush cabinet—until, that is, the 2006 appointment of Wall Street's Henry Paulson as secretary of the U.S. Treasury. The commitment and leadership of the USTR seems important in influencing the U.S. Congress on trade issues, the FTAA and Doha included. For instance, during the brief stint of USTR Rob Portman, clearly the most politically astute of the three Bush appointees in the years 2000–09, Congress ratified the Central American Free Trade Agreement (CAFTA).

Brazil and U.S. Trade Strategies

Whether the U.S. bureaucratic process and ideological commitment toward free trade could maintain momentum under Portman's replacement at the USTR (Susan Schwab) was a source of doubt even before the 2006 U.S. midterm elections. Now, with the Democratic Party in control of both houses of Congress and the appointment of some avowed protectionists to key trade-related congressional committees, the prospects for reviving the FTAA and the Doha negotiations have been further muddied.

Brazil's External Ambitions and Strategy

Apart from the FTAA, Brazil is currently negotiating the creation or the deepening of trade integration arrangements with a number of commercial partners, including the EU countries (as part of the Mercosur-EU agreement), Mercosur and other Latin American countries (Chile, Mexico, Venezuela), and the Andean Community. In addition, Brazil has been active on the multilateral front at the WTO. Historically, Brazil's trade strategy has been to promote the multilateral forum of the General Agreement on Tariffs and Trade (GATT) and WTO as the best option for developing countries to challenge the economic hegemony of the developed countries. The current Labor Party government has been forthright in pushing this line of Brazilian economic foreign policy, which has been especially apparent since the launching of the Doha Development Round in 2001.[31]

At the Doha WTO meetings, Brazil and other countries that share similarities as large developing economies moved to form the G20 group, its purpose being to present a joint proposal for the liberalization of crucial markets (agriculture) and to protest the distorting consequences of subsidies upheld by the developed countries. Within the G20, Lula's government has pursued the goal of expanding bilateral trade among big emerging market economies like China, India, Russia, and South Africa, which have now become a priority in Brazilian commercial policy.[32] This is so despite the fact that these markets accounted for only 3.4 percent, 0.5 percent, 1.9 percent, and 0.6 percent, respectively, of Brazilian exports in 2001.[33] But Brazil's emphasis on a multilateral and autonomous strategy is understandable since its exports to large trade partners now render the country a truly global trader. (Table 7-1 shows that Brazil's exports in 2005 were 22.4 percent to the EU, 19.2 percent to the United States, 8.4 percent to Argentina, and 3.4 percent to Mexico.)

The biggest challenges for Brazil to overcome regarding either the FTAA or the Doha Round are the political and economic obstacles to integration with the more advanced economies. Obviously, for many small Latin American nations with nondiversified economies the stakes for achieving WTO-plus outcomes are very high. In Brazil the prospect of joining an FTA with the biggest and most advanced economy in the world creates economic opportunities, but it also creates problems. These challenges coincide with Brazil's need to make deeper market reforms to complement and sustain the rules around the new trade issues.[34] Reforms are needed, for example, to modernize economic institutional structures, to enforce property rights, and to encourage more flexible rules for investment and regulations to foster innovation. Broadly, Brazil will require a much-upgraded institutional and regulatory environment to succeed in a technology-driven world economy.[35]

The connection and complementarity between deeper reforms and further trade integration has yet to be fully appreciated by Brazilian economic actors and policymakers. Although the Lula administration has committed to pursuing the new trade issues at the WTO, with the breakdown of the Doha negotiations the FTAA would ostensibly be a viable fallback strategy. But the reluctance of political and economic elites to broach the discussion of deeper integration within Doha, the FTAA, and even the EU-Mercosur talks has foreclosed all of these options for the time being. This political intransigence defies the economic realities. First, sectors damaged by U.S. competition could surely be won over with the promise of some transitional support from the government.[36] And second, the long-term benefits of conceding on the new trade issues could mean a sizable increase in Brazil's international economic standing. While the habit of sitting on the fence politically in the face of badly needed economic reforms is common to the Latin American region, by continuing to do so Brazil risks losing an incredible opportunity to break out of this mold.

U.S. External Interests and Strategy

Since comparative advantage for the United States has come to rely primarily on trade in services and high-technology products, the prompt liberalization

Table 7-1. *Brazil's Export Markets, 1997, 2004, 2005*

	1997		2004		2005	
Market	*U.S.$ billion*	*Percent of total*	*U.S.$ billion*	*Percent of total*	*U.S.$ billion*	*Percent of total*
European Union	14.5	27.4	24.6	25.5	26.5	22.4
United States[a]	9.4	17.8	21.3	22.1	22.7	19.2
Argentina	6.8	12.8	7.4	7.6	9.9	8.4
China	1.1	2.1	5.4	5.6	6.8	5.8
Mexico	0.8	1.6	3.9	4.1	4.1	3.4
Japan	3.1	5.8	2.8	2.9	3.5	2.9
Others	17.3	32.7	31.0	32.1	44.8	37.9
Russia	0.8	1.4	1.7	1.7	2.9	2.5
South Africa	0.3	0.6	1.0	1.1	1.4	1.2
Iran	0.2	0.5	1.1	1.2	1.0	0.8
Uruguay	0.9	1.6	0.7	0.7	0.8	0.7
Paraguay	1.4	2.7	0.9	0.9	1.0	0.8

Sources: Central Bank of Brazil and Brazilian Ministry of Development, Industry, and Trade.
a. Includes Puerto Rico.

of Latin America's barriers in these areas would pave the way for a major incursion of U.S. service-based companies into the region. Hence U.S. interests in gaining deeper access to Latin American markets, especially in South America, have been concentrated on these sectors at the WTO. Since the outset of the FTAA proposal in 1994, the U.S. position has been that the FTAA would be meaningful only if it reached beyond what the WTO had accomplished with regard to these new trade issues: steeper liberalization in traded services and investment, the opening up of government procurement, the quick and comprehensive enforcement of intellectual property rights, and even the inclusion of labor and environmental issues on the trade negotiating agenda.

U.S. objectives in the hemisphere must also be considered in light of the difficulties that have surrounded efforts to complete the Doha Development Round at the WTO. For some, the gradualist and piecemeal nature of hemispheric integration under the auspices of the FTAA seems a more promising option for the United States.[37] Just as NAFTA enabled its members to advance in areas that had eluded agreement at the Uruguay Round (dispute settlement, services, investment, intellectual property rights), the FTAA could provide incentives for negotiating breakthroughs at the multilateral level. This appeared to be happening in 2004, when the United States and the EU expressed a willingness to negotiate the reduction of agricultural barriers at the WTO.[38]

Yet it was also the intransigence of both on this front that led to the 2006 breakdown of WTO negotiations.[39] Faced now with the collapse of both WTO and FTAA negotiations and the recent election of a Congress even more suspicious of trade deals than its predecessor, the U.S. ability to provide the necessary leadership seems greatly diminished. Concerning U.S. interests in hemispheric integration, two additional points should be emphasized. First, the FTAA was originally viewed by the United States as a means of strengthening its own bargaining position with regard to Europe and East Asia. This is so in a direct sense, as the United States continues to seek greater access to European and Asian markets and as it has pursued these same goals within the WTO's multilateral framework. Second, the FTAA is the only regional process that promises to promote Latin America's global ties while retaining the United States as a hub.

Relegating the position of Latin American countries as spokes to the U.S. hub would allow for the elimination of the patchwork of subregional schemes that has evolved since the early 1990s. However, whereas Latin American countries deemed the hub-and-spoke model acceptable and even desirable a decade ago, many have now rethought its value to them. The persistence of intraregional asymmetries and the disappointing returns on trade liberalization and market reforms are behind this change of heart, and nowhere is this more apparent than in Brazil. Ironically, this is so despite the country's impressive trade advances, as reflected in table 7-1.

Conclusion and Prospects

While Brazilian negotiators insist that the FTAA is only one option for the country's trade strategy, this specific integration project has important consequences for the economic advancement of the country. With the usual delays in the multilateral trade arena and with increasing competition from Chinese goods in world markets, the FTAA constitutes the logical next step for sustaining the external trade boom that has driven Brazil's share of exports from 9 percent of GDP in 1990 to 16 percent of GDP in 2003. The trick will be to finesse the antitrade bias on the domestic political front and to tilt responsibility for the reactivation of hemispheric talks toward the economic ministries and export-oriented interests.

As Brazil is a pluralistic and complex society, the challenge is to further broaden the trade policy debate to include not only the official and business positions but also opinions from the media, academia, and labor. Some of these civil society sectors have already embraced the notion that integration is an important instrument for the modernization of the country within today's highly competitive global context. These sectors have also gradually accepted the inevitability of incorporating environmental and labor standards into trade agreements as well as the imperative to address related social issues. There is, in other words, a growing civic awareness about the nature and importance of trade agreements, even if these are still the purview of elite, business-oriented interests.

Quantitative assessments so far show that the poorest households and the most unskilled laborers will benefit the most from further trade liberalization.[40] These findings may lead some sectors to support trade agreements, particularly with the United States. The 2006 reelection of President Lula and his pragmatism concerning economic affairs may also give extra impetus to trade talks and help diminish the influence of stiff ideological positions. Yet as the Mexican experience with NAFTA has shown, trade liberalization under a North-South FTA is no panacea: concurrent institutional modernization is crucial for realizing the projected gains.[41]

For the United States, where the stakes in an FTAA have always been low, the challenge from the start of the George W. Bush administration was to publicize the economic and political benefits of the FTAA. The acrimony that surrounded the U.S. domestic debate over the passage of TPA and then the CAFTA agreement revealed that the completion of the FTAA from the U.S. vantage point would require executive leadership and statecraft. With the collapse of the FTAA and Doha negotiations, the Bush administration simply failed to rise to this occasion. As the U.S. Congress continues to oppose even small initiatives involving trade policy (for example, bilateral deals recently negotiated by the USTR with Vietnam and Colombia), it seems likely that U.S. trade policy will remain on hold until after the 2008 presidential election. Once U.S. trade policymakers awake from their slumber, a main task will be to work to convince domestic import-competing sectors and labor and environmental groups that the benefits of further trade agreements will outweigh their costs.

With regard to the FTAA, the quantitative evidence to date shows its potential to spur economic growth, foreign direct investment, and the transfer of technology.[42] But the onus is now on U.S. politicians and policymakers to publicly convey these findings and to use them to forge the kind of coalition that came together to support the NAFTA agreement. Granted, Mexico's struggles to succeed under NAFTA may have had a negative demonstration effect on Congress and the U.S. public, but rather than shun future trade deals with developing countries, the parties should directly address the adverse aspects of NAFTA and negotiate those areas, like market access and agriculture, that address the asymmetries. In this respect, Brazil's insistence on gradualism—on holding out for agricultural and market access concessions from the United States before signing on to a new trade agreement—represents an important departure from Mexico's strategy in negotiating NAFTA.

Notes

The opinions expressed here are those of the author and do not express an official position of the Brazilian government.

1. José Guilhon de Albuquerque, "A ALCA na política externa brasileira," *Sessenta Anos de Política Externa Brasileira (1930–1990),* edited by José Guilhon de Albuquerque, Ricardo Seitenfus, and Sérgio Henrique Nabuco de Castro (Lumen Juris Editora, 2006). Gary Hufbauer and Sherry Stephenson posit that this strategy could turn out to be a pyrrhic victory for Brazil. See Gary C. Hufbauer and Sherry Stephenson, "The Free Trade Agreement of the Americas: How Deep an Integration in the Western Hemisphere?" paper prepared for the seminar Reshaping the Asia Pacific Economic Order, Jakarta, December 2003.

2. For details of the negotiations between the United States and the Mercosur countries, see Fernando Masi and Carol Wise, "Negotiating the FTAA between the Main Players: The U.S. and MERCOSUR," in *MERCOSUR and the Creation of the Free Trade Area of the Americas,* edited by Marcel Vaillant and Fernando Lorenzo (Washington: Woodrow Wilson Center for International Scholars, 2005).

3. Ronald Rogowski, *Commerce and Coalitions: How Trade Affects Domestic Political Alignments* (Princeton University Press, 1989).

4. Stephen Magee, "Three Simple Tests of the Stolper-Samuelson Theorem," in *Black Hole Tariffs and Endogenous Policy Theory,* edited by Stephen Magee, William A. Brock, and Leslie Young (Cambridge University Press, 1989).

5. Ibid.

6. Gene Grossman and Elhanan Helpman, "Protection for Sale," *American Economic Review* 84, no. 4 (1994): 833–45.

7. Marcus Noland, "Chasing Phantoms: The Political Economy of USTR," *International Organization* 51, no. 3 (1997): 365–87.

8. Otaviano Canuto, Gilberto Lima, and Michel Alexandre, "Investimentos externos em serviços e efeitos potenciais da negociação da ALCA," Texto para Discussão 942 (Brasilia: Institute for Applied Economic Research, 2003).

9. Alcides Costa Vaz, "Trade Strategies in the Context of Economic Regionalism: The Case of MERCOSUR," in *The Strategic Dynamics of Latin American Trade,* edited by Vinod Aggarwal, Ralph Espach, and Joseph Tulchin (Stanford University Press, 2004).

10. Albuquerque, "A ALCA na política externa brasileira." See also Marcos Jank and Zuleika Arashiro, "A nova moldura das negociações comerciais: investimentos, compras governamentais, serviços e propriedade intelectual," *Política Externa* 103, no. 3 (2004–05): 33–45.

11. Noland, "Chasing Phantoms," 365–87.

12. Jeffrey J. Schott, "US Brazil Trade Relations in a New Era," Peterson Institute for International Economics, 2003 (www.petersoninstitute.org).

13. For more on the protrade position of these groups, see the websites of the Coalition of Service Industries (www/uscsi.org), the National Council for Foreign Trade (www.nftc.org), and the National Association of Manufacturers (www.nam.org). In January 2005 the latter organization published a memorandum of understanding with the Federation of Industries of São Paulo, the most powerful business association in Brazil, in support of resumption of the FTAA negotiations.

14. On intra-industry trade, see Manuel Pastor and Carol Wise, "The Origins and Sustainability of Mexico's Free Trade Policy," *International Organization* 48, no. 3 (1994): 459–89; Helen Milner, "Industries, Governments, and the Creation of Regional Trade Blocs," in *The Political Economy of Regionalism,* edited by Edward Mansfield and Helen Milner (Columbia University Press, 1997); Kerry A. Chase "Economic Interests and Regional Trading Arrangements," *International Organization* 57, no. 1 (2003): 137–74. On NAFTA see William A. Orme, *Understanding NAFTA: Free Trade and the New North America* (University of Texas at Austin Press, 1996); Edward Mansfield and Helen Milner, "The New Wave of Regionalism," *International Organization* 53, no. 3 (1997): 589–629; Stephan Haggard, "Regionalism in Asia and Americas," in *The Political Economy of Regionalism,* edited by Edward Mansfield and Helen Milner (Columbia University Press, 1997); Maxwell Cameron and Brian Tomlin, *The Making of NAFTA: How the Deal Was Done* (Cornell University Press, 2000).

15. In line with these directives, the Brazilian government created the Agency for Industrial Development in January 2005 to coordinate industrial and technological policies, including input from domestic actors.

16. "The Americas: A Test of Faith in Lula; Brazil's Economy," *Economist,* May 6, 2004, p. 55.

17. Rosângela Bittar, "País fica para trás em competitividade—Eficiência dos empresários salva Brasil do último lugar," *Jornal Valor Econômico,* May 5, 2004, p. A1. See also Albuquerque, "A ALCA na política externa brasileira."

18. Clóvis Rossi, "Brasil rejeita a ALCA teológica e ataca os EUA," *Jornal Folha de São Paulo,* October 1, 2003, p. B2. See also Clovis Rossi "Ceder na ALCA é hipotecar futuro, diz Amorim," *Jornal Folha de São Paulo,* February 15, 2004, p. B2.

19. Maurice Schiff and Allan Winters, *Regional Integration and Development* (Oxford University Press, 2003). See also Mansfield and Milner, "The New Wave of Regionalism."

20. Drusilla K. Brown, Kozo Kiyota, and Robert M. Stern, "Computational Analysis of the Free Trade Area of the Americas (FTAA)," *North American Journal of Economics and Finance* 16, no. 2 (2005): 153–85.

21. "Brazil Trade Policies to Improve Efficiency, Increase Growth, and Reduce Poverty," Report 24285-BR (Washington: World Bank, 2004). For a shorter version, see Glen W. Harrison and others, "Trade Policy and Poverty Reduction in Brazil," Working Paper 276 (Santiago: Central Bank of Chile, 2004). These papers are based on a static CGE model using the Global Trade Analysis Project 5.0 database. According to the results, liberalization under an FTAA would provide net welfare gains for the Brazilian economy. Results are also positive in other scenarios: a Mercosur-EU agreement, multilateral tariff liberalization, the Doha agreement, and a unilateral tariff cut of 50 percent under Mercosur. The studies focus on the impact of liberalization on poverty and find that the poorest households in Brazil would experience gains of 1.0–5.5 percent of their consumption, about three to five times the average for the country. Protection in Brazil favors capital-intensive manufacturing relative to labor-intensive agriculture and manufacturing; therefore, trade liberalization raises the return on unskilled labor relative to capital.

22. Kevin A. Hasset and James K. Glassman, "Understanding the Role of the United States in the Global Economy," *US Foreign Policy Agenda,* August 2003 (http://usinfo. state.gov/journals/itps/0803/ijpe/pj81hassett.htm). See also National Science Foundation, Division of Science Resources Studies, "Latin America: High-Tech Manufacturing on the Rise but Outpaced by East Asia," 2002 (www.nsf.gov/statistics/infbrief/nsf02331/).

23. National Science Foundation, Division of Science Resources Studies, "Latin America: R&D Spending Jumps in Brazil, Mexico, and Costa Rica," 2002 (www.nsf.gov/statistics/nsf00316/secta.htm).

24. Albert Fishlow, "Brazil: FTA or FTAA or WTO?" in *Free Trade Agreements: US Strategies and Priorities,* edited by Jeffrey Schott (Washington: Peterson Institute for International Economics, 2004).

25. Graham Allison and Morton Halperin, "Bureaucratic Politics: A Paradigm and Some Policy Implications," *World Politics* 24, "Supplement: Theory and Policy in International Relations" (1972): 40–79.

26. Daniel W. Drezner, "Ideas, Bureaucratic Politics, and the Crafting of Foreign Policy," *American Journal of Political Science* 44, no. 4 (2000): 733–49. The interaction between ideas and institutions was pioneered by Judith Goldstein, "The Impact of Ideas on Trade Policy: The Origins of U.S. Agricultural and Manufacturing Policies," *International Organization* 43, no. 1 (1989): 31–71.

27. Pastor and Wise, "The Origins and Sustainability of Mexico's Free Trade Policy."

28. Albuquerque, "A ALCA na política externa brasileira."

29. Eduardo Viola and Carlos Pio, "Doutrinarismo e realismo na percepção do interesse nacional: política macro-econômica, segurança e ALCA na relação Brasil-EUA," *Revista Cena International* 5, no. 3 (2003): 1–33.

30. "United States: Not Exactly Major League," *Economist,* March 19, 2005, p. 57.

31. Masi and Wise, "Negotiating the FTAA between the Main Players."

32. See "The Americas: Looking South, North, or Both? Brazil's Trade Diplomacy," *Economist,* February 7, 2004, p. 51. For a more sympathetic interpretation of Brazil's trade

policy, see William Greider and Kenneth Rapoza, "Lula Raises the Stakes," *Nation,* December 1, 2003, p. 11.

33. Marcelo de Paiva Abreu, "Política comercial brasileira: limites e oportunidades," Textos para Discussão 457 (Rio de Janeiro: Departamento de Economia, PUC-Rio, 2001).

34. Manuel Pastor and Carol Wise, "The Politics of Second-Generation Reform: Latin America's Imperiled Progress," *Journal of Democracy* 10, no. 3 (1999): 34–48. See also Patricio Navia and Andrés Velasco, "The Politics of Second Generation Reforms in Latin America," in *After the Washington Consensus: Restarting Growth In Latin America,* edited by Pedro-Pablo Kuczynski and John Williamson (Washington: Peterson Institute for International Economics, 2003).

35. For instance, a safe regulatory environment creates incentives for foreign investment in knowledge-intensive sectors such as telecommunications and services. Similarly, a modern and enforceable intellectual property rights regime is more likely to stimulate investment in R & D and to foster human capital development.

36. João Bosco Mesquita Machado and Galeno Ferraz, "FTAA: Assessments and Perceptions of the Brazilian Government and Production Sectors," in *MERCOSUR and the Creation of the Free Trade Area of the Americas,* edited by Marcel Vaillant and Fernando Lorenzo (Washington: Woodrow Wilson Center for International Scholars, 2005).

37. Sydney Weintraub, "Hemispheric Free Trade: The Possibilities," *Foreign Affairs en Español* 1, no. 3 (2001) (www.foreignaffairs-esp.org/20010901faenespcomment5642/sidney-weintraub/las-posibilidades-del-libre-comercio-hemisferico.html).

38. Bill Sing, "Deal to Loosen Trade Reached," *Los Angeles Times,* August 1, 2004, p. A1.

39. Amrita Narlikar and Diana Tussie, "The G20 at the Cancún Ministerial," *World Economy* 27, no. 7 (2004): 947–66.

40. "Brazil Trade Policies to Improve Efficiency, Increase Growth, and Reduce Poverty."

41. Tornell and his colleagues discuss the case of Mexico under NAFTA. According to these authors, the lack of a proper regulatory framework, a domestic credit crunch, and lax judiciary enforcement created strains and bottlenecks within the domestic economy that impeded the realization of NAFTA's full benefits. Aaron Tornell, Frank Westermann, and Lorenza Martinez, "NAFTA and Mexico's Less-than-Stellar Performance," Working Paper 0289 (Cambridge, Mass.: National Bureau of Economic Research, 2004). The chapters by Carol Wise and Antonio Ortiz Mena L. N. in this book also elaborate on the economic problems facing Mexico in the post-NAFTA era.

42. Brown, Kiyota, and Stern, "Computational Analysis of the Free Trade Area of the Americas."

III

THE GLOBAL CONTEXT

*The New Trade Agenda
and the Doha Round*

8

THE DOHA ROUND
Problems, Challenges, and Prospects

THEODORE H. COHN

T he General Agreement on Tariffs and Trade (GATT) completed the Uruguay Round, its most ambitious round of multilateral trade negotiations, in December 1993. The Uruguay Round resulted in a stronger dispute settlement system, multilateral trade rules for services and intellectual property, more multilateral trade discipline for agriculture and textiles, and the creation of the World Trade Organization (WTO). However, the seven years required to complete the Uruguay Round were an indication of the enormous difficulties that would follow in the first formal WTO negotiating round, the Doha Round. For example, the Uruguay Round designated agriculture and services as built-in agenda items for future negotiation, and these have presented problems since the launching of the Doha Round in 2001.

After failed efforts to launch a new WTO round at the 1999 Seattle Ministerial Meeting, the round was launched instead at the November 2001 Doha Ministerial, partly because the September 11 terrorist attacks in the United States had increased the determination of the major trading countries to reach an agreement. However, WTO members papered over serious differences in launching the Doha Round, and developing countries were highly skeptical of assurances that this would be the "development round" that had been promised. Thus the September 2003 Cancún Ministerial, which was to mark the halfway point of the Doha Round, collapsed in disarray over a number of issues discussed in this chapter. The Doha Round negotiations could not resume until July 2004, when the WTO General Council finally approved a package agreement (referred to here as the July 2004 framework agreement) that "unblocked some of the most sensitive and difficult areas of the negotiations."[1] However, major differences persisted, and in July 2006 the Doha Round negotiations were suspended for an indefinite period.

This chapter begins with a general discussion of tensions and conflicts that have posed serious difficulties for the Doha Round. The second section focuses on specific issues in the negotiations, and the chapter concludes with some thoughts regarding the Doha Round's future prospects.

Challenges Confronting the Doha Round

Conflicting interests and goals among actors have posed serious obstacles to the successful conclusion of the Doha Round. Some of the most salient conflicts are in the areas of North-South relations and North-North relations.

North-South Relations

In the 1980s developing countries adopted liberal trade policies and were more involved in the Uruguay Round than in previous GATT rounds for several reasons: the South's protectionist import substitution policies (particularly in Latin America) were unsuccessful, the benefits to the South of special and differential treatment (SDT) in earlier rounds were disappointing, and structural adjustment loans to deal with the South's foreign debt crisis were linked to the adoption of trade liberalization policies. The South also functioned less as a bloc in the Uruguay Round, and a number of North-South coalitions were formed.[2] In exchange for Northern promises to liberalize trade in textiles and agriculture, the South agreed to accept the Uruguay Round agreement's full set of rights and obligations (the single undertaking), including the agreements on services and intellectual property.

However, the South realized belatedly that it "had accepted fairly weak commitments in agriculture and textiles" in the Uruguay Round, "while making substantially stronger ones" in areas of interest to the North such as intellectual property rights.[3] The South also argued that the North did not fulfill Uruguay Round promises to provide it with capacity building and technical assistance. Despite its dissatisfaction, the South eventually agreed to the launching of the Doha Round for several reasons. Although the balance of Uruguay Round benefits favored the North, there were also some significant gains for the South; for example, although the South did not achieve its objectives in agriculture and textiles, the Uruguay Round laid the foundation for further liberalization in these sectors. Perhaps most important for the South was the declaration to include a Doha development agenda, which formalized the next round's commitment to development.[4]

Nevertheless, developing countries remain dissatisfied with their role in trade decisionmaking, and this has interfered with progress in the Doha Round. The WTO's governing councils are plenary bodies open to every member, and it has nothing comparable to the twenty-four-member executive boards of the International Monetary Fund (IMF) and World Bank, in which developed countries have predominant influence. Until the early 1960s GATT had the characteristics of a small club dominated by the North, and the lack of an executive board did not affect decisionmaking; but with decolonization the South increased its GATT membership, prompting the North to turn to smaller groups within and outside the organization to preserve its influence and facilitate trade governance.

Informal groups within GATT have included the Consultative Group of Eighteen (CG18) and the green room sessions. Although large and influential developing countries have been regular participants in these meetings, the North has clearly prevailed.[5] Green room sessions are limited to the GATT-WTO director-general and about twenty-five major traders from the Organization for Economic Cooperation and Development (OECD). Many developing countries protested their exclusion from green room sessions held to prepare for the 1999 Seattle WTO Ministerial, and the director-general indicated that he would try "to move away from the green room, and thrash out issues in the General Council."[6] However, green room sessions continued in subsequent WTO Ministerials.

Outside GATT/WTO, the North has relied on plurilateral groups to form a consensus and help set the agenda in multinational trade negotiations; these include the OECD formed in the 1960s, the Group of Seven/Group of Eight (G7/G8) formed in the 1970s, and the Quadrilateral Group of trade ministers and officials from the United States, the European Union (EU), Japan, and Canada (the Quad) formed in the early 1980s.[7] The South's dissatisfaction with its exclusion from these groups has had some effect on trade decisionmaking, including the creation of an unofficial mininegotiating Group of Six (G6), composed of the United States, the EU, Brazil, India, Japan, and Australia; the G6 sought unsuccessfully to achieve a consensus on contentious issues before the Doha Round talks were suspended.[8]

A degree of minilateralism (small-group decisionmaking on global trade issues) is essential, because it is increasingly difficult to discuss contentious issues in meetings open to the WTO's 150 members.[9] Thus a number of analysts have suggested that the WTO establish a consultative or executive board patterned partly after the IMF and World Bank executive boards. In their view, such a group would have more transparency and legitimacy than the controversial green room sessions because it would be a formal part of the WTO's institutional structure.[10] However, WTO members have not agreed to establish such a group, and a statement in the 1994 Marrakesh Agreement that "the WTO shall continue the practice of decisionmaking by consensus followed under GATT" makes establishing a consultative or executive board difficult.[11]

Although the interests of developing countries are certainly not homogeneous, with China, Brazil, and India as leaders, groups of developing countries such as the Group of Twenty (G20) have been unified and powerful enough to defy the pressure of developed countries on some major issues in the Doha Round.[12] A more balanced relationship between North and South would be a welcome change, but it is also essential that the WTO develop a formal minilateral body to ensure that this balance contributes to consensus rather than stalemate and indecision in the large WTO governing councils.

North-North Relations

Global trade governance has faltered in recent years, partly because of serious trade conflicts between the United States and the EU and an attendant lack of leadership by the North. After the Uruguay Round, the United States shifted from its traditional position of favoring broad multilateral trade negotiations to calling for "a short negotiation, necessitating a limited agenda" that would produce "concrete results in priority areas for U.S. interests."[13] Two factors accounted for this change. First, despite U.S. economic prosperity, the late 1990s was a period of rapidly growing U.S. trade deficits. Second, conflict over the North American Free Trade Agreement (NAFTA) and the Uruguay Round produced a "domestication" of U.S. trade politics; that is, labor and environmental groups succeeded in politicizing the trade policy agenda, which contributed to increased protectionism in the U.S. Congress.[14]

In contrast to the United States, the EU wanted a comprehensive WTO round because this would provide EU members with gains in nonagricultural areas and thus permit the European Commission to counter opposition to the negotiations from French agricultural producers. However, the EU did not have the economic power or unity of purpose to substitute for U.S.

leadership. Although the United States eventually accepted a more comprehensive agenda in the Doha Round, major U.S.-EU differences persist, and three former GATT/WTO directors-general have warned that "the spate of disputes and the large overhang of retaliatory actions—actual or threatened—between the United States and the European Union is one of the most troublesome barriers to securing leadership from the WTO's two biggest beneficiaries."[15]

Contentious Issues in the Doha Round

Before discussing the Doha Round, it is important to note that most issues cannot be neatly categorized as North-South or North-North because there are also major differences *within* each of these realms. A prime example is the various divisions over trade in textiles. In response to Southern demands, the Uruguay Round concluded an agreement on textiles and clothing that abolished more than forty years of Northern textile import quotas on January 1, 2005. However, North-South controversy in this area continues because textile producers in the United States and other developed countries are pressuring for protection. Some developing countries that had pressured for an end to textile quotas also fear they will lose market share to "textile production superpowers such as China and India."[16]

The poorest developing countries have asked for WTO assistance to save their textile industries, and twenty-two middle- and low-income developing countries attended a meeting on textiles organized by Mexico in September 2004. Mexico is concerned that its market share in U.S. clothing imports could decrease by 70 percent.[17] Cleavages on this issue are also evident in the North and even within countries. For example, whereas U.S. textile producers are pressuring for continued protection, U.S. clothing retailers and importers such as Wal-Mart and J. C. Penney are seeking an end to import restrictions. In addition to divisions within the South and the North, developed and developing countries sometimes join in coalition groups. For example, the Cairns Group of so-called fair agricultural traders is a coalition of fourteen developing and three developed countries.[18]

Despite these North-South coalitions and divisions within the South and the North, however, North-South differences pose the major obstacle to the successful completion of the Doha Round. The remainder of this chapter therefore identifies those Doha Round issues in which the South or the North is the main demandeur for change. For example, although the Cairns Group includes developing and developed countries, the South has been the main demandeur for change in agricultural trade. Latin American members of the Cairns Group walked out of the Uruguay Round negotiations on two occasions (the Montreal and Brussels Ministerials) to protest the failure to deal with agriculture, and developing countries rejected an August 2000 U.S.-EU proposal to provide a framework for the Doha Round agricultural negotiations.

Issues in Which the South Is the Main Demandeur

The three main Doha Round issues in which the South is the main demandeur are agriculture, special and differential treatment, and technical assistance and capacity building. Below I review each of these issues in turn.

Agriculture

The United States has often joined with the Cairns Group in favoring the abolition of agricultural export subsidies, a decrease in trade-distorting domestic subsidies, and greater market access. The EU, by contrast, has joined with Japan, Norway, South Korea, and Switzerland in resisting agricultural trade liberalization and in favoring policies that support rural communities, sustainable agriculture, and other social goals.[19] Despite U.S. and EU differences, both have a Northern perspective on agriculture that distinguishes them from the South. For example, although the United States calls for freer agricultural trade, it continues to provide substantial trade-distorting subsidies in response to domestic U.S. farm pressures as well as EU subsidies.

Agriculture was not included in the GATT Kennedy and Tokyo Rounds despite U.S. pressure because the United States in the end agreed to go along with the EU in giving priority to other issues. The United States took a stronger position on the inclusion of agriculture in the Uruguay Round. The Uruguay Round Agreement on Agriculture (URAA) requires WTO members to reduce their export and domestic subsidies, but the base years used and the categorization of subsidies permit the United States and the EU to continue providing substantial trade-distorting subsidies. The URAA also requires members to convert agricultural import quotas to tariffs that will gradually be reduced, but countries often replace their import quotas with excessively high tariffs ("dirty tariffication") and tariff rate quotas. Many developing countries have a comparative advantage in agriculture; agriculture also accounts for a much larger share of employment, exports, and economic output in the South than in the North.[20]

The strong divisions on agriculture are evident in the Doha Round, and as the 2003 Cancún Ministerial approached, the United States and the EU tried to provide leadership by issuing a joint paper calling for the partial elimination of export subsidies and for a market access formula that would blend the U.S. and EU approaches. However, the paper contributed to a major impasse. On one side, the Group of Ten (G10) net food importers (Bulgaria, Iceland, Israel, Japan, Korea, Liechtenstein, Mauritius, Norway, Switzerland, and Taiwan) argued that the U.S.-EU paper did not provide enough flexibility to countries needing higher tariffs to protect producers of sensitive commodities. On the other side, the G20 developing countries, led by Brazil, India, and China, argued that the U.S.-EU proposal was not ambitious enough. The G20 called for an end to export subsidies, with an earlier deadline for products of interest to the North, and for major tariff cuts by the North to improve market access for the South. Developing countries also linked any concessions they would provide on industrial market access, services trade, and trade facilitation to developed countries' concessions in agriculture.[21]

To resolve the agricultural impasse, five "interested parties" (the United States, the EU, Brazil, India, and Australia) eventually agreed on a text that formed the basis of the July 2004 framework agreement on agriculture. Although the framework is very general and leaves many sensitive issues for future negotiation, it is significant in that it calls for the elimination of agricultural export subsidies. The EU accepted this provision only after commitments were made to eliminate U.S. agricultural export credits with repayment periods beyond 180 days, to adopt new measures to ensure that food aid does not distort trade, and to impose discipline on state-trading enterprises such as the Canadian and Australian Wheat Boards (Canada was notably unenthusiastic about this last provision). The agricultural framework also calls for substantial reductions in trade-distorting domestic subsidies, with the largest subsidizers cutting the most. It is vague, however, on market access.

In sum, progress has been made in the agriculture trade negotiations, but a number of sensitive issues like wheat and cotton require further negotiation. For example, the EU did not commit to a date for ending agricultural export subsidies, and the framework text offers little guidance on the degree to which WTO members can shield sensitive agricultural products from market access concessions.

Special and Differential Treatment

An agreement on special and differential treatment "lies at the heart of the [Doha Round] agenda," because the South has linked SDT with its willingness to negotiate issues of interest to the North.[22] SDT has a long history in GATT/WTO.[23] In 1965 a new part 4 of GATT called for special treatment for the South, but it was largely symbolic. In 1971 the South gained a more concrete concession when the North established a generalized system of preferences for developing country exports, and one result of the 1973–79 GATT Tokyo Round was the enabling clause, which "established for the first time in trade relations . . . a permanent legal basis for preferences in favor of developing countries."[24] In exchange for the enabling clause, the South had to accept the graduation principle: that countries showing notable progress in development must accept greater GATT/WTO discipline and eventually wean themselves from SDT.

However, during the crisis-ridden 1980s, developing countries began to view reciprocal trade liberalization as critical to the success of their export-oriented development strategies. SDT remained a central element of global trade, and the Uruguay Round agreement contains about 155 SDT provisions, but developing countries were willing to accept "a dilution of special and differential treatment in exchange for better market access and strengthened rules."[25] Unlike the Tokyo Round's nontariff barrier codes, in which most developing countries did not participate, the South agreed to treat the Uruguay Round as a single undertaking (that is, acceptance of the Uruguay Round accord meant acceptance of all of its agreements). Thus developing countries were more willing to extend reciprocity in the Uruguay Round partly because of these SDT provisions, and they actively participated in the negotiations.

Yet after the Uruguay Round, the South demanded that SDT provisions be clarified and strengthened for two major reasons. First, developing countries were disillusioned with the Uruguay Round results; and second, it was difficult for them to implement their WTO obligations. Developing countries want four changes to the SDT provisions: greater flexibility, such as exemptions from trade rules because of the South's development status and its difficulty in implementing agreements; stricter rules to ensure that the North provides increased market access to the South; technical assistance to enable the South to implement WTO agreements; and procedures to monitor and enforce SDT. In response to the South's demands, the 2001 Doha Ministerial declaration states that all SDT provisions "shall be reviewed with a view to strengthening them and making them more precise, effective and operational"; the WTO's Committee on Trade and Development is to carry out this mandate.[26]

Despite such inroads, SDT has become a more complex issue in recent years, and this has contributed to stalemate in the Doha Round. As a number of developing countries have become increasingly competitive, "industrial countries and the poorest countries alike" are more reluctant to consider Singapore, South Korea, Brazil, China, and India "as developing countries."[27] Thus the North is less willing to offer SDT to major developing country traders, and some landlocked and small countries in the South want to create additional categories of SDT for lower-income countries (which are not always accepted by the North).[28]

In view of these differences, two deadlines were missed for making significant recommendations on SDT, and to realize SDT gains the South will have to offer concessions on other issues in return. The failure to reach an early SDT agreement has caused a number of developing countries to question the North's sincerity in calling Doha the Development Round.[29] The July 2004 framework recognized the South's interest in SDT by calling on the WTO Committee on Trade and Development "to expeditiously complete the review of all the outstanding" STD proposals and to "report to the [WTO] General Council, with clear recommendations for a decision."[30] Of course, the status of these STD proposals is uncertain with the suspension of Doha Round negotiations.

Technical Assistance and Capacity Building

Technical assistance, in the context of the WTO, includes a wide range of activities to assist the South, including training in trade policy, negotiation skills, and dispute settlement in Geneva and abroad.[31] Although the North promised technical assistance to help the South fulfill its Uruguay Round commitments, the amount it provided was disappointing. The North's promise was not legally binding, and in 1999 the WTO technical assistance budget was less than SF 1 million. This funding was insufficient because of the increase in the number of WTO members and because trade negotiations have become much more complicated than they were in earlier years, when tariff reductions were the main preoccupation. For example, countries require substantial monetary and human resources to implement Uruguay Round agreements in complex areas such as customs valuation, sanitary and phytosanitary standards, and intellectual property. Thus the South required additional time to fulfill its Uruguay Round commitments, and it wanted more technical and capacity building assistance before agreeing to additional commitments within the Doha Round.[32]

The North has taken the technical assistance issue more seriously in the Doha Round, and the 2001 Doha declaration called for development of a plan to ensure long-term funding for this purpose. As a result, the WTO established the Global Trust Fund to help build the South's capacity to participate more fully in the Doha Round.[33] Although WTO members had pledged U.S.$18.4 million to this fund by early 2002, the North and South continue to disagree over the level and purpose of technical assistance under the Doha declaration mandate. Whereas the South argues that technical assistance should include development aid to help it implement new obligations and take advantage of new market access opportunities, the North argues that technical assistance should focus more narrowly on Doha Round negotiations.

The July 2004 framework states that developing countries "and in particular least-developed countries, should be provided with enhanced TRTA [trade-related technical assistance] and capacity building, to increase their effective participation in the negotiations, to facilitate their implementation of WTO rules, and to enable them to adjust and diversify their economies."[34] However, the WTO has only limited expertise in development, and it will require more staff and resources if it is to coordinate the work of institutions with the main responsibility in this area—institutions such as the World Bank, regional development banks, and the United Nations Conference on Trade and Development.[35]

Issues in Which the North Is the Main Demandeur

Three Doha Round issues in which the North is the main demandeur are the Singapore, or "new trade" issues, nonagricultural market access, and services trade. I discuss each of these issues below.

The Singapore Issues

At the 1996 Singapore WTO Ministerial the EU and Japan called for negotiations on investment, competition policy, government procurement, and trade facilitation, and these have henceforth been called the Singapore issues. Whereas developed countries generally argue that the WTO should acknowledge the growing importance of the Singapore issues, developing countries believe that WTO discipline in these areas would undercut their development efforts. Despite this basic North-South division, there are also differences within the South and North on these issues. For example, some Latin American countries support an EU proposal for a multilateral agreement on competition policy, because it would strengthen their domestic constituencies for reform.

The United States, by contrast, is ambivalent about a competition agreement because of concerns that it could affect U.S. antitrust law. In regard to investment, the United States is skeptical that a WTO agreement would uphold the strong provisions for protecting foreign investment in bilateral and regional investment treaties (for example, under NAFTA) because of widespread resistance from the South. However, the United States strongly supports WTO negotiations for the other two Singapore issues: government procurement and trade facilitation.[36]

Developing countries generally resist negotiating the Singapore issues for several reasons. First, the South lacks the financial and human resources to negotiate this broadened agenda. Second, based on their experience with the Uruguay Round, developing countries fear they will be subject to trade sanctions if they do not implement new agreements on the Singapore issues in a timely fashion. For example, sanctions were imposed on some developing countries that delayed in complying with the agreement on trade-related intellectual property rights. Third, since the North already meets most of the standards to be negotiated for the Singapore issues, it is the South that would take on new obligations. Finally, as Glauco Oliveira points out in chapter 7, developing countries fear that restrictions on their ability to regulate competition, investment, and government procurement would hinder their economic development.[37]

The 2001 Doha declaration tried to avoid North-South conflict with the ambiguous statement that negotiation of the Singapore issues "will take place, after the Fifth Session of the Ministerial Conference [that is, after Cancún] on the basis of a decision to be taken, by explicit consensus, at that Session on the modalities of negotiations."[38] However, the term *explicit consensus* was not clearly defined and was open to conflicting interpretations. Whereas many developing countries felt that an explicit consensus was needed at the 2003 Cancún Ministerial to launch negotiations on the Singapore issues, the EU believed that a commitment had already been made to begin negotiating these issues and that the explicit consensus requirement refers to the modalities of the negotiations. Thus the Cancún Ministerial collapsed partly because developing countries, especially in Africa, would not agree to negotiate the Singapore issues.[39]

After the failure at Cancún, the EU, the United States, and developing countries demonstrated more flexibility and reached a compromise in the July 2004 framework to begin negotiations on only one of the Singapore issues: trade facilitation, or expediting "the movement, release and clearance of goods, including goods in transit."[40] However, the framework does not specify whether trade facilitation disciplines would be subject to WTO dispute settlement and whether all WTO members would be required to participate. Although the framework clearly indicates that the other Singapore issues—investment, competition, and government procurement—will not be negotiated in the Doha Round, views differ as to whether the working groups for these issues can continue their discussions. These unanswered questions provide a warning that North-South conflict over the Singapore issues will continue.[41]

Nonagricultural Market Access

Negotiations for industrial or nonagricultural market access (NAMA) would be beneficial to the South for several reasons: developing countries apply some of their highest tariffs to nonagricultural trade with each other; developing countries would benefit from reductions in tariff escalation (imposition of higher tariffs on processed products than on raw materials); and developing countries would benefit from reductions in tariff peaks (imposition of higher tariffs on sensitive products such as textiles). Although average tariffs in the North are now relatively low, they tend to be higher for a number of products, such as textiles, imported from the South.[42]

Despite the potential benefits of a NAMA agreement for the South, the North has been the main demandeur for such an agreement in the Doha Round. The United States and the EU are united in pressing for an ambitious NAMA agreement, in which developing countries would make significant concessions. However, the South has linked the NAMA talks with progress in agriculture and has demanded more special treatment in a NAMA agreement than the United States and the EU are inclined to offer. In the talks leading to the July 2004 framework agreement, developing countries were unwilling to engage in serious discussion of NAMA until the results of the talks on agriculture were clearer. Thus the framework agreement on NAMA is even more vague than the agreement on agriculture.[43]

Services Trade

As discussed above, the Uruguay Round designated agriculture and services trade as built-in agenda items for further negotiation. The South wants to promote some aspects of services trade, such as the movement of natural persons or labor migration that could offer it considerable benefits. However, the North has been the main demandeur in the services trade area and has been impatient with the slow pace at which developing countries have tabled service trade offers. Progress has been slow because services talks are complicated and because the South wants a services safeguard to protect infant industries. Although more than thirty developing countries presented *requests* for new services market access in 2002, none met the March 2003 deadline for *offers* of services trade liberalization.[44] The July 2004 framework set a new May 2005 deadline for WTO members to table their offers.[45] However, thirty-seven non-least-developed members had yet to file services trade offers by early December 2004, and many of the offers were made in only a small number of service sectors (least developed countries are not expected to make offers).[46]

Prospects for the Doha Round

As mentioned earlier, Doha Round negotiations were suspended in July 2006. This section addresses some of the requirements for reviving the negotiations and reaching an agreement.

WTO members were able to agree on the July 2004 framework only by phrasing many issues in highly general terms and delaying decisions in contentious areas. In agriculture, for example, the framework focuses on underlying principles and "does not include most of the figures that will eventually be used to determine precisely how much reform is to be achieved."[47] Thus formulas for reducing agricultural tariffs, tariff quotas, export subsidies, and trade-distorting domestic subsidies are still up for negotiation. Related issues such as safeguards, food safety, consumer information and labeling, and geographic indications and food quality will also have to be negotiated. For industrial goods, negotiators must find a formula that meets the agreed goal of cutting tariff peaks by the largest amount while giving some flexibility to developing countries that often have the highest tariffs. For services trade, negotiators must address the problem that many countries have not even made their initial offers.

As was the case for the Uruguay Round, the Doha Round had to be extended well beyond the initial deadline, and WTO members set themselves a new deadline of April 30, 2006. This now unmet deadline would have permitted enough time for ratification of the agreement before the expiry of the U.S. president's Trade Promotion Authority (TPA) in June

2007 (TPA permits the president to negotiate trade agreements that cannot be changed by Congress).

To reach a consensus on sensitive issues, the North must accept the fact that it cannot dominate the Doha Round negotiations to the degree that it has controlled previous rounds. Until the Uruguay Round, the South was less involved in GATT, and the North largely dominated negotiations at the multilateral level. Although the South was more involved in the Uruguay Round, the Group of Seventy-Seven (G77) did not act as a bloc, and some developing countries joined in a number of alliances with developed countries. In the Doha Round, by contrast, China's membership in the WTO and the formation of several new groups of developing countries (including the G20 and the Group of Ninety, a tripartite alliance of the African Union; the African, Caribbean, and Pacific group; and the least developed countries) have made it more difficult for the North to prevail.[48] For example, the G20 successfully pressured developed countries, and particularly the EU, to agree to the removal of agricultural export subsidies.

But the large coalitions of developing countries are porous and open to divisions, and the South's influence continues to face limitations. For example, the G20 could not induce the EU to commit to a date for removing agricultural export subsidies. Nevertheless, so-called alliances of sympathy have emerged even among developing countries with divergent interests, and the North will have to agree to more concessions in the Doha Round than in previous rounds. The Doha Round, like the Uruguay Round, is also a single undertaking, and the North must acknowledge that this increases developing countries' reluctance to make new commitments "because they lack the resources to analyze all the issues . . . yet they are expected to sign all the results."[49] The North must therefore clarify SDT provisions for developing countries and provide technical and capacity building assistance to enable the South to implement new agreements.

Developing countries must also be willing to offer concessions if the negotiations are to succeed. For example, the South has demanded that the WTO provisions on SDT be clarified and strengthened. The South's demand for an "early harvest" on this issue was not realized, however, and it is evident that Northern concessions on SDT will be used as a bargaining chip to induce the South to agree to other parts of the Doha agenda. The North is also unlikely to offer significant concessions on SDT if the South does not agree to more differentiation in the definition of *developing country*, with large, middle-income developing countries being less eligible for SDT benefits.

As Jacques Delors notes, "We can no longer speak . . . about relations between North and South; now it is between the North and Souths."[50] The economic development witnessed in the Asia-Pacific and in Latin America has largely bypassed most of sub-Saharan Africa. Even poorer developing countries must realize there is a trade-off between SDT benefits they might receive and the limited influence they will have in the Doha Round. Some SDT benefits are of course essential and fully justified, especially for the least developed countries. However, experience under GATT demonstrates that there is always a price to be paid for SDT benefits.

The Doha Round, like the Uruguay Round, goes far beyond negotiating tariffs, and many sensitive behind-the-border issues must be addressed. As was the case for the Uruguay Round, a broad-ranging negotiation is most likely to succeed because WTO members can point to benefits they receive in some areas as compensation for concessions they must make in others. For example, the EU will have to commit to a date for terminating agricultural export subsidies, and both the United States and the EU will have to significantly decrease their trade-distorting domestic subsidies. Other major traders such as Japan, South Korea, and Canada may have to significantly reduce their tariffs for sensitive agricultural products.

However, these countries will expect concessions from the South in return in such areas as nonagricultural market access, services trade, and trade facilitation. Thus the European Commission strongly supported a broad-ranging Doha Round because it can only counter French objections to EU concessions in agriculture by pointing to benefits for the EU in other areas. Similarly, developing countries will not agree to significant concessions in services trade, nonagricultural market access, and trade facilitation unless they receive benefits in such areas as agricultural trade, SDT, and technical assistance and capacity building.

Several issues pose serious risks for the Doha Round. First are the growing U.S. budget, trade, and current account deficits, which have contributed to rising U.S. protectionism. A second problematic issue is the proliferation of bilateral free trade agreements, which divert attention and resources from the more difficult task of promoting trade liberalization in the broader WTO. A third problematic area is the number of conflicts between the two largest traders, the United States and the EU. A degree of consensus between the two in crucial areas will be essential for the successful completion of the Doha Round, as it was at the end of the Kennedy, Tokyo, and Uruguay Rounds. Finally, the United States and the EU have been undermining the

WTO's effectiveness by flouting some high-profile dispute settlement decisions. The major traders must be more supportive of the WTO dispute settlement system if the Doha Round is to eventually succeed.

The WTO director-general, Pascal Lamy, summed up the obstacles to the successful completion of the Doha Round by stating that "three major actors in this cycle, the United States, the European Union and the G20 (emerging countries) each has a pebble in its shoe."[51] In other words, major players in both the North and the South must be willing to make some significant concessions if we are to avoid either the failure of the Doha Round or a limited agreement that is of little value to either North or South.

Notes

1. Supachai Panitchpakdi, "Reflections on the Last Three Years of the WTO," *World Trade Review* 4, no. 3 (2005): 378; World Trade Organization, "Doha Work Programme: Decision Adopted by the General Council on 1 August 2004," WT/L/579 (Geneva: August 2, 2004).

2. Colleen Hamilton and John Whalley, "Coalitions in the Uruguay Round," *Weltwirtschaftliches Archiv* 125, no. 3 (1989): 547–61.

3. Jayashree Watal, "Developing Countries' Interests in a Development Round," in *The WTO after Seattle,* edited by Jeffrey J. Schott (Washington: Peterson Institute for International Economics, 2000), pp. 71–72.

4. Antonio G. M. La Vina and Vicente Paolo Yu III, "From Doha to Cancún: The WTO Trade Negotiations and Implications for Communities," Working Paper (Washington: World Resources Institute, August 2002), p. 3; Arvind Panagariya, "Developing Countries at Doha: A Political Economy Analysis," *World Economy* 25, no. 9 (2002): 1205. On changes from the Seattle to Doha Ministerials, see Dilip K. Das, "The Global Trading System: From Seattle to Doha," *International Journal* 57, no. 4 (2002): 605–23.

5. Richard Blackhurst and David Hartridge, "Improving the Capacity of WTO Institutions to Fulfill Their Mandate," *Journal of International Economic Law* 7, no. 3 (2004): 706.

6. Anne Anderson, Ireland's trade negotiator, quoted in Elizabeth Olson, "Patching Up Morale at the World Trade Organization," *New York Times,* October 31, 2000, p. W1.

7. On the role of the OECD, G7/G8, and the Quad in trade decisionmaking, see Theodore H. Cohn, *Governing Global Trade: International Institutions in Conflict and Convergence* (Aldershot, U.K.: Ashgate, 2002).

8. "Latest WTO Failure Makes Doha Conclusion This Year Unlikely," *Inside U.S. Trade,* July 7, 2006, pp. 14–15.

9. On minilateralism, see Miles Kahler, "Multilateralism with Small and Large Numbers," in *Multilateralism Matters: The Theory and Praxis of an Institutional Form,* edited by J. G. Ruggie (Columbia University Press, 1993), p. 296.

10. See Sylvia Ostry, "The WTO and International Governance," in *The World Trade Organization Millennium Round: Freer Trade in the Twenty-First Century,* edited by K. G. Deutsch and B. Speyer (London: Routledge, 2001), p. 292; Blackhurst and Hartridge, "Improving the Capacity of WTO Institutions to Fulfill Their Mandate." For a discussion of the numerous proposals to establish a formal group in GATT-WTO, see Cohn, *Governing Global Trade.*

11. "Marrakesh Agreement Establishing the World Trade Organization," article 9.1, in World Trade Organization, *The Results of the Uruguay Round of Multilateral Negotiations: The Legal Texts* (Geneva: 1994), p. 11.

12. Sungjoon Cho, "A Bridge Too Far: The Fall of the Fifth WTO Ministerial Conference in Cancún and the Future of Trade Constitution," *Journal of International Economic Law* 7, no. 2 (2004): 235.

13. Jeffrey J. Schott, "The WTO after Seattle," in *The WTO after Seattle,* edited by J. J. Schott (Washington: Peterson Institute for International Economics, 2000), p. 7.

14. Andreas Falke, "The USA: Why Fundamentals Do Not Always Matter; or, It's Politics, Stupid!" in *The World Trade Organization Millennium Round: Freer Trade in the Twenty-First Century,* edited by K. G. Deutsch and B. Speyer (London: Routledge, 2001), p. 22.

15. World Trade Organization, "Statement on the Multilateral Trading System by Three Former GATT/WTO Directors-General," February 1, 2001 (www.wto.org/english/news_e/news01_e/statdavos_jan01_e.htm).

16. Scott Miller and Charles Hutzler, "Poor Nations Seek WTO Aid," *Globe and Mail,* October 1, 2004, p. B9.

17. "Losing Their Shirts," *Economist,* October 16, 2004, pp. 59–60. The twenty-two countries attending the Geneva meeting were Mexico, Guatemala, Dominican Republic, El Salvador, Venezuela, Bolivia, Chile, Romania, Colombia, Sri Lanka, Bangladesh, Ecuador, Indonesia, Jordan, Tunisia, Bulgaria, Nicaragua, Morocco, Israel, Mauritius, Turkey, and Haiti.

18. Members of the Cairns Group are Argentina, Australia, Bolivia, Brazil, Canada, Chile, Colombia, Costa Rica, Guatemala, Indonesia, Malaysia, New Zealand, Paraguay, Philippines, South Africa, Thailand, and Uruguay.

19. Thomas C. Beierle, "Agricultural Trade Liberalization: Uruguay, Doha, and Beyond," *Journal of World Trade* 36, no. 6 (2002): 1101–02.

20. Ibid., 1089–91.

21. Cho, "A Bridge Too Far," pp. 227–29; various issues of *Inside U.S. Trade* and *Bridges Weekly Digest.* The current members of the G20 are Argentina, Bolivia, Brazil, Chile, China, Cuba, Egypt, Guatemala, India, Indonesia, Mexico, Nigeria, Pakistan, Paraguay, Philippines, South Africa, Tanzania, Thailand, Venezuela, and Zimbabwe.

22. Michael Hart and Bill Dymond, "Special and Differential Treatment and the Doha 'Development' Round," *Journal of World Trade* 37, no. 2 (2003): 395, 407–09.

23. Alexander Keck and Patrick Low, "Special and Differential Treatment in the WTO: Why, When and How?" Staff Working Paper ERSD-2004-3 (Geneva: Economic Research and Statistics Division, World Trade Organization, May 2004).

24. Olivier Long, *Law and Its Limitations in the GATT Multilateral Trade System* (Dordrecht, Netherlands: Martinus Nijhoff, 1985), p. 101. On GATT/WTO changes in SDT for developing countries over time, see Theodore H. Cohn, *Global Political Economy: Theory and Practice,* 3d ed. (New York: Longman, 2005), pp. 241–48; Norma Breda dos Santos, Rogério Farias, and Raphael Cunha, "Generalized System of Preferences in General Agreement on Tariffs and Trade/World Trade Organization: History and Current Issues," *Journal of World Trade* 39, no. 4 (2005): 637–70.

25. Quoted in Mari Pangestu, "Special and Differential Treatment in the Millennium: Special for Whom and How Different?" *World Economy* 23, no. 9 (2000): 1291; Robert Wolfe, "Crossing the River by Feeling the Stones: Where the WTO Is Going after Seattle, Doha, and Cancun," *Review of International Political Economy* 11, no. 3 (2004): 587.

26. World Trade Organization, *Doha Ministerial Declaration,* WT/MIN(01)/DEC/W/1 (Geneva: November 14, 2001), para. 44.

27. Patrick A. Messerlin, "Three Variations on 'the Future of the WTO,'" *Journal of International Economic Law* 8, no. 2 (2005): 307.

28. Bernard Hoekman, "Operationalizing the Concept of Policy Space in the WTO: Beyond Special and Differential Treatment," *Journal of International Economic Law* 8, no. 2 (2005): 422; Wolfe, "Crossing the River by Feeling the Stones," pp. 586–87; Claire Melamed, "Doing 'Development' at the World Trade Organization: The Doha Round and Special and Differential Treatment," *IDS Bulletin* 34, no. 2 (2003): 17–20.

29. Melamed, "Doing 'Development' at the World Trade Organization," pp. 13–17; "U.S., Allies Resist New Obligations in WTO Debate on S&D Provisions," *Inside U.S. Trade,* June 21, 2002.

30. WTO, "Doha Work Programme," para. D1.

31. Panitchpakdi, "Reflections on the Last Three Years of the WTO," p. 372.

32. J. Michael Finger and Philip Schuler, "Developing Countries and the Millennium Round," in *The World Trade Organization Millennium Round: Freer Trade in the Twenty-First Century,* edited by K. G. Deutsch and B. Speyer (London: Routledge, 2001); Hart and Dymond, "Special and Differential Treatment and the Doha 'Development' Round," pp. 407–09.

33. See World Trade Organization, "Governments Pledge CHF 30 Million to Doha Development Agenda Global Trust Fund," News Release 279, March 11, 2002.

34. WTO, "Doha Work Programme," para. D1.

35. Sylvia Ostry, "The World Trading System: In Dire Need of Reform," *Temple International and Comparative Law Journal* 17, no. 1 (2003): 116.

36. "U.S. Official Sees Staged Approach to WTO Investment Talks," *Inside U.S. Trade,* June 14, 2002, p. 1.

37. Panagariya, "Developing Countries at Doha," pp. 1216–18; La Vina and Yu, "From Doha to Cancún," pp. 4, 12; Das, "The Global Trading System," p. 613. On the South's view of a government procurement agreement, see Cohn, *Governing Global Trade,* chaps. 3, 4.

38. WTO, *Doha Ministerial Declaration,* paras. 20, 23, 26, and 27.

39. Amrita Narlikar and Rorden Wilkinson, "Collapse at the WTO: A Cancun Post Mortem," *Third World Quarterly* 25, no. 3 (2004): 417–30; Cho, "A Bridge Too Far," pp. 230–31.

40. WTO, "Doha Work Programme," para. D1.

41. "WTO Framework Leaves Open Major Questions on Singapore Issue," *Inside U.S. Trade*, August 6, 2004.

42. Wolfe, "Crossing the River by Feeling the Stones," p. 584.

43. WTO, "Doha Work Programme," paras. B1–B2; "World Trade: Now Harvest It," *Economist*, August 7, 2004, p. 59.

44. Wolfe, "Crossing the River by Feeling the Stones," pp. 584–85.

45. WTO, "Doha Work Programme," para. E1.

46. Rudolf Adlung and Martin Roy, "Turning Hills into Mountains? Current Commitments under the General Agreement on Trade in Services and Prospects for Change," *Journal of World Trade* 39, no. 6 (2005): 1170.

47. World Trade Organization, "WTO Agriculture Negotiations: The Issues and Where We Are Now" (www.wto.org/english/tratop_e/agric_e/agnegs_bkgrnd_e.pdf [updated December 1, 2004]).

48. Other new groups of developing countries in the Doha Round include a coalition on strategic products and a special safeguard mechanism and a coalition of African states proposing a phaseout of cotton subsidies.

49. Wolfe, "Crossing the River by Feeling the Stones," p. 590.

50. Jacques Delors, "The Future of Europe: Managing Economic and Social Change," in *At the Global Crossroads: The Sylvia Ostry Foundation Lectures* (McGill-Queen's University Press, 2003), p. 25.

51. "Lamy Urges Effort on Trade Talks as Deadline Approaches," *World Trade News*, April 11, 2006.

9

U.S. TRADE POLITICS DURING THE DOHA ROUND

I. M. ("MAC") DESTLER

On July 24, 2006, Pascal Lamy, director-general of the World Trade Organization (WTO), declared the Doha Development Round of global trade talks "suspended" because of the failure of the principal parties to reach agreement on agricultural trade. Then, on November 7, 2006, the domestic political context for U.S. trade was transformed as Democrats won control of the Senate and the House of Representatives in the midterm elections. No longer could President George W. Bush rely on partisan majorities and Republican control of congressional procedures to sustain his trade policy. Thus both abroad and at home, U.S. trade policy was entering a challenging new era.

The preceding years had featured important changes as well. On March 17, 2005, Bush had announced the appointment of Representative Rob Portman (R-Ohio) to serve in the Office of the United States Trade Representative (USTR) during his second term. This designation ended months of anxiety in the trade policy community, which watched as all other cabinet-level positions were filled and no word emerged about this key position. The choice was warmly received: "You couldn't have a person with a better relationship with Congress and the President," declared Benjamin L. Cardin

(D-Md.), ranking Democrat on the House Ways and Means Trade Subcommittee. A trade lawyer before his election to Congress in 1992, Portman easily won Senate confirmation.

Portman succeeded Robert B. Zoellick, who compiled a formidable record of achievement despite having a suboptimal relationship with both Congress and the White House. Neither a confidant of the president nor popular on Capitol Hill, Zoellick still won broad respect for his trade expertise and international negotiating skills. Pursuing a strategy of "competitive liberalization" during his tenure as USTR, Zoellick had negotiated free trade agreements (FTAs) with Singapore, Chile, Australia, Morocco, Central America/Dominican Republic, and Bahrain, with the first four winning easy congressional approval. He also played a key role in launching and advancing the Doha Round of multilateral trade talks under the WTO. Zoellick became deputy secretary of state in the second Bush administration.

His successor inherited a full plate. Record U.S. trade imbalances—worldwide and with China—had heightened congressional concerns about the performance of U.S. trade. Portman's first challenge was to secure congressional approval of the Central American Free Trade Agreement (CAFTA)—actually CAFTA-DR, since its broadening to include the Dominican Republic—which passed narrowly after a very acrimonious debate on Capitol Hill. Decade-long negotiations for a Free Trade Area of the Americas (FTAA) remained stalled, with the January 2005 deadline for agreement now history. Most important for U.S. interests, the Doha Round talks needed major additional attention and effort—including the offering of important new concessions by the United States.

In the fall of 2005 Portman responded to this need with a substantial offer to break the deadlock in the Doha agricultural negotiations and with an impressive performance at the December 2005 WTO Ministerial Meeting in Hong Kong. But other major trader states met him less than halfway, and Doha remained in jeopardy when President Bush, desperate to reinvigorate his flagging administration, announced in April 2006 that he was moving Portman from the trade office to the key position of director of the Office of Management and Budget.[1] Chosen to replace Portman was Deputy USTR Susan Schwab, a seasoned trade professional with senior staff experience on Capitol Hill.

Both Portman and Schwab undertook their responsibilities in a U.S. trade policy environment that had changed in fundamental ways over the past fifteen years.

Where's the New Protectionism?

In the 1980s, driven by a strong dollar, the U.S. merchandise trade deficit soared to unprecedented, twelve-digit dimensions. Industry after industry was hit and demanded new trade protection: textiles, steel, autos, shoes, machine tools, semiconductors, and so on. The Reagan administration resisted to some degree but also granted some form of trade relief to most of them.

The trade deficit receded late in that decade, facilitating compromises in (and enactment of) comprehensive trade legislation in 1988. The trade deficit dropped below U.S.$100 billion in 1991 and 1992 and then grew slowly through 1997. Thereafter it skyrocketed—from U.S.$198.1 billion in 1997 to U.S.$452.4 billion in 2000 and U.S.$782.0 billion in 2005.[2] In that year, the United States imported U.S.$1.674 trillion in goods and exported just U.S.$892.0 billion.

In absolute terms, this latest U.S. trade deficit dwarfed the U.S.$159.6 billion that had triggered so much anxiety in 1987. But total U.S. trade had soared also, roughly tripling between 1987 and 2000. As a proportion of trade, the deficit was comparable in those years: 24.0 percent in 1987, 23.0 percent in 2000. But it reached a new peak of 30.0 percent in 2005, meaning that the country imported more than U.S.$9 in goods for every U.S.$5 that it exported. As a proportion of GDP, the deficits of the early twenty-first century also came to exceed their counterparts in the 1980s, reaching a record 6.2 percent in 2005.

These trade deficits are a macroeconomic phenomenon, and the proximate causes vary.[3] Throughout, they have reflected the disagreeable fact that U.S. citizens are saving too little and consuming more than they are producing. But such lofty macroeconomic explanations have been no consolation to U.S.-based goods producers, who have felt the heat all along. And for them, the new deficits are at least comparable to those of the 1980s.

Yet the domestic political response to the more recent ballooning of the U.S. deficit has been very different. In the first period, multiple industries sought protection, Congress seized the initiative in trade policy, and many experts trembled over whether the open U.S. trade regime could survive. In the second period, only one important dog barked—the steel industry. It had won comprehensive (if temporary) protection under Reagan in 1985 in the form of a number of export restraint agreements with key producers. It won no such protection under Clinton (aside from a number of antidumping cases), and just twenty-one months of relief from the current Bush administration, which imposed tariffs on a range of steel products in March 2002 but removed them in December 2003, after the WTO ruled them illegal.

Antidumping cases have continued in the 2000s, but they haven't increased, and half of them continue to be initiated by the steel industry. The textile industry has certainly not become a free trade bastion. But with the phasing out of the Multi Fiber Arrangement at the end of 2004, its stance has shifted from limiting imports in general to maximizing the share of apparel imports made with fiber and cloth manufactured in the United States.[4]

Why weren't more injured claimants demanding and receiving import relief after 1995? One reason was certainly the overall strength of the U.S. economy compared with that of the mid 1980s: in the midst of economic prosperity and sound growth, campaigns for trade relief were harder to sustain. Another reason was the fading of Japan as the prime trade "adversary" of U.S. producers (though China seemed poised to take its place). But there was also precious little new business protectionism after the stock market bubble burst in 2000 and the economy entered into recession at the outset of the George W. Bush years.

Why has there not been more demand for new trade protection? The basic answer lies in what is commonly labeled *globalization,* the deepening international integration of the U.S. economy over recent decades. Goods production has in fact declined as a share of the total economy, from 43 percent in 1970 to 35 percent in 2000. But over the same period, trade in goods has grown from 4 percent to 10 percent of GDP.[5] Thus the ratio of trade (average of imports and exports) to goods production has risen even faster, from .09 to .29. Producers are exporting a larger share of their output and importing a larger share of their products' final value. And those who lag in exploiting the gains from international specialization face uphill competition from those who have learned to successfully exploit them.

In the context of a globalizing economy, a pure protectionist position becomes much harder for an industry to maintain, and support for open markets is easier to find. When in late 2003 the Bush trade team weighed how to respond to the WTO's finding that U.S. steel tariffs violated international trade rules, press reports highlighted the concerns of steel-user industries in key electoral states as much as they stressed the steel-producing interests in Pennsylvania, West Virginia, and Ohio. And the White House took the steel users' interests fully into account in its decision to remove the tariffs.

There remained entrenched pockets of protection, of course, most of them in the agricultural sector. The farm bill enacted in 2002 flew in the face of long-standing U.S. trade negotiating goals by increasing producer subsidies. Sugar survived under an import quota system that renders U.S. prices a multiple of those in the global market and makes domestic producers of corn sweetener competitive. Orange juice was another well-protected market that Brazil clamored to enter. The rigidity of the U.S. stance on sugar was made evident during various trade negotiations under way in 2004: Central America was granted minimal increased sugar access under CAFTA, and Australia was granted none at all in its FTA with the United States.

Lack of agreement over trade in both sugar and oranges has impeded the conclusion of a comprehensive FTAA agreement, and U.S. cotton subsidies have undercut the livelihoods of African farmers and helped trigger the breakup of the Cancún Ministerial of the Doha Round. In the spring of 2004 a WTO panel held that U.S. cotton subsidies were in excess of those allowed under the Uruguay Round agreements (a finding later affirmed by the appellate body).

These still-restricted U.S. markets remain barriers both to trade and to progress in trade negotiations, but they are now outliers in the overall U.S. economy. As recently as the 1980s it was plausible to argue that the threat of generalized, 1930's type protection was real and that concessions to one or two new industries could put the United States on a slippery slope. In the twenty-first century it is much harder to make this argument, as U.S. business is predominantly on the side of open trade.

Why, then, don't market-opening bills sail through Congress? The basic reason is that U.S. politics has become increasingly polarized along party lines, and this polarization has spread to trade policy (which was traditionally managed by a bipartisan, centrist coalition).

The Partisan Divide

In recent decades partisan polarization and interparty rancor has steadily, even relentlessly, grown in the U.S. Congress, in the House of Representatives in particular. This cleavage has been driven by broad national forces not directly related to trade policy. But it has undercut one of the enduring sources of support for trade liberalization: bipartisan leadership cooperation at the committee and chamber level.

Since 1981 the *National Journal,* a respected newsweekly focusing on government, has published sophisticated voter ratings placing every member of Congress on the ideological spectrum from liberal to conservative. The general pattern in the early years of these ratings was for most Democrats to cluster on the left side and Republicans on the right, with considerable overlap in the middle. By 1999, however, "for the first time" in the Senate, "every Democrat had an average score that was to the left of the most liberal Republican." In the House, moreover, *NJ* found that "only two Republicans . . . were in that chamber's more-liberal half on each of the three issue areas. . . . And only two Democrats . . . ranked in the more-conservative half."[6] Since then, the pattern has stayed essentially the same: two House Republicans (and no Democrats) met that criterion in 2004; just one Republican senator was more liberal than just one Democratic senator the same year.[7] Parallel data developed by political scientists underscore the same trend. In 1969–70, as noted by Sarah Binder, there was "substantial overlap between Democrats' and Republicans' right- and left-most members." A "large ideological middle dominate[d] the House." "Thirty years later, there is virtually no ideological common ground."[8]

Contrary to frequent press reporting, the polarization of Congress does not reflect a deep ideological divide among the public at large. Americans remain basically centrist: in 2004, at the end of a particularly contentious presidential election campaign, 71 percent of survey respondents described themselves as being in the ideological middle.[9] Morris Fiorina demolishes the "myth of a polarized America" in a brilliant short book that gives particular attention to the divisive issues of abortion and homosexuality. Most citizens are ambivalent about these and other public issues, in Republican as well as Democratic states. We have, he concludes, "centrist voters and polarizing elites," and the latter have taken control of the political process in what he labels "the hijacking of American democracy."[10]

Why has Congress come to reflect the polarized elite activists rather than the centrist public? One powerful force has been regular congressional redistricting. Once the Supreme Court ruled in the 1960s that congressional districts within a state have to have substantially equal populations, the lines have had to be redrawn after each decennial census. Politicians naturally shaped this process with an eye toward their own survival. This meant more "safe" districts (strongly Republican or Democratic) and fewer competitive districts. In a competitive district, candidates fight for the votes of the citizens in the center, so the representative is driven toward courting the median voter. In a one-party-dominant district, candidates are virtually assured of reelection provided they can win renomination. So candidate priorities have shifted toward maintaining the allegiance of at least the median party member in the congressional district if not the median *activist* party member in the district, both of which move the candidate away from the center.

Within the House, partisan polarization has had a major impact on how legislative business is conducted. Through most of the post–World War II period, committees dominated the process of developing and enacting legislation. The majority party ran them, but committee chairs reached for bipartisan support to improve the prospects for final passage. As parties became more ideological, however, the pattern changed. Increasingly, congressional party caucuses got into the business of shaping legislation. This was bound to cause problems for trade policy, which was politically dependent on strong, broad-based, bipartisan support in the Senate Finance and the House Ways and Means Committees. Traditionally, bills authorizing and implementing major trade agreements were worked out in subcommittees and full committees. Lopsided, bipartisan committee votes in favor of such bills paved the way for lesser, but solid, majorities in their parent chambers. And their strong role made these committees effective partners and interlocutors for successive U.S. trade representatives.

Cross-party, committee-based policy collaboration remained the congressional norm on trade well after it was fading in other policy spheres. The NAFTA battle was won through close collaboration between the Clinton White House and congressional leaders of both parties, with Republican whip Newt Gingrich (R-Ga.) and former senior Ways and Means member Bill Frenzel (R-Minn.) playing important roles. Increasingly, however, there were also occasions when Ways and Means Democrats excluded Republicans from important trade policy meetings (including the drafting of language to implement the Uruguay Round antidumping agreement in 1994).

Partisanship in the House became yet more intense when the Republicans took control following the 1994 election. House Speaker Newt Gingrich centralized policymaking and the selection of committee chairs, which were thereby pressed to respond first and foremost to party interests. On trade, partisan divisions were furthered by the commitment of unions, grassroots activists, and nongovernment organizations (NGOs) to the inclusion of labor and environmental standards in trade agreements. Democrats, who were most beholden to these constituencies, wanted such standards to be major negotiating objectives in authorizing legislation, particularly for bilateral and regional agreements; Republicans sought to exclude or minimize them on the grounds that such standards encroached too much on business and that trade agreements were not the proper venue for pursuing these objectives. This difference led Ways and Means Republicans under chairman Bill Archer (R-Tex.) to put together their own fast-track renewal proposal in 1995, while

Democrats stayed on the sidelines, and to add changes to President Bill Clinton's 1997 fast-track renewal proposal designed to limit the inclusion of these issues under fast-track procedures.[11]

Bipartisanship made a modest comeback in 2000, in the struggle over granting normal trade status to the People's Republic of China upon its entry into the WTO. This was Clinton's last major trade priority. It had enormous business support and won by a relatively comfortable margin of 237 to 197, with seventy-three Democrats in favor. Overall, however, broader polarization continued in the House, with the result that committee members came to see their colleagues across the aisle not as colleagues but as antagonists.

Against this backdrop, it was hardly surprising that bitter interparty conflict reemerged in 2001, when the Bush administration sought renewal of fast-track authority (which it renamed trade promotion authority). This legislation, essential for major trade talks, authorizes the president to submit bills implementing trade agreements to Congress for up-or-down votes, without amendments. Two senior Ways and Means Committee Democrats, Charles Rangel (ranking member, D-N.Y.) and Sandy Levin (ranking trade subcommittee member, D-Mich.), made it clear that they wanted to work with the majority to develop a compromise bill. But the new, assertive committee chair, Bill Thomas (R-Calif.), decided instead to negotiate a "bipartisan" bill with a group of more junior Democrats led by Cal Dooley (D-Calif.). Rangel and Levin then led the bulk of their colleagues into opposition, urged on by organized labor and antiglobalist NGOs.

This led to the closest, bitterest, and most partisan vote on a major trade bill since World War II: legislation on Trade Promotion Authority (TPA) passed 215 to 214, with just twenty-one Democrats in favor and twenty-three Republicans against. When the initial tally indicated defeat for the legislation, House Speaker Dennis Hastert held the vote open for twenty extra minutes, until a South Carolina Republican changed from nay to aye in exchange for a promise to tighten rules-of-origin on textiles from the Andean region and the Caribbean.[12]

In the Senate, by contrast, there was constructive bipartisan compromise, with Democrats winning a major expansion of trade adjustment assistance for workers displaced by trade. This assistance included

—A new health insurance subsidy for eligible workers

—Coverage, for the first time, of "secondary workers" (producers of inputs to trade-impacted final goods) and of certain workers who lost their jobs due to relocation of plants overseas

—A new, alternative program of "wage insurance" for trade-displaced workers taking lower-paying jobs

—A doubling of the funds authorized for worker retraining.[13]

With this addition, the legislation passed the Senate by a comfortable 66 to 30 vote. But although the bill emerged from conference with an expansion of trade adjustment assistance included, this only increased the House margin from 1 vote to 3 votes (215 to 212) and the number of favorable Democratic votes from 21 to 25.

The bill became law in August 2002. But winning this way was costly for trade policy. Since the House victory was built on a number of Republicans voting against their convictions and their constituencies, it cast doubt on the USTR's ability to win approval of controversial trade agreements in the future. And it inflated the power of those entrenched interests (like steel or sugar producers) that were determined to resist liberalization of their markets.

Competitive Liberalization

Still, for USTR Robert Zoellick, winning in this way was certainly better than not getting TPA legislation at all. He played a lesser role in lobbying for trade authority than had most of his predecessors, as congressional relations were not his forte. Rather, Zoellick's strengths were on the international bargaining side, where he more than held his own. For example, at the November 2001 WTO Ministerial Conference in Doha, Qatar, he was effective on both substance and tactics, making a U.S. concession early in the meeting to include trade remedy laws in the negotiating agenda and then joining with developing nations to strengthen the language on agriculture in the face of resistance from the European Union (EU). Not only did Zoellick play a critical role in launching the new global trade talks, he was also, as discussed below, a major player in both the problems and the progress of the Doha Round in 2003 and 2004.

Zoellick's main immediate use of the newly granted TPA, however, was the negotiation of a series of bilateral and regional FTAs. His predecessors had also pursued such deals, beginning with the U.S.-Israel and U.S.-Canada FTAs negotiated in the 1980s; these FTAs were seen both as an end in themselves for U.S. trade policy and as a means to generate pressure for concessions on global talks by signaling that the United States would pursue alternative routes if global trade talks failed. The final Uruguay Round/WTO compromise of December 1993, in fact, owed something to House passage of the NAFTA implementing legislation in November, followed immediately by Clinton's hosting the first summit meeting of leaders of the Asia-Pacific Economic Cooperation (APEC) forum in Seattle.

Zoellick expanded on this record, explicitly including political and strategic criteria in the choice of partner nations. The U.S.-Jordan FTA, completed under Clinton, was approved before TPA's enactment, but two deals initiated by Clinton (with Singapore and with Chile) were signed in early 2003 and brought up under the new TPA. (Chile had been promised such a deal since the Miami hemispheric summit of 1994, but the lapse of fast-track authority delayed the initiation of talks.) FTAs with Australia and Morocco were completed thereafter and were approved by Congress in July 2004. CAFTA was completed in late 2003, and the Dominican Republic was added in 2004 (CAFTA-DR). Talks were also initiated or ongoing with others, including Bahrain, the states of Southern Africa, Thailand, Panama, and the Andean countries of Colombia, Peru, Ecuador, and Bolivia. Finally, the Bush administration declared a long-term goal of creating a Middle East Free Trade Area.

Zoellick enveloped these initiatives in a broader strategy. In his own words, by combining global, regional, and bilateral negotiations, "the United States is creating a competition in liberalization, placing America at the heart of a network of initiatives to open markets." We will, he said, "proceed with countries that are ready" to open their markets, and success will create pressure on others.[14] Hence, in his view, FTAs were stepping stones to broader liberalization. Moreover, most FTAs were relatively popular with Congress and hence useful for muting partisan divisions. Finally, the success of the USTR in concluding this geographically diverse set of FTAs buttressed Zoellick's standing within the Bush administration. Zoellick was not a White House insider, nor was he close to the president; therefore, whatever credibility he achieved had to come from visible results. With the hemispheric FTAA talks flagging, and the Doha Round proceeding by fits and starts, bilateral deals kept his trade vessel afloat.

There was some skepticism about whether these specific FTAs provided leverage for broader negotiations. Deals with Latin nations might conceivably exert some leverage on Brazil, whose disagreements with the United States had become the prime obstacle to completion of the hemisphere-wide FTAA. But it was implausible that CAFTA-DR, for example, could generate the same pressure for progress on the Doha Round in the first decade of the twenty-first century that NAFTA and APEC had exerted on the EU at the close of the Uruguay Round in 1993, for the Central American nations were far less important in U.S. and world trade.[15] And while the domestic politics of securing congressional support for FTAs with smaller countries where U.S. trade was modest (Chile) or noncontroversial (Singapore) might be smoother, it was another matter for deals involving countries whose labor practices touched hot buttons in American trade politics. Hence CAFTA-DR, completed before the Australia or Morocco deals, was not brought to Congress until after the 2004 elections.

Cancún and Geneva

Whatever the trade and political benefits of FTAs, Zoellick realized that the completion of the WTO's Doha Round was paramount. Only in global talks could U.S. agriculture win major new market access, and only from its large trading partners could the U.S. economy add to its already considerable gains from economic openness. Only a substantial WTO deal on nonagricultural market access and services offered the possibility of reenergizing the protrade business coalition in the United States.

But the WTO was now an organization of 149 members, operating by consensus. And emerging economies like Brazil, India, Russia, and China were no longer willing to defer to the U.S.-EU duopoly that had historically prevailed over prior GATT trade rounds. Emerging economies were disappointed, they said, with their gains from the Uruguay Round, and they were upset by the rise in U.S. steel tariffs and the protectionist Farm Bill of 2002, which directly contradicted U.S. trade rhetoric in support of liberalization.

This more fractious global trade politics became manifest when, in preparation for the WTO's Cancún Ministerial Conference of September 2003, Zoellick struck a deal with his EU counterpart, Pascal Lamy, that committed to modest reductions in farm subsidies on both sides of the Atlantic. Emerging economies reacted suspiciously and refused to accept it as a basis for negotiation. Instead, Brazil joined with India and China in forming the Group of Twenty-One to demand deeper reductions in agricultural subsidies from the United States and the EU.[16] Then in the midst of the Cancún Ministerial Conference, a so-called Group of Ninety, driven by the concerns of African nations and egged on by activist NGOs, made more sweeping demands, including the immediate removal of U.S. cotton subsidies. Cancún was supposed to bring agreement, not on the final terms of the Doha Round but on the modalities, or ground rules, under which they would be hammered out. Instead, it ended in complete disarray, as the Mexican chair and host, seeing no prospect of compromise, gaveled the meeting to a close.

Initial reactions were sharp. Zoellick denounced the emerging economies in question as "can't do" nations (a label with some credibility because the G21 and G90 nations had shown little readiness to offer concessions themselves). His EU counterpart, Pascal Lamy, labeled the WTO process medieval. But the Cancún collapse did raise a broader question: Could the institutions of liberal trade be maintained in a world in which economic power no longer resided overwhelmingly in the exclusive G7 club? By early 2004, however, tempers had cooled. Zoellick took steps to relaunch Doha discussions, working with both developed and developing nations and traveling to sub-Saharan Africa to facilitate compromise with (and among) the G90. A new group of five political entities—the United States, the European Union, Brazil, India, and Australia—helped to shepherd this process.

On August 1, 2004, following round-the-clock negotiations, WTO members reached agreement on what was labeled the July package: a document combining substantive and procedural accords on agriculture (and specifically cotton), nonagricultural market access, services, trade facilitation, and a range of development-related issues. Particularly notable was the commitment to end export subsidies for farm products. The talks, it appeared, were back on track, even if an actual Doha Round agreement remained a long way off. The original Doha deadline had been set for December 2004, but the various disruptions delayed the target date for substantial agreement until the Hong Kong WTO Ministerial of December 2005.[17]

In the meantime, U.S. trade authorities were coping with some losses in WTO dispute settlement cases. Like other nations, the United States did very well when it took other nations to this global trade "court." Twenty-two of the cases the USTR brought before the WTO as of December 31, 2004, were litigated to completion, and eighteen were decided in favor of the United States.[18] This added up to an impressive 82 percent overall success rate. But the United States was submitting fewer cases: under Bush, three a year, versus eleven a year under Clinton. Although U.S. submissions were lower, the frequency of cases filed against the United States increased from about eight a year under Clinton to nearly ten a year in the first four years of the George W. Bush administration.

In those cases in which the United States was the defendant, it was U.S. law or practice that was usually found wanting. In 74 percent (twenty-five of thirty-four) of WTO panel or appellate body decisions reached by January 2005, the United States was found in violation of its trade obligations.[19] Prominent among these were a European challenge to the U.S. system of subsidizing exports through favorable tax treatment, a U.S. law banning imports of shrimp not caught with turtle-excluder devices, and President

Bush's decision in 2002 to impose section 201 (escape clause) safeguards on certain imports of steel.[20]

In the bulk of these cases, the United States complied with the adverse decision, although it often took time, especially if legislation was required. The most prominent exception as of the end of 2004 was the Byrd Amendment, which channeled the proceeds of antidumping duties to the coffers of the petitioners. The WTO authorized petitioning countries to levy penalty duties against U.S. products until the law was changed.[21]

From "Bob" to "Rob"—and Beyond

As the first term of President Bush came to an end, he and Zoellick could claim a creditable trade record. New authorizing legislation had been enacted, and a number of FTAs were concluded or in progress. Negotiations for an FTAA were stalled, but the Doha talks were alive and making some progress. Moreover, the president reversed his most protectionist act when he removed the steel tariffs in December 2003, and he maintained a free trade posture through the reelection campaign that followed. His opponent in the 2004 presidential race, John F. Kerry, complained about "outsourcing" of production and jobs by "Benedict Arnold corporations" during the Democratic primary campaign, but he did not press the issue once he had secured the Democratic nomination.

In the months after Bush's November 2004 election victory, however, trade seemed to disappear from the White House policy agenda. The USTR position went unaddressed, as the president replaced (or reaffirmed) all other members of his cabinet and as he announced the nomination of Zoellick to be deputy to the new secretary of state, Condoleezza Rice. Trade went unmentioned in the president's state of the union address, which centered on his proposal to restructure the Social Security retirement system. Anxiety over this high-level neglect spread within the U.S. trade policy community. Reports circulated that Bush might act to terminate the USTR's cabinet-level status. A president supposedly committed to free trade seemed to be undermining the institution with the statutory responsibility to pursue it.

On March 17, 2005, Bush moved to put an end to these concerns. In choosing Representative Rob Portman (R-Ohio), he named someone with whom he had personal ties, who had trade policy experience, and who had good relations with legislators of both political parties. The appointment in fact suggested a return to the long-standing USTR model and role. Portman could be expected to act as a policy broker at home and a negotiator abroad.

While the House leadership as a whole was acting more partisan than ever, a thaw on trade policy now seemed possible within the House Ways and Means Committee.[22] Its senior Democrats had voted for all four FTAs that came before Congress in 2003 and 2004. Moreover, its Subcommittee on Trade had a new chairman, Clay Shaw of Florida, and a new ranking Democrat, Ben Cardin of Maryland, both of whom were moderates within their respective parties.

The major trade business of 2005, however, was CAFTA-DR, a particularly controversial agreement because of the labor practices of the Central American countries and what critics saw as inadequate provisions to address them; in particular, CAFTA did not commit these countries to enforce core labor standards as defined by the International Labor Organization.

In June 2005, before the CAFTA vote, the House rejected a resolution calling for U.S. withdrawal from the WTO—just thirty-nine Republicans and forty-six Democrats voted in favor.[23] And at the end of that month, TPA was granted an automatic two-year extension, making July 1, 2007, the new deadline for agreements that would receive expedited legislative consideration.[24] Neither issue was seriously contested.

CAFTA was another matter entirely. Organized labor went all out in opposition, joined by NGOs that saw the agreement as exploiting workers and peasants for the benefit of multinational business. Portman reached out to Democrats, but with his late start he couldn't crack the basic partisan pattern. The House Democratic leadership pressed for a maximum negative vote, angry at the Republicans' systematic exclusion of their party from legislative influence across the board and thinking that this was a vote they might actually win. They didn't, but they forced the Bush administration and House Republican leaders to spend major political capital (and, apparently, substantial public funds) to win over undecided compatriots. In the end, their July 2005 victory was a less frantic replication of the fight over TPA in December 2001: the final count was 217 to 215, with only fifteen Democrats in favor but three additional Republicans available just in case.[25]

Portman was pleased with the victory but unhappy about the manner of its achievement. Calling the CAFTA-DR legislative process "a train wreck not of my own making," he reached out immediately to senior Ways and Means Democrats, anxious to restore communications. And by early 2006 it was clear that Republican discipline was eroding with the emergence of differences within the rank and file and with the departure—amid fundraising and lobbying scandals—of the Texas representative who had made it all work, Majority Leader Tom "The Hammer" DeLay. Meanwhile, Bill

Thomas, the highly effective and highly partisan Ways and Means chairman, announced he would be leaving the House at the end of the year.

So Portman faced not only a formidable domestic challenge but also the opportunity to rebuild bipartisan support for trade policy at a time when interparty rancor was beginning, finally, to self-destruct. But his biggest political challenge was international: completion of the Doha Round. Zoellick had helped keep it alive, but negotiators had missed every deadline. When Portman took over, the new target for a breakthrough was the Hong Kong Ministerial Conference of December 2005. The WTO was energized by the election of a dynamic new leader, Pascal Lamy of France and the EU. In an effort to propel the talks forward, Portman tabled a new U.S. proposal to curb farm subsidies. This was bold enough to be well received internationally without going so far as to undermine domestic support. But the EU negotiator, Peter Mandelson, had less negotiating leeway, and though his response went far enough to prevent a rupture in the talks, it was insufficient to move them onto firm new ground. Portman did, however, make a solid impression at Hong Kong. As reported in the *Financial Times,*

> The US trade representative was widely acclaimed as the star of this, his first WTO ministerial meeting. Many participants were impressed by his effortless command of his brief, political astuteness, polished delivery and boyish charm. . . . The US is often accused of bullying and heavy-handed tactics at WTO meetings, which have made it the main target of attacks by other, particularly developing, countries. In Hong Kong, however, Portman's light touch helped disarm US critics, even in regard to highly emotive issues such as its trade-distorting cotton subsidies. Whatever the fate of the Doha round, his performance seems likely to enhance his political stature, in Washington as well as internationally.[26]

Like Zoellick before him, Portman had the international and domestic leverage gained from TPA. And like Zoellick, he was pursuing bilateral as well as global deals. Of particular importance was the launching in February 2006 of FTA talks with Korea, a major U.S. trading partner. But the Doha Round remained the central challenge for U.S. trade policy and U.S. trade politics. The FTAA was bound to fall further behind schedule, but a Doha success on agriculture remained the most promising route toward the eventual completion of a hemispheric agreement. Brazil, in particular, wanted market access concessions on sensitive products like sugar, citrus, and cotton. The United States was unlikely to make these in the regional context, because it would need agricultural market gains beyond the hemisphere, above all from the European Union.

As WTO members moved toward the new make-or-break negotiating event—the July 2006 talks at Geneva—the United States changed its trade leader once again. The U.S. trade baton passed from the former representative (Portman, now elevated to director of the president's Office of Management and Budget) to trade policy veteran Susan C. Schwab. Nominated in April 2006, and readily confirmed by the Senate in June, she took on the daunting task of salvaging what experts increasingly saw as a negotiation destined for failure. To avert this outcome, the WTO director-general, Pascal Lamy, talked privately with each member of the Group of Six leading the negotiations, asking what it would be prepared to offer if others made substantial reciprocal moves. But he found the responses insufficient, and when nothing new was put on the table in Geneva, he declared the talks suspended. In a press conference immediately thereafter, Schwab said that the U.S. delegation had a mandate from President Bush to go further, but "most of our trading partners showed up with exactly the same positions they had two, three weeks ago." Since others had not responded in kind to Portman's earlier offer, she saw no benefit in putting forward another one, declaring that "the United States cannot be in a position of negotiating with ourselves."[27]

History is reassuring on global trade talks; it suggests that they typically falter in midcourse but bring constructive, positive-sum, trade-liberalizing compromises in the end. It also suggests they take longer and longer: five years for the Kennedy Round of the 1960s, six years for the Tokyo Round of the 1970s, and seven years plus for the Uruguay Round of the late 1980s and early 1990s. Eight years for the completion of Doha would put us in 2009, after yet another U.S. presidential election and well beyond the period authorized by current U.S. law.

That law required formal agreement by mid-2007 and, therefore, substantive agreement early in that year. As of late 2006 this was no longer possible—unless the United States acceded to a Doha "lite" outcome, which it had long steadfastly resisted. The alternative was to secure an extension of TPA from the new, Democratic-controlled 110th Congress.[28] Speaking in the wake of his party's election triumph, Ways and Means Committee chair-to-be Charles Rangel declared himself open to bipartisan cooperation on trade. He spent the opening months of 2007 negotiating with USTR Schwab (and new ranking Ways and Means Republican Jim McCrery [R-La.]) new legislative language for bilateral FTAs more friendly to Democrats' concerns. Above all, this included commitments to the core labor standards embodied in the International Labor Organization's Declaration on Fundamental Principles and Rights at Work, adopted by international consensus in June 1998. If agreement were reached, this language would be in the bilateral FTAs already negotiated with Peru, Panama, and Colombia.

On Doha, interparty differences were not so sharp. But for an extension of TPA to gain sufficient domestic support to pass in this Congress, U.S. business would have to see a substantial, beneficial Doha deal on the horizon—including new access to both goods and services markets within emerging economic powerhouses like Brazil and India. There is very little sympathy in the United States for special and differential treatment insofar as this applies to such advanced developing countries. As the United States sees it, if these big emerging markets want to get, they will have to give.

But the United States will have to give as well. On the wish lists of U.S. trading partners are not just farm subsidies and cotton, orange juice, and sugar but also the reform of antidumping laws and the movement of persons. And any changes in U.S. farm support programs have to be coordinated between the extension of TPA and the renewal of agriculture legislation likely to come up around the same time. To make U.S. market-opening concessions possible, the USTR will have to build a domestic coalition of potential winners such that it can beat the well-fortified redoubts of protection in legislative battle. To make it worth the winners' while, Schwab will need to work with a broad group of nations committed to major Doha results.

In hopes that this might yet be possible, Schwab consulted actively with potential allies in the aftermath of the July breakup, flying twice to Brazil and once to Argentina. She also accompanied the president to the November 2006 Hanoi meeting of the APEC Forum, where the United States proposed the launch of negotiations for a Free Trade Area of the Asia Pacific (FTAAP). The hope, in part, was that the threat of such a group would make players like the EU, Brazil, and India more flexible in their Doha Round positions. The result was a modest victory for Bush. The final communiqué called on members to "undertake further studies on ways and means to promote regional economic integration, including a Free Trade Area of the Asia Pacific as a long-term prospect, and report to the 2007 APEC Economic Leaders' Meeting in Australia."[29]

But the challenges remain formidable. In spite of Schwab's talents, a weakened Bush administration and the complexities that impede the completion of Doha will be difficult to overcome, even if the goal remains well worth the pursuit.

Notes

1. The position was vacant because of Bush's designation of its director, Josh Bolten, to be his new White House chief of staff.

2. Throughout this chapter the focus is on the U.S. trade balance in goods, not the overall balance in goods and services now highlighted by the Department of Commerce nor the still broader balance on current account. The reason is that trade policy is still mostly about goods (though services have undeniably grown in importance), so that the products of farms and factories (and their producers) have dominated the trade policy process.

3. In the late 1990s a strong dollar and a surge in investment demand precipitated capital inflows and the Asian financial crisis that dampened exports. By 2003 the new Bush budget deficit was playing a role, as had Reagan's in the 1980s.

4. For comprehensive treatment, see Craig VanGrasstek, *U.S. Policy in Textile and Apparel Trade: From Managed Protection to Managed Liberalization* (Washington: Washington Trade Reports, 2003).

5. Trade here is the average of exports and imports $(X + M)/2$. Properly speaking, trade/GDP and trade/goods production should be seen as ratios, not percentages, since trade statistics represent final value of goods bought and sold, and GDP and goods production represent just value added in the United States. (All statistics are calculated from *Economic Report of the President,* 2004, tables B-1, B-8, and B-13.)

6. Richard E. Cohen, "Going to Extremes: Our Annual Vote Ratings," special supplement, *National Journal,* February 26, 2000, p. 4. One of the two Democratic outliers left the party in 2000; one of the two Republicans was defeated for reelection in 2002.

7. *National Journal,* February 12, 2005, pp. 427 and 440–54.

8. Sarah A. Binder, *Stalemate: Causes and Consequences of Legislative Gridlock* (Brookings, 2003), pp. 23–24.

9. As it has for over thirty years, the National Election Survey, based at the University of Michigan, asked 2004 voters the following question: "When it comes to politics do you usually think of yourself as extremely liberal, liberal, slightly liberal, moderate or middle of the road, slightly conservative, conservative, extremely conservative, or haven't you thought much about this?" A total of 71 percent either chose one of the three middle categories or said they hadn't thought about it (www.umich.edu/~nes/nesguide/toptable/tab3_1.htm).

10. Morris P. Fiorina with Samuel J. Abrams and Jeremy C. Pope, *Culture War? The Myth of a Polarized America* (New York: Pearson Longman, 2005); quotations on pp. 78 and 99.

11. After this proposal failed to win a House majority, Gingrich infuriated Democrats by bringing it up for a vote a year later, even though it had no chance to pass, in order to put a political squeeze on Democrats. In response to this, senior Ways and Means Democrat Robert Matsui (D-Calif.), long a stalwart free trader, moved to the opposition camp.

12. For the detailed story, see I. M. Destler, *American Trade Politics,* 4th ed. (Washington: Peterson Institute for International Economics, 2005), appendix A.

13. Lori G. Kletzer and Howard Rosen, "Easing the Adjustment Burden on US Workers," in *The United States and the World Economy,* edited by C. Fred Bergsten (Washington: Peterson Institute for International Economics, 2005), pp. 319–20. Rosen played a key role in developing an expansion of trade adjustment assistance legislation.

14. "Remarks by Ambassador Robert B. Zoellick, Phoenix, April 30, 2002" (Washington: Office of the U.S. Trade Representative, 2002), p. 81.

15. For a comprehensive review of the pros and cons, see Jeffrey J. Schott, ed., *Free Trade Agreements: US Strategies and Priorities* (Washington: Peterson Institute for International Economics, 2004).

16. Membership varied, so the group is sometimes referred to as the G20/21 and sometimes as the G22.

17. For details see Jeffrey J. Schott, "Confronting Current Challenges to US Trade Policy," in *The United States and the World Economy,* edited by C. Fred Bergsten (Washington: Peterson Institute for International Economics, 2005).

18. Cases submitted separately but reviewed together are here counted as single cases (for example, three linked cases against the EU's import regime for bananas). If such cases were counted individually, the United States won twenty-two and lost six, a success rate of 79 percent. This excludes twenty-five (twenty-seven) that were negotiated, nine that are pending, and fourteen (sixteen) that are inactive.

19. If cases were counted individually (for example, the eight separate country filings in 2002 against U.S. steel safeguards), the United States won nine and lost thirty-seven, or 80 percent of WTO cases that were litigated to completion. Excluded are fourteen (sixteen) cases that were negotiated, seventeen that are pending, and nine that are inactive.

20. The Bush administration reported, in mid-2004, an overall WTO won-lost record of thirteen to ten (56 percent) during its tenure and eighteen to fifteen (54 percent) during the Clinton years. (See "Real Results: Leveling the Playing Field for American Workers and Farmers," news release, Office of the U.S. Trade Representative, July 8, 2004.)

21. The Byrd Amendment was finally repealed in January 2006, but the effective date was put off until October 1, 2007.

22. In the fall of 2004, Speaker Dennis Hastert refused to let the conference report on a major intelligence reorganization bill go to the House floor for a vote because, in spite of strong opposition from the Republican caucus, it clearly would have passed (further, President Bush supported it). What should govern, Hastert implied, was not the majority of the House but the majority of House *Republicans.* Eventually, prominent critics were mollified, and the bill was enacted.

23. This was the result of a provision authored by none other than free trader Newt Gingrich who, faced with an anti-WTO primary appointment in 1994, had gotten a provision added to the Uruguay Round implementing legislation providing for such a resolution to be voted on every five years. In 2000 just fifty-six members of the House had backed it: thirty-three Republicans, twenty-one Democrats, and two Independents.

24. TPA legislation enacted in 2002 provided for such an extension if the president sought it and neither the House nor the Senate voted against it. For a negative vote to occur, moreover, the House Ways and Means Committee or the Senate Finance Committee would have to report a negative resolution to the floor. Neither did so, and the authority was therefore extended by inaction. In 1991, under an identical provision in the 1988 trade law, both committees reported out such resolutions with a negative recommendation, and they were defeated. However, the committees used administration concern over the forthcoming votes as leverage to extract policy commitments from the first Bush administration. In 2005 neither committee was inclined to use this process for oversight purposes.

25. The vote was 214 to 211 when time expired. But according to one who was in the room with the leadership, the Republicans wanted 217 votes in favor and also to allow the maximum number of colleagues to vote their constituencies. So they held six on-the-fence members in abeyance until the final Democrat voted nay, had three of these Republicans vote aye, and then let the three most politically vulnerable off the hook. Such was the power of party discipline that twenty-five of the thirty-nine Republicans who voted to withdraw from the WTO in June voted in favor of CAFTA in July. On the other side of the aisle, the fifteen pro-CAFTA Democrats represented the smallest Democratic support ever for a trade agreement.

26. Guy de Jonquières and Frances Williams, "The Diverse Styles of the Figures on WTO's Stage," *Financial Times,* December 18, 2005.

27. "Evening Press Availability on the Doha Development Agenda with Ambassador Susan C. Schwab and Mike Johanns, Secretary of Agriculture," WTO Headquarters, Geneva, July 24, 2006.

28. Arguably the easiest legislation to enact would be the sort of extension granted President Bill Clinton in 1993—one that applied only to the WTO talks. Harder to enact would be a proposal that applied that authority to all negotiations then in progress; most difficult would be a blanket extension. For a discussion of the politics as of early spring 2006, see Bruce Stokes, "Fast-Track on the Fast Track?" *National Journal,* April 1, 2006, pp. 64–65.

29. Hanoi Declaration, Fourteenth APEC Economic Leaders' Meeting, November 18–19, 2006. In 1993 the first APEC economic leaders' meeting at Seattle raised the prospect of free trade among member nations, and this (plus congressional approval of NAFTA a week before) was credited with securing additional concessions from the EU sufficient to complete the Uruguay Round agreement. Advocates like C. Fred Bergsten, director of the Peterson Institute for International Economics, were clearly hoping for a repeat.

10

MEXICO IN THE MULTILATERAL TRADING SYSTEM

A Long and Winding Road

ANTONIO ORTIZ MENA L. N.

I n the two decades since Mexico joined the General Agreement on Tariffs and Trade (GATT), it has become an important trader in Latin America, participates actively in multilateral trade negotiations, and has been one of the most dynamic participants in regional trade agreements. Currently, more than 70 percent of the country's GDP derives from trade.[1] The present situation stands in stark contrast to Mexico's trade practices of relatively recent times. In 1982 it still had a closed economy and delayed joining GATT until 1986. Even in 1980, during the oil price boom, its exports amounted to only U.S.$33 billion, compared with U.S.$178 billion in 2003.[2]

When Mexico finally joined GATT in 1986, it was after a period of unilateral trade liberalization ushered in as part of a larger macroeconomic stabilization effort. Throughout the 1990s Mexico negotiated a series of free trade agreements (FTAs), chief among them the North American Free Trade Agreement (NAFTA). Thereafter, Mexico's multilateral commitments were not as pressing in light of the importance that NAFTA came to play as a regional initiative.

More recently, this has begun to change. In 2004 a panel set up under the World Trade Organization (WTO) Dispute Settlement Understanding issued a report stating that Mexico had breached several obligations regarding its commitment to liberalize trade in the telecommunications sector. This was the first WTO dispute settlement case involving trade in telecommunications services, and it reflected the increasing scope and depth of Mexico's multilateral commitments. While the WTO is clearly having an impact on Mexico, current discussions are reminiscent of those that prevailed some sixty years ago: Do multilateral trade rules favor developed country interests? What does the multilateral trading system have to offer in terms of a developing country's need for job creation and employment?

This chapter provides an overview of Mexico's role in the multilateral arena and traces its transition from a closed economy to that of a leading actor in the world trading system. The chapter covers Mexico's long-delayed decision to join GATT, deals with its participation in the various GATT/WTO Rounds, critiques its trade policy formulation process, and highlights some of Mexico's challenges regarding the multilateral trading system and development.

Accession to GATT

Mexico remained a highly protected economy from the post–World War II era up until the mid-1980s. It would take three economic shocks for trade policy to be altered in a significant way. The first was the macroeconomic instability of the early 1970s and a devaluation of the peso in 1976 (after twenty-two years of fixed parity to the U.S. dollar); the second a severe economic downturn in 1982–83 caused by a drop in the world price of oil and a rise in international interest rates (which pushed Mexico to the verge of defaulting on its foreign debt); the third shock was the 1986 stock market crash and a devaluation of the peso in 1987.

From the late 1940s until the mid-1970s the basic thrust of trade policy was the use of high tariffs and import licensing requirements for a broad range of products, with the aim of fostering import substitution industrialization.[3] The policy was quite successful, especially from the mid-1950s until the early 1970s. Mexico's economy grew at an annual average rate of 6.8 percent during this period, surpassed only by Japan, Singapore, and South Korea. However, trade volumes were low compared to these Asian trading states, accounting for less than 15 percent of GDP, and about three-quarters of total exports were made up of agricultural goods and minerals.[4]

Under the Echeverria government (1970–76), annual inflation rates approached 16 percent, the public sector and current account deficits ballooned, and the public foreign debt grew from U.S.$4.5 billion to U.S.$19.1

billion.[5] A balance of payments crisis in August 1976 forced the government to devalue the peso, which had remained at a fixed parity with the U.S. dollar since 1954. Stabilization measures included an increase in export taxes and a reinstatement of import permits for products that had previously been liberalized. By the end of the Echeverria administration 90 percent of imports were so covered, and an export promotion program that had been started in 1971 was suspended.[6]

Apart from an economic crisis, the Lopez Portillo administration (1976–82) inherited a commitment to the International Monetary Fund (IMF) to stabilize the economy. Trade policy reform was spurred by IMF conditionality, a rise in U.S. protectionism, and the need to have a coherent trade policy after the erratic swings of the Echeverria era. The trade reforms pursued from 1977 to 1980 consisted of export promotion through fiscal, financial, and energy subsidies, available as a result of oil price hikes by the Organization of Petroleum Exporting Countries (OPEC). Oil was becoming increasingly important for the Mexican economy after the discovery of significant reserves in the mid-1970s. Some trade liberalization also occurred during this window of time: import licensing requirements decreased to 60 percent of all products by 1980, and quantitative restrictions were to be completely phased out by 1982.

Mexico's accession to GATT also became a key element of trade policy reform. In 1978 the U.S. government, seeking to avoid a permanent trade deficit with Mexico, whereby the United States imported oil from its southern neighbor while the latter maintained a closed economy, issued "emphatic invitations" for Mexico to join GATT before the end of the Tokyo Round (1973–79).[7] During the early stages of the Tokyo Round, an Office for Trade Negotiations and Tariffs was established at the Mexican Finance Ministry, as well as an interministerial commission dealing with the same topics. This incipient interest in GATT was maintained when Lopez Portillo became president in 1976, and in January 1979 Mexico finally began negotiations for GATT accession. Negotiations were successfully completed within a relatively short time.

But government policymakers made clear that Mexico would accept accession only if three basic principles were upheld: that Mexico be recognized as a developing country, that it be allowed to implement the measures required to achieve the aims of domestic economic and social development policies, and that its liberalization commitments made during the Tokyo Round be considered as part of the concessions given for GATT accession. The protocol of accession fulfilled all of these requirements. The country's industrial promotion strategy was left intact, even though it violated several of the new GATT plurilateral codes of conduct. The Mexican government was also allowed to maintain export subsidies for a certain time period as well as ample protection for the agricultural sector and the highly regulated automotive industry. The oil industry, moreover, was completely omitted from the protocol.[8]

In the draft protocol Mexico would have granted tariff concessions on 300 products, with an import value of U.S.$504 million at 1976 prices (8 percent of total imports), and bound tariffs were negotiated at a higher level (50 percent) than those currently applied. In exchange, Mexico would have received concessions on 373 products with an export value of about U.S.$1.9 billion and an average tariff reduction of 34 percent.[9] In addition, Mexico could have made ample use of GATT's safeguard provisions (articles 12 and 18) to deal with balance of payments problems as they arose, which India and Brazil had been doing for some time.[10]

An acrimonious national debate that continued throughout 1979 and early 1980 involving government officials, politicians, academics, public intellectuals, and business leaders on the merits of GATT accession, however, sidelined these patently successful negotiations. The bulk of this debate, it should be emphasized, went on before the terms of accession were agreed upon and without analyzing the specifics of the protocol once it became available! Nevertheless, the question over GATT accession became a lightning rod for a much larger and general debate on national development strategies, a debate that pitted those favoring an interventionist approach within a closed economy against those pushing for greater economic liberalization. The discussion was very doctrinaire, and it did not take long for public opinion to conclude that GATT membership would threaten national sovereignty.[11]

In March 1980 Lopez Portillo made public his decision to postpone Mexico's accession to GATT. The announcement, made on the anniversary of the nationalization of the oil industry in 1938—and thus a highly symbolic date—stated that it was not the appropriate time for Mexico to join GATT. Chief among the reasons given was the world energy plan that Mexico had proposed at the United Nations, the idea being that Mexico's new status as an oil exporter could be incompatible with some GATT provisions, such as those related to supply commitments.[12] Lopez Portillo went on to say that bilateral negotiations were preferable to multilateral ones as a way to bridge the gap between North and South. In the end, the crux of the matter was the philosophy of GATT itself and not the truly remarkable protocol obtained by Mexican negotiators.[13]

The 1978–81 period was one of impressive economic growth based on oil exports: GDP grew at more than 8 percent annually and oil exports outpaced the increase in production, growing at an average annual rate of 53 percent.[14] The cost of the strategy was extremely high, however. Instead of addressing severe macroeconomic imbalances (the current account deficit grew by 69 percent in 1978 and by 81 percent in 1979), the government spent as if there were no tomorrow. The strategy started to unravel by mid-1981, when oil prices began to fall and the U.S. Federal Reserve cranked up interest rates in order to combat double-digit inflation. To cover the revenue gap, the Mexican government turned to short-term borrowing at ever increasing interest rates, so that the debt fueled a spiral of inflation and an impending recession.

The situation imploded in 1982, when the banks halted lending, Lopez Portillo devalued the peso, and Mexico's economic fundamentals literally collapsed. The devaluation, however, was not accompanied by sensible policies to lessen its costs and make the most of its benefits. Rather, the devaluation created uncertainty and further downward pressures on the peso. Exchange controls were imposed, and the banks were nationalized. Lopez Portillo basically bequeathed his successor, Miguel de la Madrid (1982–88), what he had inherited from Echeverria: an economy in crisis and under IMF surveillance, with many urgent reforms, including trade policy, still pending.

By the time Mexico decided to restart GATT accession negotiations in late 1985, national economic circumstances had changed drastically. For lack of any viable alternatives in the aftermath of the 1982 crisis, the country had embarked on a rapid course of unilateral trade liberalization.[15] This time around, the argument made by domestic proponents of GATT accession was that, since Mexico was already liberalizing on a unilateral basis, it should receive some concessions in return through GATT accession.[16] This would also signal Mexico's commitment to the completion of liberal economic reforms, much as NAFTA entry would do later on.

The decision to liberalize unilaterally just before it was about to undertake trade negotiations reflects the dire economic straits that had befallen Mexico and the extent to which trade opening and GATT entry had become part of an overall economic reform program aimed at stabilizing the economy and restoring growth. The policy shift was thus the result of a pragmatic decision by the government and largely forced on it by the prevailing economic circumstances; tellingly, there was no significant business sector pressure in favor of trade liberalization.[17]

As had been the case in 1979, the 1986 GATT protocol fulfilled all of Mexico's basic requirements. Mexico successfully negotiated a 50 percent bound tariff level, higher than the rates it was currently applying, and an eight-year phase-in period, during which tariffs could be higher than the bound level for certain products.[18] At last, Mexico joined GATT in 1986, although the decision turned out to be much ado about nothing. The protocol allowed leeway in all areas of economic policy, and the most far-reaching trade policy reforms were ultimately carried out unilaterally and through regional commitments.

The Uruguay Round

The unilateral trade liberalization carried out in the 1980s and the launching of the NAFTA negotiations among Canada, Mexico, and the United States in 1991 made Mexico's position in the Uruguay Round different from that of other developing countries.[19] In marked contrast to its recent past, Mexico was at the forefront in some areas, such as investment and intellectual property rights; Mexican negotiators, moreover, gradually softened their position on agriculture, acquiescing to the elimination of export subsidies and the setting of binding tariffs on agricultural imports.[20]

Mexico gained improved access for some of its exports without significant concessions in return, given the large margin that prevailed between its bound rate and applied rate levels (under Uruguay Round commitments, Mexico's bound tariff rates for industrial goods were reduced from 50 percent to 35 percent in a five-year transition period). In addition, by the end of the Uruguay Round, most of Mexico's trade legislation was already in compliance with its commitments, due to changes in domestic legislation implemented as a result of, or concomitantly with, its NAFTA commitments.[21]

The economic impact of Mexico's Uruguay Round commitments was very limited, as was the legal impact. This was largely due to NAFTA, as most of the increased trade flows after 1994 involved bilateral trade with the United States.[22] The most significant impact derived from the Uruguay Round was thus indirect, related to commitments undertaken to continue negotiating trade in services (the so-called built-in agenda). One of the most contentious issues was Mexico's multilateral commitment to liberalize trade in telecommunications services. Mexico was one of sixty-eight countries that subscribed to the WTO Basic Telecommunications Agreement, which came into force in February 1998, and it also adopted the Reference Paper on Regulatory

Principles in all aspects except resale. But adherence to these commitments turned out to be another matter entirely.

As mentioned earlier, in July 2000 the Office of the United States Trade Representative (USTR) requested WTO consultations with Mexico regarding alleged barriers to competition in this sector. This matter, unfortunately, was not resolved through consultations, and in April 2004 a WTO panel issued its report: of its seven conclusions, four ruled in favor of the USTR's claims.[23] The telecommunications dispute was a wake-up call for Mexico, as it showed that WTO commitments could not be ignored. Up to that point, given the far-reaching commitments undertaken within NAFTA and other regional trade agreements, there was a sense of complacency regarding the WTO, as Mexico was now a step ahead of multilateral commitments through its regional initiatives.

The Doha Round

Mexico's participation in the Fourth WTO Ministerial Conference held in Doha, Qatar, in November 2001 followed a successful decade in terms of trade policy aims and achievements.[24] During the 1990s Mexico subscribed to a large number of FTAs, foremost among them NAFTA, and capped this activity off with the negotiation of its Association Agreement with the European Union in 2000. In terms of trade volume, Mexico's total trade grew from U.S.\$67 billion in 1986, at the time of GATT accession, to U.S.\$367 billion in 2003, an impressive increase of 448 percent.[25]

Mexico's overall aim is to contribute to a more open, fair, and stable international trading system through its participation at the WTO and to ensure that the significant gains it has made through its FTA memberships are maintained. In August 2000 Mexico hosted a preparatory meeting for the WTO's Fourth Ministerial Conference, which was attended by Argentina, Australia, Brazil, Canada, the European Union, Egypt, Hong Kong, India, Jamaica, Japan, Malaysia, Pakistan, Singapore, South Africa, Switzerland, Tanzania, the United States, and Uruguay. It also chaired the working group on intellectual property rights during the Fourth Ministerial Conference and was instrumental in helping to broker a decision in August 2003 involving an agreement on trade-related intellectual property rights, under which the export of generic copies of patented drugs to poor countries was allowed. And in September 2003 Mexico chaired and hosted the Fifth Ministerial Conference of the WTO, which was held in Cancún in September 2003. At Doha Mexico favored the built-in agenda but also regarded it as insufficient.

At a minimum, Mexican policymakers wanted a full binding of the tariff structure for industrial goods; they were wary of contaminating the trade agenda with environmental and labor issues that could negate the gains from trade liberalization.[26] Likewise, Mexico took the view that these issues would make it difficult for developing countries to fully address issues such as investment, competition policy, transparency in government procurement, and trade facilitation that had been brought up during the 1996 Singapore Ministerial Meeting.

Implementation of the Uruguay Round Agreements

From Mexico's standpoint, the implementation of market access commitments in agriculture and textiles has not translated into improved access for developing country exports; special and differential treatment for developing countries has not materialized in practice; and legitimate implementation difficulties faced by developing countries should be recognized and adequately addressed. Mexico itself has benefited from the implementation of the Uruguay Round agreements by other countries and has upheld its own commitments.[27]

On the built-in agenda, Mexico's stance is as follows:

—Rules for antidumping and countervailing duties: Mexico favors rules that allow the legitimate use of antidumping measures and at the same time curtails their use for strictly protectionist aims.

—Agriculture: Among Mexico's priorities are the reduction and eventual elimination of export subsidies and improved market access for agricultural trade.

—Trade-related investment measures: Mexico has to eliminate trade-related performance requirements in its automotive industry. It agreed, under NAFTA rules, to eliminate a number of provisions of the automotive decree by 2004, but under this agreement it would have been forced to eliminate them by 2001, thus losing important concessions it had gained under NAFTA. In July 2001 Mexico requested an additional moratorium on bringing its decrees into full compliance with the agreement. An extension was granted, so that Mexico's automotive sector decrees had to comply by January 1, 2004.[28] It has since complied, with the publication of amendments to the automotive decree in the *Daily Register* on December 31, 2003.

—Services: As the most important exporter of services in Latin America, Mexico is interested in wide coverage of this sector. It would gain from the Doha negotiations by attaining greater market diversification and wants to ensure that there is sufficient flexibility for developing countries regarding negotiations over trade in services.

—Intellectual property rights: Mexico seeks the establishment of a multilateral system of registry and notification of distinctive products for wine and spirits. This interest pertains basically to tequila and mezcal, which are recognized as distinctive products under NAFTA's annex 313. However, Mexico opposes the extensive use of geographical indications, which could constitute a new nontariff barrier. Regarding intellectual property rights and public health issues, Mexico believes a balance must be struck between the legitimate needs of developing countries and respect for the agreement on trade-related aspects of intellectual property. Mexico believes that the correct balance was struck in the Doha declaration on the topic.[29]

On the Singapore issues, Mexico did not request negotiation of the four topics covered by the Singapore Ministerial (investment, transparency in government procurement, trade facilitation, and competition policy), although it accepted the agreement to discuss them during the Fifth Ministerial. Its FTAs already cover these issues, so multilateral agreements will probably not imply any significant new commitments for Mexico.[30]

Regarding foreign direct investment, Mexico takes the view that an eventual multilateral agreement on investment should not be linked with environmental and labor issues, nor should it inhibit the regulatory oversight of the state. As mentioned, Mexico wants to incorporate competition policy criteria into the application of antidumping laws. Mexico favors transparency in government procurement but has given no indication that it intends to endorse the WTO agreement on government procurement. Finally, Mexico has made some progress in areas such as customs procedures and is not opposed to their inclusion, but trade facilitation is not an area of paramount concern.

Other issues are

—Industrial goods: Mexico favors the full binding of the industrial goods tariff structure by all WTO members. It is opposed to a sectoral approach, preferring the inclusion of all sectors so that a more balanced final deal is possible. It believes that a significant reduction and binding of the full tariff structure for industrial goods will improve its market access to countries with which it does not have an FTA.

—Electronic commerce: Mexico maintains its position that there should be no tariffs on electronic commerce.

—Labor and environmental issues: Mexico accepts the need for their discussion but is opposed to formal commitments within the realm of the WTO that could result in disguised protectionism by developed countries. It believes that the proper instruments and venues must be used to deal with these issues, such as the International Labor Organization for trade-related labor issues. Mexico also holds that trade and environmental protection are not mutually exclusive, and that greater economic growth can help free up the resources to better protect the environment.[31]

The Cancún Ministerial of the WTO

When Mexico offered to host the Fifth Ministerial conference in mid-2003 it had little idea of the challenges involved. The Doha negotiations were slated to conclude in December 2004, but as of mid-2003 meager progress had been made. Several countries (among them members of the European Union, Japan, and South Korea) insisted on the importance of negotiating the Singapore issues. But many developed countries were loath to negotiate those issues and, regarding agriculture, insisted on the need to eliminate export subsidies and radically reduce and if possible eliminate domestic supports. With these entrenched positions, there seemed to be little room for progress in the negotiations.

One ray of hope for Cancún was the successful negotiation of the agreement on trade-related intellectual property rights, which allowed for the sale of generic copies of patent medicines in poor countries facing public health crises. The deal had come just days before the start of the Cancún meeting and showed the importance of the WTO as a negotiation venue and an instrument to bridge the apparently irreconcilable differences between some developed and developing countries, but its political effect turned out to be negligible. Also, in the days before the Cancún meeting, a new coalition of developing countries with similar concerns regarding trade in agricultural products had been formed. The Group of Twenty (G20) advocated an elimination of export subsidies, substantial reductions in domestic supports, and special and differential treatment for developing countries.[32]

During Cancún, the European Union, Japan, and South Korea insisted on retaining at least two of the Singapore issues (trade facilitation and transparency in government procurement), but some G20 members, such as India, did not want to negotiate any part of the Singapore agenda. In addition, the United States and the European Union were less ambitious in their proposals regarding the elimination of export subsidies, reduction of domestic supports, and special and differential treatment as requested by the G20.

While Mexico was not particularly concerned about the Singapore issues, it had taken a strong position on agriculture by joining the G20. Given the rapid pace and considerable depth of its liberalization through FTAs, Mexico's position had on many occasions been at odds with that of other developing countries. Now it found itself allied with countries such as Brazil, despite not always seeing eye-to-eye with this country regarding multilateral trade rules.

Once the Cancún meeting was under way, the complexity of issues and alliances that emerged was not adequately grasped by the Mexican press. For example, not even the G20 members were all of one mind: while some developing countries are efficient producers and net exporters of agricultural products and advocate a radical liberalization of trade in agriculture, others are net food importers or have privileged access to certain markets (such as the European Union) and are reluctant to see any radical change in the status quo.

Sensational local press coverage was an exacerbation, to say the least, but things spun out of control when a demonstrating Korean farmer—wishing to attract attention to the plight of Korean farmers with the liberalization of trade in agriculture—stabbed himself. The self-inflicted wound proved to be fatal, and despite the enormous press coverage of the Cancún meeting, what most commentators failed to see was that Korea heavily subsidizes its agriculture (just like the European Union, Japan, and the United States) and that countries such as those that had formed the G20 were clamoring for an end to practices like the ones the Korean farmer had tragically defended.[33]

The July Package in Cancún

Multilateral trade negotiations virtually ground to a halt after Cancún.[34] It was not until the final hours of the Fifth Ministerial that a breakthrough was possible in what became known as the July package, which covered four issue areas: agriculture, industrial goods, trade facilitation, and services.

Regarding agriculture, the major achievement was an agreement to eliminate export subsidies (at a date to be set). Mexican exporters of sugar, wheat, beef, chicken, and pork were expected to benefit from the implementation of this measure. A basic agreement that sets out guidelines for the reduction of domestic support was also reached, which would favor Mexican producers of cotton and apples. A nonlinear tariff reduction schedule was agreed upon for trade in industrial goods. Although Mexico has excellent access for industrial goods with its FTA partners, it could benefit by improved access to economies that are growing at high rates (such as China and India) but with which it does not have an FTA. Trade facilitation is the only one of the original four Singapore issues that is still subject to negotiation. Developing countries accepted this insofar as there is a commitment to provide them with technical assistance for implementing their Doha commitments.

A final gain for Mexico was the commitments by developing countries to undertake negotiations to further liberalize the provision of services in mode 4 (the temporary movement of the service provider). Mexico wants both qualified and nonqualified workers to be allowed temporary entry to provide a service in markets where there are labor shortages or where labor is expensive. Even though Mexico has made some important gains in multilateral trade negotiations, there is still some disquiet about how national positions on trade policy are arrived at and what all of these alleged gains will add up to in terms of economic development.

The Hong Kong Ministerial of the WTO

The Sixth WTO Ministerial Conference took place in Hong Kong in December 2005. Despite pressing deadlines, with U.S. Trade Promotion Authority set to expire in the summer of 2007, there was scant progress at Hong Kong.[35] Impasses in agriculture, compounded by deadlock in nonagricultural market access, put the entire Doha agenda at risk.

On agriculture, Mexico has maintained its backing of the G20 position, which consists of an average reduction in tariffs of 54 percent for developed countries and 36 percent for developing ones. Given the lack of progress in agriculture, there was no agreement regarding tariff reduction formulas for nonagricultural market access. Mexico concurs with the position that participation in sectoral initiatives should be done on a voluntary basis.

Mexico has offensive interests in services negotiations and has presented requests to twenty-one WTO members in the areas of communications, tourism, construction and engineering services, transportation, financial services, and environmental and recreational services.[36] It is also interested in the liberalization of trade in services in mode 4 (presence of natural persons).

Mexico believes that special and differential treatment is an essential component of the development dimension of the Doha agenda and is against the OECD's position that the more advanced developing countries, such as Mexico, should be excluded from eligibility. At the same time, Mexico emphasizes that the best support for development is improved market access for goods and services of developing countries.

Mexico also gives priority to negotiations on norms and especially those pertaining to antidumping. It is working with two groups of countries in this regard: it seeks ambitious reforms of WTO antidumping provisions through actions with the Friends of Anti-Dumping Negotiations.[37] At the same time it is working with the European Union, Brazil, Australia, Canada, New Zealand, and Turkey, which also seek improvement to the WTO antidumping agreement.

Negotiations on improvements to the Dispute Settlement Understanding did not loom large in Hong Kong, but Mexico regards it as salient. Mexico remains an active participant in seeking improvements to the Dispute Settlement Understanding, especially regarding ways to accelerate proceedings to obtain WTO authorization for retaliation against countries that maintain WTO-inconsistent measures.[38] These issues will remain of paramount importance for Mexico, especially if Doha falters.

The Politics of Trade Policymaking in Mexico

As chapter 5, by Jaime Zabludovsky and Sergio Gómez, emphasizes, Mexico is the country with the most FTAs in the world. At the time of this writing, it has FTAs with forty-two countries.[39] All of these agreements were negotiated with relatively little input from the legislature, but this has changed. In September 2004 a new law on international economic agreements went into effect, granting unprecedented oversight powers to the Mexican Senate. While in the past the Senate could ratify an agreement only after it had been concluded, the new law provides for consultations both before and during negotiations. Inasmuch as Mexico has FTAs with all of its major trade partners, this law may have a significant impact on Mexico's multilateral trade commitments.

From the time of Mexico's first overtures to GATT in the post–World War II era until 2000, a single political party, the Institutional Revolutionary Party (PRI), controlled the presidency; and until 1987 the party had at least a simple majority in the legislature. Under this political system, which relied on strong control of the party and the legislature by the chief executive and was supported by a corporatist mode of interest representation (including not only labor but also business), the chief executive had ample discretion to pursue economic policies, including trade policy.[40] Such heavy concentration of power in the executive often proved disastrous in terms of economic policy, as demonstrated by the 1976 and 1982 crises.

During most of the import substitution era, there was close coordination between the public and private sectors, both through established institutional channels and through the close rapport between political and economic elites.[41] The system began to show signs of strain in the late 1960s but survived until the early 1980s. However, after Mexico's 1986 accession to GATT a novel consultative mechanism came into being. To implement a badly needed stabilization program aimed at reducing inflation, which approached 160 percent in 1987, tripartite consultations among representatives from government, labor, and business were established. This tripartite mechanism was the centerpiece of the Economic Solidarity Pact, a major component of which was the deepening of trade liberalization with the aim of reducing inflation through greater competition from imports of traded goods.[42]

The true sea change in Mexico's trade policy formulation process came with NAFTA. An innovative scheme worked out by government and business representatives permitted extremely close collaboration before, during, and after the negotiations. The mechanism set up for the NAFTA negotiations was used in all subsequent trade negotiations and has survived, with some modifications, to the present. The main channel of communication for interest groups is the Foreign Trade Business Coordination Council (COECE), an umbrella organization that encompasses all major business organizations.[43] The system still works well in terms of business-government consultations on trade policy, but effective representation of small and medium-size enterprises and a more pluralistic representation of civil society are still lacking.

The Ministry of the Economy (known until 2001 as the Ministry of Trade and Industrial Development, or Secofi) is still in charge of trade policy, although intermittent frictions between the Economics Ministry and the Foreign Ministry over foreign economic policy still come to the fore periodically.[44] An interministerial commission on trade policy, currently called Cocex, carries out intra-executive coordination.[45]

A challenge that is emerging for trade policy formulation is the role of the legislature, which is becoming increasingly active and assertive in the foreign policy area since the passage of the 2004 law on international economic agreements.[46] With a growing number of actors interested in and affected by trade policy, new mechanisms must be designed and implemented in order to strike an adequate balance between this heightened participation and efficient policymaking. While greater transparency and accountability on foreign economic policy is to be welcomed, this new level of legislative involvement could undermine the executive's ability to negotiate international economic agreements.

For example, article 3.1 of this new international economic agreement states that for a trade accord to be approved it must contribute to an improvement in the quality of life and welfare of all Mexicans. This worthy goal can, however, lead to an unwarranted questioning of trade agreements. While most economists agree that trade liberalization enhances productivity, many are agnostic as to its job creating and distributional effects. Likewise, most trade agreements have short-term costs and long-term benefits. How are these issues to be properly assessed by Mexico's increasingly activist legislature?

Article 8 states that the Senate can initiate hearings in the presence of trade negotiators and during the negotiation process. If this faculty is abused, it could easily be used to disrupt negotiations. Article 9.3 states that at the conclusion of negotiations over a given trade agreement, the executive must provide documentation to the Senate attesting to Mexico's concessions during the negotiations. This could cast a mercantilist shadow over future trade negotiations, as it implies that a concession is necessarily costly or undesirable for Mexico, when the opposite case could be made.

Article 12 states that the Senate shall take into account the proposals made by local governments and legislatures. This can translate into an over-representation of local interests versus national ones and could hijack a potentially positive agreement because of some specific local qualm. This closer scrutiny of the policymaking process is due in large part to concerns about the effects of economic liberalization on the welfare of Mexicans. Unless there is a clearer understanding about what trade can and cannot deliver in terms of concrete development gains, these new legislative powers could translate into large opportunity costs for Mexico.

Mexico, the WTO, and Development

Mexico's entry into GATT, and its subsequent participation in the WTO, did not have a significant impact on trade composition or volumes nor on market diversification. Unilateral liberalization and regional initiatives, foremost among them NAFTA, were the main forces behind changes in Mexico's trade regime and performance.

Shortly before it joined GATT in 1986, Mexico still had a relatively closed economy with low export volumes and a high degree of dependence on oil exports. It managed to diversify its export structure in a very short time span, so that by the end of the 1980s oil accounted for less than 25 percent of exports, and non-oil exports were mostly made up of manufactures.[47] The change in the composition of exports was associated with the downward evolution of oil prices and an increase in exports to the United States favored by a weak Mexican peso.

During the 1990s the most significant benchmarks for Mexican trade policy were the entry into force of NAFTA and several other FTAs. In terms of export composition there were no significant changes, but export volumes grew dramatically. The remarkable growth was closely linked to bilateral trade with the United States, whose economy performed extremely well during the second half of the 1990s. While by 2004, 74 percent of Mexico's trade was with the United States and Canada, its trade with Europe decreased from 12 percent of total trade in 1993 to 8 percent in 2004.[48]

The WTO is, however, becoming increasingly relevant for Mexico as its scope and coverage increases and as it encompasses issues that were previously dealt with at the regional level, such as agriculture and services. The strengthened dispute settlement mechanism in force since 1995 has also made the WTO especially salient in terms of international economic governance.[49] Given that Mexico's FTAs are of a basically static nature in terms of scope, coverage, and institutional makeup, while the multilateral trading system is dynamic, Mexico will not be able to rely permanently on regional preferences to deal with its foreign economic relations.

Like the discussions over GATT membership in the 1970s, current debates on the WTO center on the relationship between trade and development. There is, however, a major difference between past and present. While in previous instances the debate was to a certain degree symbolic insofar as GATT agreements were not a single undertaking, and the 1979 accession protocol awarded ample leeway for the maintenance of Mexican industrial policy and established bound tariffs at 50 percent, current and future multilateral trade negotiations will have a real impact on Mexico.

After two decades of trade liberalization in Mexico (unilateral, regional, and multilateral), economic growth has not been as high as expected (or needed), and poverty is still prevalent, as is a highly skewed distribution of income. To what extent is further participation in the multilateral trading system a valuable instrument to help alleviate Mexico's developmental challenges?

Five issues dominate current trade policy debates in Mexico: agriculture, export subsidies, cartels, dumping, and development. Regarding the protection of agriculture in developed countries and the related issue of export subsidies, it has taken more than half a century to register any real progress. As a result of the Uruguay Round agreements, quotas have been tariffed, and under the July 2003 package there is finally an agreement to end agricultural export subsidies and curtail domestic supports. This may not be an ideal world for those seeking free trade in agriculture (and developing countries are divided on the matter), but it is progress nevertheless.

Regarding cartels and dumping, there has been some improvement but not nearly as much as needed. The GATT codes on subsidies and countervailing measures, and on antidumping, were not compulsory for GATT members when they were first established. Since the Uruguay Round they have become part of the single undertaking, and it is now a matter of improving upon those rules. There is also a tinge of hypocrisy in this regard by some developing countries, as they are the most active users of antidumping duties. For instance, in April 1993 Mexico imposed a record number of antidumping duties on Chinese imports, in terms of the number of tariff lines covered and the level of tariffs.

Mexico has also paid lip service to competition policy. When it negotiated NAFTA, it proposed that antidumping be made illegal in North America and that competition policy be used in its stead. The United States balked at the proposal and instead offered a binational panel review of the application of each country's domestic legislation on unfair trade practices.[50] However, in its other free trade agreements Mexico has not opted for the use of competition policy over antidumping rules; Chile and Canada opted to use competition policy instead of antidumping laws in their FTA, but Mexico did not follow this approach in its FTA with Chile. As discussed previously, Mexico has also been strongly criticized for weak enforcement of competition laws in its telecommunications sector.[51] One wonders whether the main challenges in combating cartels reside in WTO rules; in any case, ducking out of the purview of multilateral trade liberalization and hampering competition in the domestic market is no way to curtail the power of oligopolies.

In the area of growth and development, at least in Mexico, civil society discussions led by nongovernmental organizations have dominated—but in quite emotional ways, and have been low on analytic content. The WTO is sometimes brought up in these discussions without specific reference to the Uruguay or Doha Rounds but rather is lumped together with such organizations like the IMF and the World Bank, entities that are supposedly the drivers of rampant globalization. These multilateral institutions, in turn, have been blamed for a vast array of ills, such as low economic growth, environmental degradation, poverty, and unequal income distribution.[52] The Mexican government, along with professional groups and institutions undertaking serious academic studies of trade policy and development, has an uphill battle explaining how the multilateral trading system is not the cause of these problems or how they can be part of their solution.

The Mexican public is generally wary of globalization and the WTO.[53] In 2004 only 34 percent of Mexicans thought globalization was mostly good for

Mexico, 66 percent of them strongly or somewhat strongly disagreed that rich countries are playing fairly in trade negotiations with poor countries, and less than half of Mexicans (48 percent) believed that Mexico should comply with WTO rulings that go against it as a result of trade disputes. These opinions, nevertheless, do not translate into a preference for economic isolationism: 85 percent of Mexicans believe that promoting the sale of Mexican products in other countries should be a very important foreign policy goal, and, in fact, they rank it as the second most important foreign policy goal, after the protection of the interests of Mexicans in other countries.

What can the WTO do for countries like Mexico in terms of leveling the economic playing field and more generally promoting growth and development? The World Bank holds that sustained economic growth helps to reduce poverty and that for countries to grow they must integrate into the world economy.[54] Some well-crafted econometric studies have nevertheless shown that there is no systematic relationship between trade openness and growth, while others note that openness is a necessary but not sufficient condition for economic growth.[55] Even leading critics of the so-called Washington consensus grant that for countries to grow they must engage in the world economy and that the WTO can help developing countries by imposing limits on antidumping actions, by facilitating the provision of services, and by providing a venue for the settlement of disputes.[56] In short, there is no magic recipe or single route to achieve growth and development. The WTO need not be part of the problem and can be part of the solution for some developing country concerns.

It is also up to the Mexican government to establish closer links between its domestic policies and its international commitments. Trade liberalization has helped Mexico grow and create new employment opportunities, although the benefits of increased trade have not been equally shared. Small and medium-size enterprises still do not have adequate financing or political representation, especially in the area of trade policy, where they account for less than 7 percent of exports.[57] Regional disparities have also grown, with the northern part of Mexico benefiting from economic openness while the southeast has seen few benefits.

The burden is now on Mexican policymakers to show that trade openness, and specifically participation in the multilateral trading system, can be an instrument for spurring growth. The government must also take greater care to design incentives that would spread the benefits of growth in a more equitable manner. But this is not an automatic process and will take consistent and concerted effort by the government and the groups it represents. Mexico must make openness work if it is to maintain an open economy and continue to participate in the multilateral trading system.[58]

Notes

This chapter is an updated version of the chapter on Mexico that I wrote for *The World Trade Organization: Economic, Legal, and Political Analysis,* edited by Patrick F. J. Macrory, Arthur E. Appleton, and Michael J. Plummer (New York: Springer, 2005). Marilea Fried kindly gave permission to use the chapter as the basis for this updated version. Mónica Colín provided valuable research assistance, for which I am grateful.

1. World Trade Organization, *Trade Policy Review: Mexico—Report by the Secretariat,* WT/TPR/S/97 (Geneva: 2002).

2. World Bank, *World Development Indicators on CD-ROM 05* (Washington: 2005). All figures reported herein that are taken from the World Bank database are expressed in constant 2000 U.S. dollars.

3. Import substitution industrialization was pursued before that time, but less as a clear strategy than as a default option resulting from the dire international economic circumstances of the 1930s. See Leopoldo Solís, *La realidad económica mexicana: Retrovisión y perspectivas* (Mexico City: Siglo XXI, 1991).

4. Solís, *La realidad económica mexicana,* p. 92; Antonio Ortiz Mena, *El Desarrollo estabilizador: reflexiones sobre una época* (Mexico City: Fondo de Cultura Económica, 1998), p. 88.

5. Antonio Ortiz Mena L. N., "An Inquiry into the Causes of the 1982 Economic Crisis in Mexico," master's thesis, University of London, 1987, p. 60.

6. Aldo Flores, *Proteccionismo versus librecambismo: La economía política de la protección comercial en México 1970–1994 (*Mexico City: Fondo de Cultura Económica, 1998), pp. 184–93.

7. Ibid., p. 203.

8. Ibid., pp. 240–41.

9. Fernando De Mateo, "Del ¡No! al ¡Sí! Historia de Un matrimonio por conveniencia: México frente al GATT," in *México en el GATT: Ventajas y desventajas* (Tijuana: El Colegio de la Frontera Norte, 1986), pp. 47–48. A comparison between the 1979 and the 1986 protocols is presented in Gabinete de Comercio Exterior, *El proceso de adhesión de México al Acuerdo General Sobre Aranceles Aduaneros y Comercio, GATT* (Mexico City: 1986), pp. 233–41.

10. Lustig notes that at the time Mexico lacked antidumping and countervailing duty laws, but in my view those laws could have been enacted without much trouble, given the hold of the ruling Institutional Revolutionary Party (PRI) over congress and the president's de facto mandate over PRI issues. See Nora Lustig, *Mexico: The Remaking of an Economy* (Brookings, 1992).

11. Dionisio Meade, interview with author, February 12, 2002; De Mateo, "Del ¡No! al ¡Sí!"

12. Lopez Portillo did not make a more explicit reference regarding supply conditions, but he probably was referring to GATT rules against restrictions on exports.

13. The March 18, 1980, speech by Lopez Portillo is summarized in Luis Malpica de la Madrid, *¿Qué es el GATT? Las consecuencias prácticas del ingreso de México al Acuerdo General* (Mexico City: Grijalbo, 1988).

14. Ortiz Mena, "An Inquiry into the Causes of the 1982 Economic Crisis in Mexico," p. 40.

15. An excellent overview of Mexican economic reforms during the de la Madrid administration is Lustig, *Mexico*. Regarding trade policy reform, see Organization for Economic Cooperation and Development, *Trade Liberalisation Policies in Mexico* (Paris: 1996). An influential diagnosis of the Mexican economy in the early 1980s and a cogent program for a turn toward renewed growth based on a more open economy and export growth is Bela Balassa and others, eds., *Toward Renewed Economic Growth in Latin America* (Washington: [Peterson] Institute for International Economics, 1986).

16. Luis Bravo Aguilera, interview with author, February 11, 2002.

17. De Mateo, "Del ¡No! al ¡Sí!" Flores, *Proteccionismo versus librecambismo*, takes a different view, arguing that the shift in trade policy had a significant impetus from business sectors looking for secure access to new markets.

18. Gabinete de Comercio Exterior, *El proceso de adhesión*, pp. 11–23.

19. For an overview of Mexico's Uruguay Round commitments, see Antonio Ortiz Mena L. N., "Mexico," in *The World Trade Organization: Legal, Economic and Political Analysis,* edited by Patrick F. J. Macrory, Arthur E. Appleton, and Michael G. Plummer, vol. 3 (New York: Springer, 2005).

20. Mexico's willingness to eliminate export subsidies may have been partly due to the scarcity of public resources for export subsidies rather than to a policy switch on principle.

21. Under article 133 of the Mexican Constitution, international agreements subscribed to by the president and ratified by the Senate have the highest legal status and require no implementing legislation. See Organización Mundial del Comercio, *Examen de las políticas comerciales: México 1997,* WTO WT/TPR/S/29 (Geneva: 1998).

22. Presidencia de la República, *IV Informe de Gobierno,* vol. 2 (Mexico City: 2004), annex.

23. See Antonio Ortiz Mena L. N. and Ricardo Rodríguez, "Mexico's International Telecommunications Policy: Origins, the WTO Dispute, and Future Challenges," *Telecommunications Policy* 29 (2005): 429–48.

24. Unless otherwise noted, the sources for this section are Secretaría de Economía, "México y la quinta conferencia ministerial de la Organización Mundial del Comercio" (Mexico City: 2001); and Secretaría de Economía, "México y la Organización Mundial del Comercio" (Mexico City: 2002).

25. World Bank, *World Development Indicators.*

26. SECOFI, "Reunión ministerial de Seattle y la posibilidad de una nueva ronda de negociaciones" (Mexico City: 1999).

27. Secretaría de Economía, "México y la Organización Mundial del Comercio."

28. Organización Mundial del Comercio, *Examen de las políticas comerciales: México,* WT/TPR/S/97 (Geneva: WTO, 2002), p. 86.

29. Secretaría de Economía, "México y la Organización Mundial del Comercio."

30. In addition, in August 2004 WTO members decided to drop all Singapore issues, except trade facilitation, from the Doha negotiations.

31. Secretaría de Economía, "México y la Organización Mundial del Comercio."

32. Membership in the G20 has varied, creating confusion (it has also been referred to as the G21, the G22, and the G20 plus). The original sixteen members were Argentina, Brazil, Bolivia, Chile, China, Colombia, Costa Rica, Ecuador, Guatemala, India, Mexico, Paraguay, Peru, Philippines, Thailand, and South Africa. See International Center for Trade and Sustainable Development (Geneva), "Cairns Joint Text," August 20, 2003.

33. See, for example, Silvia Ribeiro, "Cancún, paredón, y después," *La Jornada,* September 18, 2003.

34. The information of the July package was obtained from Secretaría de Economía 2004.

35. The information regarding Mexico's position at Honk Kong is taken from Fernando de Mateo's presentation, "La Política Comercial de México en la Organización Mundial del Comercio," Mexico City, January 18, 2006.

36. The European Community is counted as one WTO member.

37. The countries that have participated as "friends of antidumping negotiations" are Brazil, Chile, Colombia, Costa Rica, Israel, Japan, Korea, Norway, Chinese Taipei, Switzerland, Thailand, Turkey, and China.

38. See www.ictsd.org/weekly/02-11-20/story3.htm [May 23, 2006]).

39. At the time of this writing (May 2006), Mexico has FTAs with forty-three countries, but on May 21 Hugo Chávez announced that Venezuela would withdraw from the Group of Three (G3) Free Trade Agreement made up of Colombia, Mexico, and Venezuela.

40. See Wayne A. Cornelius, *Mexican Politics in Transition: The Breakdown of a One-Party-Dominant Regime* (La Jolla, Calif.: Center for U.S.-Mexican Studies, University of California, 1996). See also Gabriel Zaid, *La economía presidencial* (Mexico City: Vuelta, 1987).

41. Ortiz Mena, *El desarrollo estabilizador.*

42. The pacts were reborn under several guises until 1998. See Robert Kaufman, Carlos Bazdresch, and Blanca Heredia, "Mexico: Radical Reform in a Dominant Party System," in *Voting for Reform: Democracy, Political Liberalization, and Economic Adjustment,* edited by Stephan Haggard and Steven R. Webb (Oxford University Press, 1994). See also Lustig, *Mexico,* pp. 50–60.

43. For an overview of business organizations in Mexico, see Matilde Luna, "Entrepreneurial Interests and Political Action in Mexico: Facing the Demands of Economic Modernization," in *The Challenge of Institutional Reform in Mexico,* edited by Riordan Roett (Boulder, Colo.: Lynne Rienner, 1995); Carlos Arriola, "La Ley de Cámaras Empresariales y sus confederaciones," *Foro Internacional* 37, no. 4 (1997): 634–60.

44. Jorge Schiavon and Antonio Ortiz Mena L. N., "Apertura comercial y reforma institucional en México 1988–2000: Un análisis comparado del TLCAN y el TLCUE," *Foro Internacional* 41, no. 4 (2001): 731–60.

45. The Cocex comprises the following ministries: Foreign Relations, Finance, Social Development, Economy, Agriculture, Environment, and Health. The central bank (*Banco de México*) and the Federal Competition Commission are also represented.

46. The Senate has the faculty to ratify treaties negotiated by the executive, while the Chamber of Deputies has an influence on trade policy through its say on fiscal policy, given that tariffs are considered an integral part thereof.

47. Banco de México, *Informe Anual 1989* (Mexico City: 1990).

48. Presidencia de la República, *Quinto Informe de Gobierno* (Mexico City: 2005), p. 173.

49. It is worth noting that the WTO Dispute Settlement Understanding provides for binding decisions, while NAFTA's general mechanism, contained in chapter 20, provides for recommendations only. For a comparison between these two mechanisms, see Antonio Ortiz Mena L. N. "La solución de controversias en el Tratado de Libre Comercio de América del Norte: Un esbozo sobre su desempeño y retos," Working Paper 2 (Hamburg: Institut für Iberoamerika-Kunde, 2002).

50. See Antonio Ortiz Mena, L. N., "The Politics of Institutional Choice: International Trade and Dispute Settlement," Ph.D. dissertation, University of California–San Diego, 2001.

51. See Antonio Ortiz Mena L. N. and Ricardo Rodríguez, "Mexico's International Telecommunications Policy: Origins, the WTO Dispute, and Future Challenges," *Telecommunications Policy* 29 (2005): 429–48.

52. See, for example, the publications and press bulletins available at the Mexican Trade Action Network (www.rmalc.org.mx/index.shtml).

53. Information for this paragraph was obtained from Centro de Investigación y Docencia Económicas and Consejo Mexicano de Asuntos Internacionales, *México y el mundo: visiones globales 2004* (Mexico City: CIDE-COMEXI, 2004) (http://mexicoy elmundo.cide.edu/2004). In 2006 a new survey was carried out. It is available at http://mexicoyelmundo.cide.edu.

54. World Bank, *World Development Report 2001: Attacking Poverty* (Washington: 2001).

55. One work showing no systematic relationship is Francisco Rodriguez and Dani Rodrik, "Trade Policy and Economic Growth: A Skeptic's Guide to the Cross-national Evidence," Working Paper 7081 (Cambridge, Mass.: National Bureau of Economic Research, 1999). For a study showing that openness is not enough, see Arvind Panagariya, "Developing Countries at Doha: A Political Economy Analysis," *World Economy* 25, no. 9 (2002): 1205.

56. Dani Rodrik, *The Global Governance of Trade as if Development Really Mattered* (New York: United Nations Development Program, 2001).

57. Approximately 50 percent of exports are carried out by large corporations, and the remainder is accounted for by maquiladoras. See Antonio Ortiz Mena L. N., "Ten Years of NAFTA: A Mexican Perspective," *Voices of Mexico* 60 (2002): 60.

58. For specific policies that can be followed to favor a more equitable distribution of the gains from trade, see Dani Rodrik, *The New Global Economy and Developing Countries: Making Openness Work* (Washington: Overseas Development Council, 1999).

PART IV

BEYOND TRADE

Energy, Migration, and North American Integration

11

The Politics of Energy Markets in North America

Challenges and Prospects for a Continental Partnership

ISIDRO MORALES

With global energy prices reaching new heights since 2000, the United States has turned its attention more closely to the prospects for forging an explicit and cohesive energy policy that involves Canada and Mexico. The U.S. energy strategy up until now has bet on market mechanisms and blind faith that price incentives for Canada and Mexico will encourage the development of their unconventional and conventional resources in order to maintain the flow of energy supplies to the U.S. market. Although there is no consensus in North America on how to proceed with a continental strategy that pools the benefits and risks, the Security and Prosperity Partnership (SPP) of North America, an initiative launched by the three countries in 2005, calls for the design of a common policy framework for energy issues.

Although the SPP could constitute the space within which the three countries of North America can work to better accommodate their respective interests in the energy field, I argue in this chapter that key policy decisions in the energy field will remain grounded in national and subnational priorities. A main obstacle to forging a continental policy is the fundamentally different approaches to energy development between Mexico, on the one hand,

and Canada and the United States, on the other. The U.S. strategy for enhancing energy security is rooted in a market-oriented model that seeks to establish incentives for developing conventional and nonconventional resources in an era of historically high oil prices. This strategy, which also envisions strong regulatory intervention and the development of nonconventional oil resources (tar sands, bitumen, and synthetic oil) in western Canada, fits well with Canadian energy strategy: Prime Minister Stephen Harper's Conservative Party government in Canada stands ready and willing to deepen market integration in oil and gas markets with its southern neighbor, although regulatory and environmental concerns must still be better coordinated between the western province of Alberta, where oil sands lie, and federal agencies in Ottawa.

Mexico's energy strategy is worlds apart from that of Canada and the United States: the bulk of this sector remains under state control. Further, the future of Mexico's oil and gas production is highly uncertain, with a divided federal congress and contrasting energy proposals put forth by the three major candidates who ran for president in 2006. These proposals raised the politically sensitive question of whether to open Mexico's energy sector to private participation.

The chapter begins with a discussion of how U.S. security and energy concerns have become more tightly linked since the terrorist attacks of September 11, 2001. The second section analyzes how U.S. strategy complements current energy policies in Canada, a country that has emerged as an oil power with the development of its huge nonconventional petroleum resources. The third section examines the Mexican side of the equation. Although Mexico's energy sector was largely excluded from the North American Free Trade Agreement (NAFTA), the United States has traditionally relied on Mexico's oil production to quell its energy security concerns. Given the inability of the Mexican government to fully modernize the country's energy sector, the United States can no longer take Mexico for granted as an oil supplier. As sensible as it might be for Mexico to enlarge the coverage of NAFTA's disciplines to its energy sector, a large swath of domestic public opinion continues to oppose the marketization of oil and gas production.[1]

The analysis is confined to the oil and gas sectors of the three countries. Although the three North American economies are rich in coal and uranium resources as well as in renewable energy (hydroelectric, wind, solar), hydrocarbons remain at the core of the U.S. security agenda and constitute the major energy resources exchanged at the regional level.

U.S. Energy Security Revisited: Looking North and South

Energy cooperation in North America started when Canada and the United States joined the International Energy Agency (IEA) in 1974 in order to deal with soaring oil prices provoked by political instability in the Persian Gulf and the ability of the Organization of Petroleum Exporting Countries (OPEC) to fix global prices. At this time, Canada and all of IEA's oil producing countries committed to a sharing mechanism in the event that a major disruption in oil supplies affected one of its members.[2] The spirit of this cooperation mechanism was embedded in command and control security strategies meant to accommodate member countries according to their varying needs and circumstances. While the Europeans decided to enforce energy security by curbing consumption, Canada and the United States relied on price controls and trade quotas.

A new era in energy cooperation between Canada and the United States started with the implementation of the Canada-U.S. Free Trade Agreement (CUSFTA) in 1989. Through this agreement, barriers to cross-border energy trade were eliminated, dual pricing (different treatment for domestic and foreign producers) was prohibited, and Canada committed to maintaining its share of energy exports to the United States (based on the previous three years) in case of a major reduction in overall supply. Energy cooperation in North America was strengthened by the 1994 implementation of NAFTA. NAFTA upheld the Canada-U.S. commitments agreed to earlier and prompted Mexico to liberalize its cross-border energy trade in gas and electricity. Mexico also began to permit private investment in domestic gas distribution and transportation as well as in independent electricity production, provided these producers sell their output through the national electricity network. At the same time, Mexico's state monopoly on upstream and downstream activities was maintained. From this point on, and keeping in mind Mexico's reluctance to privatize, energy trade and cooperation among the three countries has been framed in those market-based principles preferred by Canada and the United States.

In 2001 President George W. Bush, Mexican president Vicente Fox, and Prime Minister Jean Chrétien created the North American Energy Working Group, an interministerial task force assigned the goal of sharing information and data for improving energy trade and interconnections within North America.[3] The meetings and publications of this trilateral group became more relevant after the September 11 terrorist attacks and the devastating

2005 hurricane season in the Gulf of Mexico. The launching of the SPP that same year and the designation of energy cooperation as one of its major pillars reflect the escalation of North American energy concerns to crisis levels.

The June 2005 SPP report called for the creation of a policy environment in which a sustainable supply and efficient use of energy could be promoted. It also recognized that energy had become "critical to the prosperity and security" of the three nations.[4] This type of regional partnership is fully consistent with what U.S. secretary of state Condoleezza Rice has called transformational diplomacy, a new postdeterrence diplomatic order that the second term of the Bush administration has struggled to articulate. Through this new approach, major U.S. goals for combating terrorism, weapons of mass destruction, and rogue states and for expanding democratic institutions will be pursued through regional alliances.[5]

Although these new security partnerships entail in some cases political alliances and strong state involvement, the securitization of energy markets in North America combines market-oriented incentives with strong regulatory intervention at the state, provincial, and federal levels. That is, in contrast with other post–September 11 security concerns in the region (such as border surveillance, migratory flows, and air and space defense, all of which require different degrees of state involvement and interagency collaboration), the security of energy flows is still perceived as better guaranteed if market signals drive the decisions of major stakeholders (consumers, producing companies, energy developers, government interests).

The governance of risk and uncertainty is another consideration intrinsic to this strategy. Risk concerns possible unexpected shocks that affect the stability of energy supplies (mainly oil and gas). These could include natural depletion (the decline of energy stocks in reservoirs), natural disasters (such as hurricanes Katrina and Rita, which catapulted oil prices above U.S.$50 a barrel in 2005), and geopolitical changes (political instability in the oil producing countries of the Persian Gulf, the proliferation of weapons of mass production in a sensitive country or region, or a radical change in the oil and gas regime of a country, as was the case in Bolivia). These supply shocks may at the same time unleash uncertainties in energy markets and undermine policy options. For the Bush administration the best option for dealing with these risks and uncertainties is the development of conventional and nonconventional energy resources either at home or outside of high-risk areas.

The Bush administration's market-driven approach for ensuring energy inflows is anchored in an optimistic perception of energy market fundamentals. At present, high oil prices are not perceived as fueling inflation or hampering economic growth, as was the case during the oils shocks of the 1970s; it seems, rather, that the current American administration is resigned to a new era of "expensive oil" (ranging around or above U.S.$40 a barrel for the next twenty-five years), during which several energy options could become possible: the development of nonconventional hydrocarbon resources (tar sands, synthetic oil, shale oil); a new generation of nuclear energy; a boost to coal consumption as an input for electricity (as technological advances have reduced damages to the environment); or the growth of renewable sources of energy and the technological feasibility of synthetic fuels. The U.S. Environmental Protection Agency launched incentives for promoting these possibilities in 2005.[6] In other words, the Bush administration is looking to a new era in which oil continues to be a major source of world energy, but mainly for fueling the transportation sector, while a more diversified energy mix based on synthetic oil and fuels comes to the fore.[7]

The rationale by which expensive oil is not seen as a disadvantage (as in the past) lies in the fact that the U.S. economy is less dependent on energy-intensive industries, such as cement, steel, paper, and chemicals. According to recent estimates, future growth will come from service industries (which currently account for 80 percent of U.S. GDP) and nonenergy-intensive manufacturing. This—combined with a secular decline in energy intensity ratios (that is, less energy is needed per unit of GDP), a rapid pace of technological innovation, and growing labor productivity—means that the U.S. economy is expected to grow at an average rate of 3 percent in real terms over the next twenty-five years in spite of the prevalence of high oil prices.[8]

Another optimistic supposition of the Bush administration is that international oil prices will remain high because of economic fundamentals; that is, major consumers and importers such as the United States, China, and India will sustain high energy demand due to sound economic growth. Since OPEC countries remain the residual suppliers, the development of additional spare capacity in these countries is crucial for the evolution of prices. To date, the increase in OPEC's spare capacity has lagged behind demand growth. However, U.S. Department of Energy estimates do not fully account for the geopolitical fundamentals that could prompt a drop in the supply capacity of the main oil producers: the de facto embargo that the United States has with key oil producing countries such as Iraq, Iran, and to a lesser extent Libya; and the various uncertainties raised by the war on terror. If OPEC production returns to precrisis levels, and the spare capacity of the Persian Gulf countries is increased, this would obviously have a downward impact on oil prices.

In light of these uncertainties, the major goal of a strategic North American energy partnership will be to retain both Canada and Mexico as reliable and safe suppliers to the United States. The strategic role that both Canada and Mexico will play in this new security partnership agenda becomes clear if we take into account that, in spite of recent policy efforts, the United States shows all signs of remaining a country addicted to oil and natural gas. According to most recent available scenarios, by the year 2030 oil and natural gas will still amount to 61 percent of overall U.S. energy consumption.[9] Canada and Mexico are the two single largest suppliers of oil to the United States. In 2005 Canada supplied 16 percent of U.S. oil imports and Mexico supplied 15 percent.[10]

Canada is also the major exporter of natural gas to the United States, providing around 15 percent of its domestic consumption. The energy grids of Canada and Mexico are highly interconnected with U.S. markets (especially in the case of Canada), rendering these two countries extensions of the U.S. homeland, at least in terms of security. The United States is interested not only in the steady development of both conventional and nonconventional sources of oil and gas in each of its North American partners but also in the infrastructure to ensure a steady inflow of energy. Needless to say, the United States is intent on keeping and increasing its share of energy imports from these two countries into the foreseeable future.

Canada's Role as the Largest Continental Energy Supplier

Canada's amazingly huge oil sands have become the most important energy reservoir in North America. With the equivalent of 179 billion barrels of proven reserves, oil sands in Canada's western Alberta province rank the country second only to Saudi Arabia as the largest reserve in the world.[11] Taking into account current levels of production, both the United States and Mexico will deplete their respective proven reserves in less than a decade, while Canada's are projected to last 195 years. It is worth noting that estimates of Mexico's proven reserves were lowered following two major reclassifications made by the state-owned monopoly Petroleos Mexicanos (Pemex) in 2003 in order to comply with international standards. This also reflects the inability of Pemex to replenish its energy stock by investing in exploration and development. In the Western Hemisphere, only Venezuela has significant proven reserves of crude oil similar in quality to Canada's heavy oil.

Canada is thus well positioned to become an energy powerhouse.[12] In 2004 Canadian crude production reached 2.5 million barrels per day, of which 90 percent came from western Canada. It is in fact in the Western Canadian Sedimentary Basin (WCSB), a vast region encompassing most of Alberta, parts of British Columbia, Saskatchewan, and Manitoba, where most of Canada's conventional and nonconventional crude oil and natural gas reserves are located. Conventional oil production located mainly offshore in the maritime provinces of eastern Canada is also anticipated and, if successfully developed, could help offset the expected decline in crude production in the WCSB. However, production from the western oil sands will be the main source for compensating the depletion of conventional oil.[13] This will eventually offset the pivotal role that central Canada has played in the North American economy, since Ontario and Quebec have traditionally been the major sources and destinations of overall trade between Canada and the United States. The fact that Alberta is the political base of Prime Minister Stephen Harper's Conservative Party government reflects this geographical rebalancing of political and economic power in Canada.

Nonconventional Oil Resources

Crude from oil sands is normally recovered as bitumen, a high-viscosity hydrocarbon with high concentrations of sulfur and metals.[14] In principle, the most attractive option for oil sands producers is to upgrade their bitumen to lighter blends, which most readily meet the demands of gasoline consumption. But the transformation of bitumen into synthetic light blends has become the most expensive process in the production of unconventional oils. Supply costs should decrease in time, as the normal trend (due to investment and technological innovation) is toward cost reduction.[15]

Currently, experts estimate that a return on investment from oil sands becomes possible if crude oil prices per barrel remain about U.S.$25–$30.[16] If prices remain above U.S.$40 a barrel over the long term, as stated in 2006 forecasts, a boom in oil sands production is anticipated.[17] However, any number of geopolitical scenarios could push oil prices in either direction. If for any reason the Gulf oil producing countries succeed in raising their current production capacity of cheap conventional oil, prices could plummet as they did in the 1980s. Albertans and the Canadian federal government alike are keen to see international oil markets stabilize in the range of U.S.$25–$30 a barrel.

If prices remain attractive enough there will be no major structural barrier to the development of this enormous source of nonconventional oil. Canada and the United States mutually liberalized their oil and gas markets with the coming into force of CUSFTA, and now major American, as well as Asian, firms are investing in the development of the oil sands.[18] Public officials from Canada's western provinces are fully devoted to the development of their natural resource wealth. As Alberta's premier has emphasized, Canadian resources have become more competitive because Alberta offers a safe and predictable investment environment and a stable fiscal regime compared to the Middle East and Latin America.[19]

There remains the question of infrastructure development and the design of horizontal regulatory measures to ensure the exploitation of nonconventional oil for export. Practically all of Canada's crude exports go to the United States, with the consumption of fuels concentrated in the northern and central states. Exports are shipped through a grid of seven pipelines going from north to south, the largest of which is Enbridge, carrying around 72 percent of western Canadian crude oil shipments. This line crosses the western provinces and goes south to Chicago, creating a cross-border economic region between western Canada and the U.S. Midwest. This means that the central and eastern Canadian provinces are supplied either by oil from the maritime provinces or by oil imported from foreign suppliers.[20] According to official estimates, the anticipated production of oil from bitumen will increase exports to the United States in the near term and will reach Canada's central provinces in the mid to long term. This is because the existing transport infrastructure is connected to U.S. markets, not to mention the physical constraints inherent in exploiting nonconventional reservoirs.

The bitumen upgrading process could be done at the point of extraction (as some producers are currently doing) or during the refinery process. Currently, 27 percent of total Canadian supply is synthetic oil, while 41 percent is heavy blend. Some of this oil is processed by refineries in the U.S. Midwest; since some of these refineries are increasing their capacities, they will be able to continue to refine Canadian heavy blend.[21] However, as oil sands production continues to expand, other refineries must be used. According to some market analysts, it makes sense for oil sands producers to ship heavy blend to Texas and Gulf of Mexico refineries because of their economies of scale.[22] Another possible outlet is the Pacific coast, through which Canadian oil could be shipped to California or Asia.

Scheduled investment plans indicate that both of these options will be pursued. In 2008 Enbridge will undertake the first phase of a new line linking its terminal in Chicago with Wood River, a point from which it will be possible to connect with the Gulf of Mexico refinery cluster. The same company has plans for piping in up to 400,000 barrels a day to the Pacific coast in British Columbia by 2010. The pipeline could be co-financed with Chinese capital to open an export outlet to Asia and California. Other pipeline companies, including TransCanada (operating as a major west-east gas line), are planning to increase their transmission capacities in order to profit from the anticipated boom in nonconventional oil.[23]

Canada's oil boom has also prompted the planning and construction of new refinery plants.[24] A new one is about to be constructed in southern California, which in principle could be supplied by oil from Mexico. Since Mexican authorities could not guarantee a ten-year supply of crude for reasons I discuss below, Canadian suppliers have shown interest. Thus the expansion of Canadian exports to the U.S. South and the Gulf of Mexico will directly compete with (and could substitute for) oil from Mexico and Venezuela, since these two countries also export great volumes of heavy blend.

Apart from these infrastructure logistics, the further deepening of energy markets between Canada and the United States must accommodate regulatory constraints. Transmission lines and import connections are regulated at the federal level in the two countries, but operating permits must be obtained at the local, state or provincial, and federal levels, which heightens political risks. However, the most controversial issues are environmental. Since exploitation of oil sands is in itself an energy-intensive activity, requiring high consumption of natural gas in order to upgrade bitumen, environmental and advocacy groups are pressing for stricter supervision of this development by Canadian agencies. Recently, the Sierra Legal Defense Fund, followed by other organizations, appealed to the Supreme Court of Canada to broaden the federal government's environmental oversight of the oil sands project.[25]

A major environmental battle that Alberta and WCSB producers must confront will be compliance with the commitments that Ottawa has made under the Kyoto Protocol. In September 2002 the Chrétien government announced the ratification of this multilateral protocol, which compels Canada to reduce greenhouse emissions by 6 percent below 1990 levels. For Albertans this signals a return of federal government regulation of the oil and gas industry. Albertans thus oppose the Kyoto Protocol and suggest a Canadian-made alternative. Alberta's concerns stem from the cost impact that an eventual carbon tax could have on oil sands production, since some estimates show that environmental commitments could add an additional U.S.$6 a barrel to the cost of nonconventional oil.[26]

Conventional Natural Gas

Currently, 97 percent of Canada's natural gas production comes from the WCSB and just 3 percent from the Atlantic provinces. However, it is estimated that 23 percent of ultimate recoverable reserves lie in the Arctic zone of the country, mainly in the Mackenzie Delta region.[27] Since Canadian domestic consumption is estimated to keep growing while production from the WCSB appears to be flattening, Canadian agencies have sought for two decades to develop the Arctic reserves by building a pipeline to connect the Mackenzie Delta with Alberta's gas lines in order to maintain current supply levels of natural gas.[28] Hearings are now taking place to reconcile environmental and land and Native rights with the imperatives of energy development. If the Mackenzie line comes into operation (scheduled for 2011), it will be a major infrastructure accomplishment in terms of Canada's ability to maintain gas exports to the United States.

However, estimates are that U.S. imports of Canadian gas will decline from a peak reached in 2001 to the levels of the early 1990s just before gas from the Arctic region comes onstream. In spite of this Arctic opening, Canada's net gas exports to the United States will continue to decline until nonconventional gas becomes economically feasible, which will take until the year 2020. Thus Canadian gas will not be enough to supply a growing demand for gas imports driven by the needs of U.S. power generation.[29] Canadian agencies estimate as well that conventional gas production from the WCSB will start a fairly dramatic decline from the year 2008. From then on, this decline could be compensated for by gas coming from offshore production on the east coast, nonconventional gas (obtained mainly from coal), Mackenzie Delta production, and growing imports of liquefied natural gas (LNG).[30]

There are at present eight proposals for building terminals to import LNG. Most of them are in the Atlantic and Quebec region and are scheduled to start operation at the end of the decade. The development of these terminals will also exacerbate regulatory and environmental concerns at the provincial and federal levels, since re-exports to the United States are also scheduled from some of these terminals. The building of LNG terminals either in Canada or in Mexico has become a highlight of the SPP. There are now five terminals along the Gulf of Mexico to provide for LNG imports by the United States, and this capacity will only increase in years to come. It is projected that most U.S. imports of gas will come from overseas LNG and will grow from less than 1 trillion cubic feet in 2005 to more than 4 trillion cubic feet in 2030. Since Canadian net exports will decline and the future of Mexico's gas production is uncertain, it has become strategic to develop LNG terminal clusters throughout North America for the growing requirements of natural gas for all three economies.[31]

Mexico as a Net Oil Exporter

The uncertainties of Mexico's oil and gas production have become a security concern for North America. The Mexican quandary is how to maintain, even increase, current levels of oil and gas production in light of the political obstacles to energy sector privatization. According to Mexico's constitution and energy-related legislation, hydrocarbon resources belong to the state, and only the state is entitled to authorize the exploration, development, and production of hydrocarbon resources. This includes the nationwide generation and distribution of electricity and the transport and sale of crude oil downstream. Before NAFTA the participation of private national and international companies was prohibited in Mexico's energy sector. The exceptions were turnkey projects and specific services by subcontractors to one of the two major state monopolies, Pemex and Comisión Federal de Electricidad (CFE), Mexico's federal electricity commission.

Legislation reflects Mexico's history, during which a state monopoly on energy played a major role in the country's industrialization during most of the twentieth century. Since these monopolies survived NAFTA, the Mexican government may still differentiate between national and international markets when fixing energy prices. From the early 1980s up to the present, when it became an oil exporting company Pemex also emerged as the major source of fiscal income for the government (currently accounting for 35 percent of overall government revenues). Thus for the Mexican government oil rents have become necessary for financing government expenditures and for backing debt held by the government and Pemex. This is why no one within the Mexican political elite has been willing to openly support the privatization of the oil sector. Needless to say, the investment climate in Mexico's energy sector has been less than inviting for private capital.

Mexico's nationalistic energy policies, while periodically causing tensions with the United States, have never directly challenged U.S. strategic interests. Only in the 1980s, when Mexico became a major oil exporter—a time when the United States and other Western countries were dealing with oil shortages and price instability—did Mexico agree to sell oil to supply the U.S. strategic petroleum reserve. In spite of a sovereignty discourse within Mexican political circles that highlights Mexico's nationalism and autonomy on energy matters, Mexico never joined OPEC and never threatened to use its oil exports to leverage strategic concessions from the United States.[32]

Domestic stakeholders and public opinion have always perceived Mexico's oil rent as a tool for supporting social and industrial policies. However, from the early 1980s to the present, political elites have also used this oil rent for dealing with successive financial crises. This was the case during the 1982 debt default, in 1986 when oil prices collapsed, and in 1995 during the peso crisis. At all of these crisis junctures Mexico's oil income was put on the table in order to restructure unpaid loans and to guarantee the repayment of new ones. This helps to explain why Mexico made a strong effort to increase its oil exports during the past decade, in spite of diminishing investment in its energy sector. Further, the United States has progressively become the country of destination for its oil exports, going from 73 percent of Mexican oil exports in 1994 to 85 percent at the end of 2004.[33] These trends clearly indicate that Mexico's energy policies have been compatible with U.S. interests and concerns in the oil market. However, in terms of Mexico's participation in a continental energy partnership, it is unclear if Mexico can supply its own energy needs let alone those of the United States.

Oil Exports

The lack of modernizing reforms in Mexico's energy sector has placed the sustainability of its oil and gas production at risk. During the past fifteen years most investments in Pemex were channeled toward increasing production for export. The result has been a decline in Mexico's proven stock of crude oil and a deficit in gasoline and natural gas production for supplying domestic demand. Even more concerning is that most of the country's current oil production is sustained by just one field, Cantarell, the offshore reservoir south of the Gulf of Mexico. In 2004, 72 percent of Mexico's oil production and 17 percent of natural gas came from this field.[34] Experts estimate that Cantarell's reserves will have declined by half in the year 2010.[35] Estimates from Mexico's secretary of energy and the director of Pemex agree that it will require at least U.S.$10 billion in annual investment if oil production is to be sustained at present levels. According to these same officials, investments should be as high as U.S.$15 billion to U.S.$25 billion annually over a period of twelve years if Mexico is to increase its production to 5 million to 6 million barrels a day.[36]

During the Fox administration (2000–06) investments did increase over previous years, reaching almost U.S.$11 billion in 2004. However, since 1997 a rising share of energy investments has not been from Pemex but rather from private companies hired for drilling and exploration. Those service companies leverage the funding for Pemex, and once their contracts are completed Pemex "pays" them. In 2004 private companies funded 90 percent of Pemex's overall investments through this outsourcing mechanism.[37] The

Fox administration has praised this investment design as the way for Pemex to increase its production without directly violating constitutional restrictions on private investment in this industry. At the same time, this formula has enabled the government to capture oil rents to cover its own budgetary needs without entirely sacrificing energy exploration and development.

Such de facto privatization of some of Pemex's upstream operations unleashed a major debate in Mexico concerning the need to reform investment in the energy industry. There was no agreement during the Fox administration on this, and it became a hot point of debate in the 2006 presidential campaign. There seems to be a general consensus that the status quo is not sustainable, but the debate has turned quite contentious regarding the various alternatives for updating and modernizing Mexico's energy investment regime. This is well reflected in the case of gas and power generation.

Gas and Electricity

For Mexico, NAFTA stipulates the participation of private utilities in the production of electricity and in cross-border transactions if they are small producers or produce for self-consumption or through cogeneration. In all cases power production can be traded only through the national transmission network, which is in the hands of the CFE (the Mexican power monopoly). In early 1999 President Ernesto Zedillo submitted a constitutional reform proposal to the congress that would have released power generation from the state monopoly, leaving just the transmission network under the purview of the CFE. If the Mexican congress had approved the reform, NAFTA treatment would have been extended to Mexico's power sector, enabling private utilities to increase their share in a growing national market.[38]

Two years later, President Fox submitted a more timid regulatory reform, through which private utilities could increase their market shares in the power sector while still selling through the CFE. The opposition in the congress challenged the proposal at the Supreme Court of Justice, alleging that the executive branch did not have sufficient competence in the matter and that, therefore, the legislative branch should decide. This open confrontation between key opposition legislators and the president set the stage for a bruising battle over the energy investment regime during the entire Fox administration, which never was successful in passing major reforms in this regard.

On the natural gas front, while Mexico exported marginal amounts of natural gas in the early 1980s, during the 1990s it started to import growing volumes of this fuel. Mexico still has large gas reserves, although most of these are either tied to oil exploitation or remain untapped. Furthermore,

Pemex has traditionally lacked the transmission pipelines to supply the growing demand for natural gas in the country's northern industrialized states. Imports from Texas have thus become more attractive than pumping gas from Mexico's southern fields. When the country shifted from oil to gas inputs for electricity generation in the 1990s the demand for natural gas increased dramatically. Natural gas imports now account for 27 percent of domestic consumption. If consumption trends continue at this pace, imports could reach 50 percent of overall consumption by 2012.[39]

Mexico's dependence on natural gas imports reflects the failure of the state monopoly to capitalize on and ensure national self-sufficiency in an era of higher international gas prices. Nonetheless, the government is anticipating that growing imports could be supplied by liquefied natural gas shipments entering through Altamira and Baja California. Infrastructure and regasification plants are being developed in both locations, and the government expects that part of those shipments could eventually be exported to the United States.

This is why the development of the Burgos Basin became important for the Fox administration, since this northern reservoir could easily supply additional gas to the Nuevo León border region. From 2003 to 2005 Pemex bid out multiple service contracts for developing the Burgos reserves. These contracts continue the Pemex practice of outsourcing specific services that exceed its capabilities. As in the past, these contracts do not allow for any private share or direct participation in Mexico's natural gas industry. A fixed amount is paid for the services provided by companies on a yearly basis, regardless of the output yield from the gas fields they develop. According to Pemex's estimates, private companies have invested U.S.$5.9 billion through this mechanism, which will boost gas production from the Burgos fields to 605 million cubic feet daily by 2008.[40]

The Fox administration's reliance on multiple service contracts has been criticized on several fronts. On one side are the major oil and gas companies, none of which has applied for contracts, perhaps because the contracts do not allow them to own shares in the country's gas reserves and because the fee paid may not cover the development of some fields. Another argument against the contracts is that they give away too much: that the constitution does not allow private companies to develop any fields at all. This is the stand of the opposition parties in the government.

The controversial aspects of the contracts have discouraged potential investors in the Burgos Basin and have embittered the debate over the need to change the status quo in the energy sector. While President Fox pushed hard for constitutional changes that would allow private investors to participate in the exploration and production of natural gas in Mexico, the congress has just as heatedly debated the need to push through a fiscal reform package to reduce the government's reliance on Pemex transfers to the Treasury. In December 2005 the congress passed a new fiscal regime for Pemex, through which the company was entitled to use approximately U.S.$2.5 billion to U.S.$3.0 billion annually to fund energy sector investments.

These two themes—Fox's unmet plea for opening exploration and production activities in the gas sector to private companies and the need for further fiscal reform to free up Pemex—framed the energy reform debate in the 2006 presidential campaign. The two poles of the debate were represented by the leading presidential contenders: Felipe Calderón, the candidate of the incumbent Partido Acción Nacional (PAN), who eventually won the election by a small margin in July 2006; and Andrés Manuel López Obrador, of the left-leaning Partido de la Revolución Democrática (PRD). Calderón's proposals seek to revive and deepen Fox's earlier reform efforts in the electricity, gas, and oil sectors. Arguing that technological skills for exploiting Mexico's potential gas reserves in the Gulf of Mexico cannot be obtained via the Pemex model, Calderón proposes a public-private ownership structure that will most likely require a constitutional amendment. Calderón also proposes fiscal reform geared toward replenishing the financial resources of Pemex. Other proposed reforms in the governance of Pemex would render it more accountable and transparent and less overstaffed.[41]

By contrast, López Obrador's energy program was geared toward ensuring energy self-sufficiency. Here, the idea was to maintain current oil production levels while reducing Mexico's imports of gas. The means for achieving this was a fiscal reform to increase Pemex's financial resources; oil production would have been enhanced from known reservoirs and shallow waters (rather than tapping deep-water fields located in the Gulf of Mexico, as Calderón plans to do); three new refineries were to be built to increase the domestic production of gasoline; gas exploitation from the Burgos Basin would have also been enhanced, although the financing mechanism for this was not clear. To reduce natural gas imports, López Obrador planned to increase the use of heavy oil as an electricity input and release natural gas for industrial use. If done, this would have been a major departure from past policies, as the use of gas in power generation has long been preferred because it is an environmentally cleaner fuel.[42]

The reform proposals differed, but there was a common thread in that both sides recognized that the status quo was unsustainable: if Mexico's oil output is to be maintained, investments must obviously be increased, but state ownership in the oil and electricity sectors shouldn't be eliminated. This common ground between political opponents was fully compatible with U.S. energy security concerns discussed earlier.

I would argue, however, that the proposal of President Calderón (2006–12) better suits current U.S. and Canadian energy interests. Widening the scope of private participation in the production of electricity and in upstream oil and gas activities will mean the extension of NAFTA treatment to these activities. That is, investors and the services they provide would be fully covered by NAFTA obligations on government procurement, services, property rights, and investments; legal disputes, moreover, could eventually be solved under NAFTA's dispute resolution mechanisms.[43] The extension of NAFTA treatment to these activities would increase legal protection and certainty for foreign investors, such as Canadian and U.S. firms looking to participate in the development of Mexico's energy sector. Such a strategy would be optimal for both U.S. and Canadian interests, since both countries would benefit from a further opening of Mexico's energy markets.

But for Mexico to extend NAFTA treatment to oil and gas would still require a constitutional amendment, a feat that perpetually eluded the Fox administration. Chapter 6 of the NAFTA charter is clear in stating that in case of a conflict of interpretation between that chapter and the Mexican constitution the constitution would prevail. To pass a constitutional amendment, two-thirds of the votes of the federal congress are required as well as a two-thirds vote in each of the state legislatures. Given the divisions between a majority congressional opposition and a minority party in the executive office, which plagued the entire Fox sexenio, a constitutional reform was not in the political cards. Since divided government is expected to prevail into the next sexenio, there are few signs that sweeping energy reform will be anything but an uphill battle.

Conclusions

Whereas numerous cross-border problems such as illegal migration, drug trafficking, and deepening inequalities remain bogged down at the government level in each NAFTA country, energy issues have shown greater potential for a market-oriented continentalized strategy. This is partly explained by the market approach of the United States for dealing with soaring oil prices and political instability in key oil producing regions and countries. Faced with these incentives, the Bush administration is now actively developing unconventional oil and gas resources at home and within its own North American neighborhood.

So far a market-based governance approach has worked reasonably well in North America. Canada's development of nonconventional oil sands reflects flexible innovation in response to an era of expensive oil. In years to come, producers and developers from Alberta could eventually double Canada's production, making the country an energy powerhouse and a stable supplier to its southern neighbor. The Conservative Party government elected in January 2006 is poised to support the further continentalization of oil and gas grids and flows. Canada's strategy makes especially good sense in light of the high costs of oil sands production, as prices above U.S.$50 a barrel offer a financial means for consolidating its market for synthetic oil.

However, Canada's strategy is far from risk free. Although the U.S. economy has thus far weathered high oil prices, it remains to be seen if other high consuming countries and regions—like India, China, and Europe—can follow suit. If a recession looms in a key country or area, let alone in the United States, Canada will be pinched. In other words, the era of expensive oil that has so benefited Canada could be compromised by the revival of energy production in the Middle East. If prices dwindle, Canada could act in concert with other key producers to stabilize the market according to its own interests. Already, Canada is gaining the market power necessary to play this role.

Mexico has also benefited from the surge in oil prices, as oil revenues, which go directly into government coffers, have compensated for low domestic tax collections. But in contrast to Canada, there is no domestic consensus on how to fully tap the development of Mexico's energy potential. The tone of the 2006 presidential race confirmed that Mexican political parties and elites are divided on the best formula for developing their conventional reserves located in the deep waters of the Gulf of Mexico. Calderón remains convinced that NAFTA must be expanded to apply to upstream gas and oil activities but without privatizing Pemex. This proposal would allow for the further integration of energy markets under an arrangement that links Pemex with private firms. López Obrador, the losing presidential candidate in 2006, argued for the opposite: the preservation of state-led policies and minimal participation of private (foreign) firms.

Calderón's proposal best suits American and Canadian interests, since energy firms in these countries are eager to participate in new opportunities for private investment. Under such a scenario, Mexican production could eventually increase and any surplus could be exported to the U.S. market. Further, any opening of Mexico's energy sector that might be supported by a constitutional amendment would be regulated by the principles and obligations of NAFTA. In this sense, Mexico's energy markets would move closer to a market-based governance approach and could increase sales to the United States without requiring major political or strategic concessions.

Nevertheless, Calderón's immediate challenge is to build political support within a divided congress in order to move his energy reforms forward. Since López Obrador and many of his followers in the PRD continue to contest Calderón's victory in the July 2006 elections, it will be difficult for the PAN to secure congressional support from the PRD for any reform whatsoever in the investment climate of the energy sector. But Calderón could continue with Pemex's fiscal and corporate governance reforms that were started during the previous administration, since most of the political opposition in both the Partido Revolucionario Institucional (PRI) and the PRD has already expressed a policy preference for this option.

Notes

I thank the School of International Service and the Center for North American Studies (CNAS) at American University for hosting me during the 2005–06 academic year. The financial sponsorship of CNAS made this research possible.

1. Antonio Ortiz Mena L. N., "Getting to 'No': Defending against Demands in NAFTA Energy Negotiations," in *Negotiating Trade: Developing Countries in the WTO and NAFTA,* edited by John S. Odell (Cambridge University Press, 2006).

2. In 1993 IEA countries included this principle in their shared goals. See International Energy Agency, *Energy Policies of IEA Countries: Canada 2004 Review* (Paris: OECD, 2004), pp. 169–70.

3. Released in March 2001, before the terrorist attacks on New York and the Pentagon, the Bush administration's national energy policy called for energy conservation through technological innovation, infrastructure development, the increase of domestic energy supplies (other than oil and gas), and stronger links with both Canada and Mexico. See National Energy Policy Development Group, *National Energy Policy* (Washington: 2001).

4. "Security and Prosperity Partnership of North America: Report to Leaders," June 2005 (www.spp.gov/spp/report_to_leaders).

5. Condoleezza Rice, remarks at Georgetown University School of International Service, Washington, January 18, 2006.

6. See Senate Committee on Energy and Natural Resources, *Energy Policy Act of 2005.*

7. Energy Information Administration, *Annual Energy Outlook 2006 with Projection to 2030* (U.S. Department of Energy, 2006). According to some authors, it is irrelevant for the United States to reduce its oil imports from Persian Gulf producers (which accounted for about 22 percent of its oil imports in 2005), since oil markets are globally integrated.

See Anthony Cordesman and Khalid R. Al-Rodhan, "The Changing Risks in Global Oil Supply and Demand: Crisis or Evolving Solution?" (Washington: Center for Strategic and International Studies, 2005). This is true in terms of the evolution of crude oil prices, where a disruption in any part of the world is immediately transmitted to all importing countries. However, in terms of strategic options, the growing U.S. reliance on high-risk countries or areas could become a liability. If the war on terror persists, Washington will be keen to increase its oil imports from lower risk regions.

8. See Energy Information Administration, *Annual Energy Outlook 2006*, p. 63.

9. Ibid., p. 64.

10. Import shares from Saudi Arabia and Venezuela amount to 14.3 percent and 12.24 percent, respectively. Imports from Gulf oil producing countries (including Saudi Arabia) amount to 21.7 percent (U.S. Department of Energy [www.eia.doe.gov]).

11. National Energy Board, *Canada's Oil Sands: Opportunities and Challenges to 2015* (Calgary: 2004), p. 4. In contrast, the proven oil reserves of the other two North American countries are paltry: 22 billion barrels in the United States and 15 billion barrels in Mexico.

12. Barbara Shook, "Northwest Territories Want to Get into the Energy Act," *Natural Gas Week,* March 21, 2005.

13. National Energy Board, *Short Term Outlook for Canadian Crude Oil to 2006* (Calgary: 2005), pp. 20–28.

14. For the technicalities involved in oil sands production, see National Energy Board, *Canada's Oil Sands.*

15. For supply costs of Canadian oil sands, see ibid., p. 7. In the past decade, costs for bitumen ranged from U.S.$30 to U.S.$35 a barrel. Kathleen McFall, "Feeding the American Addiction," *Platts Energy Economist,* March 1, 2006.

16. This is established by American experts; see Energy Information Administration, *Annual Energy Outlook 2006,* p. 52.

17. The U.S. Energy Information Administration assumes that the higher the price, the higher the volume that will be produced from unconventional oil. In Mexico, the opposite trend is anticipated, since Pemex is a statist company that will attempt to optimize the value of its oil according to the fluctuation of prices. See Energy Information Administration, *Annual Energy Outlook 2006,* p. 182.

18. Currently, Imperial Oil, Exxon, Mobil, Chevron, and Conoco Philips are operating in the country. Firms from Japan and China have also shown interest in the WCSB resources. The participation of these firms is facilitating the expansion of transmission and refinery capacities in the United States. See International Energy Agency, *Energy Policies of IEA Countries: Canada, 2004 Review* (Paris: OECD, 2004), p. 80; Takeo Kumagai, "Japan Weighs Running Canadian Synthetic," *Platts Oilgram News,* March 13, 2006.

19. Alberta has offered fiscal incentives for investors to participate in oil sands development. Since the 1990s the government takes a 1 percent royalty of the gross revenue of a company until it pays out of its capital. Once this is done, royalties amount to 25 percent. See McFall, "Feeding the American Addiction."

20. In 2004 Canada imported 950,000 barrels a day mainly for the needs of central and eastern Canada. However, the country remains a net oil exporter.

21. National Energy Board, *Short Term Outlook,* p. 33.

22. David J. Hawkins, "Canadian Bitumen Stands Poised to Expand to U.S. Markets," *Oil and Gas Journal* 102, no. 29 (August 2004): 52–57.

23. National Energy Board, *Short Term Outlook,* p. 41.

24. Canada is currently exporting 500,000 barrels of petroleum products a day. This amount could dramatically increase if the costs of building new refineries for upgrading bitumen and exporting fuels to the United States are attractive to oil companies.

25. "Groups Seek Oil Sands Review," *Oil Daily,* March 29, 2006.

26. Keith Brownsey, "Alberta's Oil and Gas Industry in the Era of the Kyoto Protocol," in *Canadian Energy Policy and the Struggle for Sustainable Development,* edited by Bruce Coern (University of Toronto Press, 2005), p. 216. For the Alberta plan for greenhouse emissions, see Alastair Lucas, "The Alberta Energy Sector's Voluntary Approach to Climate Change: Context, Prospects, and Limits," in *Canadian Energy Policy and the Struggle for Sustainable Development,* edited by Bruce Coern (University of Toronto Press, 2005).

27. National Energy Board, *Canada's Conventional Natural Gas Resources: A Status Report* (Calgary: 2004), p. 3.

28. National Energy Board, *Short Term Outlook,* p. 20.

29. Energy Information Administration, *Annual Energy Outlook 2006,* p. 86.

30. For this forecast, see North American Energy Working Group, *North American Natural Gas Vision* (Washington: 2005), p. 82.

31. See National Energy Board, *Short Term Outlook 2006,* p. 15; Energy Information Administration, *Annual Energy Outlook,* p. 86.

32. Lorenzo Meyer and Isidro Morales, *Petróleo y nación (1900–1987): La política petrolera en México* (Mexico City: Fondo de Cultura Económica, 1990).

33. David Shields, *PEMEX: La reforma petrolera* (Mexico City: Editorial Planeta, 2005), p. 45.

34. PEMEX, *Anuario Estadístico* (Mexico City: 2005).

35. George Baker, "Mexico's Presidential Elections Trigger Oil Policy Debate," *Oil and Gas Journal* 103, no. 42 (2005): 20–24.

36. Shields, *PEMEX,* p. 87.

37. PEMEX, *Anuario Estadístico,* p. 8.

38. José Antonio Beltrán Mata, *México: Crónica de los negros intereses del petróleo* (Mexico City: Grupo Editorial Diez, 2005), pp. 152–53.

39. Shields, *PEMEX,* p. 63.

40. See www.csm.pemex.com.

41. Felipe Calderón, "El reto de México" (2005) (www.felipe.org.mx/fc/html/elreto.htm).

42. Andrés Manuel López Obrador, "50 compromisos para recuperar el orgullo nacional" (2005) (www.amlo.org.mx/). For the substitution of gas for heavy oil in the power sector, see the annexes to Commitment 22 (energy), especially the section

"Aprovechar al máximo y diversificar la capacidad instalada del sector eléctrico nacional (SEN)," pp. 9-5 to 9-9.

43. Eduardo Nuñez-Rodriguez, "Mexico's Changing Energy Regulatory Framework: Liberalization under NAFTA Chapter 6," in *The First Decade of NAFTA: The Future of Free Trade in North America,* edited by Kevin C. Kennedy (Ardsley, N.Y.: Transnational, 2004).

12

International Energy Security and North America

CHARLES F. DORAN

A tendency exists among analysts of international relations to believe that an international energy crisis cannot occur through a supply disruption because such a crisis has not happened before—or at least has not happened recently. But such logic concerning the long term—namely, that oil exporters must sell their oil and therefore are not likely to disrupt supply—could in the short term break down under certain political and economic circumstances. Common wisdom holds that those who could disrupt supply, and thereby trigger a crisis, will not do so. This is because supplier countries rely heavily on the revenue from oil and are thus not willing to forgo it by provoking an energy crisis. However, in the short term, such constraints may not hold. It is the possible short-term propensity to disrupt the supply of crude oil or natural gas and the impact of such disruption on North America that this chapter explores.

The purpose of the chapter is to convince the reader that the threat to the international energy market is real and that it can best be comprehended by analyzing the motivations and mechanisms that drive oil markets. Once these fundamentals are understood, through evaluation of scenarios and examples, such a crisis could be averted or at least mitigated in terms of effect. North America is a complex place, and not all three countries would be affected in the same way by an energy crisis. Yet each member of the North American community clearly seeks a stable international political environment wherein the continuous supply of energy to the global economy is a foundational principle.

All Oil Comes from a Single Barrel

While most people know that the United States is the largest consumer of energy in the world, few are aware that it is also the largest producer of energy. But the sizable and growing disparity between the level of U.S. consumption and the level of U.S. production, as well as similar disparities elsewhere in the world, is creating economic and political problems. Moreover, despite conventional notions that the U.S. energy supply is secure because it derives from two reliable local suppliers (Canada and Mexico), in reality only a third of U.S. energy imports come from these suppliers. Canada provides about 24 percent of U.S. imported oil and natural gas, and Mexico supplies about 8 percent.[1] That leaves some two-thirds of U.S. energy imports coming from other parts of the world, countries in which the sources of supply are much less reliable than those of North America.

But even if all North American energy needs were met at home, the problem of energy security would not disappear for these countries. During a severe international energy crisis, prices would rise in North America on par with prices elsewhere. Because of the efficiency of the world oil industry and of world oil markets, all oil does indeed come from a single (extremely large) barrel. Any disruption of oil supply in one region is immediately transmitted to the world market through decisive and proportionate price increases.

Moreover, as Mexico's population and economy continue to grow, indigenous energy will increasingly be used to meet its own needs, especially if Mexico's domestic legislation concerning foreign investment in the energy industry continues to constrain energy development.[2] This constraint will have a particularly negative impact in high-cost areas such as the Gulf of Mexico, where the sophisticated technology of the international oil industry is most needed.

Underlined by the reality that North America alone accounts for 29 percent of total world energy demand, the problem of energy vulnerability is large and troublesome. This energy vulnerability will only truly be ameliorated when alternative energy sources become available at prices competitive with petroleum and natural gas prices.[3] Fusion, for example, looks on paper to be an ideal energy source, but the complex engineering necessary to achieve commercial-grade energy outputs from fusion is far from being resolved. Most other alternative energy sources either possess undesirable side effects, such as damage to the environment, or are not cost-effective. Ethanol, for example, may help the corn grower in Illinois since corn is a source of ethanol production, and this form of energy replacement is therefore politically popular. But in terms of energy equivalents, once total real costs are factored in, ethanol is actually a poor substitute for petroleum. Given the marginal cost of producing a barrel-equivalent of ethanol, ethanol is no cheaper than petroleum, and its price rises with the cost of petroleum.

Why should anyone outside the United States be convinced there is a threat to the international energy market as long as the United States refuses to sign the Kyoto agreement to reduce energy consumption? Coupled with this salient question is sometimes a statement heard in Canada, which is that U.S. overreliance on oil is an obstacle to a continental energy deal.

Taking the latter observation first, a misunderstanding seems to exist about a possible continental energy deal. There is no plan for a formulaic sharing of energy in North America, as no one in this energy community accepts the rigidity inherent in such a plan. What any continental energy deal would likely entail is an agreement to deregulate markets and retain open borders for flows of capital and energy. Under this market-based regime, transportation costs would become the most important factor in determining direction and magnitude of energy flows.

Regarding the hypothesized link between conservation and international energy security, the problem here is that, however necessary and attractive energy conservation is, it cannot solve the problem of energy security because the true threat to that security arises from political matters exogenous to the energy market itself. This threat of supply disruption is not innate to the energy market but merely uses that market for political purpose. Supply disruption could occur at any time regardless of the effectiveness or ineffectiveness of energy conservation.

Regarding Kyoto, while energy warming is a huge environmental problem that is indeed linked to the burning of fossil fuels, Kyoto is a sadly flawed environmental treaty that is not being upheld by its signatories any more than by those, like the United States, that have refused to sign. Canada, although a signatory to the treaty, is not even close to observing the terms of the treaty, nor would its citizens allow such observation were they to fully comprehend the treaty's impact. The projected time required to obtain the supposed results from Kyoto reach to the end of the twenty-first century.

Kyoto lacks, among other things, an energy-trading provision. Had such a provision been included, the United States would have signed. But such a provision alone is not sufficient to promote energy conservation. Currently, Europe has an energy-trading arrangement within the European Union that is badly crafted and therefore yields little in the way of conservation. If Canada and the United States were truly committed to the merits of energy conservation, other than that which occurs when the oil price rises, they would legislate a hefty gasoline tax. But as Joe Clark's short-lived Progressive-Conservative government in Canada learned, an energy tax in North America could raise explosive political conflicts.

Despite the fact that each North American country is a heavy energy user, declines in relative demand have occurred in the United States and Canada. As a percentage of GDP, for example, energy consumption in the United States has fallen sharply over the past three decades.[4] Such decline in relative energy consumption is sometimes taken as conservation. But important as this may be, conservation of energy alone cannot solve the problem of energy supply vulnerability.

It is true that proven reserves of petroleum and natural gas in North America seem large. For instance, the United States possesses about 21 billion barrels of crude petroleum; Mexico claims to have on hand about 15 billion barrels of crude; and Canada records about 4 billion barrels of conventional reserves. But set against the size of North American energy needs, these reserves will not meet a constant share of North America's needs over time, because much of this oil and natural gas entails high-cost production.

A bright spot in this not very bright portrait is the Canadian oil sands in the western province of Alberta, estimated to hold 175 billion barrels of oil.[5] But limited by technical and environmental constraints, oil production from the Canadian oil sands is currently in the half-million-barrel-a-day range. By 2015 Canada's objective is to produce about 3 million barrels a day. When expressed in 2004 parameters, even if all of that energy from the Canadian oil sands were to go solely to the U.S. market, 3 million barrels a day still covers only 14 percent of U.S. energy needs. Thus as welcome as the Canadian oil sands contribution would be in meeting North American energy needs, North America is still quite far from producing enough energy to eliminate the problem of supply vulnerability. This is a problem that the United States will be obliged to confront, and sooner rather than later.

Another truth is that the United States has peaked in terms of domestic production of so-called easy oil. First explored analytically by M. King Hubbert regarding the United States, the dynamic of the peaking of easy oil has now been considered in world terms. The question facing the world energy system is whether world petroleum production will likewise peak in terms of the oil and natural gas that is of high quality, close to markets, and not too expensive to extract.[6] A peaking of easy oil worldwide would set up a situation in which energy substitutes would have to be found at prices roughly comparable to petroleum so as to prevent tumult in the international energy market. This is the setting in which supply disruptions would have their most serious effect.

Much debated is the issue of whether substitutes can be found at prices that are not sharply higher; substitutes may be known, such as coal or nuclear energy, or unknown.[7] Even today surplus capacity worldwide is perilously thin and is largely located in one country, Saudi Arabia. The peaking of easy oil globally would only worsen the matter of supply vulnerability for all consumers in the world, especially for the largest importers.

Still, the impact of supply vulnerability in North America is quite different for the three countries. Despite a highly interdependent North American energy market, which could be rendered more efficient with additional deregulation, the United States is the most vulnerable of the three countries because it alone is a net importer of energy (notwithstanding that it is a net exporter of coal to its North American partners). Mexico, now an exporter of petroleum to the United States, could in the reasonably near future become a net importer of petroleum and natural gas unless it accelerates the development of its own reserves. Canada, because of its very large oil sands reserves, is likely to remain a net exporter of energy for some time to come. Given its own supply and demand situation, each North American energy partner is likely to look at global energy vulnerability in its own way and from quite diverse commercial and political perspectives.

How the World Petroleum Market Operates

The potential for energy supply vulnerability lies in the inner workings of the international energy market. All kinds of models, including partial equilibrium, general equilibrium, and international political economy models, have attempted to deconstruct and reconstruct the mechanisms of global energy markets. Textbook explanations start with the simple observation that the behavior of this particular market is similar to that of any other.[8]

First, every actor in the world except one produces a level of output that the actor is desirous and capable of producing. Second, a calculation is made regarding worldwide energy demand. This calculation is modified by the experience of the 1979 demand crisis, which revealed the importance of the amount of oil in storage or in transit. Third, the largest oil exporter in the world, Saudi Arabia, then makes up the difference between the amounts of production equivalent to the aggregate demand for world oil and the amount equivalent to the aggregate supply of world oil. As long as this difference is greater than the minimum that Saudi Arabia needs to meet its basic financial and other requirements (about 3 million barrels a day) and less than the maximum it is able to pump without damaging its oil fields (about 10 million barrels a day), Saudi Arabia theoretically sets the world price for oil.

I say theoretically because Saudi Arabia is a very small country with only a few million citizens (much fewer than the 24 million it is credited with) and because it is located in a sea of domestic and international political instability.[9] Notwithstanding help from friends, Saudi Arabia is in no strategic position to dictate oil prices recklessly to hostile producers and consumers, nor does it relish the prospect of doing so. And yet dictation of a sort is exactly what in practice happens, a dictation that is informed by not only Saudi Arabia's own internal political and economic preferences and constraints but also by the Organization of Petroleum Exporting Countries (OPEC), by powerful consumer nations, and by the Saudi Arabian Oil Company (Aramco).

Any simple characterization of the oil market thus misses a crucial element of the motivations and mechanisms that underpin crude oil pricing. Saudi Arabia does not just fill the gap between aggregate world demand and the amount of oil that must be supplied and then determine market-clearing prices in a neutral and numerical fashion. For example, in 1984–85, tired of cheating by OPEC members against agreed upon quotas, Saudi Arabia employed an administered approach to oil pricing.[10] From the Saudi perspective, it was trying to restore discipline to the international oil market. However, since it is the low-cost producer worldwide, Saudi Arabia could drop prices, drive high-cost OPEC producers out of the market, and thereby retain adequate market share.

From the U.S. perspective the problem with this form of discipline is that it imposes as much pressure on high-cost wells in the United States as on those of OPEC producers. Following a brief visit from Vice President George Bush to the Saudi capitol of Riyadh, the price, which had plunged to single digits, returned to about $18 a barrel. As a producer as well as a consumer of energy, the United States was interested not in bargain oil prices so much as orderly oil prices, prices that would offer a stable point for producers to build upon in the expansion of their drilling operations. Stable prices would also benefit commuters, industrial users, and household users. Strictly economic models often ignore this political dimension of decisions regarding oil production.

When Venezuela challenged the size of its OPEC production quota in 1996–97 by increasing production, Saudi Arabia sought to retain market share within OPEC by driving prices down temporarily. Although this strategy of price leadership cost Saudi Arabia income in the short term, it also ensured that Saudi Arabia remained the swing producer in the world oil market.

Some experts in the industry and in academia initially questioned whether Saudi Arabia could (or would) choose to determine prices in ways predicted by the administered price model, which was proposed to explain how the world oil market would operate immediately after the shift of oil power from the Texas Gulf of Mexico to the Arab Persian Gulf. The model first appeared in published form in 1977. But as an explanation for how the world oil market operates, the model has continued to account for both the motivation and the mechanism of price management. In particular, the model explains how price is actually managed in crucial intervals of market stress.

From time to time, energy prices move outside the bounds of what Saudi Arabia can manage. On the upside this can create a price that in the short term goes so high that it is vulnerable to a massive adjustment downward during some future economic recession, when the world will use far less energy than at its peak level of consumption.[11] Sometimes coalitions of OPEC states try to finesse a preferred price based on the particular characteristics of their own industrial situation. As recent OPEC history shows, sooner or later these coalitions collapse.[12]

In short, a number of variants of the basic model of oil price determination are possible. Prices are invariably shaped by long-term market conditions, which are the final arbiter and which are based on an account of all energy forms and all changes in demand and on emerging technologies. One simple rule applies throughout: in the short term, if the swing producer (Saudi Arabia) runs out of spare supply capacity, the price of oil is susceptible to manipulation by another state contemplating a supply disruption. When spare capacity is very small and the market is tight, the temptation to interrupt supply in order to drive price upward or to extort other foreign policy objectives from consumers is at its greatest and most ominous. Politics aside, the economics of oil supply create certain historic intervals when energy price manipulation by a state or states contemplating mischief is most tempting and most dangerous.

Oil Supply Disruption: How and When and What

Energy security has not been regarded as particularly problematic from the U.S. standpoint, since in the last two Iraq wars, although the price of oil rose sharply during each supply interruption, it came down just as sharply thereafter (even before the war ended, in anticipation of that outcome). Oil prices in each crisis followed the classic pattern of a price spike. In each case, the interval encompassed by the price spike was remarkably short. All of this supports those who believe that energy insecurity is a chimera, since oil exporters will always prefer selling oil to disrupting supply and that no other circumstances could account for such a supply disruption.[13]

Yet for those who mistrust history as an augur of things to come, other possibilities warrant consideration. A relevant example is the view held before the first Gulf War in 1991 that oil fields would never be targeted militarily. During the prior eight-year war between Iraq and Iran, neither side, despite very bitter warfare and large losses of life, targeted the other's oil fields. Indeed, proponents of the view that the oil fields would not come under fire invented an explanation that seemed to account for the facts, holding that each opponent's oil field was the hostage of the other. Hence the parties were mutually deterred from destroying the oil field of the other.

The problem with this thesis of oil field deterrence is that it does not encompass all possibilities. No one foresaw, for instance, that when withdrawing from Kuwait, Saddam Hussein would set fire to the very Kuwaiti fields he had hoped to tap upon occupation. History, it seems, is an imperfect guide to what might happen in the future. Those concerned about matters of energy security and insecurity will want to consider alternative outcomes in addition to those that have occurred in the past, some of which may not turn out as favorably.[14]

Between Iraq and a Hard Place

Iran's president, Mahmoud Ahmadinejad, has made proclamations from seemingly opposite sides of the argument. He has emphasized that the world has nothing to fear from Iran regarding an oil supply disruption, for there is no possible circumstance in which Iran would want to do anything other than sell petroleum and natural gas. At the same time, however, he has remonstrated against the United States for its challenges to Iran regarding its purported nuclear weapons program. Ahmadinejad has in fact repeatedly threatened that Iran will, under any circumstances involving use of U.S. force against it, strike back at U.S. interests anywhere in the world. Similarly, polls show that the average Iranian is willing to use oil as a weapon of Iranian foreign policy, thus adding further weight to the possibility that the Iranian government would contemplate supply disruptions as a foreign policy instrument.

Iran could play its oil card in either of two ways. First, in the case of tight oil markets it could powerfully affect prices by stopping oil production for a certain interval. Simulations show heuristically that a cutback of 4 percent of production could drive the price of crude to at least U.S.$150 a barrel under tight market conditions. Iran produces roughly 4 percent of the world's import needs on any given day and so could use such a stoppage to bargain politically with the principal importers of the world.

A downside for Iran is that selective boycotts make for blunt policy instruments and can inflict unintended consequences. This means that Iran, like other potential supply disrupters, would hurt its friends as much as its enemies with such an interruption of supply. It could try to sustain supplies to China and India with natural gas from pipelines to these importers dedicated exclusively to this purpose. But Iran could not prevent either country from surreptitiously selling natural gas or the equivalent value of some other energy source to third parties for the very high prices these supplies would earn. All oil, as I said, comes from a single barrel.

If it did not seek to push oil prices to their limit by cutting all exports, Iran could theoretically earn a very high return on the fewer barrels it exported. Manipulating supply in this way for commercial gain could become almost as attractive as cutting supply for punitive foreign policy purposes.

One additional factor would make this stratagem of supply interruption attractive. Even though Iran is perhaps far from acquiring a nuclear weapon, and even further from developing second-strike nuclear capability by acquiring a weapon of mass destruction, the country could thwart challenges that might be out of reach of the Iranian army or state-sponsored acts of terrorism. Possession of a nuclear weapon along with a means of transport, such as a missile obtained from North Korea, could function to shelter a mischief maker in the world oil market. It is for this reason that acquisition of a nuclear weapon by Iran is regarded by oil importers as a problem for continuity of supply at market prices. In the end, security and economics become inextricably linked.

A second scenario is a possible attempt by the West to use force to destroy Iranian nuclear installations, no matter how partial such destruction would be. This could lead to an Iranian boycott of oil markets. The paradox here is that to supposedly prevent Iran from being able to interrupt energy supply in the future, the United States and its allies might actually precipitate a supply interruption.

One issue to consider is the magnitude and territorial scope of any future supply interruption.[15] If Teheran subscribes to the oil-field-as-hostage thesis, it might restrict its response to reductions of supply from its own fields and pipelines. If Iran is indeed a rogue state, as some claim, it might seek to broaden the crisis by attempting to attack pipelines, pumping facilities, refineries, and port facilities in Abu Dhabi, Kuwait, or Saudi Arabia. This almost assuredly would trigger a defensive response by local authorities and by U.S. and British forces and a possible counterresponse against Iranian facilities as well. Such an escalation of crisis could quickly lead to counterproductive actions that might extend the duration of the crisis, transforming a price spike into a high price plateau. Any use of force against Iranian nuclear facilities would put at risk not only whatever Iran would in turn attack but also the security of all oil production and distribution in the Arab Persian Gulf area. Ironically, because of the asymmetry in attitudes toward the management of oil and natural gas prices, the government in Teheran may exaggerate its strengths, since it is likely to enjoy high energy prices under any of these scenarios.

Asymmetry is indeed at the core of the strategic problem of energy supply. If a supply disruption occurs, the price of oil will skyrocket, and exporters will flourish at the expense of importers. Thus importers will universally abhor supply disruptions, but exporters will be ambivalent. Although exporters may be wary of angering importers, who are more numerous and more powerful than exporters, exporters will always find such a disruption tempting because of windfall profits.

A corollary of this asymmetry principle regarding oil supply disruption is that exporters will either seek strong allies to defend themselves under all circumstances of market setting or will attempt to acquire the instruments of force—such as weapons of mass destruction—that they believe will enhance their security as well as their leverage, political and military.

Scenarios of Supply Disruption

At least four types of oil and natural gas supply disruption could directly affect North America. These are unilateral supply manipulation, war-based supply interruption, supply interruption plus intimidation, and supply disruption plus emulation. These scenarios vary as to motivation and circumstance but also according to strategy—that is, the decisions that oil and natural gas exporters must make to effectively achieve their goals. The U.S. strategic oil reserve, the energy futures market, the desire of firms and governments to break rank with an attempted oil embargo so as to take advantage of abnormally high prices—each of these factors is arrayed against the impulse on the part of exporters to use an energy supply disruption for a strategic purpose.

Unilateral Supply Manipulation

In its first serious test following the October War of 1973, unilateral supply manipulation by Arab oil producers led to one enormous failure and to one great success. Taking the failure first, the purpose of the supply disruption was to target the Dutch and U.S. economies in a selective boycott because of the perception that the two governments had been unusually supportive of Israel during the October War. But the selective boycott failed utterly. Neither economy experienced disproportionate suffering or a price increase. Indeed, the lesson of this effort to target individual economies was that such focused punitive action against single governments, especially the advanced governments of the Organization for Economic Cooperation and Development (OECD), is virtually impossible. What happened was that some firms and governments diverted supplies to these two economies, not as a political statement but to take advantage of the relatively higher prices in these markets. Thus the world oil market acted, as any relatively efficient market would, as though all oil was flowing from a single barrel.

But in contrast to the failure of selective oil boycotts, the conspicuous success of supply disruption was to drive up the world oil price overall. Although the purpose was political and it failed, the consequence of the attempted oil embargo was to discover that only Saudi Arabia had significant spare oil capacity. When that spare capacity is removed from the market, the stabilizer is gone; in this case, the world price of oil shot up severalfold in the following months. Political failure led to economic success. This was true for the oil exporters in the Arab Middle East, but that economic success was transmitted to oil producers everywhere.

Unilateral supply interruptions are feasible only for exporters with the following characteristics:

—Very large petroleum or natural gas reserves

—Large annual levels of production

—Small populations and thus low domestic demand for oil for revenue

—Large financial reserves that can carry the government through an interval when revenue from energy might decline.

Not many producers meet these criteria, and consequently few are by themselves capable of manipulating the price of oil, whatever their political propensity may be to do so.

War-Based Supply Interruption in the Arab Persian Gulf

An entirely different scenario of supply interruption involves that caused by war. To some extent the thesis that the oil fields of opposing parties are mutual hostages is true. But the problem with this thesis is that the bulk of the world's exportable oil and natural gas comes from one small region of the world, where fields, pipelines, refineries, and port facilities are within a few miles of each other. Iraq is a possible model for what the production situation could look like in other countries of the Persian Gulf after a war.[16]

Optimistic models of oil field recovery after a war may consider Kuwait as an example. But the lesson of the rapid recovery of the Kuwaiti fields after Saddam's slash-and-burn tactics must be qualified by awareness that all situations might not be as secure and clear-cut as with the withdrawal of Iraqi forces from Kuwait in 1991. They may, instead, look like Iraq.

Supply Interruption plus Intimidation

A rule of Middle East politics, as of the politics of any region where security is precarious, is that a government does not need to occupy another state to obtain that state's adherence to a policy. All that a powerful government in the region must do to exact compliance is to intimidate the smaller state. This is what Saddam Hussein had in mind after invading Kuwait. By invading Kuwait, Saddam doubled his energy production and revenue without altering the OPEC quota. His next objective was to threaten militarily (intimidate) but not necessarily invade Saudi Arabia and the United Arab Emirates—at the appropriate time. This tactic would signal to them that unless they complied with a common strategy of a partial cutback of crude oil and natural gas production, perhaps disguised as a technical oil field problem, they would face the possibility of military intervention by Iraq. Depending upon the elasticity of supply and demand, the loss of face involved in yielding to Saddam's intimidation could at least be ameliorated by the enjoyment of more revenue for less oil shipped abroad in the short term. Tactics of intimidation might thus be surprisingly persuasive.

From the perspective of the world's consumer states, especially the United States (with its special responsibilities for ensuring a steady supply of oil and natural gas at market-based prices), this brand of supply interruption is particularly annoying. Acquisition of a nuclear weapon by the supply disrupter raises the stakes and the costs of countering this form of oil blackmail. During the cold war and afterward, the United States has had its share of experience with nuclear crisis threats.

Given the size and sophistication of the U.S. nuclear arsenal, the small, primitive nuclear force of the supply disrupter would be neither unique nor especially impressive. Yet anything that potentially involves crossing the nuclear threshold, even in the abstract or as a tactical form of threat, is worrisome, not only for the United States but also for its neighbors and allies in the region.[17] Such nuclear saber rattling would bring back echoes of the cold war and in addition would allow energy pricing to be determined by the barrel of a gun or in the shadow of a nuclear weapon. Supply disruption plus intimidation is the most formidable, if not necessarily the most likely, of the scenarios of energy crisis accompanying tight energy markets.

Supply Disruption plus Emulation

In the past, greed could always be counted on to save energy markets. Collusion, notwithstanding OPEC member quotas, has never worked because a producer's desire for increased revenue through increased production always has won out over the producer's impulse to cooperate in the interest of production constraint and higher prices.

But will this individual desire for increased revenue always overwhelm the capacity of determined energy exporters to drive the price of oil and natural gas higher? That is the matter for analysts to contemplate as international energy markets become increasingly tight and prices are sustained at high levels over longer time periods. To the extent that large energy exporters discover that shared cutbacks actually generate more revenue because of the resulting higher prices, they may learn to work out collusive arrangements.

Security of Energy Supply and Its Perils: Impact on North America

Supply interruptions of various sorts lead to the same short-term economic result: abrupt price increases. Whether one is a producer or a consumer is very significant in determining how one views such large, abrupt price increases. Mexico and Canada, for example, are likely to view such price manipulation of petroleum and natural gas markets with far more equanimity than the United States will. But in addition to being on the net importing side of the energy equation, the United States has further cause for concern about supply disruptions in that it must contend with the consequences for world order politically and militarily.[18]

Energy crises are automatically diffused across the entire international system and hence go to the heart of every polity and every citizenry.[19] Energy crises, in short, cause political disputes of a most serious and enveloping kind. A situation with panicky governments facing strident demands from frightened and unhappy constituents during a sustained energy crisis brought on by some type of energy supply disruption is likely to lead to global turmoil. If a crisis developed in the Arab Persian Gulf, there would be no way to buffer the commercial effects from affecting all of North America as well as other parts of the international system. With the possibility that the world energy system may soon peak in terms of the availability of easy oil, set against a background of already tight markets and razor-thin spare capacity, the prospect of difficult times ahead is a concern that every prudent foreign policy decisionmaker ought to seriously assess.

Notes

1. Unless otherwise indicated, all data are drawn from International Energy Agency, "Energy Security in a Dangerous World," *World Energy Outlook* (Paris: OECD, 2004). All calculations are my own, as are any errors or omissions.

2. Greg Anderson, "Hemispheric Integration in the Post-Seattle Era: The Promise and Problems of the FTAA," *International Journal* 56 (Spring 2001): 207–33; José Antonio Beltrán Mata, *México: Crónica de los negros intereses del petróleo* (Mexico City: Grupo Editorial Diez, 2005); Carol Wise, ed., *The Post-NAFTA Political Economy: Mexico and the Western Hemisphere* (Penn State University Press, 1998).

3. See, for example, Rupert Gammon and others, "Hydrogen and Renewables Integration" (Centre of Renewable Energy Systems Technology, Loughborough University, 2006).

4. For the degree to which these trends were taken into consideration by the North American automobile industry, see Isabel Studer-Noguez, *Ford and the Global Strategies of the Multinationals* (London: Routledge, 2002).

5. Christopher M. Sands, "North American Energy: At Long Last, One Continent" (Washington: Center for Strategic and International Studies, 2005); National Energy Board, *Canada's Oil Sands: Opportunities and Challenges to 2015* (Calgary: 2006).

6. Matthew R. Simmons, *Twilight in the Desert: The Coming Saudi Oil Shock and the World Economy* (New York: Wiley, 2005).

7. Leonardo Maugeri, "Two Cheers for Expensive Oil," *Foreign Affairs,* March/April 2006, pp. 149–63.

8. Gregory Mankiw, *Principles of Economics* (Orlando: Dryden, 1997), p. 106.

9. *World in Figures* (London: Economist, 2006), p. 54.

10. Charles F. Doran, *Myth, Oil, and Politics* (New York: Free Press, 1977), pp. 138–41.

11. In a speculative but highly interesting assessment, Edward Morse and James Richard challenge the idea that Saudi Arabia will or can remain the swing producer. See Edward L. Morse and James Richard, "The Battle for Energy Dominance," *Foreign Affairs,* March/April 2002, pp. 16–31.

12. Charles F. Doran, "OPEC Structure and Cohesion: Exploring the Determinants of Cartel Policy," *Journal of Politics* 42 (1980): 82–101.

13. John Gault, "Has Iraq Helped America's Energy Security?" *International Herald Tribune,* December 14, 2005, op-ed. Gault says that many in the world believe the purpose of the U.S. invasion of Iraq was to "seize control of the country's oil." If that were true, then given current production levels, the plan must have disappointed. What does "seize control" mean when the government that benefits from the sale of Iraqi oil is Iraq? These analysts mistake security of oil supply at orderly prices for appropriation of oil, which is not what the U.S.-British presence in the Persian Gulf concerns.

14. Anthony H. Cordesman and Khalid R. Al-Rodhan, *The Global Oil Market* (Washington: Center for Strategic and International Studies, 2006).

15. Michael A. Toman, *International Oil Security: Problems and Policies* (Washington: Resources for the Future, 2002).

16. Consider the discussion in Thomas E. Ricks, "Merits of Partitioning Iraq; or, Allowing Civil War Weighed," *Washington Post,* April 30, 2006, p. A18.

17. Patrick Clauson and Simon Henderson, "Reducing Vulnerability to Middle East Energy Shocks: A Key Element in Strengthening U.S. Energy Security" (Washington: Washington Institute for Near East Policy, 2005).

18. E. Anthony Wayne, "Energy Security: A Global Challenge" (Brussels: European Policy Centre, 2006).

19. Erica S. Downs, "National Energy Security Depends on International Energy Security" (Brookings, 2006).

13

NORTH AMERICAN IMMIGRATION
The Search for Positive-Sum Returns

TAMARA M. WOROBY

The 1994 North American Free Trade Agreement (NAFTA) was mainly about the free flow of goods and services among the three signatories and, with the exception of visas for a limited group of professionals, did not address migration issues. Since that time, the number of people crossing Mexican, Canadian, and especially U.S. borders has increased, creating in the minds of some a causal link between trade liberalization under NAFTA and increased migration flows. In the midst of this, academics and policymakers have contemplated the deepening of NAFTA, a process that could in theory include the creation of a North American common market and thus a freer flow of the North American population across national borders.

However, the cloud of September 11, 2001, has made border security in the United States a dominant issue, steering public discussion away from a rational assessment of the social and economic impacts of immigration. In this chapter, I examine various facets of immigration in North America with an eye toward understanding the motives for migration, the importance of using the term *immigration* correctly, the actual patterns of migration, and the distinction between border enforcement and immigration reform.

Not All Migrants are Immigrants

People cross international borders for various reasons and can be classified into two groups: *immigrants* and nonimmigrants. Immigrants are those who take up permanent residence in a new country. This may be for the purposes of a new job (economic), to join family members already permanently residing in the new country (family reunification), or to seek safe haven (refuge).

Although all three countries in North America experience both immigration and emigration, Canada and the United States are net receiving countries, whereas Mexico is overwhelmingly a net sending country.[1] Between 2000 and 2005 the annual increase in legal immigrants living in the United States averaged 900,000, with only 400,000 being first-time entrants and the remaining 500,000 representing adjustments to the permanent legal status of foreigners already residing in the United States. In comparison, the annual inflow of legal immigrants to Canada averaged 230,000 and to Mexico just 15,000.[2]

Nonimmigrants are migrants who enter a country with the intention to reside for a temporary period of time. This group consists of foreign students, temporary workers, business visitors, and tourists. They may or may not be required to enter with a visa.[3] The length of stay will vary according to the purpose of the visit and can range from days (in which case there is the possibility of multiple entries by one person within a given year) to several years. Nonimmigrants wishing to remain permanently in a country must apply for an adjustment of their legal status to that of an immigrant.

There is also an illegal dimension to migration in that both immigrants and nonimmigrants might enter a country unlawfully. It is incorrect to refer to such undocumented (or illegal) *migration* as undocumented (or illegal) *immigration,* as the intention of these migrants—to stay temporarily (such as agricultural workers) or permanently—may vary.[4] Undocumented migration has emerged as an important problem for the United States.[5] As I discuss below, despite the fact that Mexico has very low levels of legal immigration, undocumented migration into Mexico (which tends to be predominantly nonimmigrant and headed for the United States) poses serious challenges. The annual inflow of undocumented migrants to the United States may be as high as 500,000 and to Mexico at least 150,000.[6] Paradoxically, tighter border controls can turn an undocumented migrant's intended temporary stay into a permanent one, since the risk of not being able to reenter at a future date increases.

Border Enforcement Is Not Immigration Reform

The number of nonimmigrants dwarfs the number of immigrants in the data on migration flows. For example, in a recent year, approximately 1.4 million immigrants (including legal and illegal) and 33.0 million nonimmigrants entered the United States. For Canada, these numbers were 250,000 immigrants and 6.2 million nonimmigrants.[7] Thus when we refer to a country's immigration policy, we limit the discussion to a small fraction of those who actually cross that country's borders.

In light of this, a successful immigration policy should, at the very least, consider immigrant admissions in terms of optimal size as well as the demographic and labor market characteristics of immigrants. In other words, what specific socioeconomic characteristics would be desired of someone who is going to become a permanent member of the receiving country's society? What proportion of immigrants should be admitted on the basis of skills and human capital? What proportion should be refugees or family members? How different might the economic consequences be if one group is favored over others?

Furthermore, can it be assumed that selection criteria that were once considered valid are still appropriate? If they are not, what flexibility exists to allow for a policy adjustment? Effective immigration reform must address such questions, and at a minimum it should be transparent and designed with informed public input. Very little of this appears to have occurred in the United States. As Mark Krikorian observes about U.S. immigration policy, "Even by the standards of lawmaking in a democracy, immigration policy has developed in a remarkably haphazard, politicized, and aimless fashion."[8]

A major reason that the United States has found it difficult to undertake an open and informed discussion about immigration reform is its preoccupation with border security since September 11 and its reaction to the increasing number of undocumented migrants headed its way. Border enforcement, however, does not constitute immigration reform. Border enforcement is about effectively controlling the flow of all migrants, be they temporary or permanent, legal or illegal. It is about establishing the integrity of borders so that those who should get into a country are able to and those who should not, do not. It is also a prerequisite for effective immigration reform, for when there is integrity of the national border, public policy can turn more easily to addressing questions concerning the characteristics of permanent residents. Put differently, without successful border enforcement, successful immigration reform cannot be achieved.

Trends in North American Immigration Policy

What then has been the experience of immigration reform in North America and what are the prospects for a more rational and humane immigration policy within the NAFTA region? To evaluate the policy choices that have been made, I examine recent trends on the basis of geographic patterns. I begin with a comparison of Canada and the United States as immigrant receiving countries, with Mexico in this case a sending country. I then consider two other flows that are significant in the context of North America: migrant flows out of Canada and migrant flows into Mexico. The discussion is at first limited to legal immigration, but I conclude with an examination of undocumented migration.

Canada and the United States as Receiving Countries with Divergent Paths

A good starting point in assessing the importance of immigration within a country is to examine the proportion of foreign-born in that country's population, since this figure represents the cumulative effect of all previous annual inflows of legal permanent residents. Proportionately, the United States, whose legal foreign-born population is 12 percent of its population, appears to be less open than Canada, whose foreign-born population accounts for almost 19 percent of its population. Based on this measure, Canada is one of the most open countries in the world, with only a few countries such as Australia (where 23 percent of the population is foreign-born) and Switzerland (where 20 percent of the population is foreign-born) being more open. In contrast, less than 1 percent of Mexico's population is foreign-born.[9]

Canada's pattern of greater openness to immigrants dates back more than a hundred years (see table 13-1). At the beginning of the twentieth century, the share of foreign-born in the total population was almost identical for both countries (13.6 percent for the United States and 13.5 percent for Canada), but since then the Canadian foreign-born have consistently comprised a larger share of total population than the U.S. foreign-born. In some years this difference has been as great as a factor of three. (For example, in 1960 the foreign-born share in Canada was 15.3 percent but was only 5.4 percent in the United States.) Both countries saw immigration's relative importance increase in the early 1900s, decline after 1930, and then begin to rise again after 1970.

This increase in immigration, however, has been far more significant in the United States, resulting in almost a threefold increase since 1970 (4.7 percent to 12.1 percent) and increasing 50 percent since 1990 (7.9 percent to

Table 13-1. *Foreign-Born in the United States and Canada, Various Years, 1900–2005*

Percent of total population

Year	United States	Canada
1900	13.6	13.5
1920	13.2	23.7
1940	8.8	17.2
1960	5.4	15.3
1970	4.7	14.6
1980	6.2	16.1
1990	7.9	16.4
2005 or 2001[a]	12.1	18.8

Source: U.S. Census of the Population, 1960, 1980, and 2000; Census Population Survey 2006; Statistics Canada, Catalogue 99-936; Census of Canada 2001.

a. Data are for 2005 in the United States and 2001 in Canada.

12.1 percent). This has no doubt contributed to the perception by the American public that U.S. immigration has run amok.

A second difference between Canadian and U.S. immigration lies in the geographic origin of immigrants. One in three foreign-born residents in the United States arrived from Mexico. Overall, more than 50 percent of the U.S. foreign-born comes from Latin America and the Caribbean. Almost one-quarter is from Asia, and only about 10 percent are from Europe. Immigrants from Africa, Canada, the Middle East, and Oceania together make up less than one-tenth of total U.S. foreign-born.[10] Recent immigration patterns, reflected in annual inflows, suggest that for the most part these trends will continue, with the geographic origin of U.S. immigrants remaining basically the same.

In contrast, the Western Hemisphere is not a major source of Canadian immigration, nor does one single country play as significant a role in Canadian immigration as Mexico does in U.S. immigration. In fact, Mexican immigration to Canada accounts for barely 1 percent of all foreign-born. The continent of Europe has dominated Canadian immigration in the past and continues to account for about 40 percent of all foreign-born.[11] However, new geographic patterns are emerging in Canada. Whereas immigrants from East and Southeast Asia make up a third of all the foreign-born in Canada, they account for more than half of recent flows. Should these trends continue, the predominant geographic origin of the foreign-born in Canada will shift from Europe to Asia.[12]

The trends outlined above reveal that a South-North flow will continue to dominate U.S. immigration issues, whereas an increasing East-West flow will preoccupy Canadian policymakers. In addition, there is a clear need for U.S. immigration policy to develop a bilateral component vis-à-vis Mexico.

During the 1960s both Canadian and U.S. immigration policies, which had been based on country of origin as the main selection criterion, underwent significant but different changes, which continue to the present day. In the United States family reunification—the notion that an immigrant should be given priority if he or she already has close family residing in the country—became the overriding principle for immigrant selection. In Canada the more important factor was whether the immigrant had the economic skills that Canada required. Canada introduced an assessment technique for economic skills, allocating points on the basis of desired economic characteristics. The attractive feature of this system is that the maximum number of points allocated to each of the categories can be easily adjusted to reflect changes in the economic needs of the country.

Since 1994 Canada has systematically increased the emphasis placed on the skill level of the immigrant by raising the points assigned to higher education. For example, twenty-five points are now allotted to education: a doctorate or master's degree earns an applicant the full twenty-five points, but a secondary school education is given only five points.[13] During this same time period, the United States has continued to consider family reunification first. The result of these diverging positions in immigrant selection is that approximately two-thirds of immigrants entering the United States do so on the basis of family reunification criteria and only one-fifth because of their skills. In contrast, some 60 percent of immigrants entering Canada do so based on their skill levels and only one quarter because of family reunification criteria (see table 13-2). The economic implications of these differences have been profound.

The skill level among immigrants to the United States has markedly deteriorated. In an analysis undertaken in 2002 the Center for Immigration Studies found that almost one-third of all U.S. immigrants had less than a high school education, more than triple the numbers of native-born Americans; immigrants, moreover, accounted for some 40 percent of all high school dropouts. At the upper end of the skill continuum, immigrants were no longer more highly educated than their U.S. counterparts, having proportionately almost the same number of graduate or professional degrees and slightly fewer bachelor's degrees than the native-born. This was not the case in the period before 1970, but it is now a firm trend.[14] In contrast, Canadian

Table 13-2. *U.S. and Canadian Immigrant Population, by Category of Visa,*
2000–04 Average
Percent of total immigration

Category	United States	Canada
Family	67	26
Economic	21	61
Refugee	8	13
Lottery	4	...

Source: *Yearbook of Immigration Statistics,* 2002, 2004, and 2006; Citizenship and Immigration Canada, *Facts and Figures Immigration Overview,* 2001–2005.

immigrants are 50 percent more likely than native-born Canadians to hold a university degree.[15]

For native-born Americans, the proportion of high school dropouts is about 8 percent; yet for Mexican immigrants this figure is over 65 percent (see table 13-3). The proportion of high school dropouts for other Latin American immigrants is also high, significantly above that of most other countries. Recall that one of three U.S. foreign-born is from Mexico, over half are from Latin America, and since 1965 family reunification has dominated U.S. immigrant selection criteria.

The primary reason for the well-documented decline in the skills of U.S. immigrants is the selection criteria. Put simply, if immigrants arrive from countries where the skill level is low, and if family reunification is used as the primary selection criterion, then over time (because unskilled immigrants are more likely to have unskilled relatives) this lower skill level will be magnified in the foreign-born population. In this way, family reunification creates an economic multiplier effect.

Based on the above evidence, it becomes easier to understand the major failure of U.S. immigration policy: a combination of geographic origin and family reunification criteria has created an economic immigrant underclass in the United States. Immigration experts have, for this reason, long recommended that the United States reevaluate its immigration selection criteria.[16] In the current political climate, however, with the focus on undocumented migration and border security, this reassessment of immigration policy—in other words true immigration reform—will be postponed for some time to come.

The mismatch between the emphasis on postgraduate degrees in Canadian immigrant selection and the low skill set of Mexican and other Latin

Table 13-3. *Adult High School Dropout Rates, by Country of Origin,*
U.S. Immigrant Population, 2002
Percent

Country of origin	Dropout rate
Mexico	65.5
El Salvador	63.5
Guatemala	49.1
Vietnam	29.0
Jamaica	19.3
China/Taiwan/Hong Kong	14.1
Poland	14.0
India	9.2
Native-born	7.6
Iran	7.4
United Kingdom	5.9

Source: Steve Camarota, *Analysis of Current Population Survey 2002* (Washington: Center for Immigration Studies, 2002).

American immigrants helps to explain why immigration to Canada from the Western Hemisphere is so low. As long as Canadian immigration policy continues to emphasize high educational achievement, there is little likelihood that Mexican labor flows to Canada will increase. However, at least two economic pressures may drive Canadian policymakers to relax this preference in the near term. First, Canada is now riding out a global commodities boom and facing severe labor shortages, especially in the oil-rich West, where unemployment is half the national average. Second, there is evidence that the more recently arrived Canadian immigrants, who in fact have more education than previous immigrant groups, are not being successfully absorbed into labor markets. It has been noted that "Toronto is . . . full of taxi-driving doctors and nuclear physicists."[17]

The causes for this mismatch are unclear, and various hypotheses have been presented.[18] One concerns institutional barriers such as professional qualifications not being recognized, while another points to fundamental demand changes in the Canadian economy. There have also been charges of racial discrimination in the workplace. On the positive side, Canadians are engaged in public discussion of this situation, and Canadian immigration policy is sufficiently flexible such that a change in the points allotted to a particular economic characteristic can allow for an adjustment to be made.

Canada as a Sending Country—A Loss of Skills?

Another dimension of North American migration worth examining is the movement of Canadians to the United States. Unlike the United States and most other receiving countries, Canada has historically been concerned with both labor inflows and labor outflows. While net migration has been positive and has contributed substantially to population growth for most of the past century, there is the question of whether Canada loses human capital to the United States and in effect suffers a brain drain. While the number of Canadians moving to the United States may not be high in either absolute or relative terms, it is the quality of exiting workers that matters, and it is possible that Canada is losing its best and its brightest.

A study undertaken in 2000 by Statistics Canada found that during the 1990s the number of highly skilled workers migrating to the United States from Canada increased, especially skilled workers in certain economically important occupations. Yet during this same time period, the number of highly skilled workers entering Canada also increased (due to the Canadian immigrant selection preferences discussed above) and was more than enough to offset losses. In all, four times as many foreign university graduates immigrated to Canada as Canadian graduates emigrated to the United States, implying a brain gain rather than a brain drain.

Researchers who contest this conclusion tend to compare the quality of those skilled workers leaving with the quality of those arriving. For example, when "churning costs" associated with the integration and adaptation of new immigrants (such as administrative fees, language study, retraining and recertification costs, as well as loss of income before finding a job) are factored in, it appears that new arrivals do not replace the Canadians who have left.[19]

To appreciate the difficulty in establishing the size or existence of any brain drain, consider the following results from a survey of newly graduated Canadian Ph.D.'s. The survey found that 20 percent of these graduates were planning to emigrate, with only 13 percent intending to move to the United States and 7 percent intending to go elsewhere. However, this same survey found that of new Ph.D.'s in the biological and health sciences, more than 40 percent intended to move to the United States.[20] At present, without more detailed data and the ability to assess the quality of all skilled workers moving, one can argue as easily that there is a brain drain as that there is not. It has been put best as follows:

> Canada may well lose skilled workers to the United States and import skilled human capital from other countries. However, the quality of the

two-way flow is key, though it is difficult to calculate whether the loss of a top genetics researcher at a public lab can be compensated for by the arrival of even several hundred IT specialists. On the other hand, as skilled migration between advanced countries is often temporary, there may be a double gain from the circulation of the highly skilled, first from the overseas experience acquired by their genetics researcher, and second from the constant inflow of skilled workers.[21]

Analysts agree that since the early 1990s an average of about 10,000 highly skilled and educated Canadians have emigrated annually to the United States.[22] For those who believe that there is a brain drain, the debate should consider those Canadians working in the United States on TN visas. Section 341 of the NAFTA Implementation Act, enacted in December 1993, created the TN visa to allow Mexican, U.S., and Canadian professionals in sixty-three specific occupations to work temporarily within North America. The suspicion is that this visa has created an easy way for some Canadian professionals (brains) to, de facto, reside permanently in the United States, since these visas can be renewed annually and indefinitely.[23]

The issuance of TN visas to Canadians and Mexicans seeking entry into the United States was at first subject to differing conditions. For Canadians there was no limit on the number of TN visas that could be issued, and while valid for a year, these visas could be renewed indefinitely. This continues to be the case today. For Mexicans there were labor certification requirements, and the total number of visas that could be issued was subject to an annual limit of 5,000. These conditions were both removed in 2004. It is not yet clear what effect this will have on Mexican professional out-migration, but the Canadian case may yield some insights.

The number of Canadians entering the United States annually under TN visas has increased significantly since 1996, declining somewhat after 2001 and stabilizing in recent years at nearly three times the baseline level in 1996 (table 13-4). In particular, annual permits have risen from about 24,000 in 1996 to over 64,000 in 2004. As there is a lack of detailed data on the longer-term intentions of the Canadian NAFTA workers, it is difficult to assess what these much higher numbers imply for Canada. While it can be argued that these may be brains intending to permanently reside in the United States, the counter argument—that many of these workers will return to Canada after some time and bring home improved human capital—can also be made. Only with time will this become clear.

Table 13-4. *Annual Number of Canadian and Mexican Professionals Entering the United States on TN Visas, 1996–2004* [a]

Number

Country	1996	1998	1999	2000	2001	2002	2003	2004
Canada[b]	23,600	58,200	66,600	88,500	92,100	71,300	58,200	4,200
Mexico	243	824	1,737	2,720	3,341	2,366	1,268	2,000

Source: *Yearbook of Immigration Statistics,* selected years, 1997–2005.

a. Numbers are for workers only and exclusive of visas granted to NAFTA dependents.

b. Numbers are rounded for Canada.

One is also struck by the staggering difference in the number of TN permits issued to Canadians and Mexicans. Recall that Canadian permits were not subject to a numerical limit, whereas Mexican permits (until 2004) were subject to a 5,000 cap. At the same time, this cap has never been reached. This may be due to structural economic conditions or to labor certification procedures, as these could have slowed the visa review process. It is also too soon to predict what the effect of removing the TN cap will imply for Mexican entrants, but if the case of Canada is any indication, there is the possibility that Mexico will find itself debating the threat of a brain drain to the United States as well.

Mexico as a Receiving Country—A Major Stopover Point

As discussed earlier, Mexico is a country of out-migration, with most migrants moving to the United States and proportionately few to Canada. It is estimated that almost 10 percent of the Mexican population resides in the United States.[24] The primary cause of this migration lies in the sizable Mexican-U.S. income differential, which is the highest in the world between any two geographically contiguous countries. Specifically, U.S. per capita income is four times that of Mexico.[25] As long as this disparity persists, economic theory assures us that pressures to migrate will continue. So what then can be said about migration inflows to Mexico, and what is their significance within the context of North America?

As noted earlier, the total number of foreign-born residing in Mexico is very small, amounting to just 0.5 percent of the population, or less than 500,000 residents. Citizens from the United States dominate this legal flow, comprising some 70 percent of Mexico's foreign-born, while Central Americans and Europeans each account for almost 10 percent, followed by South Americans, who total just 6 percent.[26]

The demographic characteristics of the foreign-born vary significantly by region of origin, indicating different motives for migration. A 2004 study, for example, found that 68.4 percent of U.S. immigrants are less than fifteen years old, suggesting that most of this flow consists of children of Mexican return migrants, children who were born in the United States. In the case of immigrants from Central and South America, however, most are between the ages of twenty and forty-five, revealing an economic motive for migration; and one-third of immigrants from Europe are over the age of fifty, suggesting that leisure and retirement are the main motives.[27]

Recently, because of civil unrest in Guatemala, Mexico has also had to address the issue of refugees. In concert with the Office of the United Nations High Commissioner for Refugees (UNHCR), Mexico has instituted policies that have resulted in successful repatriation. Seasonal workers are also of note in Mexico, consisting of agricultural laborers from Central America, mainly Guatemala. The annual inflow of this group has declined since 2000, averaging about 40,000 annually, although the number may actually be as high as 70,000, since part of this inflow is also undocumented.[28]

In the context of North American migration, undocumented workers are a far more important aspect of Mexico's migratory inflows, since Mexico serves as a transit country for the large numbers of undocumented migrants en route to the United States. The majority of these migrants cross into the Mexican state of Chiapas, at Mexico's southern border with Guatemala. Undocumented migrants are primarily from Guatemala, Honduras, and El Salvador. One estimate puts the number of undocumented entrants into Mexico since 1990 at an annual average of 130,000, with an observed increase from 157,000 in 2000 to 182,000 in 2003.[29] Other estimates are as high as 400,000 in 2004, which saw 204,000 Central Americans detained by Mexican authorities at the southern border and 50,000 detained by U.S. authorities at the U.S.-Mexico border.[30] To appreciate the size of this flow of undocumented migrants, compare it with the 44,000 Central American legal immigrants in Mexico.

The Illegal Dimension of Migration

To say that the topic of immigration is now on the U.S. radar screen is an understatement. At the same time, there is confusion in the press and in public discourse as to just who the focus of this debate is: legal immigrants or undocumented migrants? Invariably, the adjective *Mexican* also appears. The reason for this is that the socioeconomic characteristics of undocumented migrants living in the United States appear to be similar to those of legal immigrants but in exaggerated form. Evidence on undocumented migration is, of course, more difficult to gather, and the number is an estimate at best. Nevertheless, there is consensus on several aspects and trends.

The first is that the number of undocumented migrants is large and growing. Almost one-third of the foreign-born in the United States are undocumented residents. When the 1986 Immigration Reform and Control Act (IRCA) was implemented, an act that included amnesty, it was estimated that the total number of undocumented migrants living in the United States was about 3 million. Today, most estimates place the total between 11 million and 12 million, amounting to 4 percent of the U.S. population and as much as 5 percent of the workforce.[31] It is also estimated that 35 percent of this population arrived between 2000 and 2005. When this number is added to the number of legal foreign-born listed in Table 13-1, and given the fact that Canada does not register notable levels of undocumented migration, my earlier conclusion that the United States has proportionately far fewer foreign residents than Canada is no longer as valid.

Second, as with legal immigration, unauthorized migrants are predominantly from Mexico. While over 80 percent come from Latin America, of these 55 percent are from Mexico. It is believed that most unauthorized workers are less skilled than legal immigrants, with three-quarters not having completed high school (compare with data in table 13-3). This lower skill level, coupled with the fact that unauthorized workers have a negotiating disadvantage in the labor market, is reflected in lower weekly earnings. These have been estimated at around $380, compared to $700 for legal permanent residents and $930 for U.S. citizens.[32]

The existence of this sizable undocumented population provoked reactionary legislation in the U.S. House of Representatives in the fall of 2005, which in turn opened the floodgates to a huge public debate on "immigration." The remainder of this chapter reviews some of the main arguments to consider in the search for solutions to the unauthorized migrant problem in the United States. Two separate and distinct factors must be addressed: the first is what to do with those unauthorized migrants who are already residing in the United States; the second is to identify those policies that will best prevent future unauthorized migration.

How to Deal with Existing Unauthorized Immigration

The stark reality is that there is no practical way for the United States to identify and deport 12 million people, and therefore one has to think about how best to manage this population. Whatever steps are undertaken, the solution will involve compromise. The notion that most of these migrants will eventually be allowed to stay should be balanced with an imposition on them of some cost, because, in fact, they have broken the law. Otherwise the message will be sent globally that if one waits long enough (in this case twenty years—that is, from the passage of the IRCA to the present) the United States inevitably will grant an unauthorized migrant legal status.

Unauthorized migrants have not only ignored the boundaries and laws of the United States, they have also been unfair to their fellow citizens who like them seek better economic opportunities through migration (a faultless goal); but unlike them, they have followed procedure, applied for legal immigration, and are waiting at home for the process to work. Unauthorized migrants have unfairly jumped to the head of the queue and should not be given legal resident status without first paying some sort of penalty.

The creation of an intermediate immigrant category, something between unauthorized and legal resident status, could be a starting point. For this reason, the granting of temporary status (as in a guest worker program) is reasonable, for it would bring the unauthorized into the open. Conditions for proof of economic contribution, such as a required number of years in active employment before applying for change of status to legal resident, could be set forth. If these conditions are not met, there would need to be a mechanism that would allow the government to readily identify individuals and to deport them.

Additionally, a penalty could be considered such as not allowing these immigrants, once they obtain legal status, to sponsor other family members as soon as they could have had they entered as legal immigrants. However, in tandem with this policy of amnesty with conditions would have to be a parallel system giving integrity to the border and halting the flow of unauthorized migrants. Without this parallel system, ten years from now the United States will find itself in the same position as today but perhaps with another 20 million undocumented migrants.

Policies to Prevent Future Undocumented Migration

While building walls at the border may seem to be an immediate solution to preventing further undocumented migration, such a policy will simply encourage other more creative ways to enter the United States. This could include tunnels dug underground or increased entry through ocean ports and across the mostly open Canadian border. The only permanent solution, therefore, is to address the underlying causes of such undocumented migration. Put simply, people will continue to come to the United States as long as they can obtain higher paying employment there. It is only by focusing on this fact that specific permanent solutions can be found.

Sanctions on U.S. employers who hire undocumented workers can go a long way to stop the flow, but this option has for the most part been ignored.[33] Such laws already exist, having been introduced as part of the IRCA, and require no further legislative action. Rather, it is the enforcement of these laws that needs to be undertaken, since this has been virtually nonexistent. For example, according to a study by the U.S. Government Accountability Office, only three fines on employers who hired illegal workers were imposed in 2004.[34] Undocumented workers are the supply side of the labor market, but they cannot become employed without the demand side, which is provided by U.S. employers.

Markets working freely will eliminate shortages. Thus where there are no migrants to fill jobs, employers will have to pay higher wages to hire American workers. It is therefore important to understand that effective employer sanctions will result in an increase in wages at the bottom end of the labor market, which in turn will be passed on to the consumer in higher prices. This economic reality is no doubt the primary reason that there has been such reluctance in the United States to enforcing employer sanctions.

While employer sanctions can significantly reduce the draw of U.S. jobs, policies that help create more and better jobs in the sending countries, particularly in Mexico, are also imperative. To achieve this, there are several roads to consider. First, the amount of direct aid should be increased. While the United States has committed to the G-8 goal of raising its total global aid, or official development assistance, to 0.7 percent of gross national income, the sad reality is that this number amounts to less than 0.2 percent of U.S. gross domestic product.[35] Mexico receives 17.7 percent of this meager amount.[36]

A second way to improve labor opportunities is to consider the "trade as aid" approach. This, of course, was one of the original intentions of NAFTA. Thus policymakers truly concerned with immigration should examine the questions of why the Mexican economy has not obtained the expected benefits of NAFTA and what can be done to deliver on the promise of NAFTA. The reality is that remittances have become a vital alternative to the economic impetus that should have come from increased trade opportunities. Mexico receives the greatest remittances of any country in the world, this estimate being at least $16 billion annually.[37]

Finally, increasing legal immigration is yet another policy alternative that should be considered to control undocumented migration, in that this will encourage potential immigrants to join the legal immigration queue. One step is to shorten the waiting time for the completion of official immigration procedures. The present backlog in the processing of applications is significant when compared to immigration flows. For example, in May 2006 U.S. Citizenship and Immigration Services had a backlog of 420,000 applications, and the U.S. Department of Labor, which also processes applications, had an additional 235,000 applicants waiting to be processed.[38]

Concluding Summary

In this chapter I examine North American immigration trends so as to clarify the emerging issues associated with North American integration. My assessment of immigration patterns is based on geographic flows and migrant types. This has flushed out the difference between government policies that focus on border enforcement and those that focus on immigration reform. Border enforcement is about providing security, controlling the entry of temporary and permanent legal migrants, and preventing illegal migrant flows. Immigration reform, in distinction, deals with a small subset of the total number of people crossing borders, since immigrants are those migrants who have been screened and approved for permanent legal residency (and eventual citizenship if they so choose) in the receiving country.

Economic motives are key to understanding why people move, with family reunification being the ripple effect of the initial decision. This being the case, the pressure to migrate will continue as long as significant income differentials exist, such as those between Mexico and the United States. One simply cannot separate economic development issues from migration issues. This is a reality that has not fully resonated with U.S. policymakers, who focus on strengthening barriers to entry and so avoid addressing the causes of undocumented migration. The Mexican government, in turn, has the opportunity to become a more effective partner in managing North American migration by strengthening controls at its own southern border, as the United States continues to struggle with an estimated half million undocumented entries annually.

If a country is to view immigration in a positive light, its social and economic benefits must be included in any public discussion. The size of immigration as well as immigrant selection criteria should be openly debated. The two net receiving countries in this present discussion—Canada and the United States—follow different paths in this respect.

Canadian immigration policy emphasizes the economic returns from migration, with a resulting focus on selecting skilled immigrants. There is short-run evidence that this has not been to Canada's full advantage. For example, it does not follow that increasing the supply of highly educated workers guarantees that the national economy will be able to absorb these new arrivals. Nor does a preoccupation with postgraduate education address worker shortages in Canada's oil-rich West. However, Canada has in place a flexible immigration system so that, should it be deemed preferable, adjustments to meet the changing demands of the economy can be made.

In the United States preoccupation with security and border enforcement is likely to relegate to the back burner for some time to come a long overdue debate on the social and economic benefits and costs of immigration.

Notes

1. According to the World Bank, in the period 1995–2000 official net migration (defined as legal immigration minus emigration) into the United States was 6,200,000; into Canada it was 733,000; whereas in Mexico there was a net out-migration of 2,000,000. At the global level, the United States received 44 percent of total official world inflows. World Bank, *World Development Report 2006* (Washington: 2006), pp. 298–99.

2. Specifically, the number of U.S. permanent admissions in 2000 was 850,000; in 2001 and again in 2002 the number was 1,064,000; in 2003 it was 706,000; and in 2004 it was 946,000 (www.uscis.gov/graphics/shared/aboutus/statistics). For Canada, the annual immigrant inflow surpassed 250,000 in 2001 but decreased to 236,000 in 2004 (www.cic.gc.ca/statistics). Annual inflows for Mexico have been estimated as an average based on the difference in census estimates of Mexican foreign-born in 1990 and 2000. Consejo Nacional de Población, "La inmigracion en México," in *Nueva era de las migracions: Caracteristicas de la migracion internacional en México* (December 2004), p. 94.

3. For example, the U.S. Visa Waiver Program allows eligible citizens from twenty-seven countries to enter the United States for a maximum stay of ninety days if the visit is for purposes of business or tourism (www.travel.state.gov/visa/about/report). Increased security coordination at the Canada-U.S. border has resulted in both countries now having common visa policies for 144 countries.

4. While some prefer the term *undocumented* and object to the term *illegal*—on the grounds that a person cannot be illegal, only their actions can—both the Canadian and U.S. governments refer to "illegal immigrants" in official publications. Thus I use the terms *undocumented* and *illegal* interchangeably in this chapter.

5. Estimates of the total number of undocumented immigrants living in Canada range from 100,000 to 200,000, or about 0.5 percent of the total population. For a summary of this issue, see M. Jimenéz, "Illegal Immigrants Toiling in Canada's Underground Economy," *Globe and Mail,* November 15, 2003, p. 17.

6. Although some estimates of undocumented inflows into the United States range between 350,000 and 400,000 annually, estimates by the Pew Hispanic Center place the

number of annual unlawful admissions at 500,000 during the period 2000–04. See Jeffrey S. Passel, *Estimates of the Size and Characteristics of the Undocumented Migrant Population in the United States* (Washington: Pew Hispanic Center, 2005). The Instituto Nacional de Migracion in Mexico estimates, on the basis of survey evidence, that almost 150,000 illegal border crossings occurred in 2004, exclusive of 204,000 non-Mexicans detained at the Mexican border and 54,000 non-Mexicans detained at the U.S. border. Instituto Nacional de Migracion, *Foros hacia una politica migratoria integral en la frontera sur de México* (Mexico City: Secretaria de Gobernacion, 2005), p. 35.

7. Peter Rekai, *U.S. and Canadian Immigration Policies: Marching Together to Different Tunes* (Toronto: C. D. Howe Institute, 2002).

8. Mark Krikorian, "Legal Immigration: What Is to Be Done?" in *Blueprints for an Ideal Immigration Policy,* edited by Richard Lamm and Alan Simpson (Washington: Center for Immigration Studies, 2001), p. 48.

9. Organization for Economic Cooperation and Development, *Trends in International Migration* (Paris: 2005).

10. Calculated using data from Migration Information Source, Migration Policy Institute (www.migrationinformation.org/globaldata/countrydata/data.cfm).

11. Ibid.

12. It should be noted also that China is now the number-one sending country, and its importance in Canadian immigration is growing, with annual flows to Canada increasing from 6.7 percent in 1990 to 15.8 percent in 2004.

13. The passing score was lowered in September 2003 from seventy-five to sixty-seven points. The government at any time can adjust the passing score and also the weight of each attribute. Other attributes in Canada's selection grid are language (twenty-four points), experience (twenty-one points), age (ten points), arranged employment (ten points), and adaptability (ten points).

14. For more detail on this point see Steve Camarota, *Analysis of Current Population Survey 2002* (Washington: Center for Immigration Studies, 2002).

15. Organization for Economic Cooperation and Development, *Trends in International Migration* (Paris: 2003), p. 45. Note that these figures are for all immigrants and not just for the newest arrivals, which of course would have even higher skilled proportions, since the points for a university degree have increased since 1994.

16. This is the consensus that emerges from the compelling essays in the edited collection by Lamm and Simpson, *Blueprints for an Ideal Immigration Policy.* See also George Borjas, "Making It Worse," *National Review,* February 2, 2004, pp. 88–94; Jagdish Bhagwati, "El Norte," *Wall Street Journal,* March 28, 2006; "Sense, not Sensenbrenner," *Economist,* April 1, 2006, p. 18; James Goldsborough, "Out of Control Immigration," *Foreign Affairs,* September–October 2000, pp. 89–102.

17. "Help Wanted," *Economist,* May 27, 2006, p. 35.

18. For more on the debate surrounding these various hypotheses, see *Immigrant Occupations: Recent Trends and Issues* (Ottawa: Citizenship and Immigration Canada, 2003).

19. Specifically, DeVoretz finds that the total churning costs of replacing all highly skilled managers, scientists, and health care professionals who left Canada between 1989 and 1996 would have been Can$11.5 billion dollars. Don DeVoretz, *Canadian Human Capital Transfers* (Toronto: C. D. Howe Institute, 1998). For other perspectives on the brain drain, see John Helliwell, "Checking the Brain Drain: Evidence and Implications," *Policy Options* 20, no. 7 (1999): 6–17; Daniel Schwanen, *Putting the Brain Drain in Context: Canada and the Global Competition for Scientists and Engineers* (Toronto: C. D. Howe Institute, 2000).

20. *The Survey of Earned Doctorates* (Ottawa: Statistics Canada, 2005).

21. "Brain Drain: Old Myths, New Realities," *OECD Observer,* May 2002, p. 64.

22. For a summary of consistent empirical results from three different sources, see Statistics Canada, "Brain Drain and Brain Gain" (Ottawa: 2000), pp. 10–12.

23. Compare these conditions with those of the H1-B visa, which is also granted to skilled labor but is subject to a time limitation and cannot be renewed after three years.

24. Gordon Hanson, *Emigration, Labor Supply, and Earnings in Mexico* (Cambridge, Mass.: National Bureau of Economic Research, 2005). This proportion has quadrupled during the past three decades. It is estimated that in 1970, 1.7 percent of the Mexican population was residing in the United States but that by 2000 this number had increased to 8.6 percent. Also see George Borjas and Lawrence Katz, "The Evolution of the Mexican-Born Workforce in the United States," Working Paper 11281 (Cambridge, Mass.: National Bureau of Economic Research, 2005); Steve Camarota, *Immigration from Mexico: Assessing the Impact on the United States* (Washington: Center for Immigration Studies, 2001).

25. Per capita income is measured on a purchasing-power-parity basis. On a non-purchasing-power-parity basis, this differential is a factor of six. World Bank, *World Development Indicators 2006* (Washington: 2006), table 1.

26. *Censo General de Población y Vivienda* (Mexico City: 2000).

27. Consejo Nacional de Población, "La inmigracion en México," p. 97.

28. Manuel Castillo, *Mexico: Caught between the United States and Central America* (Washington: Migration Policy Institute, 2006).

29. Consejo Nacional de Población, "La inmigracion en México," p. 99.

30. Instituto Nacional de Migracion, *Foros hacia una politica migratoria,* p. 35.

31. The Pew Hispanic Center estimates that about 12 million unauthorized persons were living in the United States in April 2006; 60 percent of them had crossed the border illegally, 40 percent were overstaying their visas. Of the 12 million, about 7.2 million were unauthorized workers (http://pewhispanic.org/files/factsheets/16.pdf). One cannot be certain how many undocumented workers leave the United States; studies suggest a third to a half return home within five years of entry. A 2002 U.S. Census Bureau study estimates that approximately one-quarter to one-third of legal immigrants permanently leave the United States, with most leaving within several years of admission. Tammany Mulder and others, "Evaluating Components of International Migration: Foreign-Born Emigration," Working Paper 62 (Population Division, Bureau of the Census, 2002).

32. For one of the most thorough and widely referenced recent profiles of the undocumented population, see Passel, *Estimates of the Size and Characteristics of the Undocumented Migrant Population.*

33. Spencer S. Hsu and Kari Lyderson, "Illegal Hiring Is Rarely Penalized," *Washington Post,* June 19, 2006, p. A1.

34. *Immigration Enforcement Weaknesses Hindering Employment Verification and Worksite Enforcement Efforts,* GAO-05-813 (U.S. Government Accountability Office, 2005).

35. World Bank, *World Development Indicators 2006,* table 6.9.

36. For more detailed information on U.S. development assistance to Mexico, see www.usaid.gov/fani/overview/overview_devassistance.htm.

37. This number has been confirmed by Catalina Amuedo Dorantes, Cynthia Bansak, and Susan Page, "On the Remitting Patterns of Immigrants: Evidence from Mexican Survey Data," in *Economic Review, First Quarter* (Atlanta: Federal Reserve Bank of Atlanta, 2005); World Bank, *Global Economic Prospects 2006: Economic Implications of Remittances and Migration* (Washington: 2005).

38. Figures were provided to the author by the U.S. Department of Homeland Security, Office of Immigration Statistics.

14

Migration and Citizenship Rights in a New North American Space

CHRISTINA GABRIEL AND LAURA MACDONALD

S treet protests across the United States and tense debates in the U.S. Congress have brought to the fore one of the unresolved issues of North American integration: migration. Proponents of the North American Free Trade Agreement (NAFTA) argued that by bringing wealth and jobs to Mexico, NAFTA would stem the flow of undocumented workers to the United States. Migration was therefore largely left out of the NAFTA agreement. However, Mexicans have continued to travel to the United States in large numbers and under increasingly dangerous conditions, despite U.S. attempts to police its border with Mexico. Migration has thus become a contentious and politicized issue that threatens to undermine the U.S.-Mexico relationship.

Contemporary debates on migration both resurrect issues of citizenship and mobility that were not directly addressed during the NAFTA negotiations and undermine assumptions about the primacy of the nation-state. Insofar as globalization raises questions about state sovereignty, borders, and governance, it challenges fundamental understandings of citizenship.[1] While this outcome has prompted some scholars to express nostalgia for the nation-state, others have responded by developing new concepts of citizenship that capture these changes: postnational, transnational, and cosmopolitan.[2] Much of this latter scholarship has used Europe as a reference point, which is understandable given that the European Union (EU) permits the free flow of workers among its member states. In this chapter, we examine regional integration, migration, and citizenship in the North American context.

Like Europe, North America is a highly integrated region. Trade, investment, and production structures are all regional, as are both licit and illicit migration. But unlike the EU, political elites in North America resist designing institutions to facilitate political integration. New forms of citizenship and liberalized labor mobility have been largely absent from the debate on North American integration as formulated by state and business elites, policy communities, and even critics of NAFTA. Despite a growing consensus that economic integration has been one of the causes (at least indirectly) for increased Mexico-U.S. migration, since the 1994 launching of NAFTA there has been little progress in efforts to clarify and strengthen mobility rights in North America.

Discussions about deepening integration along these lines have, on the contrary, taken place against the backdrop of a politically charged and at times xenophobic debate in the United States on immigration and border control. Here, the logic of national citizenship and the closure of territorial borders have been reasserted through calls for an extension of the wall along the U.S.-Mexico border and the design of punitive measures to criminalize undocumented migrants. Yet even as this acrimonious debate is taking center stage, other understandings of citizenship are beginning to find expression within the North American region.

Our chapter begins with a brief review of some of the trends and debates in the literature on globalization, migration, and citizenship. In the second section we review theories of regional integration and citizenship and note that the dominant theories of regional integration are heavily Eurocentric; as such, they do little to account for the problems of citizenship, migration, and integration that exist under NAFTA. These two sections frame the next, which reviews some of the proposals for migration reform that have been developed, whether for the United States or for the North American region as a whole. We argue that, although regional integration does indeed destabilize conventional models of citizenship, there seems to be no necessary relationship between regional integration and broader citizenship rights, such as mobility rights, as has occurred in the European context.

Citizenship, Migration, and Globalization

Theories of citizenship historically assume a direct and natural link between the nation-state and citizenship.[3] The status of citizenship is, by definition, linked to membership in a political community, which in modern times has been identified as the nation-state. Stephen Castles and Alastair Davidson argue, however, that globalization has created new challenges for citizenship (never an uncontested concept).[4] New forces—such as increasing cross-border mobility; the growing cultural, racial, and ethnic heterogeneity of national communities; and erosion of the power of elected governments to control the economy and to provide social rights through the welfare state—have undermined the assumptions associated with territorial citizenship.[5]

The dynamics of economic globalization have also had an impact on cross-border flows of people, whether as permanent migrants, temporary workers, students, visitors, or refugees and asylum seekers. Yet as many have pointed out, it is not simply the volume of cross-border traffic that distinguishes current flows (indeed, other historic periods have been characterized by even more significant population movements) but also the changing nature of these flows.[6] On this count, at least five trends can be distinguished.

—First, public perceptions of migration in developed countries have changed significantly. While international migrants account for just 2–4 percent of the global population, current trends are perceived as having a disproportionately heavier impact on the developed world.[7]

—Second, many developed countries are increasing border controls against those deemed less desirable (asylum seekers and the low skilled) while simultaneously selectively opening borders to high-skilled and more professional workers.[8]

—Third, changes in information, communications, and transportation technology have produced, in Anthony Richmond's words, an "experiential compression of time and space," resulting in an increase in the volume of circular migration and cross-border linkages.[9]

—Fourth, irregular migration flows have increased as low-paid, undocumented workers have become integral to the smooth economic functioning of many developed countries.[10] In the United States, although NAFTA may have played a role in the surge of Mexican migrants, "financial crisis and restructuring both preceded and followed the agreement's [1994] enactment."[11] The Mexican government has failed to create enough jobs to keep pace with the country's population growth, and simultaneously the U.S. industrial, agricultural, and service sectors have become dependent on cheap migrant labor.[12]

—Fifth, throughout the 1990s the mobility of high-skilled professionals emerged as an important component of migration flows.[13] This took place through the use of work permits, as Canada and the United States attempted to address skill shortages and to respond to their changing economic conditions. Additionally, processes of globalization spurred an increase in international mobility for those working for transnational corporations.[14] This movement has been facilitated both through existing national immigration regimes and through new mobility provisions of the kind written into NAFTA.

Taken together, these five trends have destabilized the familiar dichotomies used by migration studies, such as sending or receiving countries and permanent or temporary migration. But more significantly, these trends raise the broader question of how we think about citizenship.

Regionalism and New Conceptions of Citizenship

The concept of citizenship revolves around issues of belonging—inclusion and exclusion as well as membership—and issues of rights within the shared community and duties toward it.[15] Not surprisingly, all of these issues come to the fore when considering the cross-border movement of people. Foreign workers, students, visitors, asylum seekers, and other migrants do not necessarily enjoy full membership, participation, or access to citizenship rights when they reside outside of their home country. In a globalizing environment, "the transnational existence of many migrants, evident in their continued citizenship affiliation in their home countries, their globally dispersed households and networks, international labor markets, internationalist politics, and strategic reference to human rights suggests that these global forces have significantly altered the spatial envelope of individuals' rights, entitlements and affiliations."[16]

Contesting Citizenship: New Models of Membership

Aristide Zolberg argues that current configurations of citizenship are "hyper nationalist" insofar as they have become tightly linked to a particular understanding of national belonging and identity.[17] These understandings "provided the underpinnings for widespread acceptance of a conceptualization of citizenship grounded in a global system of mutually exclusive State jurisdictions and concomitant national loyalties."[18] Consequently, membership within the political community (the basis of rights, privilege, and the ability to make claims) is frequently predicated on loyalty to a single nation-state, often expressed in terms of one's duty to the country. Yet as processes of globalization transform political, social, and economic arenas, the issue of national identity becomes more complex.

International migration flows are changing the racial, ethnic, and national composition of many countries. The cultures and identities of the inhabitants of many nation-states are becoming plural.[19] Zolberg further asserts that these hypernational versions of citizenship require nation-states to police the conditions of entry and to secure their borders against foreign populations. International law recognizes that individual states have the right to determine who qualifies as a citizen. It is in this respect that immigration has become central to the exercise of state sovereignty.[20] Through this power, nation-states determine which border-crossing rights, if any, will be bestowed on migrants.[21] Thus the movement of workers and other groups of people across borders, however regulated, poses a number of challenges to traditional models of citizenship premised on membership in a territorial nation-state.

In an effort to transcend these dichotomies and to challenge hypernationalist approaches, other writers put forward definitions of transnationalism that attempt to de-territorialize notions of citizenship and belonging.[22] "De-territorialized nation-states claim their dispersed populations as 'citizens,' because members of their diasporas conduct economic, political, social and cultural transactions that are essential for the maintenance of the home state's survival."[23]

One approach to transnationalism focuses on dual or multiple citizenship as a way of properly recognizing that "immigrants' lives transcend borders."[24] Dual citizenship refers to a situation in which an individual holds more than one country's citizenship.[25] In contrast to hypernationalist forms of citizenship, "in which you are either a citizen of your home country or you adopt the nationality of the host country," dual citizenship raises questions about competing loyalties and conflicting identities.[26] It also challenges dominant assumptions about assimilationist models of migrant incorporation. As Irene Bloemraad notes, "Dual citizenship is both a cause and effect of transnationalism. Dual citizenship can facilitate transnationalism—multiple passports provide easy access to and rights in different geopolitical spaces—and it designates dual identities."[27]

At least ninety-three countries in the world allow for some form of multiple citizenship.[28] However, as Stanley Renshon emphasizes, "Countries that allow multiple citizenships vary substantially in the specific ways and extent to which they encourage or limit the responsibilities and advantages of their multi-citizenship nationals."[29] Canada embraced dual citizenship as early as 1977, and its promotion can be linked to the government's encouragement of multiculturalism, while the United States tolerates but does not promote dual citizenship. Mexico, as discussed in the following section, has reformed its laws to allow dual nationality.

Other models of membership emphasize forms of citizenship that are not confined to the nation-state or to cross-border relations. Particularly influential is the idea of cosmopolitan citizenship. For example, according to David Held and colleagues,

> In the millennium ahead each citizen of a state will have to learn to become a "cosmopolitan citizen" as well: that is, a person capable of mediating between national traditions, communities of fate and alternative forms of life. . . . Political agents who can "reason from the point of view of others" will be better equipped to resolve, and resolve fairly, the new and challenging transboundary issues and processes that create overlapping communities of fate.[30]

In contrast to this rather idealistic notion, other accounts emphasize the way in which civil rights and social welfare have evolved through a regime of international human rights and legal norms. Yasemin Soysal advances one particularly influential account in her work *Limits of Citizenship: Migrants and Postnational Membership in Europe*.[31] Soysal does not reject the nation-state as the reference point for the construction of national identity and citizenship rights, but she does argue that this is not the only arena within which citizenship is exercised. For example, Soysal defines postnational citizenship as the process by which rights and identities converge through "multilevel discourses" and in "multiple public spheres," of which the nation-state is only one.[32]

When taken together, these models of membership—whether transnational, cosmopolitan, or postnational—suggest that hypernationalist constructions of citizenship are being questioned. These questions are being posed in political disputes about membership, inequality, and social exclusion in an era of globalization. Most of the debate centers on the European Union, where increased mobility rights for European citizens have gone hand in hand with economic integration. To what extent do such models of membership find expression in the North American case?

Regionalization and Citizenship

The only published account of North American integration to focus explicitly on the question of citizenship is provided by Jennifer Welsh, who argues that Europe is not a helpful guide for tackling this question.[33] Based on her study of the European experience, Welsh contends that a shared sense of identity is not a necessary prerequisite for the development of North American citizenship. However, she argues that if North American integration is to advance beyond the level of the NAFTA agreement, a greater sense of legitimacy would have to be generated, for example through the development of a sense of a "North American common good and a common set of expectations among the peoples of the continent."[34] In this light, discussions of deepening North American integration raise new questions about citizenship and civic rights.

Although the conceptual map may be too fuzzy and real-world lessons too limited for understanding the politics (or lack thereof) of North American citizenship, there are some trends worth reviewing. At tension are two main membership themes, one that pertains to U.S.-Mexico migration and the other to U.S.-Canada relations. The former, framed by anti-immigrant discourse and attempts to reassert a rigid conception of citizenship, is premised upon narrow understandings of national boundaries.

These debates are unfolding in the context of the demographic realities of North America, chief among these the fact that in 2000 Mexican nationals in the United States "accounted for 29.8 per cent of the total foreign born population" and reportedly sent some US$14 billion in remittances back to Mexico.[35] While the demographic realities are clearly different in the northern part of the continent, some recent proposals regarding deeper integration seek to expand mobility rights between Canada and the United States.[36] Tellingly, these discussions do not embrace Mexico. Thus the most pressing mobility problem in North America is viewed as a criminal problem.

The most interesting attempt to reconfigure national citizenship is the efforts of the Mexican state to respond to the material reality that a significant portion of its nationals reside in the United States. Since the 1990s, successive Mexican administrations have sought to identify and govern this dispersed population, including through the creation of the General Directorate for Mexican Communities Abroad (DGMCA), a special institute within the Ministry of Foreign Relations, and the granting of absentee voting rights to these Mexican nationals living abroad. This impetus to govern or manage its extraterritorial population can be linked to short-term instrumental, and sometimes partisan, calculations on the part of Mexico. However, it is likely in the longer term that these state actions are helping to create a particular transnational social space.

One reason that federal and state administrations in Mexico cater to Mexicans living across the border is the importance of their remittances to the Mexican economy.[37] As is true for many other developing countries, remittances are crucial sources of foreign exchange; since 2004 remittances to

Mexico have surpassed its annual inflow of foreign direct investment. The figures on remittances do not include funds transferred informally or brought back by individuals "in the form of cash or consumer goods during visits or return migration."[38] At any rate, since 2001 Mexico has been "the number one recipient of migrant remittances in Latin America and the number two [recipient] in the world."[39] Earnings from Mexico's foreign laborers outpace tourism and agricultural exports in the country's balance of payments.[40]

Successive administrations in Mexico have thus embarked on a number of initiatives to encourage and channel remittances. The DGMCA encourages hometown and state-level associations that raise money within émigré communities for public works in Mexico. These organizations originated through migrants' own initiatives and predate governmental action. However, significantly different in recent years are the greater involvement of state officials in these organizations and the use of matching funds to support their initiatives. Mexican president Ernesto Zedillo (1994–2000) promoted the DGMCA's activities through his vision of a Mexican nation that transcends the existing territorial borders of Mexico. The Fox administration (2000–06) continued this vision with, for example, its Adopt a Community proposal.[41]

Given this rise in emigration and remittances, Mexico has undertaken the reform of its nationality and citizenship laws. In 1996, for example, Mexican political parties agreed that three articles in the Mexican constitution should be amended to allow for dual nationality.[42] Under this change, dual nationals had the right to buy and sell land free of restrictions, to attend schools in Mexico, and to hold public service jobs; they could not hold office, vote, or serve in the Mexican armed forces.[43] Subsequently, the Mexican government moved to adopt constitutional amendments to allow voting from abroad. Measures to reform dual-citizenship and nationality laws promote loyalty to the Mexican nation and may play a role in maintaining the flow of remittances into the domestic economy.

The population of Mexicans in the United States is also emerging as a political resource, as reflected in the use of street protests in U.S. cities to pressure for reform of immigration laws. One of the early milestones in the rise of a transnational community of Mexicans dates to 1988, when Mexican migrants in the United States organized against the long-standing Institutional Revolutionary Party (PRI) government and campaigned (unsuccessfully) in California for an opposition presidential candidate.[44] More recently, there have been exhortations for Mexicans abroad to return home to vote in elections and to encourage their family members and friends at home to vote as well. During the 2000 presidential election Fox campaigned in California and Chicago.[45] In 2005 the Fox administration passed a law granting Mexicans abroad the right to vote in national elections by absentee ballot.

In the 2006 Mexican election campaign, registration of Mexicans residing outside of Mexico to vote was much lower than expected.[46] In U.S. politics, however, the Mexican vote is emerging as an important force (in the early twenty-first century, about 60 percent of the 35.3 million Hispanics in the United States were of Mexican origin).[47] The Bush administration's 2004 guest worker proposal was announced with this constituency in mind, even if the more conservative elements in the Republican Party favor criminal penalties over some form of citizenship for these migrants. Their opposition, however, does not change the fact that Mexico has undertaken a number of initiatives to identify and manage its dispersed transnational populations.

Managing Migration in a Regional Context: Migrant Work and Citizenship

In the European context, Italy, which in the early stages of integration was a major exporter of labor, was able to bargain for mobility rights for its workers.[48] In contrast, Mexico was not able to gain similar rights in NAFTA negotiations. At a November 1990 meeting in Houston, U.S. chief negotiator Jules Katz told the Mexicans that there would be no NAFTA if the Mexicans insisted on the inclusion of the free movement of labor.[49] Instead, chapter 16 of NAFTA, "Temporary Entry for Business Persons," identifies only four eligible categories for temporary entry into the other NAFTA countries: business visitors, intracompany transferees, traders or investors, and those working in high-skilled professions listed in a schedule annexed to the agreement. The chapter does not address either the supply of unskilled Mexicans who wish to work in the United States or the demand in the U.S. private sector market for these workers.

In fact, few Mexicans, even the most highly educated, take advantage of the so-called NAFTA visa established under chapter 16, since the granting of the NAFTA visa is contingent upon obtaining a visa to enter the United States. While Canada offered equal treatment to Mexican and U.S. professionals, the United States imposed a quota, which lasted ten years, on Mexican professionals.[50] In 2003, for example, 65,739 NAFTA (TN) visas were issued to Canadians, in contrast with 1,268 issued to Mexicans.[51]

Tighter border security since September 11, 2001, has made it increasingly difficult, often perilous, for Mexican migrants to enter the United States without authorization. As a result, those migrants who are able to get across the U.S. border are more likely to stay in the country rather than engaging in the circular pattern of migration that characterized earlier survival strategies. A study by the Pew Hispanic Center estimates that these workers make up almost 5 percent of the U.S. labor force and that their numbers grew by at least 400,000 in 2005 alone.[52] Migrants from Mexico now make up about 56 percent of the undocumented U.S. population.[53]

The convergence of several forces, including continued demand for low-wage workers in the U.S. economy, the failure of the Mexican economy to generate sufficient labor demand, and increasing hostility toward Mexican migrants in the United States, has prompted several proposals to rectify this situation. As a result, an intense immigration battle has broken out on Capitol Hill between "reformers" and "restrictionists." Because the details of the various proposals are intricate, we focus here only on the implications of each proposal for access to citizenship. As Sean Garcia notes,

> Most immigration reform advocates believe that a path to citizenship is an essential component of any successful immigration reform proposal. Migrants faced with becoming legal and then being deported before they are ready to return to their home country may opt to maintain their illegal status in order to stay in the country as long as they want. More dangerously, new migrants may opt to risk their lives entering the United States illegally rather than accept a process that limits how long they can work in the country. Either way, as long as residents are working, law-abiding members of a society, they should be allowed to join that society officially if they choose to do so.[54]

Nevertheless, most of the proposals currently being discussed in Washington do not include paths to national citizenship.

Fox's Proposals: Expanded Guest Worker Program and Regularization

Upon his election to the Mexican presidency in 2000, Vicente Fox sought to establish an agreement with the United States to permit labor mobility within North America. Just before the attacks of September 11 such an agreement looked likely. Apart from expending considerable political capital on this issue, Fox no doubt hoped that such a move would deflect Mexican voters' discontent regarding his failure to deliver on jobs and income gains for the average Mexican.[55] Fox called not just for an expansion for the existing temporary worker program but also for an "amnesty," or "regularization," of the immigration status of Mexicans already in the United States without documentation. As the former Mexican foreign minister Jorge Castañeda argues:

Any program that's temporary is, up to a point, meaningless. If you tell somebody, "You can stay [in the United States] legally for six months, but then you leave," the guy will say, "Where are you going to find me?" Nobody is going to leave voluntarily who is already [in the United States] unless they have the guarantee of coming back. . . . Different countries have different citizenship laws. This is not something of huge significance to us. What is of huge significance to us is all the other rights [attached to permanent residency].[56]

Bush's Proposals: The Bracero Program Revisited

In 2004 continued demand by U.S. businesses for Mexican labor and the failure of U.S. border control measures to limit Mexican migration prompted President Bush to revive his support for migration reform. Compared to the more conservative and punitive proposals put forth by some in Bush's own Republican Party, his proposals seem rather moderate. However, to gain the support of conservative Republicans, Bush's speeches place heavy emphasis on tight border control. In a November 2005 speech to border agents at a Tucson air force base, he advocated reducing illegal immigration by increasing the number of U.S. Border Patrol agents as well as by installing more sophisticated technology and infrastructure for detection of illegals at the border. Bush also launched a pilot program called the "interior repatriation" of Mexicans, meaning that those caught crossing the border illegally would be flown to Mexico and then bused to their hometowns, as opposed to dropping them off just across the border.[57]

In May 2006 Bush announced a controversial plan to send thousands of National Guard troops to the U.S.-Mexican border to reinforce border security.[58] At the same time, and in contrast to the right wing of his own party, Bush advocates a temporary worker program to alleviate border tensions. "This program would create a legal way to match willing foreign workers with willing American employers to fill jobs that Americans will not do. Workers would be able to register for legal status for a fixed period of time and then be required to go home."[59]

Bush rejected Fox's proposal for the regularization of immigration status for Mexicans already in the United States on the grounds that such a program would reward those who have broken the law and thus encourage others to do so. Bush's proposals thus fail to provide a path to citizenship for Mexican migrants and are instead reminiscent of the bracero program that admitted 4.6 million Mexicans to the United States between 1942 and 1964 to work in agriculture. The program was designed to address the shortage of labor during World War II, but U.S. farmers pushed to maintain and expand the program. The program was eventually cancelled, but a group of former braceros continues to struggle for back payment for time already worked.[60]

There is currently a small guest worker program in the United States under which 42,000 workers receive H-2A visas for jobs in agriculture on a temporary basis. This program, however, is associated with widespread worker abuse, including forced and unpaid overtime.[61] Advocates of immigration reform fear that Bush's proposed guest worker program would lead to similar kinds of infractions and thus would not address the situation of millions of undocumented Mexicans already residing in the United States.

Reassertions of the National: Exclusionary Citizenship and Immigration Restrictionists

Bush's support for a guest worker program has resulted in a major split within the Republican Party. Until recently, anti-immigrant forces that favored draconian measures against immigration were relatively marginalized in Washington. However, the ideological context of the "war on terror" as well as the failure of the U.S. economy to generate well-paying jobs for millions of Americans have stoked anti-immigrant sentiments. A *Washington Post*–ABC News poll conducted in mid-December 2005 found that four in five Americans thought the government was not doing enough to prevent illegal immigration, while three in five held that view strongly.[62] Proponents of restricting immigration have gained influence both in states bordering Mexico and in Washington.

In the House of Representatives, the Immigration Reform Caucus created by Tom Tancredo (R-Colorado) has more than ninety members. The caucus initially focused on the following objectives: "Addressing the explosive growth in illegal immigration, reversing the growth in legal immigration, and stopping a further extension of Section 245(i) of the Immigration and Nationality Act—a 'mini-amnesty.'"[63] After September 11, according to the caucus's website, it "continued to establish and emphasize the link between open borders, unregulated immigration, and the potential for terrorism."[64] The caucus "gives members an opportunity to address the strong concerns about immigration that constituents have relayed to them. It also exists as an outlet for members and staff to discuss how current laws and regulation pose a threat to the security of America." The caucus views trade agreements like NAFTA as a threat to the national well-being. Tancredo spokesman Will

Adams states, "There's a huge chasm between us and big business. . . . They're addicted to cheap labor, which illegal aliens provide. It's in their interests to keep the border porous and to keep the labor flowing."[65]

In December 2005 the House passed a bill designed by House Judiciary Committee chairman F. James Sensenbrenner Jr. (R-Wisconsin) to crack down on illegal immigration: 203 Republicans and 36 Democrats supported the bill, which passed 239 to 182, while 164 Democrats, 17 Republicans, and 1 independent voted against it. The House bill called for tougher sanctions on employers who fail to verify that all of their workers are in the United States legally; the imprisonment and deportation of non-Mexican migrants without documentation; stiffer criminal penalties for smuggling immigrants; the spending of US$2.2 billion to build five double-layer border fences in California and Arizona; and the empowerment of local law enforcement agencies to enforce federal immigration law.

The House did reject proposed amendments that would eliminate automatic citizenship for babies born to undocumented migrants in the United States and that would authorize the building of a fence along the entire U.S.-Mexico border. While Tancredo's coalition greeted the bill as a major victory, the law was criticized harshly by Latino organizations in the United States and by the Mexican government on the grounds that it treats as criminals both undocumented workers and the businesses that hire.[66]

The House bill was followed by long negotiations within the Senate Judiciary Committee, led by committee chair Arlen Specter (R-Pennsylvania), to write a more moderate bill. The committee's bill would have authorized the hiring of new border agents, the use of unmanned aerial vehicles and other new technological approaches to border control, an expansion of the definition of alien smuggling to combat those who shelter illegal immigrants, and an imposition of tougher penalties on smugglers and repeat border crossers. But it would also have included a new H-2C visa, good for six years, which would allow employers to hire immigrants if they are unable to find an American worker to fill jobs in hotel work, cleaning, restaurants, and meat processing. The visa, like Bush's plan, would offer no special path toward citizenship for migrants.

A more liberal bipartisan proposal was put forward by Senators McCain (R-Ariz.) and Kennedy (D-Mass.). Their proposal not only advocated greater border security and a temporary visa program but also contained provisions that would allow undocumented workers already in the country to apply for citizenship status, albeit after paying a fine, staying employed for a prescribed period, paying back taxes, and going to the back of the line of applicants.[67]

The Senate ultimately passed an immigration reform bill on May 25, 2006, that did contain a "path to citizenship," which would permit some 8 million undocumented immigrants to eventually gain permanent residence. The bill also increased family visas and provided for a new temporary worker program that would issue temporary visas to up to 200,000 applicants a year. The temporary worker program would contain worker protections, give workers the ability to change employers, and provide a path to permanent residence for those who wish to stay. However, immigration reform advocates have strong reservations about some aspects of the bill, such as the English-only provision aimed at establishing a "national language" and the criminalization of immigrants. They are also concerned that significant numbers of undocumented workers might be barred from applying for legalization of their status.[68]

In any case, the Senate bill faced fierce resistance in the House, and any compromise would have required strong support from President Bush. In response to the Senate's proposals, Bush has made vague references to his willingness to entertain the possibility that immigrants currently in the United States on an unauthorized basis might be able to apply for citizenship after paying a fine. At an appearance in California in April 2006, Bush asserted that "A person ought to be allowed to . . . pay a penalty for being here illegally, commit him or herself to learn English, which is part of the American system, and get in the back of the line" for citizenship.[69]

Unfortunately, Bush subsequently signed into law in October 2006 a bill to authorize the construction of a 700-mile-long fence along the U.S.-Mexico border, although it was unclear whether Congress would appropriate money for its construction.[70] In the congressional elections of November 2006, the Republicans made illegal immigration a priority issue. The defeat of several high-profile Republican opponents of immigration reform and the Democrats' new majority status in both the House and the Senate suggest that a more rational and humane solution may lie ahead. Moreover, Bush's own position on immigration remains closer to that of moderate Democrats than to that of many in his own party. However, immigration is still a highly controversial issue, and any positive legislative breakthrough will obviously depend on whether Democrats can muster the collective political will to push this issue forward.[71]

North American Citizenship: A New Proposal for Membership?

What are the prospects for a new model of membership in North America? Writing on the eve of the March 2006 Cancún meeting of NAFTA leaders,

Robert Pastor called upon the three member countries to embrace the idea of a North American community to address the "most pressing problems in the region—immigration, security, and declining competitiveness."[72] Pastor wrote, "North America isn't Europe. But the region's three countries should draw on the EU's experience and think more in regional terms. The leaders of the United States, Canada and Mexico must articulate a vision that recognizes how instability or recession in one affects the other two. At the same time they need to remind their constituents that when the value of a neighbor's house rises, so too does theirs."[73]

Specifically, Pastor emphasized the way EU member countries provided development funds to countries such as Greece, Spain, and Portugal to close the gap between the latter and the more prosperous EU members. He noted that in the short term measures to narrow the income gap between Mexico and its NAFTA counterparts would not curb undocumented migration from Mexico northward but that in the long run Mexican economic development would address this regional problem. This said, Pastor correctly acknowledged that there is currently little political will among the leaders of the three countries to tackle this challenge.[74]

The March 2006 meeting of the three NAFTA leaders in Cancún proved Pastor's reading of the situation. President Bush, President Fox, and Prime Minister Harper underlined their support for the Security and Prosperity Partnership of North America, which had been signed by the three countries in March 2005. In their progress report to the three leaders in September 2006, ministers of the three countries outlined the measures they were pursuing to promote security and prosperity in North America. Included among these were commitments to "develop and implement compatible immigration security measures to enhance North American security, including requirements for admission and length of stay; visa decision-making standards; lookout systems; and examining the feasibility of entry and exit procedures and systems."[75] These initiatives clearly represented efforts to meet the demands of North American businesses for efficient cross-border travel by "low-risk travelers," while also addressing U.S. security concerns. The initiative did not, however, address the needs and demands of low-skilled migrant workers.

In short, proposals to deepen integration and, by extension, to address labor mobility issues have been generated largely by business groups and elites.[76] The 2005 Task Force Report *Building a North American Community* published by the Council on Foreign Relations (CFR) provides a case in point and to some extent may offer some insights into future trajectories. The report suggests that "people are North America's greatest asset" and that to "make the most of the impressive pool of skill and talent within North America, the three countries should look beyond the NAFTA visa system."[77] Even as the report suggests moving beyond the provisions of the NAFTA agreement, however, the recommendations are still bound to the NAFTA framework. The CFR report has two short-term proposals:

—Canada and the United States should expand programs for temporary labor migration from Mexico.

—The United States and Mexico should implement a Social Security agreement that would recognize payroll contributions across the two country systems.

There may be some efforts to expand temporary work programs. Shortly before the Cancún summit President Fox urged Canada to expand its temporary workers program beyond agriculture, to include, for example, construction and services.[78] Canada's temporary worker programs have been touted as a means to address acute labor shortages in certain sectors, such as construction, and in particular provinces, notably Alberta.[79] These programs are often seen by Mexicans as preferable to the lack of guest worker programs in the United States.

This said, temporary worker programs raise questions in respect to worker rights and citizenship. For example, to what extent would the status of temporary workers be contingent on maintaining employment with the same employer? Would these workers be protected by existing domestic employment standards legislation? Would they be allowed to join existing labor unions? Would they be allowed access to social programs? What would be the status of their families? Further, in terms of citizenship would there be a provision that allows foreign temporary workers who wished to stay once their employment has ended to change their status?

The Council on Foreign Relations task force report also had two long-term proposals:

—By 2010 all three NAFTA countries should streamline their immigration and labor mobility rules to enable citizens of all three countries to work elsewhere in North America with far fewer restrictions than immigrants from other countries.

—By 2010 Canada and the United States should move to full labor mobility between their countries, eliminating all remaining barriers to the ability of their citizens to live and work in the other country.[80] These provisions should eventually be extended to Mexico.

These two proposals fall short of a robust conception of regional membership. There is, in fact, a conspicuous lack of attention to the rights of migrant workers and their families. For the most part, proposals to deepen integration sideline broader questions of citizenship and membership. Moreover, the fact that they have been generated by elites and business groups raises concerns about their legitimacy among all citizens in the three countries.[81]

Conclusion

Since the inception of NAFTA, the debate about North American integration has commonly focused on the deepening of ties among the three countries. Although NAFTA has successfully facilitated the intraregional movement of goods, services, and capital, labor markets remain legally segmented and have not been rationally restructured.

The failure of NAFTA to address labor market restructuring is not just about economic costs and benefits but also about rights, identity, and belonging. Globalization and regionalization in North America have resulted in an increased movement of people, yet the option of legalizing these migration flows and obtaining formal citizenship status for unauthorized workers has basically been foreclosed. In the EU similar pressures were accompanied by expanded and multiple forms of citizenship, although European approaches have not proven transferable to North America. For example, migrant-sending states like Italy have been able to press for a bargain within the EU that includes labor mobility, a feat for which Mexico has lacked the bargaining power and political leverage to accomplish in North America.

As a result, hypernationalist forms of citizenship have been reinforced, especially in the United States, while potentially more progressive and humane notions of postnational or cosmopolitan citizenship have been rejected out of hand, particularly since September 11. The ongoing debate within the U.S. Congress reveals these tensions. Nevertheless, migrants continue their northward march, developing new forms of identity and making claims for citizens' rights.

One irony is that the revival of hypernationalist narratives of citizenship by advocates of tighter immigration reform has led to the emergence of a vocal and vibrant immigrant rights movement in the United States. Hundreds of thousands of people across the country participated in protests beginning in March 2006 and culminating in a May 1, 2006, boycott of work, school, and shops. These protests brought out into the open alternative conceptions of citizenship, which will continue to be claimed despite political obstacles to their recognition. Clearly, recognition of these citizenship claims will remain an intrinsic part of the pending North American agenda for years to come.

Notes

The Social Sciences and Humanities Federation of Canada supported our work and the writing of this chapter. We thank the federation and also the editors and anonymous reviewers for their comments.

1. Jan Aart Scholte, "The Globalization of World Politics," in *The Globalization of World Politics,* 2d ed., edited by John Baylis and Steve Smith (Oxford University Press, 2001).

2. Dominique Schnapper, "The European Debate on Citizenship," *Daedalus* 126, no. 3 (1997): 199–222. See also Yasemin Soysal, *Limits of Citizenship: Migrants and Postnational Membership in Europe* (University of Chicago Press, 1994); Gerard Delanty, "Models of Citizenship: Defining European Identity and Citizenship," *Citizenship Studies* 1, no. 3 (1997): 285–03.

3. Delanty, "Models of Citizenship."

4. Stephen Castles and Alastair Davidson, *Citizenship and Migration: Globalization and the Politics of Belonging* (New York: Routledge, 2000).

5. Ibid., p. vii.

6. Stephen Castles, "Migration and Community Formation under Conditions of Globalization," *International Migration Review* 36, no. 4 (2002): 1143–68; Peter Stalker, *Workers without Frontiers: The Impact of Globalization on International Migration* (Boulder, Colo.: Lynne Rienner, 2000).

7. Castles, "Migration and Community Formation," p. 1147.

8. Christina Gabriel, "A Question of Skills: Gender, Migration Policy, and the Global Political Economy," in *Global Regulation: Managing Crisis after the Imperial Turn,* edited by Kees van der Pijl and others (London: Palgrave-Macmillan, 2004).

9. Anthony Richmond, "Globalization: Implications for Immigrants and Refugees," *Ethnic and Racial Studies* 25, no. 5 (2002): 707–27, quotation on p. 708.

10. It is estimated that the "population of unauthorized Mexican immigrants in the U.S. more than doubled between 1990 and 2000 (with most of the growth occurring after 1994)." Demetrius Papademetriou, "The Shifting Expectations of Trade and Migration: NAFTA's Promise and Reality," in *NAFTA's Promise and Reality,* edited by John Audley and others (Washington: Carnegie Endowment for International Peace, 2003), p. 40.

11. Ibid.

12. An estimated 5.3 million undocumented Mexicans were living in the United States in 2002. Deborah Meyers and Kevin O'Neil, "Immigration: Mapping the New North American Reality," *Policy Options* 25, no. 6 (2004): 46–47.

13. Khalid Koser and John Salt, "The Geography of Highly Skilled Migration," *International Journal of Population Geography* 3, no. 4 (1997): 285–303; Robyn Iredale, "The Migration of Professionals: Theories and Typologies," *International Migration* 39, no. 5 (2001): 7–26.

14. Reginald Appleyard, "International Migration and Developing Countries," in *The Impact of International Migration on Developing Countries,* edited by Reginald Appleyard (Paris: OECD, 1989), cited by Stephen Castles and Mark Miller, *The Age of Migration* (New York: Guildford, 1993), p. 161.

15. Stuart Hall and David Held, "Citizens and Citizenship," in *New Times,* edited by Stuart Hall and Martin Jacques (London: Verso, 1989), p. 175.

16. Daiva Stasiulis and Abigail Bakan, *Negotiating Citizenship: Migrant Women in Canada and the Global System* (London: Palgrave-Macmillan, 2003), p. 15.

17. Aristide Zolberg, "The Dawn of Cosmopolitan Denizenship," *Indiana Journal of Global Legal Studies* 7, no. 2 (2000): 511–18.

18. Ibid., p. 511.

19. Stuart Hall, "The Question of Cultural Identity," in *Modernity and Its Futures,* edited by Stuart Hall and Tony McGrew (Cambridge, Mass.: Polity, 1992), p. 306.

20. Zolberg, "The Dawn of Cosmopolitan Denizenship," p. 514.

21. Stasiulis and Bakan, *Negotiating Citizenship,* p. 38.

22. Linda Basch, Nina Glick Schiller, and Cristina Blanc, eds., *Nations Unbound: Transnational Projects, Post Colonial Predicaments, and Deterritorialized Nation States* (Amsterdam: Gordon and Breach, 1994). See also Peggy Levitt and Rafael de la Dehesa, "Transnational Migration and the Redefinition of the State: Variations and Explanations," *Ethnic and Racial Studies* 26, no. 4 (2003): 587–611. Michael Smith, "Transnationalism, the State, and the Extraterritorial Citizen," *Politics and Society* 31, no. 4 (2003): 467–502.

23. Basch, Schiller, and Blanc, *Nations Unbound,* p. 270.

24. Irene Bloemraad, "Who Claims Dual Citizenship? The Limits of Postnationalism, the Possibilities of Transnationalism, and the Persistence of Traditional Citizenship," *International Migration Review* 38, no. 2 (2004): 389–426, quotation on p. 394.

25. See Stanley A. Renshon, *Dual Citizenship and American National Identity* (Washington: Center for Immigration Studies, 2002), p. 6.

26. Bloemraad, "Who Claims Dual Citizenship?" p. 393.

27. Ibid., p. 394.

28. See Renshon, *Dual Citizenship and American National Identity,* p. 45.

29. Stanley A. Renshon, *Backgrounder: Dual Citizens in America. An Issue of Vast Proportions and Broad Significance* (Washington: Center for Immigration Studies, 2000), p. 5.

30. David Held and others, *Global Transformations: Politics, Economics, and Culture* (Stanford University Press, 1999), p. 449.

31. Soysal, *Limits of Citizenship.*

32. Yasemin Soysal, "Postnational Citizenship: Reconfiguring a Familiar Terrain," in *Blackwell Companion to Political Sociology,* edited by Kate Nash and A. Scott (Oxford: Blackwell, 2001), p. 339.

33. Jennifer M. Welsh, "North American Citizenship: Possibilities and Limits," in *The Art of the State: Thinking North America,* edited by Thomas Courchene, Donald J. Savoie, and Daniel Schwanen (Montreal: Institute for Research on Public Policy, 2004).

34. Ibid., p. 46.

35. Deborah Meyers and Kevin O'Neil, "Immigration: Mapping the New North American Reality," *Policy Options* 25, no. 6 (2004): 45–49, quotation on p. 46.

36. Council on Foreign Relations, *Building a North American Community* (New York, 2005), p. 27.

37. See Smith, "Transnationalism, the State, and the Extraterritorial Citizen," pp. 467–502; Renshon, *Dual Citizenship and American National Identity,* p. 34.

38. Bhargavi Ramamurthy, *International Labour Migrants: Unsung Heroes of Globalization* (Stockholm: Swedish International Development Corporation Agency, 2003), p. 10.

39. Raul Delgado Wise, "Labour and Migration Policies under Vicente Fox: Subordination to US Economic and Geopolitical Interests," in *Mexico in Transition: Neoliberal Globalism, the State, and Civil Society,* edited by Gerardo Otero (London: Zed/Fernwood, 2004), p. 145.

40. Ibid.

41. Levitt and de la Dehesa, "Transnational Migration and the Redefinition of the State," p. 592; Delgado Wise, "Labour and Migration Policies under Vicente Fox," p. 152.

42. Levitt and de la Dehesa, "Transnational Migration and the Redefinition of the State," p. 595.

43. Delgado Wise, "Labour and Migration Policies under Vicente Fox," p. 149.

44. Levitt and de la Dehesa, "Transnational Migration and the Redefinition of the State," p. 603.

45. Ibid., p. 604.

46. See, for example, Sam Enriquez, "No Loud Voice for Expats in Mexican Vote," *Los Angeles Times,* January 14, 2006 (www.latimes.com).

47. Robert Pastor, *Toward a North American Community: Lessons from the Old World to the New* (Washington: Institute for International Economics, 2001), p. 132.

48. Willem Maas, "The Genesis of European Rights," *Journal of Common Market Studies* 43, no. 5 (2005): 1009–25.

49. Maxwell A. Cameron and Brian W. Tomlin, *The Making of NAFTA: How the Deal Was Done* (Cornell University Press, 2000), p. 71.

50. Christina Gabriel and Laura Macdonald, "The Hypermobile, the Mobile, and the Rest: Patterns of Inclusion and Exclusion in an Emerging North American Migration Regime," *Canadian Journal of Latin American and Caribbean Studies* 29, nos. 57–58 (2004): 67–91.

51. Jessica Vaughan, "Be Our Guest: Trade Agreements and Visas," *Backgrounder* (Washington: Center for Immigration Studies, 2003), p. 4.

52. Jeffrey S. Passel, "Size and Characteristics of the Unauthorized Migrant Population in the U.S." (Washington: Pew Hispanic Center, 2006).

53. S. Mitra Kalita, "Illegal Workers' Presence Growing," *Washington Post,* March 8, 2006, p. A6.

54. Sean Garcia, "The ABCs of Immigration Reform," *Foreign Policy in Focus (FPIF)*, May 28, 2004, p. 1.

55. Manuel Pastor and Susan Alva, "Guest Workers and the New Transnationalism: Possibilities and Realities in an Age of Repression," *Social Justice* 31, nos. 1–2 (2004): 92–112.

56. Cited in Sergio Muñoz, "Jorge Castañeda: Mexico's Man Abroad," *Los Angeles Times*, August 12, 2001, p. M3.

57. George W. Bush, "Remarks by the President on Border Security and Immigration Reform," 2005 (www.gop.com).

58. "Bush Calls for 6,000 Troops along Border," May 15, 2006 (www.cnn.com).

59. Jim Rutenberg, "Bush Calls for Compromise on Immigration," *New York Times*, May 16, 2006.

60. Pastor and Alva, "Guest Workers and the New Transnationalism," p. 95.

61. Ibid., p. 96.

62. Dan Balz, "Political Splits on Immigration Reflect Voters' Ambivalence," *Washington Post*, January 3, 2006, p. A7.

63. "Congressional Immigration Reform Caucus," 2004 (http://tancredo.house.gov/irc/about.html).

64. Ibid.

65. Jeffrey H. Birnbaum, "Immigration Pushes Apart GOP, Chamber," *Washington Post*, December 14, 2005, p. A1.

66. José Carreño, "Nueva ley en EU define a braceros como criminales," *El Universal*, December 17, 2005, p. 1.

67. "Enter McCain-Kennedy," *Washington Post*, May 14, 2005, p. A20.

68. National Council of La Raza, "NCLR Commends Senate for Historic Immigration Vote," news release, May 25, 2006 (www.nclr.org).

69. Jonathan Weisman and Jim VandeHei, "Immigration Bill Lobbying Focuses on House Leaders," *Washington Post*, May 1, 2006, p. A5.

70. "The Fence Campaign," *New York Times*, October 30, 2006.

71. "Signs of Hope on Immigration," *New York Times*, November 20, 2006.

72. Robert A. Pastor, "North America: How to Solve Illegal Immigration," *Newsweek International*, March 27, 2006, p. 1.

73. Ibid., p. 2.

74. Ibid., pp. 2–3.

75. *Security and Prosperity Partnership of North America, Report to Leaders, June 2005* (Washington: SPP, 2005), Security Annex, p. 50.

76. See, for example, Christina Gabriel and Laura Macdonald, "Of Borders and Business: Canadian Corporate Proposals for Deep Integration," *Studies in Political Economy* 74 (Fall-Winter 2004): 79–100.

77. Council on Foreign Relations, *Building a North American Community*, Independent Task Force Report 53 (Washington, 2005), p. 26.

78. Alan Freeman, "The Mexican Leader Urges Canada to Open Doors to 'Guest Workers,'" *Globe and Mail*, March 28, 2006, p. A1.

79. Comment: "How to Retain Workers without a Big Amnesty," *Globe and Mail*, March 28, 2006, p. A16.

80. Ibid., pp. 27–28.

81. See, for example, Maude Barlow, *Too Close for Comfort: Canada's Future within Fortress North America* (Toronto: McClelland and Stewart, 2005).

Contributors

Theodore H. Cohn is professor emeritus of political science at Simon Fraser University in British Columbia, Canada. He has written a number of books, articles, and smaller monographs on international political economy, international trade, global food and agricultural issues, and Canada-U.S.-Mexico relations. Professor Cohn's books include *Global Political Economy: Theory and Practice* (Longman, 2005, 3rd ed.), *Governing Global Trade: International Institutions in Conflict and Convergence* (Ashgate, 2002), *The International Politics of Agricultural Trade: Canadian-American Relations in a Global Agricultural Context* (University of British Columbia Press, 1990), and *Canadian Food Aid: Domestic and Foreign Policy Implications* (University of Denver, 1979). He is currently writing the fourth edition of *Global Political Economy* and cowriting a book on international organization.

I. M. ("Mac") Destler is professor at the School of Public Policy, University of Maryland, and director of its International Security and Economic Policy Program. He is also a senior fellow at the Peterson Institute for International Economics. Professor Destler is the author of numerous works on U.S. trade policymaking, the most prominent being *American Trade Politics,* the fourth edition of which was published by the Peterson Institute in 2005.

CHARLES F. DORAN is the Andrew W. Mellon Professor of International Relations at the School of Advanced International Studies (SAIS), Johns Hopkins University. There, he directs the Program of Global Theory and History as well as the Program of Canadian Studies. He is also a senior associate at the Center for Strategic and International Studies. Professor Doran's books on Canada include *Forgotten Partnership* (selected as the most noteworthy book on foreign policy across thirty years of Canadian studies scholarship, Johns Hopkins University Press, 1984) and *Why Canadian Unity Matters* (University of Toronto Press, 2001). Among his works in energy security are *Myth, Oil, and Politics* (Free Press, 1977) and *The Gulf, Energy, and Global Security* (coedited with Stephen W. Buck, Rienner Publishers, 1991). He received the Donner Medal for distinguished scholarship in Canadian Studies and the prestigious Governor General's Award.

CHRISTINA GABRIEL is associate professor in the Department of Political Science and the Pauline Jewett Institute of Women's Studies at Carleton University in Ottawa, Canada. She has published numerous articles in the areas of citizenship and migration, gender and politics, and globalization. She is coauthor with Yasmeen Abu-Laban of *Selling Diversity: Immigration, Multiculturalism, Employment Equity, and Globalization* (Broadview Press, 2002).

SERGIO GÓMEZ LORA has served at the Mexican Ministry of Trade and Industry (now called the Ministry of Economy) in the capacity of trade counselor in Mexico's NAFTA office in Ottawa, Canada, and as a member of the team in charge of preparing the implementation of NAFTA. He was director for NAFTA accession procedures and for international trade agreements, and he participated in the Mexico-EU free trade agreement negotiations. He was a senior consultant at Soluciones Estratégicas and since 2005 has been general director of IQOM Inteligencia Comercial, which is a firm that specializes in the provision of electronic data and information on all aspects of Mexico's foreign trade to companies established in Mexico.

LAURA MACDONALD is professor and chair in the Department of Political Science and the director of the Centre on North American Politics and Society at Carleton University in Ottawa, Canada. She has published numerous articles in journals and edited collections on such issues as the role of nongovernmental organizations in development, global civil society, citizenship struggles in Latin America, and Canadian development assistance. She has also published extensively on the political impact of NAFTA on human rights and democracy in the three member states.

GORDON MACE is director of the Inter-American Studies Center at Université Laval in Québec City, Canada. He is also the editor of the journal *Études Internationales*. His main research interests are inter-American cooperation, regional integration, and Canadian foreign policy. He has written or cowritten six books and more than sixty articles and book chapters on various subjects related to the aforementioned themes. He is currently working on an edited book on inter-American institutions and on a team project on regionalism and foreign policy convergence in the context of NAFTA.

ISIDRO MORALES is professor of international relations at the Universidad de las Américas (UDLA), in Puebla, Mexico. At UDLA he has held the positions of dean of the School of Social Sciences and chairman of the Department of International Relations and Political Science. In 2005–06 Professor Morales was a Fulbright Visiting Scholar in the Center for North American Studies at American University in Washington, D.C. He has taught previously at El Colegio de México, Brown University, University of Copenhagen, and University of Gothenburg. He has cowritten two books on energy issues and published several articles in specialized journals, dealing mainly with integration and trade-related topics. Professor Morales is a member of Mexico's National Research System, the Academic Council for the United Nations System (ACUNS), and the Mexican Council for Foreign Affairs.

GLAUCO OLIVEIRA is a doctoral candidate in political economy and public policy at the University of Southern California and a public policy analyst at the Ministry of Finance in Brazil. He has been a Brazilian career civil servant for more than ten years, working with international economic policy issues at the Ministry of Planning and at the Ministry of Finance.

ANTONIO ORTIZ MENA L. N. is professor of International Relations at CIDE (Centro de Investigación y Docencia Económicas) in Mexico City where he also chairs the Division of International Studies. He was previously a member of the Mexican government's NAFTA negotiation office and writes on international political economy issues. His latest publications include: "Mexico's International Telecommunications Policy: Origins, the WTO Dispute, and Future Challenges" (cowritten with Ricardo Rodríguez),

Telecommunications Policy, 29, nos. 5-6 (June-July 2005): 429–48; "Mexico," in *The World Trade Organization: Legal, Economic and Political Analysis,* edited by Patrick F. J. Macrory and others (Springer, 2005); and "Getting to No: Mexico in the NAFTA Energy Negotiations," in *Negotiating Trade: Developing Countries in the WTO and NAFTA,* edited by John S. Odell (Cambridge University Press, 2006).

JEFFREY J. SCHOTT is a senior fellow at the Peterson Institute for International Economics. He has been a visiting lecturer at Princeton University (1994) and an adjunct professor at Georgetown University (1986–88). He was a senior associate at the Carnegie Endowment for International Peace (1982–83) and an official of the U.S. Treasury Department (1974–82) in international trade and energy policy. During the Tokyo Round of multilateral trade negotiations, he was a member of the U.S. delegation that negotiated the GATT Subsidies Code. Since January 2003 he has been a member of the Trade and Environment Policy Advisory Committee of the U.S. government. Schott is the author, coauthor, or editor of several recent books on trade, including *NAFTA Revisited: Achievements and Challenges* (Peterson Institute for International Economics, 2005), *Free Trade Agreements: US Strategies and Priorities* (Peterson Institute, 2004), *Prospects for Free Trade in the Americas* (Peterson Institute, 2001), and *The WTO after Seattle* (Peterson Institute, 2000).

ISABEL STUDER is senior policy adviser to the under-secretary for North American affairs at the Mexican Ministry of Foreign Affairs. She has been research director at the North American Commission for Labor Cooperation and general director for North America at the Mexican Ministry of the Environment and Natural Resources, as well as alternate representative of the minister before the Environmental Cooperation Commission for North America. Dr. Studer has been professor and researcher at various Mexican universities, including the Instituto Tecnológico Autónomo de México (ITAM), the Centro de Investigación y Docencia Económicas, and the Facultad Latinoamericana de Ciencias Sociales (FLACSO). She is the author of *Ford and the Global Strategies of Multinationals* (Routledge, 2002) and has published widely on issues related to the processes of regional integration in North America.

CAROL WISE is associate professor of international relations in the School of International Relations at the University of Southern California. In 2005 she held the Carleton University Fulbright Chair in North American Studies in

Ottawa, Canada, and the Fulbright-Hays Senior Fulbright Specialist Award in the Department of International Relations and Political Science at the Universidad de las Américas (UDLA), in Puebla, Mexico, and was a 2006 Public Policy Scholar in the Canada Institute at the Woodrow Wilson International Center for Scholars in Washington, D.C. Professor Wise has written widely on issues pertaining to Latin American political economy, including three edited collections that analyze exchange rate regimes, trade integration, and political responses to market reform in the region. In 2003 she published *Reinventing the State: Economic Strategy and Institutional Change in Peru* (University of Michigan Press), and she is currently completing a coauthored book with Manuel Pastor on the transformation of the Mexican political economy under NAFTA.

TAMARA M. WOROBY is professor of economics at Towson University (University of Maryland System) and an affiliated professor of international economics and Western Hemisphere studies at Johns Hopkins University's School of Advanced International Studies in Washington, D.C. She has published in the fields of economic history, international economics, and immigration policy, most recently having completed a study on resettlement issues for the European Commission. She has served as an economic consultant to the World Bank; the government of Ontario, Canada; the Canadian International Development Agency; and the U.S. Department of State.

JAIME ZABLUDOVSKY is a managing partner at Soluciones Estratégicas, a consulting firm that advises Latin American governments, multilateral organizations, transnational companies, and business associations on matters related to international trade and competitiveness. He is also executive vice president of IQOM Inteligencia Comercial. From 1990–94 Dr. Zabludovsky was Mexico's sub-director in charge of the NAFTA negotiations, was named sub-secretary for international trade negotiations in 1994, and assumed responsibility for the design and implementation of Mexico's commercial strategy in the principal international organizations (WTO, OECD, APEC, and FTAA). During this time Dr. Zabludovsky also played the lead role in negotiating bilateral free trade agreements among Mexico and Chile, Costa Rica, Bolivia, Colombia, and Venezuela, as well as a number of other bilateral accords. From 1998 to 2001 he served as Mexico's ambassador to the European Union and was the chief negotiator for the free trade agreement between Mexico and the EU.

INDEX